Designing Web Navigation

James Kalbach

O'REILLY®

BEIJING · CAMBRIDGE · FARNHAM · KÖLN · PARIS · SEBASTOPOL · TAIPEI · TOKYO

Designing Web Navigation BY JAMES KALBACH

Published by O'Reilly Media, Inc., 1005 Gravenstein Highway North, Sebastopol, CA 95472.

O'Reilly books may be purchased for educational, business, or sales promotional use. Online editions are also available for most titles (*safari.oreilly.com*). For more information, contact our corporate/institutional sales department: 800.998.9938 or *corporate@oreilly.com*.

Editor: Linda Laflamme

Production Editor: Philip Dangler

Cover Design: Karen Montgomery

Interior Design: NOON

Compositor: Ron Bilodeau

Indexer: Julie Hawks

Graphic Production: Robert Romano

Printing History: August 2007, First Edition.

ISBN-10: 0-596-52810-8
ISBN-13: 978-0-596-52810-2
[L]

To Nathalie, with all my love

Contents

PART II
A Framework for Navigation Design

Preface

In 1998, the dot-com boom was in full swing, bringing with it an extreme amount of activity in web development. In that same year we saw the appearance of Jennifer Fleming's *Web Navigation: Designing the User Experience*, the predecessor to this book. With certainty and clarity, she demonstrated techniques for creating successful web navigation that focused on users. This was a sober and welcome contrast to the hype of the time, and it influenced my own thinking.

Much has changed since 1998. Using the Web has become commonplace. Reading news, hunting for a job, shopping for gifts, looking up telephone numbers, ordering pizza, planning trips, and selling items are just some of the activities that many people do solely on the Web. The notion of Web 2.0 marks a second phase of the Web, characterized by user-generated content, collaboration, communities, and broader participation in general. And new technologies, such as Ajax and Flex, point to a more interactive Web with highly functional applications.

Amidst all this change, the problems of creating good web navigation systems remain. In many respects, they get even more complicated. Business objectives increasingly rely on the assumption that people will be able to find, access, and use the information and services they provide. In order for web sites to be successful, people must be able to navigate effectively. A "cool" site with lots of interactivity and user participation will still be lousy if the navigation doesn't work.

Designing Web Navigation offers a fresh look at a fundamental topic of web site development: navigation design. In its pages, you'll find insight and practical advice for approaching a range of navigation design problems. Though inspired by Fleming's *Web Navigation*, this book explores topics not found in the original, and it has been completely rewritten.

SCOPE OF THIS BOOK

Web navigation design touches most other aspects of web site development in some way. Defining where it begins and ends is difficult. This book situates navigation design in a broader context of site development, at times overlapping with other disciplines and concerns. But, as much as possible, the focus throughout remains clearly on creating an effective navigation system.

My intent is to provide you with some of the primary tools of navigation design and ways to solve navigation problems. Relevant theory and related material are discussed and credited where appropriate. Each chapter ends with suggested reading and a set of questions. The questions are not meant to quiz you on the chapter contents, but to offer some exercises and help you experience concepts in action. They may also require you to do some investigative research on your own. Use them as a springboard to further exploration of related topics.

The focus of this book is on creating navigation systems for large, information-rich sites serving a business purpose. At times, it also assumes you are working in a large project team with diverse roles. Don't be daunted, however; the principles and techniques in the book can apply to small sites with small teams, too. Navigation design is ultimately about the thought processes and steps in designing navigation in general, regardless of the site type, size of the team, and your overall objectives in creating a site.

Note also that I use the term *design* in its broadest sense, referring to all of the activities involved in designing web navigation, not just the graphic or visual aspects of it. Further, the use of *designer* or *navigation designer* doesn't necessarily mean that there is a single person with that job title who creates a web navigation system from beginning to end. Most often, the decisions made in creating a navigation system cross roles and teams over the entire lifespan of a project. The *designer*, then, refers to the person or group of people who make decisions about a particular aspect of the navigation at a given point in a project.

Web navigation design is a craft. You must employ creative problem-solving skills to arrive at a practical solution by considering and examining different possibilities. Intuition plays as much a role as skill, experience, and science. Rarely is there a single, optimal solution. As with any design practice, navigation design is about balance, trade-offs, and exploring alternatives. For this reason, you won't find all the answers in this book. Instead, I offer a systematic approach to the problems of navigation design. Navigation design is really about asking the right questions at the right time.

With that in mind, you should also be aware of what this book is *not* about:

This book is not about rules

> The recommendations made in this book are not to be taken as absolute truths.

This book is not about search

> Though related to web navigation, this book doesn't cover the issues of search systems. Chapter 11 offers some insight into how search and browse mechanisms can be integrated, but even there, the focus is on navigation.

This book is not about programming or implementation

> There are no examples of code or how to implement a navigation system; instead, I focus on the conception and definition of navigation systems.

AUDIENCE FOR THIS BOOK

Essentially anyone involved in web site development can benefit from *Designing Web Navigation*, including managers and other non-designers. Specifically, this book is intended for people new to the field of web design and students who want to learn more about the topic. I hope that experts may get a fresh look at the perennial problem of web navigation as well.

Although this book covers the basics of web navigation, I make a few assumptions about your prior knowledge. It's taken for granted that you are familiar with the Web and how it works in general. You may have even already been involved in web development projects in some way. If you're not yet comfortable with the terminology of web design, you might consider reading *Learning Web Design* (3rd Ed.) by Jennifer Robbins (O'Reilly, 2007) first.

ORGANIZATION OF THIS BOOK

There are three larger parts to this book. It begins with a tour of aspects and elements of web navigation, introduces a framework for navigation design, and finally explores some special topics of navigation.

Designing Web Navigation begins by introducing two basic areas of navigation design that you should understand before starting a project: human information behavior and web navigation elements. How do we navigate on the Web? How do we find information in general? Understanding these broader concerns can help you arrive at an appropriate solution for your navigation system. Also keep in mind that for any one problem, there may be a large palette of navigation mechanisms and navigation types that solve it. You need to be familiar with the tools of craft. Part 1 provides an overview of web navigation, navigation behavior, and some of the building blocks needed to create effective systems.

Every completed web project has a process because there is an outcome. Something had to have happened to get to the final result. The question is if the process was planned or unplanned, implicit or explicit, organized or chaotic. Part 2 offers a systematic framework for navigation design. Describing the process in terms of phases helps us focus on individual aspects and learn from the method more easily. In practice, however, the steps you'll take to create navigation probably won't be linear, but instead, you'll move back to previous steps or skip ahead. The phases presented here represent modes of thinking, not blocks of time on a project plan. Overall, web navigation design is about moving from an abstract concept to a concrete solution.

Navigation underlies most aspects of web design. As new design techniques, new types of web services, and new technologies emerge, good navigation design continues to play a critical role in their success. The last part of this book surveys several different contexts for web navigation: integrating navigation and search, creating effective navigation systems for social classifications and tagging services, and developing navigation with rich web applications.

ACCESSIBILITY AND INTERNATIONALIZATION

Two overarching principles of web design recur throughout the book: accessibility and internationalization. These are not afterthoughts in the design process, nor do they fit neatly into any one phase or activity. You don't create a site and then make it accessible, for instance. Retrofitting a site for compliance with accessibility guidelines is much harder than planning for it ahead of time. Instead, issues of accessibility and internationalization underlie the navigation design from beginning to end.

ACCESSIBILITY

Web accessibility commonly refers to building sites so that people with disabilities can use them. Guidelines and current practices focus on seeing-impaired users, and much of the text here is geared toward this group as well. But keep in mind that other disabilities, such as mobility or learning impairments, also fall under accessibility.

Assistive technologies are a class of devices that aid disabled people in using the Web. *Screen readers* are the most common assistive technology and receive a great deal attention in web design. After accessing a page, these programs read it out aloud in a computerized voice.

Accessibility is the law in many countries.[1] Most legislation for making accessible web sites points to or relies on the guidelines from the World Wide Web Consortium's (W3C) Web Accessibility Initiative (WAI) in some way. If you're interested in web accessibility, you should become familiar with this standard (see *www.w3.org/WAI*).

But beyond complying with legal regulations, accessibility is simply good practice. Sites that are accessible have benefits for others, too. In the real world, for instance, building curbs that dip down to meet the road not only help people in wheelchairs, they also help people with carts, bicycles, or rolling luggage. On the Web, clear easy-to-click labels with sufficient contrast help the disabled and non-disabled alike.

For more on accessibility see:

Constructing Accessible Web Sites, by Jim Thatcher, Cynthia Waddell, Shawn Henry, Sarah Swierenga, Mark Urban, Michael Burks, Bob Regan, and Paul Bohman (Peer Information, Inc., 2002).

> This is a collection of articles on web accessibility from the top professionals in the field. It's a great resource for anyone trying to develop accessible web sites. Topics range from accessibility laws to technical aspects of making Flash accessible.

Building Accessible Websites, by Joe Clark (New Riders, 2003).

> This book takes an in-depth look at a broad range of web accessibility issues, including specific techniques for implementation. Though full of detailed technical advice for expert programmers, it is approachable by novices.

INTERNATIONALIZATION

By default, sites on the Web have a global reach. Companies that previously had only a local clientele may now have a worldwide audience. Internationalization looks at the issues of designing sites so they are appropriate in a global setting, taking language, culture, and legal regulations into account. Where appropriate, I attempt to point out how issues of internationalization may affect your navigation design. Again, the hope is to sensitize you to consider internationalization as you go along and not treat it as an unplanned afterthought.

For more on internationalization see:

Beyond Borders: Web Globalization Strategies, by John Yunker (New Riders, 2002).

> This is a thorough and focused book that contains a wealth of practical details on the internationalization of web sites, including various content formats, issues regarding character sets, and step-by-step guides on how to translate web sites effectively, to name just a few. Several case studies illustrate the principles in real life.

Globalization Step-by Step, *www.microsoft.com/globaldev/getwr/steps/wrguide.mspx*.

> This is a very informative site from developers and designers at Microsoft. It includes practical advice on developing software for global markets, and many of the suggestions also apply to web site design.

---

1   See the resource page on the World Wide Web Consortium's site for international policies on accessibility: *www.w3.org/WAI/Policy*.

W3C Internationalization Activity, *www.w3.org/International.*

This is a working group of the W3C whose mission is to "ensure that W3C's formats and protocols are usable worldwide in all languages and in all writing systems." The focus is mainly on implementation and technical aspects, such as the coding of characters sets, but the site contains some information about interface design, including navigation.

ACKNOWLEDGMENTS

It's quite amazing to me how many people contributed to the completion of this book. I thank you all. Hopefully I won't leave anyone out.

First, my deepest thanks go out to the primary technical reviewers of this book, Dr. Mark Edwards and Aaron Gustafson. Your comments, critiques, and hard work are much appreciated.

A special debt of gratitude also goes out to the contributors of the sidebars: Ariane Kempken, my first real mentor in user-centered design, for her thoughts on the subject; Misha Vaughan, for her inspiring work with information shape and her sidebar on that topic; Eric Reiss, entertaining and fascinating as always with "Shared References"; Donna Maurer, for her incredible energy and brilliant insight into card sorting; Victor Lombardi, for his expert knowledge and opinion, and for helping make this book possible; Andrea Resmini, Emanuele Quintarelli, and Luca Rosati for their inspiration and great work on the FaceTag project; and Mark Edwards, for his expert knowledge and experience with interaction design and documentation techniques.

Of course, many others pitched in by reading and reviewing chapters, listening to my questions, and contributing in many other ways. Thank you all for your feedback and for your time: Peter Boersma, Liz Danzico, Jochen Fassbender, Margaret Hanley, Michael Hatscher, Andrea Hill, Theba Islam, Jeff Lash, Victor Lombardi, Ariane Kempken, Michael Kopcsak, Eric Mahleb, Kathryn McDonnell, Donna Maurer, Wolf Nöding Andrew Otwell, Tanya Raybourn, Eric Reiss, Andrea Resmini, Steffen Schilb, Gene Smith, and Joseph Veehoff. I wouldn't have been able to write this book without your support.

A huge debt of gratitude goes to my editor, Linda Laflamme for her expert opinion and insight, and for calming me down or pushing things along as needed. I'd also like to thank Steve Weiss for showing me the way. I'm very grateful for the hard work of the whole team at O'Reilly.

Finally, thanks to all the great working colleagues over the years from whom I learned the contents of this book. And, of course, thanks to my family and friends for their encouragement and support.

Danke schön!

James Kalbach

Hamburg, Germany

james.kalbach@gmail.com

HOW TO CONTACT US

Please address comments and questions concerning this book to the publisher:

O'Reilly & Associates, Inc.
1005 Gravenstein Highway North
Sebastopol, CA 95472
(800) 998-9938 (in the United States or Canada)
(707) 829-0515 (international/local)
(707) 829-0104 (fax)

There is a web page for this book, which lists errata and additional information. You can access this page at:

www.oreilly.com/catalog/9780596528102

To comment or ask technical questions about this book, send email to:

bookquestions@oreilly.com

For more information about books, conferences, software, Resource Centers, and the O'Reilly Network, see the O'Reilly web site at:

www.oreilly.com

SAFARI® ENABLED

When you see a Safari® Enabled icon on the cover of your favorite technology book, it means that book is available online through the O'Reilly Network Safari Bookshelf.

Safari offers a solution that's better than eBooks. It's a virtual library that lets you easily search thousands of top tech books, cut and paste code samples, download chapters, and find quick answers when you need the most accurate, current information. Try it for free at *http://safari.oreilly.com*.

ABOUT THE AUTHOR

James Kalbach is a human factors engineer at LexisNexis, a leading provider of legal and news information, where he develops interfaces for web-based search applications. He previously served as head of information architecture with Razorfish, Germany. James holds a degree in library and information science from Rutgers University, as well as a Master's degree in music theory and composition.

James is an assistant editor at Boxes and Arrows, a leading online journal for user experience information (*www.boxesandarrows.com*). He also serves on the advisory board of the Information Architecture Institute and is on the organizing committee for the European Information Architecture conferences (*www.euroia.org*).

Music is his main creative outlet outside of work, and James plays bass in a local jazz combo in Hamburg, Germany, where he lives with his wife, Nathalie, and cat, Niles. James is also a craft beer aficionado and regularly contributes ratings and stories to RateBeer.com, a leading online beer community, under the user name *pivo* (*www.ratebeer.com*).

ABOUT THE TECHNICAL REVIEWERS

Dr. Mark Edwards is a user experience consultant working for LexisNexis in the UK and specializing in commercial ethnography and online product design. In addition to electronic publishing, Mark has worked in the telecom and healthcare industries as a usability expert for many years. He has taught and carried out research into Human-Computer Interaction in U.K. Universities. Mark has degrees in Computing and HCI.

After getting hooked on the Web in 1996 and spending several years pushing pixels and bits for the likes of IBM and Konica Minolta, **Aaron Gustafson** decided to focus full-time on his own web consultancy, Easy! Designs LLC. Aaron is a member of the Web Standards Project (WaSP) and the Guild of Accessible Web Designers (GAWDS). He also serves as Technical Editor for *A List Apart*, is a contributing writer for *Digital Web Magazine*, and is quickly building a library of writing and editing credits in the real world. He has graced the stage at numerous conferences including An Event Apart, COMDEX, SXSW, The Ajax Experience, and Web Directions. He is frequently called on to provide web standards training in both the public and private sector.

PART I

Foundations of Web Navigation

The navigation designer must first be comfortable with the tools and elements that comprise web navigation, and realize that for any one navigation problem there may be a number of mechanisms that solve it. To help you, Part 1 presents a general overview of web navigation and the wide range of considerations you must take into account for its design.

The first two chapters, "Introducing Web Navigation" and "Understanding Navigation," paint a broad picture of web navigation and basic human information behavior, covering a lot of ground in a short space. These chapters are less practical and more theoretical than later chapters, presenting a sampling of views from other experts, as well as introducing key concepts.

Chapter 2, for instance, condenses the field of information seeking into a few pages, distilling decades of research and volumes of literature on the subject. I encourage you to explore the topics of interest further. Follow the references in the text or see the "Further Reading" section at the end of each chapter.

The next three chapters shift gears to discuss specific elements of navigation in detail:

- Chapter 3, "Mechanisms of Navigation," details various types of devices used in navigation.
- Chapter 4, "Types of Navigation," shows how mechanisms are used and reviews different categories of navigation.
- Chapter 5, "Labeling Navigation," digs into crafting the text and language used to label navigation options.

Together, these chapters offer a tour of navigation basics and establish a common language for discussing navigation.

Introducing Web Navigation

01

IN THIS CHAPTER

- Definition of navigation
- Overview of web navigation
- Roles of navigation
- Navigation design and design perspectives

Navigation plays a major role in shaping our experiences on the Web. It provides access to information in a way that enhances understanding, reflects brand, and lends to overall credibility of a site. And ultimately, web navigation and the ability to find information have a financial impact for stakeholders.

Navigation design is a task that is not merely limited to choosing a row of buttons. It's much broader, and, at the same time, more subtle than that. The navigation designer coordinates user goals with business goals. This requires an understanding of each, as well as a deep knowledge of information organization, page layout, and design presentation. This chapter paints a broad context for web navigation to help you better appreciate not just its purpose, but its potential scope of importance.

CONSIDERING NAVIGATION

When web navigation works well, it's underwhelming. Navigation is best when it's not noticed at all. It's like the officiating of a sports match. The referee may make dozens of good decisions throughout the game, and you may not even know he's there. But with one bad call, the ref is suddenly the center of attention for thousands of booing spectators.

Figure 1-1 shows a news article from the international version of the BBC web site (*www.bbc.co.uk*). It's the kind of page that we all come across regularly on the Web. There is nothing particularly interesting about the navigation. It's there when you need it, and out of the way when you don't. But this page illustrates some typical navigational features.

Figure 1-1 / An article from BBC news

Where did your focus of attention first land? If you're not looking for a specific topic, your eyes may wander across the page. You might have first seen the logo in the upper left, or perhaps the article title. Maybe the image grabbed your attention. But you probably didn't notice the E-Mail This to a Friend link above the headline or the search input field in the upper right. If you were looking for those functions, however, you could have found them easily.

Without knowing it, you made out a scheme for the page to help you understand its navigation and content. Even before you read any text, you had already created a mental image of how this page is put together in your mind: over here are the main options, over there is the article text, and down below are more options. People do this quickly and automatically.

People also rapidly scan pages for the words that meet their information needs. If you were looking for a local weather report, you'd figure out quickly that this is the wrong page. But you might have then seen the Weather option at the very top of the page. In clicking on this option, you'd expect to go to the section of the site for weather. For this reason, the labels and texts of navigation are critical.

What's more, the organization and grouping of labels also communicate valuable information about how to navigate. For instance, the first seven options on the left side of the page communicate a geographical organization of the news articles. Or, the collection of links on the right under the Climate Change—In Depth header in Figure 1-1 clearly let you know how you can find further information on the topic.

Overall, the various elements come together to create *system* of navigation. Though visitors might perceive this system as whole, we can dissect its individual components. For instance, the tabs at the top center of the page (starting with Home) are referred to as the *main navigation*. This page is in the News section. Within News, the local navigation is represented by a vertical menu on the left, which indicates where you are (Science/Nature is highlighted) and where else you can go, such as to articles about Africa or the business news section.

Is this a good navigation system? The answer is ultimately relative. You must consider a range of factors, from business goals to user goals. Still, there are common principles of good navigation that we can use to evaluate the quality of navigation. For instance, navigation on the BBC page is balanced, consistent, and provides a clear indication of where you are. Overall, it's appropriate for this type of site and probably gets people to where they want to go—the most important factor for judging success in navigation design.

DEFINING WEB NAVIGATION

Think about a link—the most basic ingredient of the Web. Links are text or graphics in one page that connect to another page or a different location within a single page. They allow for the associative leap from one idea to the next—a powerful concept. If you're reading a story about China's foreign policy you can then jump to a page with detailed information about the demographics of the country, thanks to a link. But, links do more than just associate one page with another. They also show importance. Links show relevance.

Web navigation is defined three ways:

1. The theory and practice of how people move from page to page on the Web.

2. The process of goal-directed seeking and locating hyperlinked information; browsing the Web.

3. All of the links, labels, and other elements that provide access to pages and help people orient themselves while interacting with a given web site.[1]

Web navigation design is about linking. It's about determining importance and relevance of the pages and content on your site. This requires judgment in establishing meaningful relationships between pages of information. Together, the elements of navigation determine not only if you can find the information people are looking for, but also how you experience that information.

THE NEED FOR NAVIGATION

Critics of navigation conclude that it should be eliminated from web sites all together. Author and interaction design advocate Alan Cooper, for one, suggests that navigation is unnecessary. He writes:

> " *The artless web sites created during the Web's infancy were of necessity built only with simple HTML tags, and were forced to divide up their functionality and content into a maze (a web?) of separate pages. This made a navigation scheme an unavoidable component of any web site design, and of course, a clear, visually arresting navigation scheme was better than an obscure or hidden one. But many web designers have incorrectly deduced from this that users want navigation schemes. Actually, they'd be happy if there were no navigation at all.* "

He then encourages a different paradigm for the Web:

> " *Skilled web developers using modern browsers and site construction tools such as ActiveX and JavaScript can create easier to use single-screen interactions that don't require jumping around from page to page. Yet many web designers continue to divide, and divide again, their sites into many fractured pages. These hierarchical arrangements of screens force them to impose a navigational burden on their users.*[2] "

True, people don't particularly want to navigate and risk getting lost. They come to a site to get answers or accomplish a task. As such, web navigation can be considered a means to an end. But is it a necessary evil? If navigating isn't fun, why impose a burden on people with something that could potentially confuse them?

It would be hard to image a web site without the familiar navigation we've grown accustomed to on the Web. To better understand the need for navigation, it might help to look at the some of the different functions web navigation potentially has. Web navigation:

- Provides access to information
- Shows location in a site
- Shows "aboutness" of a site
- Reflects brand

---

1   Although linking between separate sites on the Web is clearly important, the focus in this book is on designing intra-site navigation systems.

2   Alan Cooper, "Navigating isn't fun," *Cooper Interaction Design Newsletter* (October 2001). *www.cooper.com/newsletters/2001_10/navigating_isnt_fun.htm*.

- Affects site credibility
- Impacts the bottom line

Consider each of these points in greater detail.

NAVIGATION PROVIDES ACCESS TO INFORMATION

Sometimes it's hard not to state the obvious. Of course, web navigation provides access to information. Everyone knows that; we navigate the Web for information every day. However, alternative means of access also exist. Consider some possible alternative models of *how* information on your site can be accessed:

The content-linking-only model

Imagine a collection of pages linked to one another with no particular hierarchical organization or pattern of linking. All the links are embedded in the text. They aren't isolated in a way that serves as a navigational scheme, and there's no concept of a traditional home page. The site is just a big web of related information. Conceptually, it might look like Figure 1-2.

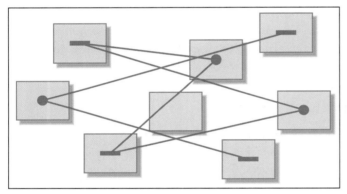

Figure 1-2 / The content-linking-only model

You might argue this would provide strong relationships between documents. A linked term or phrase on one page has a close association with the content on the destination page. But overall findability is low with this model. People wouldn't have a sense of beginning or end in their search for information, and orientation would be difficult. Also, access time would be much longer. You'd have to scan the text in its entirety to get a sense of all related content. This is certainly not the most efficient way to access information.

The "liquid information" model

This is similar to the content-linking model, but there are no links. Instead, each and every word is interactive for all texts. There is no distinction between text and hypertext, or between content and navigation. All texts are links, and all links are texts. Figure 1-3 depicts this model. From a single word on a given page, any number of navigation actions is possible, leading to new content pages.

The University College of London Interaction Centre (UCLIC, *www.uclic.ucl.ac.uk*) hosts a research project that explores the possibility of making all online text interactive—right down to

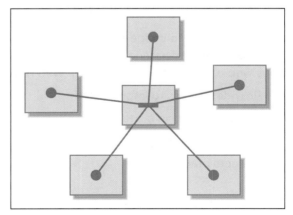

Figure 1-3 / The "liquid information" model

the individual words.[3] Instead of hypertext, the researchers refer to this as Hyperwords. The basic idea is that when a word is clicked, an option menu appears (as shown in Figure 1-4). You can then conduct a search, link to related documents, define the term, translate it, and so on. As they put it, the goal is to put an "end to the tyranny of links." This would also mean an end to navigation design.

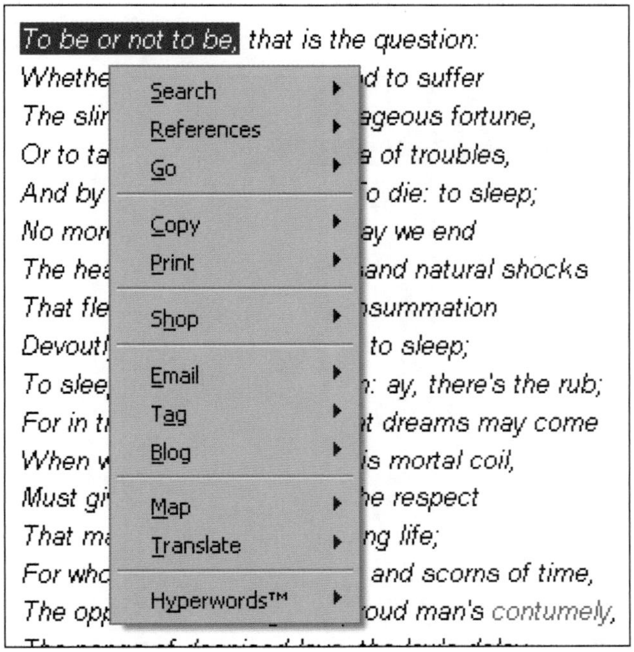

To be or not to be, that is the question:
Whethe   Search   ▶ d to suffer
The slir   References   ▶ ageous fortune,
Or to ta   Go   ▶ e of troubles,
And by   To die: to sleep;
No mor   Copy   ▶ ay we end
The hea   Print   ▶ and natural shocks
That fle   summation
Devoutl   Shop   ▶ to sleep;
To slee   Email   ▶ n: ay, there's the rub;
For in t   Tag   ▶ t dreams may come
When v   Blog   ▶ is mortal coil,
Must gi   Map   ▶ he respect
That ma   Translate   ▶ ng life;
For who   and scorns of time,
The opp   Hyperwords™   ▶ oud man's contumely,

Figure 1-4 / Navigation options with the Hyperwords menu

The filter model

Imagine accessing all the content of a web site through a single page. This page contains controls for filtering and sorting to present different chunks of material at a time. It would be highly interactive, for sure. A list of documents in the collection shrinks and expands with each interaction. Clicking on an individual item in the list would reveal its full text and images. Figure 1-5 shows this concept. A single control on a given page leads to new content, but that content is presented within the same page. The motion is therefore circular: you never leave the page, just continuously update its content.

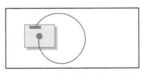

Figure 1-5 / The filter model

This model suggests a potentially efficient way to access information, similar to the model Alan Cooper proposes at the beginning of this section. But the experience would be quite different from navigating or browsing. First-time visitors would not get a good overview of the type of content available on the site. It might also be difficult for users to know when a search is completed: you could potentially filter and sort all day and still arrive at new lists of content. Bookmarking and general accessibility are also complicated.

---

3   See the liquid information project at *www.liquidinformation.org* and Hyperwords at *www.hyperwords.net*.

A working example of this model can be found in an experimental interface developed by researchers at IBM to browse the works of American composer Philip Glass (*www.philipglass.com/html/pages/glass-engine.html*). As shown in Figure 1-6, the Glass Engine filters the works of Philip Glass by various facets within a single page: the blue bars are sliders that can be moved left and right to locate pieces of music. The title and short description of each work are displayed in the center of the page, in this case, for *Einstein on the Beach*.

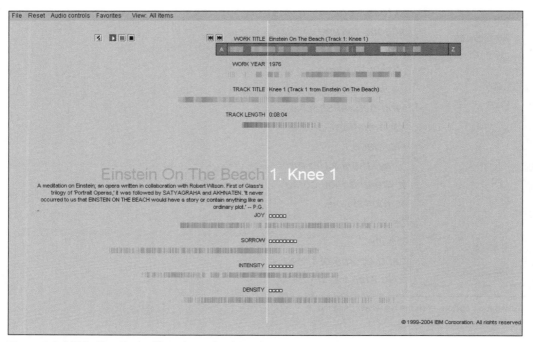

Figure 1-6 / IBM's Glass Engine filters the works of American composer Philip Glass

The search model

In this model of access, there is no navigation or linking to internal documents. Instead, visitors to the site can only perform keyword searches for information. Users type a keyword or two into a box and click the Search button. This produces a list of pages they can access. On the individual content pages, the only option is to return to the list or conduct a new search. Figure 1-7 shows these three steps from left to right.

Search is certainly an efficient way to get to content. We search on the Web all the time. But keyword searching is effective only if the item being sought is known in advance. It assumes that people will be able to accurately and completely express their information needs as a query. However, this may not always be the case.

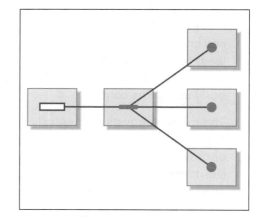

Figure 1-7 / The search model

The structural-browse model

In this model, there is only a set of links, perhaps on the side of each page, that provide access to information on a web site. This area is visually separated from the page content in the layout. You can click through a hierarchy of navigation options, refreshing the page content each time, as shown graphically in Figure 1-8. To get to a page in another area of the site, you'd have to navigate back up the tree and back down another branch. There are no embedded links within the text and no search function. Compare this with the content-only linking model, in which associations can be made in any direction from any page.

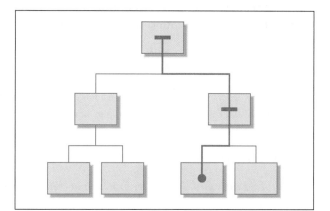

Figure 1-8 / The structural browse model

BALANCED NAVIGATION

Discussion of these too-pure models is intentionally one-sided. Generally, web sites have a mix of the models including structural navigation, content linking, and search and filtering mechanisms. Each supports a potentially different mode of seeking. Therefore, navigation tools for information on the Web come in multiple forms. Overall, a web navigation system provides efficient and balanced access.

In reality, web navigation might look more like something depicted in Figure 1-9, where various types of access are blended together. Navigation design is about creating a *system* of access to information. It is this system that gives rise to the web navigation experience.

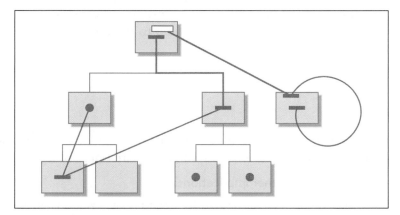

Figure 1-9 / Web navigation: multiple forms of access to information

What's more, navigating can be a more engaging information experience than, say, just a keyword search. For instance, usability expert Jared Spool and his colleagues found that people tend to continue shopping more often when navigating than after doing a direct keyword search:

> " *So, users come to the site with a purpose and they do their best to achieve that purpose. The question is: what happens after they've achieved it? How do we get them to that valuable content that they didn't know was there?*
>
> *Well, our recent studies have turned up some surprising statistics. Apparently, the way you get to the target content affects whether you'll continue looking or not.*
>
> *In a recent study of 30 users, we found that if the users used Search to locate their target content on the site, only 20% of them continued looking at other content after they found the target content.*
>
> *But if the users used the category links to find their target, 62% continued browsing the site. Users who started with the category links ended up looking at almost 10 times as many non-target content pages as those who started with Search.[4]* "

When browsing a web site, people seem to learn about other available content. For e-commerce sites, this could equal more sales; for a non-profit organization, it could result in more support; for a medical information site, it could provide a deeper understanding of a disease or cure. In other words, it's *how* navigation systems provide access to important information.

People prefer information that involves sequence. They like to browse. Navigation provides a narrative for people to follow on the Web. It tells a story—the story of your site. In this respect, there is something both familiar and comforting about web navigation. The widespread, seemingly natural use of navigation to access content on the Web reflects its strength as a narrative device.

NAVIGATION SHOWS LOCATION

Navigation isn't just about getting from one page to another; it's also about *orientation*. Sometimes people need to know where they are in a web site. Research on hypertext systems in the '80s showed this to be the case—location information helps people navigate. Many have pointed to the three basic needs in web orientation. While navigating a site, users generally need to know:

- Where am I?
- What's here?
- Where can I go from here?

Location is often indicated by highlighting the currently selected option in a navigation menu or displaying the path with a *breadcrumb trail*. Some sites even stamp location with a You Are Here notation.

Beyond orientation, knowing your location in a site has other implications:

- Comprehension of a given page may improve—or even require—understanding its relationship to other pages. This is particularly prevalent when entering a site at a page on lower levels in the site structure rather than through the home page, such as via external search results. In other words, navigation isn't just about where you are, but also about the meaning of the content. Navigation helps set context along with page titles and other elements.

---

4   Jared Spool, "Users Continue After Category Links" (December 2001). *www.uie.com/articles/continue_after_categories*.

- Pages that are deeper in a site structure may be seen as more precise. Knowing how deep you are in a site can give cues as to granularity and detail of information encountered. The natural expectation is that pages higher in a site are more general in nature, and the detail comes out as you move further down the structure.

- Knowing where you are in a site gives cues into exhaustiveness in seeking information. Location can signify if you should keep looking or not. The site navigation, then, potentially provides a sense of closure while looking for information.

For instance, Figure 1-10 shows the page for financial support for students in Europe on the Open University web site (*www.open.ac.uk*). To get to this page, you have to make several clicks: Becoming a student > Financial Support > Students Resident in Continental Europe. The relatively deep location of this page indicates that there isn't more on this subject on the site, and to find more information you'd have to call the phone number or write to the email address provided. Additionally, by itself, Students Resident in Continental Europe could refer to many things. Knowing that this is within the category Financial Support gives it a clear meaning.

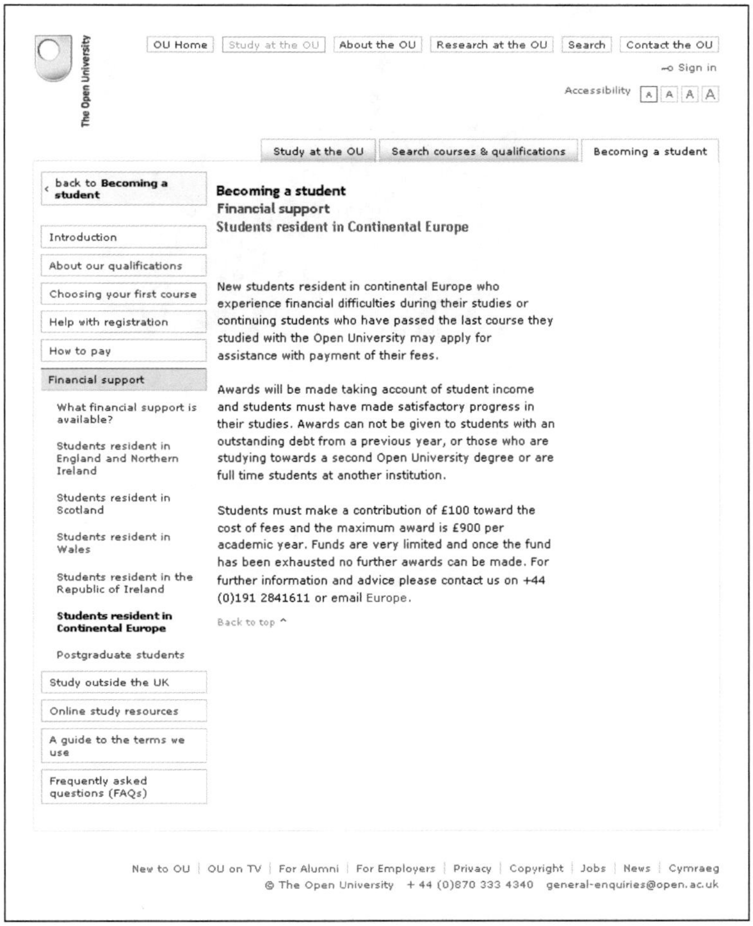

Figure 1-10 / Location information in the navigation of the Open University web site

Navigation conveys the breadth and type of a web site's content and offerings, or the "aboutness" of the site. It creates an overall, meaningful coherence of subject matter of the site and sets expectations. In turn, knowledge of main topics of a site can affect the approach people take to finding information there. Note that this does not imply that navigation shows the scope of the site in terms of quantity of pages. Instead, it reflects the depth of the subject of a site.

Imagine you want to buy a new stereo receiver from Sony. You know to go to the Sony Style web site (Figure 1-11, *www.sonystyle.com*) to find out about their products. When you get there, you find categories for all kinds of electronic equipment: computers, cameras, TVs, and more.

Figure 1-11 / Stereo receivers on the Sony Style site under TV & Home Entertainment and Home Audio Components

The navigation at top of the page is clear, and you're able to work your way to the home audio section to find stereo receivers. Along the way, you also understand that Sony offers a wide range of all kinds of electronics.

Now compare Sony's site to the Harman/Kardon site (Figure 1-12, *www.harmankardon.com*).

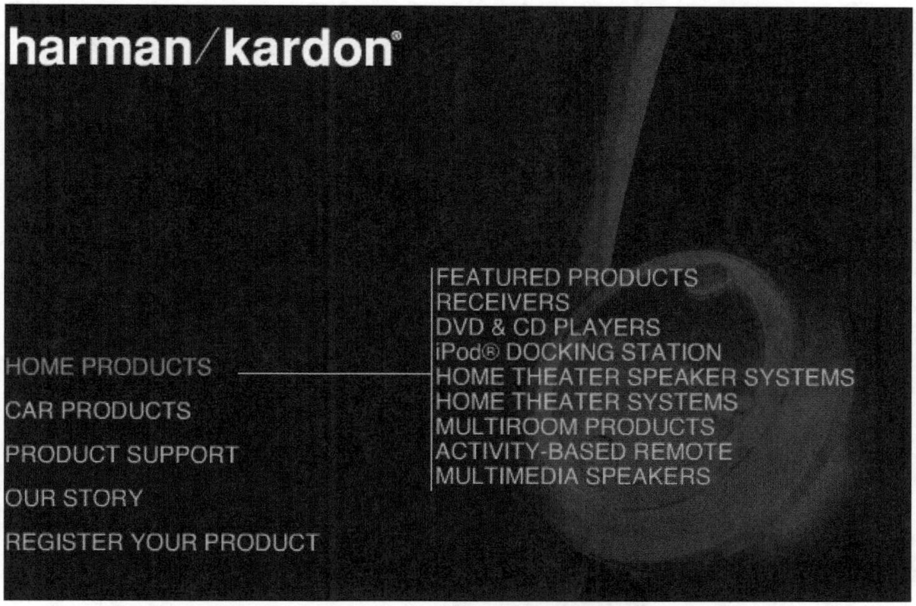

Figure 1-12 / Receivers under Home Products on the Harman/Kardon web site

Harman/Kardon makes a select range of high-end audio products. The navigation here is quite different than the Sony site shown in Figure 1-11. The browsing experience on the Harman/Kardon site is much more focused. This breadth is reflected by the site's navigation. Also note that Harman/Kardon places emphasis on car products, something you won't find on Sony's site. The two sites reflect a different depth and breadth on a similar topic, and these differences are reflected in the navigation.

In general, navigation offers visitors a semantic peripheral vision of a site's content. This provides cues for its relevance to your information needs. It reveals what's available and what's not, and lets you know you're exploring the right topic.

NAVIGATION REFLECTS BRAND

Brand is often thought of in terms of its visual manifestation: logo, colors, font, etc. These elements— commonly referred to as trade dress—help people identify with your company and its products. But a brand is much more than that. Brand position affects essentially every aspect of a product or service, including web navigation. Ultimately, a brand is a promise to the consumer about the goods and services offered.

Brands have values and character. For instance, one company brand may value its tradition and quality of products, while another may value being on the cutting edge and providing friendly customer service. Navigation reflects and supports aspects of the brand. The navigation options displayed, order of elements, tone of voice for labels, and visual style of navigation all contribute to a holistic brand experience on the Web.

Compare the main navigation areas of the watch makers Swatch (Figure 1-13; *www.swatch.com*) and Rolex (Figure 1-14; *www.rolex.com*).

Figure 1-13 / The home page for Swatch.com, featuring rotating navigation

Swatches are fashionable and modern, and are targeted at young, first-time watch buyers. The web site navigation reflects a youthful, fun brand. For instance:

- The main options are presented in a spinning circle in a playful way.

- In addition to an option for the main collections, there are links to such things as The Club and Beach Volley, which are special programs and activities the company sponsors.

- Teaser ads above the navigation (in the center of the page) include things like Flashmob Competition, as a way of attracting new customers.

Figure 1-14 / The Rolex home page

In contrast, the navigation on Rolex.com is more somber and in line with the Rolex brand. The company values tradition and quality, and generally caters to a much more upscale clientele. This comes through in the site's navigation:

- Collections is the first option in the upper-left. Rolex clearly places value on their traditional line of quality watches. Instead of a seasonal collection, as with Swatch, there are long-standing product lines such as The Oyster Professional.

- The category Sports & Culture contains information about opera, golf, and yachting. Beach volleyball is nowhere to be found on the Rolex site.

- Instead of a Club, as with Swatch, there is The Rolex Institute. And within The Rolex Institute, visitors find options for Awards for Enterprises and Rolex Mentors and Protégés.

Neither of these examples is right nor wrong, better or worse. The point is that these site navigations reflect their respective brands. You won't find Flashmob Competition on the Rolex site, for instance, just as you won't find options for yachting on the Swatch site.

Another example is the Bose Corporation, which makes a range of quality sound system products, from speakers, to home entertainment products, to car audio system. Key company values are research and innovation. Bose also has web sites in countries around the world. In most, these values are clearly reflected in the navigation. This is an excellent way to reinforce the brand beyond just visual branding elements.

Figure 1-15 shows the top portion of the home page for Bose Ireland (*www.bose.ie*). The first option, New from Bose, communicates that the company is moving forward with new products and research. Two options to the right of this is the Innovations link. The message: Bose is on the cutting edge of sound system and related products.

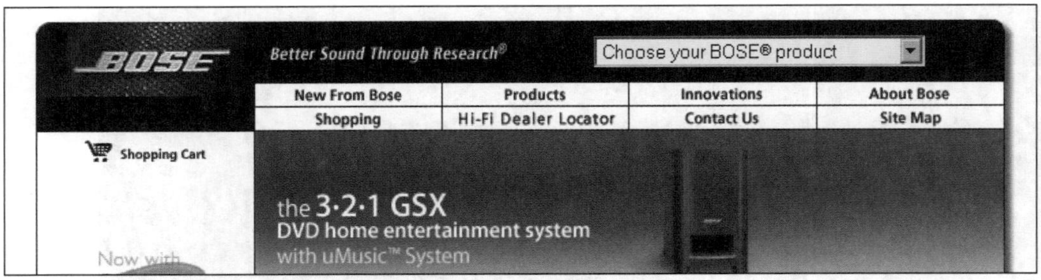

Figure 1-15 / Brand values reinforced in the navigation on the Bose web site in Ireland (*www.bose.ie*)

Color, images, and layout obviously play a more immediate role in the brand perception. But navigation labels, categories, and order of those options do as well. This perhaps more subtle type of branding is all too often excluded from conversations of web design. But all elements of a site contribute to the brand experience, including the navigation.

NAVIGATION AFFECTS SITE CREDIBILITY

Credibility refers to how believable a web site is; it's a perceived quality as judged by the visitor. A common goal in web site design is making the site more credible. This helps get a message across. The more believable your site is, the more effectively you can reach your audience and attain your goals. Good navigation helps you persuade and encourage visitors to do what you want them to.

Note that the term "persuasion" is not necessarily a negative concept. In fact, the ancient Greeks believed persuasion to be a cornerstone of democracy. It is the *abuse* of persuasion that is negative. Making your site more credible, and therefore potentially more persuasive, doesn't mean relying on coercion and deception. Your organization has objectives. Your site has objectives. You want visitors to register for a service, read specific content, go shopping, or perhaps even convince them to improve their own lives. Making a credible site helps your cause.

B.J. Fogg, director of Stanford University's Persuasive Technology Lab (*http://captology.stanford.edu*), has done the most extensive work on understanding web credibility to date.[5] His book *Persuasive Technology: Using Computers to Change What We Think and Do* (Morgan Koffmann; 2002), is highly recommended.

In a large-scale study, design look was the most important factor influencing web site credibility, and information organization was the second.[6] When judging credibility, participants commented on how easy or hard it was to navigate the site and on how well or poorly the information fit together. The results show that easily navigable sites are likely to carry more credibility.

Consider the web site for India's national broadcaster, Doordarshan (*www.ddindia.gov.in*), as an example (Figure 1-16). The site's navigation is full of problems:

---

5   See also the Stanford Web Credibility Research web site: *credibility.stanford.edu*.

6   BJ Fogg, Cathy Soohoo, David Danielson, Leslie Marable, Julianne Stanford, and Ellen R. Tauber, "How Do People Evaluate a Web Site's Credibility?" *Consumer Reports WebWatch* (2002). *www.consumerwebwatch.org/dynamic/web-credibility-report-evaluate.cfm*.

Broad, vague categories

For instance, you'll find categories such as Business, Information, and even Miscellaneous.

Abbreviations

Some visitors may not know what PB (BCI) and TAM Ratings mean.

Poor organization of menu options

Figure 1-16 shows Acts & Guidelines separated from The Right to Information Act 2005 by unrelated options.

Poor grouping of categories

Job Opportunities is under the main category Business, while Advertise on DD is under Information. You might expect this categorization to be the other way around.

Unexpected navigation behavior

Contact Us (under the Information main tab) leads to a page with a single link for a telephone directory. This link then opens an Excel document with names and addresses. In other cases, navigation options lead to blank pages.

Misspelled navigation options

Archieve instead of Archive.

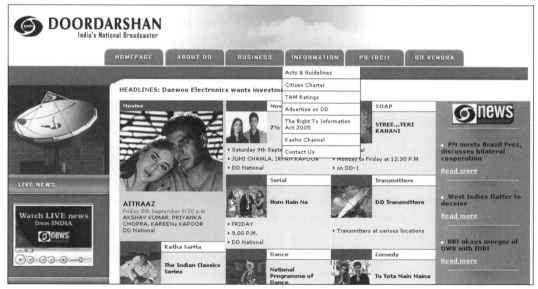

Figure 1-16 / Poor navigation reduces site credibility

Overall, the navigation experience is quite poor. This detracts from the credibility of the site and the organization as a whole. Of course, there are potentially many other influencing factors, such as visual design, content, and the reputation of the organization. But one thing holds true: well-designed, easy-to-use navigation is important in establishing credibility, authority, and trust.

Information is useless if it can't be found. Organizations spend so much time and money making information available on the Web without really knowing how—or even *if*—it's getting used. If a visitor can't find the information they're looking for, it can be costly to your business.

Calculating the return on investment for site navigation only can't be easily done, if at all. There are many other factors to consider as well, such as search, technical performance, user needs and behaviors, and usability of the site. Still, justifications for good navigation include:

Customers can't buy what they can't find

> For e-commerce sites, navigation is critical. As mentioned earlier, people tend to continue browsing—and buying—when they can successfully navigate to the products they want to purchase. Sure, keyword searching may also get them there, but that experience is different. Well-designed navigation plays a key role in getting people to the information or products you want to see. This ultimately helps you sell products or ideas.

Employees lose productivity when navigation is inefficient

> Companies are making more and more information available to their employees on corporate intranets, but the size of some intranets can be enormous. The time to find information is critical for employee productivity. Even the smallest increase in navigational efficiency can have huge returns for a large corporation if you multiple it by thousands of employees.

The cost of support increases with poor navigation

> If customers can't find what they're looking for, they'll either leave the site or call your help line, which increases costs at the call center. And if you don't have a call center, you've just lost a sale.

Brands become devalued with poor navigation

> Negative experiences with a site's navigation far outweigh any positive visual branding measures or marketing you may have done. Frustrated customers are hard to win back, regardless of how much you dazzle them elsewhere. And competition is not far away on the Web. So, effective navigation also brings a competitive advantage with it. Make your site useful, and people will come back and recommend the site to their friends. Similarly, frustrated users are unlikely to mention your site to another potential customer.

Plus, you must take into account the costs of training, relaunching, and so on. Mind you, well-designed navigation won't solve all your problems. But because navigation is so central to the basic Web experience, it stands to reason that its financial implications are potentially far-reaching.

WEB NAVIGATION DESIGN

Given the many potential roles web navigation plays, you can see that its design requires a mix of skills and levels of understanding. Many factors influence navigation design and, in turn, navigation affects many aspects of the site. Web navigation design can't be done in isolation. When considering a navigation design, ask yourself these fundamental questions:

Why are you building the site?

Though seemingly obvious, this question is overlooked all too often. Or, if it is asked, the answers are unclear or based on the wrong reasons. The first step in navigation design is understanding the purpose and motivation for the web site as a whole, as well as in the broader business context.

Who will use the site?

This is perhaps the most important question to ask. It's also one of the trickiest to answer. User research is the process of systematically investigating the visitors to a given site. It not only gives insight into the types of people visiting your site, but also into their needs and behaviors.

What does the navigation provide access to?

People come to a site to find answers or to perform a task. You must be providing the right content for the site to have value.

How is the site content organized?

Information architecture represents the underlying structures that give shape and meaning to the content and functionality on your site. It also has a major and direct impact on the navigation. As the designer, you must understand the content and how it is organized.

How will users navigate to the content they need?

Page layout and graphic design give the navigation its final form. This is more than just cosmetic window dressing, however. Aspects such as the order of options, their arrangement on the page, the font type and size used, and color, can be critical elements. They can make or break the navigation system.

Make no mistake: navigation is problematic, particularly on larger web sites. It's one of the thorniest parts of web design. Providing access to web pages on information-rich sites is remarkably complex. Web navigation design is ultimately a craft—a mix of art and science, intuition and facts, form and function.

DESIGN PHILOSOPHIES

Most web projects have a prevailing design perspective. Often this is implicit. It may not be written or spoken, but it's there. Understanding design perspectives can be important in creating a common team understanding and for guiding design decisions. Some of the many potential approaches to design are:

User-centered design

A user-centered design process places people at the center of attention while developing a product or service. It consists of methodologies that make the user an integral part of the development process, with activities such as interviews, observations, and various types of testing. This replaces guesswork and assumptions about user behavior with research. In the end, the overall design of the site should mirror how users understand the subject matter and how they expect to find information.

By carefully considering the actual context of use before a product hits the market, user-centered design potentially increases adoption rates and lowers learning curves. In this sense, user-centered design seeks to reduce the risk of product failure. User-centered design is not easy, however, and many point to the extra time and costs that user research adds to development. The benefits are not short term and pay off in the end.

Designer-centered design

From this perspective, the designer—in the broadest sense of the word—knows what's best. Decisions are made from a personal view of the world. The creative growth of the designer is valued, and her interests are highly valued. A type of free exploration may be encouraged, and there may be a need to make a statement through the final design. The designer-centered design approach can resemble perspectives found in art to some degree; personal expression is important.

This approach might be successful for smaller, design-focused enterprises and be able to produce successful sites. Creative teams also find this approach enjoyable and rewarding. However, such designer-centered design is also self-indulgent, and business goals may be overshadowed by personal interests. The designer-centered approach quickly becomes unsuccessful for sites that deal with vast amounts of information or complex interactions.

Enterprise-centered design

This is an all-too-common perspective. The web site is designed around the structure and needs of the stakeholder's company or organization. The main categories of a site, for instance, may reflect the departments of an enterprise. Also included in the perspective is the need to please the boss. Success may be measured by how well the key stakeholders react to the final product, perhaps even on a personal level.

This perspective may increase the efficiency for site maintenance later on: each department is responsible for only its own slice of the site. But it generally runs the risk of users becoming confused, getting lost, or going somewhere else.

Content-centered design

This is similar to enterprise-centered design, but an existing body of information is the basis for structuring navigation. For instance, you might organize content by document format rather than subject: all text pages in one place, all PDFs in another, images in another, and so forth.

You can easily argue that it's hard to provide access to something you don't have. In this sense, the content-centered design approach is only natural and to some degree constantly present. However, the amount and type of content available shouldn't be the only force determining navigation priorities.

Technology-centered design

This perspective also prevails on many web projects. Technology is the driving force here. Design might be determined by the easiest way to implement a solution. The focus is on implementation and reaching a final product.

This may also be cost effective and efficient. It may help meet a project deadline. But you run the risk that people won't be able to use or understand the final web site. In the long run, technology-centered design is generally counterproductive to project and business goals.

This book advocates a user-centered design perspective. This implies a holistic approach. It assumes that you—the web navigation designer—should consider a wide range of user behaviors. It requires you to actively validate assumptions about users' behavior by seeking various means of contact with them.

Note that user-centered design does not mean "do what users tell us to do," nor "ignore other project constraints." Of course, business goals and technology are important. Of course, the intuition of the navigation designer plays a vital role. But user-centered design methods can inform a designer's intuition, or better reach business goals in the long run. It's a question of the starting point and focus of the project. User-centered design mandates that the user experience is the primary goal: all other perspectives are secondary.

The Advantages of User-Centered Design

By Ariane Kempken

More and more, companies are turning to user-centered design (UCD) to improve their products and services. Companies have to go beyond maintaining their existing offerings. They must rethink their existing markets and explore new markets that exploit their strengths, capabilities, channels, and brands, particularly as marketplaces expand and specialize. UCD defines a set of methods that incorporate user needs into the development of products and services to save costs, foster true innovation, and provide a strategic edge over competitors.

- *Saving costs.* UCD enlists the help of users to expose problems and detect failures early on in the development process. It provides an inexpensive means to save the often exponentially greater cost of fixing problems in later development cycles and the cost of failures after a product or service is launched.

- *Fostering true innovation.* UCD studies the behavior of users while interacting with a product or service within its real life context. In doing so, it exposes needs that users either might not be aware of or might not be able to articulate. These insights and direct exposure to the user experience lead to non-obvious improvements and to the development of truly innovative products and services.

- *Providing a strategic edge.* UCD considers all factors of users' experience: cultural, social, cognitive, and physical. By creating a deeper understanding of the user, it affords the opportunity to establish long-term relationships that, over time, result in greater brand resonance, customer loyalty and strategic edge over competitors.

The goal of UCD is to establish a thorough understanding of users and their needs, allowing companies to fine tune current offerings and identify emerging opportunities to truly support users' lives.

An independent design and research consultant, Ariane Kempken has a master's degree in Human Centered Design from the Illinois Institute of Technology and has developed innovative products and services for IDEO and Razorfish. Contact her at ariane@designobjective.com.

SUMMARY

Links are the basic currency of the Web. They tie two pieces of web content together in a meaningful way. This is a powerful concept. Web navigation is a systematic organization of links to provide access to information and to make meaningful associations. Navigation plays a key role in our overall web experience. It would be hard to image the Web without it.

But it's not just that navigation provides access to information. It's *how* navigation provides access that's important. Browsing a site is a different experience than just searching it, for instance. Navigation provides context and understanding. Showing users where they are on your site helps orient them, not only within the structure of a site but also within the meaning of the content. Navigation reveals a site's thematic scope and it's relevance to a particular need.

Web navigation also plays a role in expressing a brand. It communicates corporate priorities and values through categories, the order of options, and the tone of the labels. Well-structured navigation also contributes to the overall credibility of a web site. People seem to trust a site that appears clearly organized with an easy-to-use navigational structure. Finally, web navigation can have a financial impact. The cost of finding information is high, and the cost of not finding information is perhaps even higher.

Web navigation design is necessarily a multidisciplinary endeavor. You must consider business goals, technology constraints, and content. More importantly, to design navigation well, you need to understand the people who will using it and what they are trying accomplish. The navigation designer does not only create a row of tabs and links. He balances a range of factors into a cohesive system that support the goals of the site and of visitors. Navigation design is a craft that blends skills and talents from different areas.

QUESTIONS

1. You'd like to buy a new CD in your favorite style of music. Nothing in particular, you just want the latest; something new. What is the difference between navigating an online music site, such as iTunes, and walking through the actual shop? Describe your experiences in the shop and on the web site as if you were:

    a) Someone shopping there for the first time.

    b) A regular visitor.

    c) What's the first thing you do in each situation? What's the last thing? How to you find what you are looking for?

2. You need a new computer desk for your home office. Use Ikea.com (or the Ikea site in your country) to find such a desk. First, do a search with the site search function, then browse to find a desk.

    a) What are the differences in how you locate the desk?

    b) What problems did you encounter with each method of access?

    c) Which was more helpful and why?

3. The World Wide Web is a type of hypertext system. Hypertext refers to the linking of one document to another, in this case, web pages. But the Web wasn't the first hypertext system to be imagined or developed. In 1945, an important American scientist during the Second World War, Vannevar Bush, envisioned a system that could link two documents.[7] With the hypothetical *memex machine*, as he dubbed it, people could create "trails" of related information. Later, Ted Nelson—who coined the term "hyperlink"—developed a system called Project *Xanadu*, considered the original hypertext system (although it took 30 years to complete and was not successful). Other attempts followed, including *HyperCard*, one of the first commercially viable hypertext applications, introduced by Apple Computer in 1987.

Using the Web, find out more about each of these systems and answer the following questions.

a) What were advantages and disadvantage of each of these systems? (Consider the memex as if it were a real system).

b) How did they approach solving the problem of navigating through information?

c) What are the differences between these systems and the Web?

d) Name two other hypertext systems apart from Xanadu and HyperCard. What approach did these take to linking information together and allowing people to navigate?

FURTHER READING

"As We May Think," by Vannevar Bush (*Atlantic Monthly*, July 1945).

This is the classic essay by Bush—the then scientific advisor to President Roosevelt—that inspired so many hypertext projects. This essay includes broad, sweeping discussions of the role of science, technology, and information. Though references to specific technologies are clearly outdated, the sentiments expressed here are timeless. Available online at: *www.theatlantic.com/doc/194507/bush*.

The Design of Everyday Things, by Donald A. Norman (Doubleday, 1990).

This is a seminal work in user-centered design—a must read for any designer. Norman uses many examples from everyday life to support his arguments. He points frequently to failures in design from all kinds of situation. Norman tends to repeat things and ramble at times, but the central tenet of this book is clear: the user's needs are not the same as the designer's.

Persuasive Technology: Using Computers to Change What We Think and Do, by B.J. Fogg (Morgan Kaufmann, 2002).

This book is highly recommended for anyone working with interface design. Fogg essentially defines a whole new discipline in one single volume. In painstaking detail, he describes the myriad of issues surrounding credibility and computers. Though this could easily serve as a college textbook, it has appeal to a larger audience. The discussions are easy to follow and at times mesmerizing. Rich, relevant examples bring concepts to life.

---

7   Vannevar Bush, "As We May Think," *Atlantic Monthly* (1945). *www.theatlantic.com/doc/194507/bush*.

Understanding Navigation

" Data is stored: Information is experienced "

—Andrew Dillon,
Dean of the Information School,
University of Texas at Austin

02

A man grabs the yellow pages and looks up the phone number of the local pizza delivery service. A scientist goes to the library to research her doctoral thesis using an online catalog. A woman searches the Web for beach resorts for the family vacation. These are all acts of information seeking.

Before beginning to design web navigation, you should take time to investigate how people look for information. The more you understand, the easier it is to structure your thoughts around solving design problems.

This chapter considers information seeking on three different levels:

General information seeking

How do people generally look for information? For simple fact-finding missions, information seeking may be straightforward. But for more complex problems, getting the information you need may be a long, involved process. This chapter briefly reviews a few key aspects from information seeking research and practice.

Seeking information online

How do people seek information online? This presents its own issues and challenges. The immediate availability of additional resources allows people to change seeking strategies rapidly. They don't always stay on course and may wander from page to page. They then get "lost in hyperspace," which is one of the oldest problems in a hypertext system design. You need to keep this in mind when creating web navigation.

Navigating web sites

How do people navigate the Web in particular? Research into web navigation behavior has only just begun. Some large-scale studies are beginning to build up, allowing for comparison over time. And concepts such transitional volatility, introduced by Stanford University researcher David Danielson, help us better explain how people navigate. Other considerations, such as "banner blindness" and others, also help form a larger picture of web navigation.

Information is not only sought, it is experienced. The term "experience" implies that emotions play an equal role alongside behavior and cognition. By considering the emotions people have when encountering a web site, we extend the mandate for navigation design. People can no longer be seen as rational, systematic information-seeking creatures. Given the critical role navigation plays on the Web, its design greatly influences the experience people will have while interacting with your site.

Taking the time to understand visitors' seeking patterns, emotions, and reactions now will help you better decide which navigation types you want to implement when we explore options in later chapters.

INFORMATION SEEKING

Information seeking refers to all of the various activities people undergo to find information. It's about how people gather information from their environment, usually to satisfy larger problem-solving goals. This can include everything people come in contact with over their lifetime—not just information that is actively sought.[1]

Theoretical models of information seeking help explain how people find information by taking holistic look at the ways in which people hunt for information in their lives. Understanding them may not solve your immediate web design problems, but an awareness of their basic principles can help you understand broader navigation issues. (See the sidebar "Theoretical Models of Seeking" for a discussion of some of the traditional academic models.)

Of particular interest for navigation designers is a behavioral model of information seeking proposed by David Ellis, professor at the University of Wales Aberystwyth.[2] This oft-cited framework has had a profound impact on information-seeking research because it demonstrates patterns across situations and contexts. Professor Ellis identifies six primary behaviors in information seeking:

- Starting: identifying relevant sources of interest
- Chaining: following and connecting new leads found in an initial source
- Browsing: scanning contents of identified sources for subject affinity
- Differentiating: filtering and assessing sources for usefulness
- Monitoring: keeping abreast of developments in a given subject area
- Extracting: systematically working through a given source for material of interest

Ellis' categorization of behaviors does not indicate a unidirectional process for finding information. Instead, the importance and involvement of each behavior in a given search is variable and situational. People move back and forth between them as they look for information. As a result, information seeking is a non-linear activity.[3]

When designing navigation, how might you support each of these types of information behaviors? Consider the starting behavior, for instance, and the different ways people get to a web site in the first place:

- Typing in a URL directly
- Referring to a bookmarked URL
- Following a link from another site
- Using a search engine

---

1 Professor Marcia Bates makes the point that information seeking can be active and passive. We come in contact with a great deal of information over our lifetimes in various ways. See Marcia Bates, "Toward an Integrated Model of Information Seeking," *The Fourth International Conference on Information Needs, Seeking and Use.* (Lisbon, Portugal. September, 2002). *www.gseis.ucla.edu/faculty/bates/articles/info_SeekSearch-i-030329.html.*

2 David Ellis, "A Behavioral Model for Information Retrieval System Design," *Journal of Information Science* 15, (1989): 237-247.

3 Alan Foster, "A Non-linear Model of Information Seeking Behavior," *Information Research* 10 (2005). *http://InformationR.net/ir/10-2/paper222.html.*

Theoretical Models of Seeking

Early models of information retrieval, or searching of electronic databases, tended to oversimplify the seeking process. Such models were black and white: the seeker simply enters a query and is given matching results. In the mid-'80s, however, there was a shift in information research and in information behavior studies. Researchers explicitly recognized the need for more holistic approaches in assessing information needs and uses.[1] Information seeking was seen as complex set of tasks with many variables.

New perspectives in research reversed traditional models of information system design. In particular, three different—yet complementary—research perspectives mark this shift:

- *Sense-Making.*[2] This needs-based model (Figure 2-1) focuses on everyday behaviors people exhibit when coming in contact with information, and was developed by Brenda Dervin, professor at Ohio State University. Sense-Making analyzes a broad spectrum of complex human activity and aims at understanding three key elements: people's situations, gaps in knowledge, and the use of information. Of particular interest are the strategies that people employ to bridge the gap and reach their information goals. Understanding the gaps in knowledge people have is critical to navigation design, discussed further in Chapter 9.

Figure 2-1 / Sense-Making Model (recreated after Dervin)

- *Anomalous states of knowledge (ASK).* This term was coined by Nicholas Belkin, professor at Rutgers University, who focused on the notion that seekers—sometimes even experts in a given information system—are not able to properly formulate queries to access the information they need.[3] How can a searcher begin to query an information system if he doesn't know the right question to ask or how to phrase it? In his view, the failures in information retrieval are caused by the system, not with the seeker.

- *Value-added seeking.* This model focuses on the perceived utility and value a user gets from a system and how this effects their decisions; it was proposed by Robert Taylor, a pioneer in the information-seeking research.[4] He placed the user's problems at the center of attention and was concerned with linking problems with information traits from a user's perspective.

For more on such academic models of information seeking, see Tom Wilson, "Models in Information Behaviour Research," *Journal of Documentation* 55, 3 (1999): 249-270. *http://informationr.net/tdw/publ/papers/1999JDoc.html*.

---

1 See in particular Brenda Dervin and M. Nilan, "Information Needs and Uses," *Annual Review of Information Science and Technology 21* (1986): 3-33.

2 Brenda Dervin, "From the Mind's Eye of the User: The Sense-Making Qualitative-Quantitative Methodology," *Qualitative Research in Information Management*, Ed. J. D. Glazier and R. R. Powell . Engelwood, CO: Libraries Unlimited (1992).

3 Nicholas Belkin, "Anomalous States of Knowledge as the Basis for Information Retrieval," *Canadian Journal of Information Science* 5 (1980): 133-143.

4 Taylor, Robert S. Taylor, "Value-added Processes in Document Based Systems: Abstracting and Indexing Services," *Information Services and Use* 4 (1984): 127-146 ; Taylor, Robert S., "Information Values in Decision Contexts." *Information Management Review* 1 (1985): 47-55.

Then consider the implications for design. How can you make it easier for people to get started? Some possible ways might be:

- Thoughtfully designed, human-readable URLs that are easy to remember.

- Alternate spellings for URLs to anticipate typos.

- Page construction that allows for easy and accurate bookmarking.

- Carefully worded browser titles that provide a useful context. (These are often displayed in search results as the linked element to your site.)

- Appropriate use of metatags to describe the site for meaning descriptions in search engine results lists.

There may be other ways that people get started, such as having to log in or enter a search query. The point is that even a generic model of information-seeking behavior such as Ellis' can help you determine useful navigation solutions.

_____ **Note** _____

For more information on how Ellis' behaviors correlate to the Web, consult "Information Seeking on the Web: An Integrated Model of Browsing and Searching," Chun Wei Choo and Don Turnbull, *FirstMonday* 5, 2 (2000). *http://firstmonday.org/issues/issue5_2/choo/index.html*.

_____

MODES OF INFORMATION SEEKING

Not all information seeking is the same. Sometimes you may know exactly what you're looking for. Let's say you just need the phone number of neighbor. You know his name and address, and can retrieve the number from an online directory quickly. Other times, you may have only a general idea of what you're after. For instance, you may want to learn more about gardening, with no particular end goal in mind.

The different approaches people take are called modes of information seeking. Sometimes people go about a search systematically. Sometimes they're just surfing or digressing from another task. Gary Marchionini, professor of information and library science at the University of North Carolina, has identified a scale of browsing modes:[4]

Directed browsing

This is systematic and focused on a specific object or target, such as scanning a list for a known item or verifying facts. In this mode, people have a small number of topics of interest or a specific information need.

Semi-directed browsing

This is less systematic, arising from a generally purposeful but less definite need. There may still be a goal of sorts, yet the seeker may not be able to express it fully. People who are new to a subject, for instance, and are still learning about the material, may exhibit semi-directed browsing behavior.

_____

4   Gary N. Marchionini, *Information Seeking in Electronic Environments* (Cambridge University Press, 1995): 106.

Undirected browsing

This implies there is no goal and little focus, as in flipping through a magazine or "channel-surfing" on TV. With undirected browsing, serendipitous discovery may be high. Curiosity is often the underlining motivation for this mode of browsing.

Donna Maurer, a freelance information architect in Australia (see her sidebar in Chapter 7), describes four similar modes in information seeking with some differences:[5]

Known-item search

This is when people know what they want, can describe it in words, and may also know where to start looking. Although known-item seeking is often associated with searching because keywords are known, a site visitor may also browse navigation with an item in mind.

Exploratory seeking

In this mode, there may be some idea of a need, but people may not be able to articulate that need clearly. Or, if the need can be identified, it may be so broad that it can't be solved quickly and the starting point may not be known. People can recognize a right answer, but may not know when they've covered the topic exhaustively. The original goal often changes as more information is discovered.

"Don't know what you need to know"

This is when people need information they didn't know existed. Or, they may think they need one thing but really need another.

Re-finding

This often overlooked mode refers to looking for things people have already seen.

These modes are not dispositional or mutually exclusive. That is, someone is generally not a "known-item searcher" by nature. Instead, modes of seeking are situational. Any one person could approach a web site in any mode at any time. For this reason, it is difficult to predict how people will approach your site. Still, if you can identify the key modes of seeking on your site, you should be better able to support your visitors' needs with the navigation.

For instance, while shopping online for a digital camera, people may compare brands and models over time. They may visit several sites to evaluate the pros and cons of various cameras. When they return to your site (assuming, of course, you're in the business of selling digital cameras), you want customers to easily re-find the last few products they viewed. This could be done passively so visitors don't have to take any action; for example, a Recently Viewed Items list might appear (Figure 2-2). Or, you could provide a "wish list" to allow them to actively save items.

---

5   Donna Maurer, "Four Modes of Seeking Information and How to Design for Them," *Boxes and Arrows* (March, 2006). *www.boxesandarrows.com/ view/four_modes_of_seeking_information_and_how_to_design_for_them.*

Figure 2-2 / Re-finding: recently viewed items on Amazon.de (Germany) with thumbnail images

SEEKING INFORMATION ONLINE

Online information-seeking behavior presents some unique problems and situations. Because linking from one source to another is simple and immediate, people can cover a great deal of information quickly. They tend to zigzag through online systems, moving from resource to resource, varying seeking strategies rapidly.

Marcia Bates, a professor at UCLA, likens online seeking to berrypicking.[6] If you've ever picked raspberries or blueberries, you know they don't come in bunches. Instead, you have to collect them one at time until your pail is full. You also move from bush to bush as you spot even riper berries, changing your approach fluidly. Similarly, when searching for information online, the solution to the original question is the culmination of many steps. It's not an all-or-nothing process. People constantly evaluate and re-evaluate what the find for relevance to their information need. People berrypick online.

Within Bates' Berrypicking Model, browsing and searching are complementary and not mutually exclusive activities. What's more, information needs evolve as people seek information. New information encountered sheds light onto the original problem, which itself changes and becomes compromised. Online information seeking is more like a negotiation between the seeker and the system.

When creating navigation, web designers often assume people will take a single, direct path to the information they are looking for. They don't. Instead, users may enter the site from a search engine on a page deep in the site's structure, move up to the home page, perform a keyword search, navigate to another page, and then pick one of the categories in the main navigation. Web navigation must be flexible enough to accommodate this behavior and support the evolving search.

Similar to the Berrypicking Model, Peter Pirolli and Stuart Card's theory of Information Foraging analyzes patterns in human information seeking[7] and is directly based on the food foraging theories found in biology and anthropology. Assuming we forage for information as early humans once foraged for food, we can then speak of "information ecologies" and refer to seekers as "informavores" that have "information diets."

---

6   Marcia Bates, "The Design of Browsing and Berrypicking Techniques for the Online Search Interface," *Online Review* 13 (1989): 407-424.

7   Peter Pirolli and Stuart Card, "Information Foraging in Information Access Environments," *Human Factors in Computer Systems: Proceedings of CHI95* (1995). *www.acm.org/turing/sigs/sigchi/chi95/Electronic/documnts/papers/ppp_bdy.htm.*

Foraging for information does not equate to aimless "surfing," however. Information Foraging Theory analyzes the trade-offs in the value of information gained against the cost of performing a task necessary to find information. It refers to the variety of strategies seekers exhibit in their quest for information and how humans adapt to their environments on a situational basis.

Consequently, in an information-rich world, the real design challenges are not only how to facilitate finding and collecting information, but how to optimize the seeker's time. Time optimization is a key goal of web navigation design.

But optimizing the seeker's time doesn't mean that you need to present every navigation option at all times. That could potentially confuse and overwhelm people. Instead, you want to preselect the most important links people will need while foraging for information. Chapter 9 outlines an approach to determining how much navigation is needed. This relies on identifying your primary user types and determining the key tasks and scenarios presented to your site's users while navigating. Then, design the navigation around those.

LOST IN HYPERSPACE

Even before the Web, the notion of getting "lost in hyperspace" existed, harkening back to closed hypertext systems of the 1980s.[8] Even in these relatively small systems, people got lost. Disorientation in navigation can occur for a variety of reasons:

- People can become disoriented when they do not understand the material itself.
- People can get lost in their seeking process and get to a point where they don't know what to do next.
- People can lose their sense of location in a web site, stranding them unable to get back to a prior page or even the home page.
- People digress and get distracted in online information systems, which is referred to as the embedded digression problem. People can lose track of the main tasks by lots of interesting, competing information.[9]

The enormous explosion of information on the Web has not improved the lost-in-hyperspace problem. Instead of small and independent hypertext databases, we now have a global network with billions of pages used every second of the day for work and pleasure by a wide range of people. And they get lost. Your site's visitors get lost. Even with a well-designed web site, people can still get lost.

A good navigation system can improve the experience people have with your site, however. It can help them figure out where they are in the site and where they can go. It can aid in devising a better seeking strategy and increase comprehension of your content. If you show visitors where they are in a process or within a site, for instance, it can help avoid disorientation. And be sure not to distract people from their main task at hand with unnecessary digressions.

Figure 2-3 shows a page from the Crate & Barrel web site, a large housewares retailer in the US (*www. crateandbarrel.com*). It's apparent that you are in the Furniture section of the site and looking at office

---

8   Jeff Conklin, "Hypertext: an Introduction and Survey" *IEEE Computer* 20 (1987): 17–41.

9   Carolyn Foss, "Tools for Reading and Browsing Hypertext," *Information Processing and Management* 25 (1989): 407-418.

chairs, which is also highlighted in the navigation on the left. You can easily navigate to desks, bookcases, and file cabinets from here—something people furnishing a home office may very well do. If needed, you can easily get to a completely different category in the main navigation or even perform a keyword search. At the same time, the focus of the page is clearly on the products. The navigation system provides a sense of location, offers the necessary navigation options, and doesn't distract from the main task at hand.

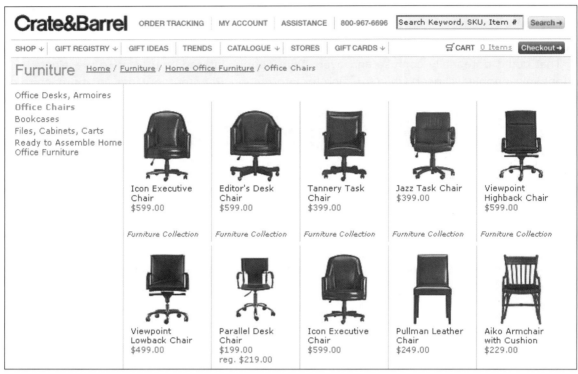

Figure 2-3 / Clear, simple navigation and a strong page focus on the Crate & Barrel web site

WEB BROWSING BEHAVIOR

We are all creatures of habit. Even in our web browsing, we rely on a limited number of pages within a site. In a 1995 study of web browsing behavior, researchers at the Georgia Institute of Technology[10] clearly showed a recurring pattern of users frequently returning to a given page or pages as a sort of home base, resulting in a hub and spoke style of navigation through a web space (Figure 2-4).

---

10 Lara Catledge and James Pitkow, "Characterizing Browsing Strategies in the World Wide Web," *Computer Systems and ISDN Systems: Proceedings of the Third International World Wide Web Conference* 10. Darmstadt, Germany. (1995): 1065-1073. *www.igd.fhg.de/archive/1995_www95/papers/80/ userpatterns/UserPatterns.Paper4.formatted.html*.

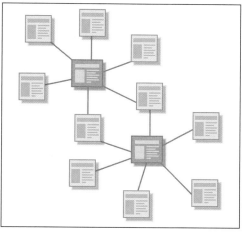

Figure 2-4 / Typical hub and spoke style of navigating

More recent studies confirm this comfort in familiarity: Andy Cockburn and Bruce McKenzie, researchers at the University of Canterbury in New Zealand, examined the surfing behavior of many web users,[11] looking at the duration of each page visit, how often people visited a page, the growth and content of bookmark collections, and many other factors. Previously, revisitation—navigating to a previously visited page—accounted for 58 to 61 percent of all page visits. In 2000, page revisitation was even more prevalent: 81 percent of page visits calculated across all users.

The results also show that browsing is rapid. People often visit several pages in a very short period of time. They move very quickly on the Web, with pages displayed for only a few seconds. This research generated a simple set of guidelines:

- Support revisitation
- Design pages to load quickly
- Shorten navigation paths
- Minimize transient pages

The revisitation pattern changed somewhat in 2006, but the speed of browsing remained, according to Harald Weinreich, at the University of Hamburg.[12] Weinreich and his colleagues noted a drop in the use of the Back button, but confirmed that people don't stay on any one page very long. Twenty-five percent of all visits lasted less than 4 seconds and 51 percent less than 10 seconds.

11 Andrew Cockburn and Bruce McKenzie, "What Do Web Users Do? An Empirical Analysis of Web Use," *International Journal of Human-Computer Studies* 54, 6 (2000): 903-922. *www.cosc.canterbury.ac.nz/andrew.cockburn/papers/ijhcsAnalysis.pdf*.

12 Harald Weinreich, Hartmut Obendorf, Eelco Herder, and Matthias Mayer, "Off the Beaten Tracks: Exploring Three Aspects of Web Navigation," *International World Wide Web Conference 2006*, Edinburgh (2006). *www2006.org/programme/files/xhtml/18/p018-weinreich/p018-weinreich.html*.

They also saw new patterns in web navigation behavior: increases in form submissions and in new window events (i.e., opening a page in a second browser). Both seem to be rooted in a change in web technologies, not necessarily people's behavior. Increased form submissions, for instance, suggest that the Web is becoming more interactive. New window events are likely to be caused by an increase in pop-up advertisements.

Although their findings differ slightly, the same overall recommendations for web design remain the same. Create concise, fast-loading pages to keep up with the high-speed pace of web navigation.

NAVIGATING WEB SITES

The movement from one page to the next is a decisive step in web navigation. It's at this point that your expectations are fulfilled or not. You click a link, the screen goes blank briefly, then the new page is displayed. Now you have to figure out if this is where you want to be and find your way again. If the new page is very different from the first, reorientation may take a considerable amount of time, relatively speaking. If the changes from one page to the next are small, you might be able to adjust very quickly—in the blink of an eye. Understanding these page-to-page transitions is critical to understanding general web navigation.

The amount that web navigation changes across a site has a name—*transitional volatility*—coined by David Danielson, a researcher at Stanford University.[13] While it may sound dangerous, volatility simply refers to the extent to which the navigation varies when moving to a new page. For instance, it's quite normal for menu position and labeling to differ from page to page while navigating. The question is, what effect do these changes have on navigation behavior?

According to Danielson, people navigate in a cycle of prediction, reorientation, and habituation (Figure 2-5):

Habituation

> While interacting with a web site, people become accustomed to its navigation mechanisms and overall system. But it's not just the currently viewed page that contributes to habituation: people may have memory of all pages they've experienced. For each navigation act, they bring prior knowledge and expectations.

Prediction

> From patterns of navigation within a web site and cues that provide "scent" to information, such as link labels and link position, people predict the attributes of destination pages. They anticipate what comes next while navigating.

Reorientation

> Once a new page is reached, people familiarize themselves with it. Reorientation occurs. The navigation on the new page now becomes incorporated into the navigator's model of the site, and the cycle begins again.

---

13 David R. Danielson, "Transitional Volatility in Web Navigation," *IT & Society* 1,3 (2003): 131-158. *www.stanford.edu/group/siqss/itandsociety/v01i03/v01i03a08.pdf.*

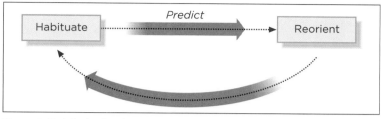

Figure 2-5 / Cycle of navigation according to Danielson

Danielson studied how participants reacted to changes in the navigation appearance from page to page in a web site. He tested three sites with different navigation schemes but with the same information architecture and content:

- The full overview version (Figure 2-6) had a full outline of all the pages in the site listed on the left of the page. This functioned like an ever-present site map, with second and third levels of the hierarchy indented. This navigation was static from page to page.

- The partial overview version (Figure 2-7) placed the main category links in a horizontal navigation bar along the top of the page. Second- and third-level categories were then listed in the left navigation bar. Once participants selected a main category, all available links were displayed on the left. Changes in navigation occurred only when a top-level category was selected.

- The local context version (Figure 2-8) also placed the main category links in horizontal navigation along the top; however, it separated the second- and third-level categories on the left. Participants saw third-level links only after selecting a second-level category. The navigation changed from page to page with a selection of both top-level and second-level categories.

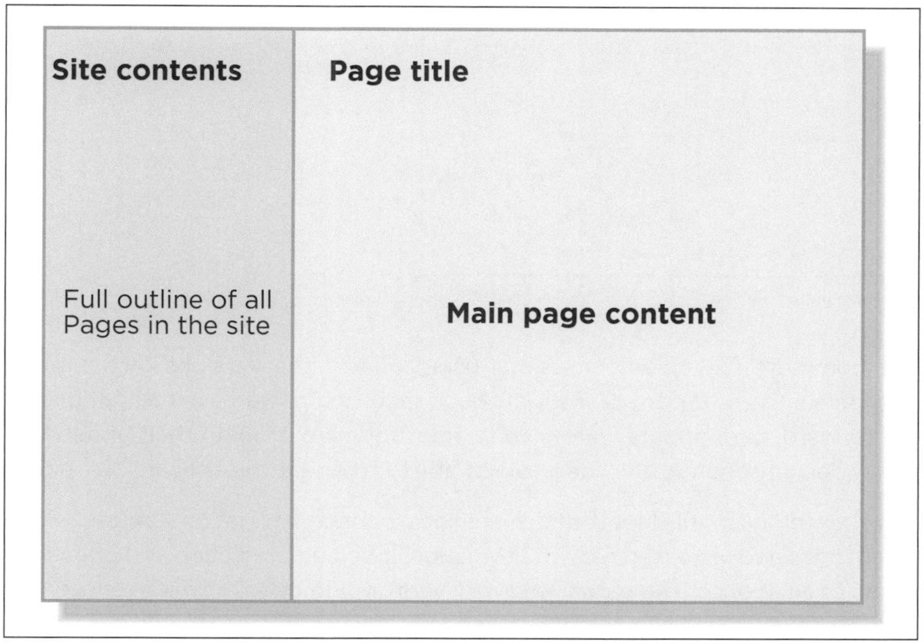

Site contents	Page title
Full outline of all Pages in the site	**Main page content**

Figure 2-6 / Recreation of Danielson's full overview layout of web site navigation

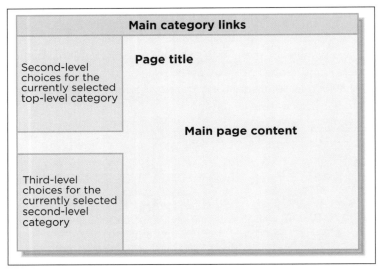

Figure 2-7 / The partial overview navigation version

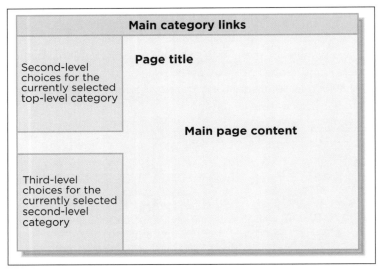

Figure 2-8 / The local context navigation version

Participants were asked to complete fact-finding missions using one of the versions of the site. This resulted in 1730 navigational acts and 2400 page visits. Danielson recorded patterns in navigation, as well as task completion rates. Afterward, participants were given a questionnaire probing their understanding of site coherence, the general design scheme, and their overall ability to orient themselves.

By changing more often and showing each third-level choice, the local context navigation (Figure 2-8) better prepared people for further changes and increased ease of navigation. It helped prediction and orientation by changing in small ways instead of all at once. The partial overview version (Figure 2-7), which reflects a lower degree of change in navigation, showed significantly higher disorientation and lower ease of navigation.

This mirrors principles of discontinuity in other media. For instance, filmmakers have long known how scene changes are either visually turbulent or give visual momentum, as Danielson points out. Or, composers use change in pitch, rhythm, texture, and so on to create drama or to move the music forward. Change and variation is vital to holding the listener's interest. As was once said about J.S. Bach's music: "it is great because it is inevitable and yet surprising."[14] This also echoes the theory of aesthetic value proposed by American mathematician George David Birkhoff:[15] for a work of art to be pleasing, it should neither be too regular nor too surprising.

Likewise, these findings show that changes in navigation show movement and progress through a site. This is important for orientation and ease of navigation. Complete consistency is not always the best route, but neither are dramatic variations from page to page. There is no fixed standard for the amount of change needed. From this research, the rule of thumb is to change navigation frequently, but keep those changes subtle, meaningful, and predictable.

In designing navigation, the choice of mechanism (Chapter 3) and the role it has within the overall scheme (Chapter 4) are critical in setting expectations. It may be jarring, for instance, if a main category link at the top of a page opens a PDF document or links to another site. Instead, people expect the main navigation to lead to pages within the current site. But a link in the lower-right of the page under the heading "Related Content" might very well contain links that open a PDF document or link to another site. Navigation design is about creating patterns that people can get accustomed to, giving them cues to help predict what will happen after clicking a link, and then helping them reorient themselves on new pages.

NAVIGATIONAL CHOICES

Another important question to ask before starting to design web navigation is: how do people make navigational choices?

Web designers often assume that people will come to a page and carefully review all the options before making an informed choice. Frequently, this isn't the case at all. People are much less systematic in their actions on the Web than you might assume. Three interrelated aspects to consider are that visitors:

- Scan pages rapidly
- Often experience "banner blindness"
- May take the first option that seems to fulfill their immediate need

SCANNING AND THE SCENT OF INFORMATION

On the Web, people scan. They aren't necessarily reading or understanding every word they come across, and they don't stay on any one page very long. For navigation design, it's critical to have key options visible. And these options must also match user expectations.

Based on Information Foraging Theory, Jared Spool and his colleagues have popularized the notion of the *scent of information*.[16] Scent refers to how well links and navigation match a visitor's information need and

---

14 Attributed to the Dutch electrical engineer Bathalzaar van der Pol as quoted in *Schroeder, Manfred Schroeder, Fractals, Chaos, Power Laws* (W.H. Freeman & Co., 1991): 109.

15 George D. Birkhoff, *Aesthetic Measure* (Harvard University Press, 1933).

16 Jared Spool, Christine Perfetti, and David Brittan, *Design for the Scent of Information* (User Interface Engineering, 2004).

how well they predict the content on the destination page. There are potentially many aspects of navigation design that contribute to scent, including position on screen, labels, icons, color, descriptive texts, and so forth.

But ultimately, scent is more complex and subtle than how links are displayed. It really has to do with creating a sense of confidence in navigating. The researchers explain:

> *Usually, however, scent is invisible. It is a product of how well the designers understand the site's users, those users' needs, and how the users access the site.*
>
> *In fact, the best way to detect scent is to measure the users' confidence...when the scent is weak, users are not confident at all. They doubt their choices. They tell us they are making 'wild guesses'. They click hesitantly, hoping the site will magically come through for them. More important, they rarely find what they are seeking.*
>
> *When scent is strong, however, their confidence builds as they draw closer to their content. They traverse the site with little hesitation. Moreover, they find what they are seeking.* [17]

Trigger words emerge to be the most critical aspect in creating information scent. These are navigation labels and texts that match a visitor's need on the page. Discussed further in Chapter 5, labels are what people scan for when they first land on a page. Spool and his team found that scanning for trigger words is a consistent pattern among all user types, tasks, and sites:

> *We've noticed that people looking for information all exhibit similar patterns. They first scan for their trigger words—words or phrases they associate with the content they're seeking—in an attempt to pick up the scent.* [18]

Trigger words help to indicate they are on the right track. They reduce uncertainty and give confidence in navigating further. For instance, pages like the home page for Staples.com (Figure 2-9) are actually more successful than pages in which options are hidden behind navigation menus. Without a specific goal in mind, this page may appear overwhelming. But when people have a focused goal and arrive here, they begin scanning without hesitation. Believe it or not, this type of design improves navigation and gets people where they want to go, which, in turn, increases business.

Figure 2-9 / Good information scent on link-rich pages such as Staples.com

---

17 Jared Spool, Christine Perfetti, and David Brittan, *Design for the Scent of Information* (User Interface Engineering, 2004): 2

18 Ibid.

BANNER BLINDNESS

Merely making an option available on a page, however, is no guarantee that people will see it. Jan Panero Benway and David M. Lane, researchers at Rice University, brought the term *banner blindness* to the attention of the web community in 1998.[19] Before this study appeared, conventional wisdom predicted that the larger an item was, the more attention it attracted.

With banner blindness, however, people simply oversee certain elements on a page, even if they are the largest items on the page. There's seeing, and there's *seeing*. Apparently, they've learned to blank out banners, or long, rectangular advertisement-like areas of a page.

Navigation behavior and information need has a large impact on whether banner blindness occurs. Researchers in Berlin studying this phenomenon conclude that the mode of seeking explains when and why people may experience banner blindness.[20] When people are focused on a specific goal (directed browsing), they are more likely to overlook banners and other elements on the page that don't fulfill that goal. When they are less focused (undirected browsing), banners tend to get noticed more.

The human visual system naturally seeks structure in information, often very rapidly.[21] Scientists refer to this as "pre-attentive" processing. This occurs in such a way that interpretation of a display is determined by the design itself. People can therefore infer relationships between elements on a web page before actively reading the page. This sets the stage for subsequent interactions.

For example, consider a page from the technology section of the Hürriyet, a national Turkish newspaper (Figure 2-10, *www.hurriyet.com.tr*). This example shows a news story announcing the arrival of Internet Explorer 7. At the top is a colorful, blinking banner. Given banner blindness, it's likely that readers will overlook these advertisements and focus instead on the content.

Figure 2-10 / Banners in the technology section of the Hürriyet, a large Turkish newspaper

---

19 Jan Panero Benway and David M. Lane, "Banner Blindness: Web Searchers Often Miss Obvious Links," *Internetworking*, 1.3 (1998). *www.internettg.org/newsletter/dec98/banner_blindness.html*.

20 Magnus Pagendarm and Heike Schaumberg, "Why Are Users Banner-Blind? The Impact of Navigation Style on the Perception of Web Banners," *Journal of Digital Information* 2, 1 (2001). *http://jodi.tamu.edu/Articles/v02/i01/Pagendarm/*.

21 V. Bruce and P.R. Green, *Visual Perception: Physiology, Psychology and Ecology*, 2nd edition (Lawrence Erlbaum Associates, 1990); N. J. Wade and M. Swanston, *Visual Perception: An Introduction* (Routledge, Chapman and Hall, Inc., 1991).

Such blind spots, however, are not just limited to rectangular banners. People can potentially overlook any element on page, including navigation mechanisms and options. Extending the banner blindness principle, we can talk of *navigation blindness* too. Page layout (Chapter 9) and visual presentation (Chapter 10) prove to be critical in overcoming navigation blindness.

SATISFICING

People also tend to *satisfice*.[22] They don't make optimal choices. They don't weigh all the advantages and disadvantages of each link. And on the Web there is no real penalty for guessing wrong. As Steve Krug puts it:

> *When we're creating sites, we act as though people are going to pore over each page, reading our finely crafted text, figuring out how we've organized things, and weighing their options before deciding which link to click.*
>
> *What they actually do most of the time (if we're lucky) is glance at each new page, scan some of the text, and click on the first link that catches their interest or vaguely resembles the thing they're looking for. There are usually large parts of the page that they don't even look at.[23]*

Of course, this is a generalization. In many situations, people don't satisfice. In specific domains, such as medicine or law, people may navigate more deliberately. But for general e-commerce sites or informational sites, never assume that visitors will evaluate all options carefully.

In designing web navigation, it's not enough to just put a link on the page and expect it will be used as intended. You must also consider many other subtle aspects such as placement of options, their relationship to other page elements, color, size, and labels. Labels are absolutely critical as well, and it's essential that you design the site so visitors' trigger words are visible and easily recognized.

INFORMATION SHAPE

There's more to navigation than providing clear, concise links, and smooth transitions from page to page. You must consider the information *shape*, as well. With shape, the form in which we experience information becomes an important navigational element itself. For instance, news articles tend to have similar shape. They start with the basic facts, then introduce people and quote them, and gradually go into more detail before tapering off. Understanding this shape potentially helps you both navigate and comprehend the article.

Andrew Dillon and Misha Vaughan proposed the notion of shape in hypertext documents, defining shape as:

> *...a property conveyed both by physical form and by information content. Separating these elements completely is perhaps impossible but one can talk of the distinction between the layout and sequencing of information as viewed by the consumer (user or reader) and the cognitive representation of meaning that employs (at least in theoretical terms) knowledge structure such as schemata, mental models and scripts.[24]*

---

22 Herbert Simon coined the term "satisfice" in 1957. In decision making, there may be a tendency to select the first option given that can work for the situation rather than seeking out or waiting for an optimal solution. See more in the Wikipedia entry for "Satisficing." *http://en.wikipedia.org/wiki/Satisficing*.

23 Steve Krug, *Don't Make Me Think* (New Riders Press, 2000).

24 Andrew Dillon and Misha Vaughan, "It's the Journey and the Destination: Shape and the Emergent Property of Genre in Evaluating Digital Documents" *New Review of Multimedia and Hypermedia* 3 (1997): 91-106. *http://ischool.utexas.edu/~adillon/publications/journey&destination.pdf*.

People naturally seek order and patterns when they come in contact with online information. This helps them predict, reorient, and habituate in the navigation process. When web content has a consistent shape (i.e., consistent physical and semantic patterns), it's easier for people to use.

DOCUMENT GENRE

The word "genre" has its roots in art and literature. In the broadest sense of the term, it refers to a distinct category of works marked by common style, form, and content—in other words, a common shape. Genre is a shared set of conventions for a given work—fairy tales versus poetry, for example. In film, a western represents a different genre than a horror movie or a comedy. Musical genres include classical, jazz, and rock.

In each example, certain identifiable elements define its categorization. A fairy tale begins with "Once upon a time..." and ends with "...and they lived happily ever after," for instance. Or, rock music is distinguished by its short songs with lyrics and a heavy back beat performed by small ensembles playing electric instruments.

STUDIES IN DOCUMENT GENRE

Elaine Toms, professor at the University of Toronto, has researched the notion of information genre and shape extensively.[25] She conducted a study comparing three different versions of a document:

* A full version. The content in its native form was intact.
* A content-only version. Text was the same as the original, but the formatting was removed and the structure was deleted.
* A form-only version. Text was replaced with Xs and 9s, but the form of the original document was maintained.

For instance, if the document in question were a telephone book, the three different versions might look like Figures 2-11, 2-12, and 2-13.

Smith Rebeca 501 Main St. 555-7133
Smith Richard E 342 Maple Ave. 555-7384
Smith Richard E & Jane M
    37 Scarborough Dr. #3D..................................555-9018
Smith Robert 1313 Grant Ave. 555-2966
Smith Robert B 12C Cherry St. 555-7485
Smith Rupert 1354 Kings Hwy...............................555-4318
Smith Samatha 13 Dogfish Head Rd 555-0074

Figure 2-11 / An example of a full version document

25 Elaine Toms, "Recognizing Digital Genre," *Bulletin of the American Society of Information Science and Technology* 27, 2 (2001). *http://asis.org/Bulletin/Dec-01/toms.html*.

Smith Rebeca 501 Main St. 555-7133, Smith
Richard E 342 Maple Ave. 555-7384, Smith
Richard E & Jane M 37 Scarborough Dr., #3D
555-9018, Smith Robert 1313 Grant Ave. 555-
2966, Smith Robert B 12C Cherry St. 555-7485,
Smith Rupert 1354 Kings Hwy 555-4318, Smith
Samatha 13 Dogfish Head Rd 555-0074

Figure 2-12 / Content-only version based on Figure 2-11

Xxxxx Xxxxxx 999 Xxxx Xx. 999-9999
Xxxxx Xxxxxxx X 999 Xxxxx Xxx. 999-9999
Xxxxx Xxxxxxx X & Xxxx X
    999 Xxxxxxxxxxx Xx. 9X.................................999-9999
Xxxxx Xxxxxx 999 Xxxxx Xxx.................................999-9999
Xxxxx Xxxxxx X 99C Xxxxxx Xx. 999-9999
Xxxxx Xxxxxx 9999 Xxxxx Xxx 999-9999
Xxxxx Xxxxxxx 99 Xxxxxxx Xxxx Xx 999-9999

Figure 2-13 / Form-only version based on Figure 2-11

Professor Toms then showed study participants one of the different versions and asked them to identify the document. The results show that people recognized the full version and content-only version more often, but recognition of the form-only version was *twice as fast*. Apparently cognitive processing of the form happens more quickly than the processing of the semantics of the content.

In another experiment, content in one genre was formatted as a different genre.[26] For example, imagine these telephone book entries in the form of a dictionary. When asked to identify the document type, participants tended to select by format, not the content. That is, even though the content was clearly from a telephone book, they may have responded with "dictionary," based solely on the form.

DESIGNING FOR INFORMATION SHAPE

Genre has found a new relevance in digital documents. The web has even spawned new genres in its short lifetime. News sites, for instance, can be recognized as such because of their common characteristics. So can personal home pages, newsletters, and blogs. Each of these has a distinct information shape.

You can use shape and genre when designing navigation and creating navigation concepts, which are discussed further in Chapter 8. The task is to identify the essential aspects of design that articulate a given genre. Find the common patterns for the genre of sites you're working in and support these in your design. It's about meeting expectations. Finding recognizable forms can improve orientation and help people predict context. In the end, shape and genre play a significant role in navigation.

---

26 Elaine G. Toms. and D. Grant Campbell. "Genre as Interface Metaphor: Exploiting Form and Function in Digital Environments." *Proceedings of the 32nd Hawaii International Conference on System Sciences* (1999).

Why Shape Matters to Web Application Designers

By Misha W. Vaughan

Information shape means that as user interface designers, interaction designers, or information architects we must concern ourselves with two key areas of design: what things mean (semantics) and getting around (navigation). Tactically, this means that we must be sure to design for:

- Content comprehension (more specifically, the correct use of language)
- The structure of the content
- Moving around the structure
- Manipulating the structure

For example, say it was your task to design a web application to automate and track time cards for McDonald's. With regard to content comprehension, your time card application would need to map to users' expectations about language. Ask these questions:

- What are the primary concepts in the system called, and is this consistent with users' expectations? For instance, are they called time cards in every geographic location where the application is used?
- What are the secondary concepts called, and again, are the terms consistent with users' expectations? Within the concept of a time card, is there a universal ability to take sick leave, medical leave, or personal leave?
- What are the actions users can take on the concepts called? For example, do users refer to "filing a time card," "submitting a time card," or "punching a time card?" The choice of terminology matters.
- How can you take advantage of the digital domain and add to the content in a new way? This is the fun part. Because you are talking about digital time cards, is there a new concept or action you want to introduce to improve the business process?

Why Shape Matters to
Web Application Designers

(Continued)

Regarding the structure of the content, your time card application needs to ensure that the time card concept in the system is structured to map to users' expectations. Again, questions will help you with your design:

- What information is consistently displayed with this kind of concept? For example, time cards often contain dates, types of time allocation (vacation, projects, etc.), and hours.

- Does it have groups of information? For example, do users expect the information to be chunked in certain ways?

- Do those groups have an order? Is one group of information more important than another?

- Are the information and groups displayed in a typical format, e.g., a table of data?

- How can you take advantage of the digital domain and extend the structure in a new way?

For moving around the structure, your time card application needs to accommodate users' navigational expectations. Find out:

- How do users' typically expect to navigate? For example, a given time card could be navigated by day, week, or month.

- Is there a current paper-based or digital analog for navigation, .e.g., page-style navigation?

- How can you extend the navigation in the digital realm in a way that is not available via paper, e.g., by allowing the enduser to navigate to past time cards and copy an old one?

For manipulating the structure, your time card application needs to support the creation, updating, deleting, and viewing of primary concepts (e.g., time cards).

By considering these aspects of information shape, the overall navigation and usability of application is improved.

Misha W. Vaughan is a Usability Architect for the Applications User Experience Group at Oracle Corporation. She holds a PhD in Information Science and a Masters in Telecommunications from Indiana University at Bloomington and can be reached at mvaughan@acm.org.

The field of user experience design, or simply experience design, attempts to address a broader range of concerns in web design. Some definitions of user experience underscore a holistic view:

> " *User experience encompasses all aspects of the end-user's interaction with the company, its services, and its products… In order to achieve high-quality user experience in a company's offerings there must be a seamless merging of the services of multiple disciplines, including engineering, marketing, graphical and industrial design, and interface design.*[27] "

Other views focus on key aspects of how people experience products and services:

Usefulness

How well the basic services, features, and functions match user needs and goals; a rational, cognitive response to the end product

Usability

How well the end product works and how well users can interact with it; the physical, objective properties of an interface

Desirability

The subjective, emotional response to the site; represents users' spontaneous feelings about the site and the site's owner

A good user experience balances these elements. A user experience is all the behaviors, thoughts, and feelings a person has when encountering a product or service over time. Your job is to take all of these factors into account when designing site navigation.

DESIGNING FOR EMOTIONS

With such definitions, you can see why emotions play a significant role in interface design. Traditional academic disciplines related to web design—human-computer interaction and information science—have long focused on the physical and cognitive aspects of computer interface design. Now, in designing for optimal user experiences, user engagement, joy of use, and just plain fun, are all part of the paradigm.

Research in psychology and neuroscience reveals a tight connection between affect and cognition: emotions are essential in human thought.[28] Emotions guide social interactions, influence decisions and judgments, affect basic understanding, and can even control physical actions. When you feel good it is easier to make decisions, brainstorm, and be creative, for instance. Attractive things really do work better.

People can no longer be modeled as purely goal-driven, task-solving agents when designing web sites. They also have affective motivations for their choices and behavior, which, more often than not, drive rational decision making. This implies an extended mandate for web design to include affective considerations.[29]

---

27 Nielsen Norman Group, "User Experience: Our Definition," (accessed December 2006). *nngroup.com/about/userexperience.html*.

28 See for instance Daniel Goleman, *Emotional Intelligence* (Bloomsbury, 1995).

29 Works such as *Funology: From Usability to Enjoyment* (edited by Blythe, Overbeek, Monk, and Wright, 2004) and *Emotional Design* (by Don Norman, 2003) articulate this line of new thought and highlight its importance.

QUALITIES OF EMOTIONS

So how do we quantify emotions to effectively factor them into the design equation? Rather than become mired in the huge diversity of definitions for emotion, focus on the aspects particularly relevant to design:

Emotions are quick

The emotional mind is far quicker than the rational mind, and people initially react to web sites on a visceral level.[30] In a Carleton University study, participants were able to assess the site's appeal after glimpsing at pages for only for 50 milliseconds—that's five one-hundredths of a second. These assessments correlated to opinions of the sites after longer examination. First impressions are critical, and the prime factor influencing the credibility of a site is the design look. There also seems to be a "halo effect" from that emotional first impression. This carries over to the interaction and comprehension of the site in general.

Emotions are situational

Emotions are grounded in a given context. A constellation of personal goals, prior knowledge, recent events, and even physical states, all contribute to the resulting emotions of an experience. What is dreadful in one situation could be delightful in another. Riding a roller coaster can be exciting and invigorating, but might be an awful experience immediately after full meal. Likewise, aimlessly surfing through a given web site can be adventurous and educational, while locating specific information on the same site under time pressure can be stressful and nerve-wracking.

Emotions are a human trait

People have emotions; web sites don't (neither do other inanimate objects, for that matter). This sounds obvious, but it's surprising how many people attribute an emotion to the web page and not to the observer. Consequently, you can't design an emotion, but you design *for* an emotion. Rather than focusing on the potential emotions an interface might suggest, web designers need to understand the real emotions users have while interacting with a site.

EMOTIONS IN INFORMATION SEEKING

Information seeking on the Web, in particular, is an emotional experience. Unfortunately, confusion and uncertainty tend to dominate feelings of enthusiasm and optimism. For many web surfers, the joy of discovery and pride of learning can be rare feelings against a backdrop of frustration and a sense of being overwhelmed.

When discussing the emotions users have while finding information on the Web, it is critical to look at common situations and user states. Here is where patterns in basic human information-seeking behaviors give rise to a framework for both evaluating and designing web-based search and navigation systems.

---

30 Gitte Lindgaard, Gary Fernandes, Cathy Dudek, and J. Brown, "Attention web designers: you have 50 milliseconds to make a good first impression!" *Behavior & Information Technology* 25, 2 (March-April 2006): 115-126.

INFORMATION SEARCH PROCESS

A holistic approach to explaining the user's experience in information seeking, the Information Search Process (ISP) is a model of searching for information with a difference: it takes emotions into account.[31] Developed by Carol Kuhlthau, a professor at Rutgers University, the ISP has six stages:

Initiation

> The user becomes conscious of a gap in knowledge. Feelings of uncertainty and apprehension are common; the main task is to recognize a need for information.

Selection

> Uncertainty often gives way to feelings of optimism and a readiness to begin searching. The task is to identify and select the topic to be investigated. Thoughts are forward-looking and attempt to predict an outcome.

Exploration

> Feelings of uncertainty, confusion, and doubt return. The general inability to precisely express an information need commonly results in an awkward interaction with the system.

Formulation

> Rising confidence and decreasing uncertainty mark a turning point in the process. Forming a focus becomes the chief task as thoughts become clearer.

Collection

> Interaction with the information system is most effective and efficient. Decisions about the scope and focus of the topic have been made and a sense of direction sets in. Confidence continues to increase.

Presentation

> The goal now is to complete the search and fulfill the information need. A sense of relief is common, as well as satisfaction or dissatisfaction (in the case of a negative outcome). Thoughts center on synthesizing and internalizing what was learned.

Kuhlthau also observed a "dip" in confidence often seen after a seeker began looking for information and started to encounter overwhelming, perhaps conflicting, information. This contradicts the previous assumption that confidence steadily increases as more information is found (Figure 2-14). A seeker "in the dip" can experience uncertainty, confusion, and even anxiety until a focus is formed or a search is broken off.

---

31 Carol C. Kuhlthau, "The Role of Experience in the Information Search Process of an Early Career Information Worker: Perceptions of Uncertainty, Complexity, Construction, and Sources." *Journal of the American Society for Information Science* 50, 5 (1991): 399-412.

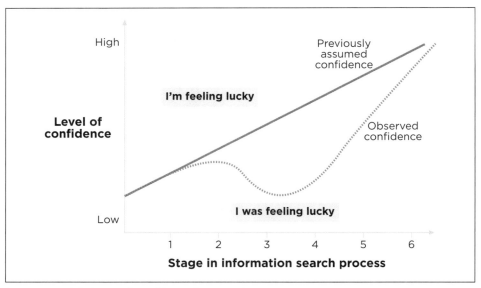

Figure 2-14 / A decrease in confidence after a search starts

The existence of that dip suggests a gap between users' natural information use and information system design. Acquiring more information in initial stages (particularly in the exploration stage) increases, rather than decreases, uncertainty. In terms of emotion, searching for information is a discontinuous endeavor with highs and low of confidence and certainty.

TAILORING THE ISP

In an attempt to avoid the dip, you can use Kuhlthau's theoretical model as the framework for navigation design, tailoring an ISP to reflect the actions, thoughts, and feelings for your site visitors. The steps are:

1. Segment users and create profiles. An ISP applies only to a particular target group.

2. Identify the information-seeking stages and user goals for each. The established phases will serve as a starting point, but must be adapted.

3. Record the typical feelings, thoughts, and actions at each stage.

4. Map stakeholder goals to each stage. What is your organization trying to achieve and how does it fit in with the natural navigation process of users?

5. Derive features and requirements for the site that map to each phase in the seeking process.

These items are best summarized in a large table. Label the columns Actions, Thoughts, Feelings, Features, and Business Goals. Make the rows the stages in your tailored ISP, then map the typical actions, thoughts, and feelings to possible site features and business goals. Table 2-1 shows an example of what this document might look like for a large corporate web site's job portal. The table attempts to describe the information searching process for job seekers: in this case, professionals who already have a job and are looking for a new position. Using this table approach ensures the flow of the navigation and its basic architecture match the natural information-seeking patterns of site visitors.

Table 2-1 / An example ISP analysis for a job portal

Phase	Actions	Thoughts	Feelings	Features	Business
1. Initiation: Recognize need to seek a job	Identifying problem and solving strategies	Vague, unclear	Uncertainty, apprehension	On- and offline campaign to raise awareness and improve image	Raise awareness of the company for job seekers
2. Selection: Choose appropriate resources	Locate starting point; Identifying job criteria	General, task oriented, open to new ideas	Curiosity, impatience; skepticism	High-quality design; self-assessment tool	Attract highly qualified job seekers
3. Searching: Locate relevant vacancies	Entering query or navigating job listings	Positive, thinking ahead to finding a job	Anticipation, optimism	Search; faceted navigation; filter by group	Make job openings publicly available over on the Web
4. Differentiation: Prioritize search results	Scanning results; prioritizing; reiterating search	Unclear, mixed	Uncertainty, confusion, feeling "underwhelmed"	Number of items next to category name; related jobs; "shopping cart"	
5. Deciding: Determine which positions are most relevant	Making a decision	Narrowed, increased interest and understanding	Feelings of clarity, satisfaction or dissatisfaction	Ability to sort; facts about company location information	Gain trust of potential applicants
6. Monitor: Check status/ availability over time	Visit site again	Remembering details	Hope, feelings of attachment	Page bookmark; newsletter; login and profile; "push" features	Relationship with potential future employees
7. Action: Apply for a job	Filling out forms online or offline; collecting necessary personal data	Clear, focused on completing tasks accurately	Relief, nervousness	Online and offline application; information about the interview	Get highly qualified applicants

INFORMATION EXPERIENCE

Design for emotions doesn't mean being flamboyant or extroverted. It doesn't mean that you now need captivating animations on each page. On the contrary, much of creating a good information experience is about avoiding negative emotions. A single negative experience—such as getting lost or feeling frustration with a complicated navigation—overrides any attempt to create positive feelings on the surface. Web navigation is best when it's not noticed at all; when it's invisible to the user.

The suggestion here, then, is to consider the entire information experience. Make emotions an explicit part of your design process. Don't deny that satisfaction, confidence, frustration, or joy of use can all be part of a viable rationale for design decisions. In usability tests or interviews with users, for instance, don't let comments people make about their emotions slip through the cracks. Capture them and use those feelings to create an overall improved information-seeking experience.

SUMMARY

Information seeking is a broad term that refers to all of the activities people engage in while hunting for information. There are decades of academic research in this area. Existing models of information seeking—though perhaps generic and abstract—can inform web navigation design. If anything, they teach us to focus on users and their needs, rather than on the technology. User research, a topic discussed in Chapter 7, is largely about understanding how visitors navigate and seek information on your site.

Studies in information seeking also reveal that finding information is complex and varied. Sometimes site visitors know what they are looking for, but often their information need is vague. The different modes of seeking people use directly impacts how they interact with your site. For instance, when focused on a specific information goal (known-item seeking), people may completely overlook page elements and experience banner blindness or even navigation blindness.

People move through different stages or states in while seeking information. It's not a linear process. The Berrypicking Model describes how people zigzag through online resources and change search strategies rapidly. Perhaps more importantly, users' confidence can vary as they seek information. As Carol Kuhlthau shows, visitors may be optimistic at the beginning, but as they progress and encounter more information, their confidence may dip. This is a critical point where people either proceed, back up and return to previously-visited pages, or break off a search completely.

Designing navigation is largely about increasing and maintaining confidence as users move through your site. There are several keys to creating this sense of certainty:

Labeling

When arriving at a page, visitors scan it quickly for trigger words. But they aren't necessarily weighing all options carefully. Instead, they may take the first link that appears to match their need. They satisfice. Creating good labels is critical for navigation, discussed further in Chapter 5.

Organization

The categories and grouping of navigation options communicates the intent of a menu or device. The overall site architecture is also important in how people move through your site. See Chapter 8 for more on structuring and organizing navigation.

Appearance

The layout and presentation of the navigation provides valuable clues to its use. Where navigation appears on the page and its visual treatment can greatly determine whether people see and understand navigation. See Chapters 9 and 10 for more.

Consistency in navigation is also important in supporting the information seeking process. But too much consistency in navigation may be a bad thing. The notion of transitional volatility shows that variations to the navigation are actually important in creating a sense of movement through a web site. These changes, however, should be subtle and predictable.

Navigation design is ultimately about creating a flow through a site—a narrative that people can follow. On a micro-level this flow is the sum of individual clicks. Navigation is a cycle of prediction, reorientation, and habituation. On a macro-level, consider other important aspects, such as shape, genre, and emotions in information seeking. Shape refers to both the physical form and the meaning of content; together, they are important to navigating and comprehending a web page. Genre refers to a set of shared conventions that define the form of a document, which people can recognize very quickly and independently of content. Finally, people are emotional while seeking information. Because emotions are grounded in a given situation, you must consider the mindset of visitors to your site. Considering the emotional aspect of navigating while you design will lead to richer information experiences on the Web.

QUESTIONS

1. Ellis' behaviors of information seeking are listed below. Some thoughts around "starting" have already been presented in this chapter. For each of the others, think of specific ways that you have experienced each on the Web.

    a) Chaining

    b) Browsing

    c) Differentiating

    d) Monitoring

    e) Extracting

2. Consider Donna Maurer's notion of the "don't know what you need to know" mode of information seeking, mentioned in this chapter. How might you design a site to support it? List three things a web site could do to help people find information they aren't directly looking for, but still need.

3. Look at the following excerpt from a familiar document and consider how form and genre might help you navigate:

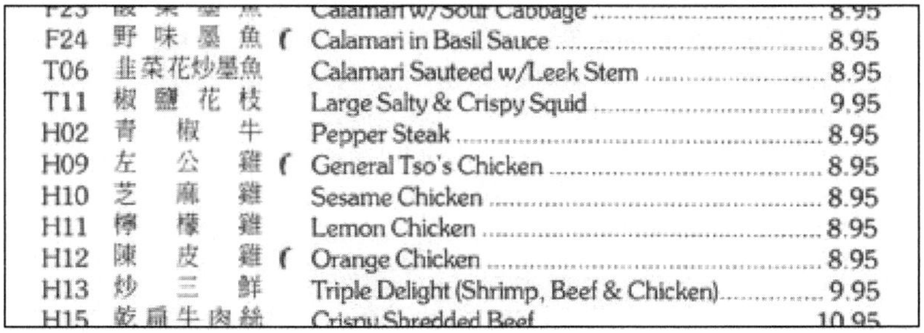

F24	野味墨魚	(	Calamari in Basil Sauce	8.95
T06	韭菜花炒墨魚		Calamari Sauteed w/Leek Stem	8.95
T11	椒鹽花枝		Large Salty & Crispy Squid	9.95
H02	青椒牛		Pepper Steak	8.95
H09	左公雞	(	General Tso's Chicken	8.95
H10	芝麻雞		Sesame Chicken	8.95
H11	檸檬雞		Lemon Chicken	8.95
H12	陳皮雞	(	Orange Chicken	8.95
H13	炒三鮮		Triple Delight (Shrimp, Beef & Chicken)	9.95

Figure 2-15 / What is it?

a) What is this image from?

b) Where are you in the document?

c) Where would go to find a list of soups?

d) Where would you go in the document to look for drinks?

e) What do the little "chili" symbols likely refer to next to three of the items?

4. Navigate to your favorite book or new best seller on Amazon.com, Amazon in your country, or another bookselling site. Compare each new page with the previous page, rapidly using the back and forward buttons on your browser. Note exactly what changes from page to page. Some changes to look out for are navigation options, layout and position of elements, as well as color, font, and text size.

a) What stays constant and what is variable?

b) How does this help or hurt navigation?

c) How do you reorient to each new page?

FURTHER READING

"The Design of Browsing and Berrypicking Techniques for the Online Search Interface," by Marcia Bates (*Online Review* 13 (1989): 407-424). *www.gseis.ucla.edu/faculty/bates/berrypicking.html*.

This oft-cited, landmark article introduces the Berrypicking Model in information seeking. There is a clear focus on the design of more effective interfaces that match real-like patterns of seeking online. Bates offers guidelines for designing better interfaces.

"Transitional Volatility in Web Navigation," by David Danielson (*IT & Society* 1, 3 (2003): 131-158). *www.stanford.edu/group/siqss/itandsociety/v01i03/v01i03a08.pdf*.

Danielson's recent work on web navigation is some of the most important to understanding the navigation process. This is an academic article, but nonetheless approachable and understandable by practitioners.

"Banner Blindness: Web Searchers Often Miss Obvious Links," by Jan Panero Benway and David M. Lane (*Internetworking* 1.3, 1998). *www.internettg.org/newsletter/dec98/banner_blindness.html*.

The concept of banner blindness reveals an important aspect of design: human behavior is complex. Logical behavioral assumptions don't always hold true. The designer's intuition is certainly important, but testing is also key. Sometimes things aren't as neat and convenient as expected. This is a fascinating and eye-opening study.

Mechanisms of Navigation

Just wait, Gretel, until the moon rises, and then we shall see the crumbs of bread which I have strewn about, they will show us our way home again. When the moon came they set out, but they found no crumbs, for the many thousands of birds which fly about in the woods and fields had picked them all up.

—Brothers Grimm
Hansel and Gretel

03

IN THIS CHAPTER

- Step and paging navigation
- Breadcrumb trails
- Tree navigation, site maps, directories, tag clouds, and A-Z indexes
- Navigation bars, tabs, and vertical menus
- Dynamic menus and drop-downs
- Visualization mechanisms

A navigational mechanism is a link or group of links that behave in a similar way and have a similar appearance. They are the tools and devices of navigation systems.

Sometimes a site's structure suggests a particular mechanism, such as a horizontal navigation bar with a site's top-level categories. Navigation mechanisms should synch up with the site's structure, and there may be negotiation between the two: a change in your structure might bring about a change in your navigation and vice-versa. For example, if your site has 20 top-level categories, a navigation bar may not be appropriate. Instead, a directory-style display or dynamic menus will probably work better.

This chapter surveys common mechanisms individually and, for the most part, stripped of overall context. In reality, these mechanisms come together to form a total navigation logic for your site. But first it's important to understand the mechanics of navigation.

STEP NAVIGATION

Step navigation allows people to move sequentially through pages. It often consists of a text label and an arrow, and is accompanied by a link to move backward in the series as well. Typically, a left-pointing arrow indicates movement to the previous page, and a right arrow indicates the next page.

Internationalization

For languages that read right to left, the direction of the arrows may be reversed. Arrows alone may not be clear or intuitive for all users in all situations. A text label in conjunction with an arrow avoids ambiguity.

The Next Blog feature on Blogger (*www.blogger.com*, Figure 3-1) is a simple example of step navigation that moves you from one blog to another, sequentially.

Figure 3-1 / Step navigation on Blogger.com

Step navigation is valuable in processes where the decision in one step affects something in the next, such as in a wizard or a checkout process. It's also appropriate for sections of a longer document or chapters in an online book, or for online surveys and exams. Step navigation provides simple access to pages, one after another.

PAGING NAVIGATION

Paging navigation is similar to step navigation, but includes additional information and options. It is often found on search results pages that show details about the pages in the results set. Results sets usually have limits on the amount of items that can be displayed at once. After this limit is reached, a second chunk of results is displayed on a new page. This is repeated until all results are represented on several pages.

The simplest form of paging navigation is step navigation with the addition of a page count. This usually appears between the links to move forward or backward. A search for men's shoes on the Lands' End web site (*www.landsend.com*, Figure 3-2), allows you to sequentially browse through the six pages of results.

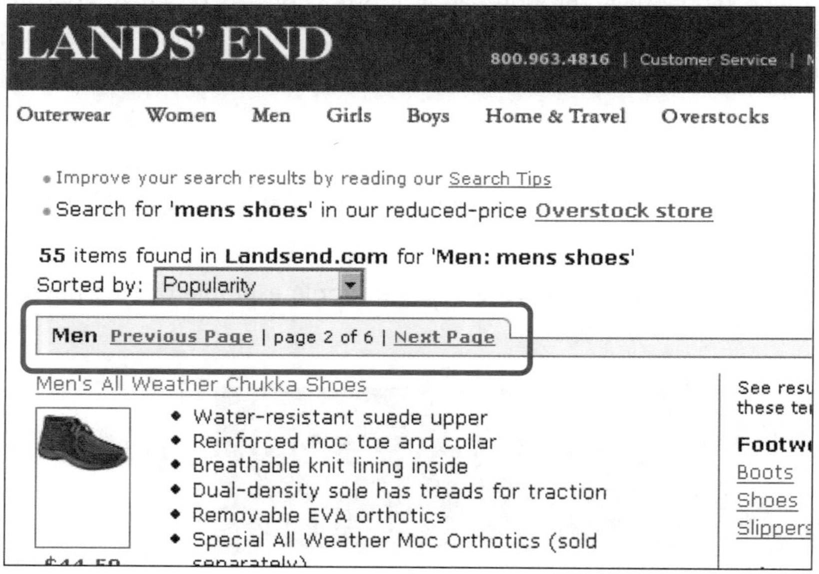

Figure 3-2 / Simple paging on Landsend.com

REWIND AND FAST-FORWARD

Sometimes visitors need to "rewind" to the first page or "fast-forward" to the last page of a set. Often a double arrow or arrow with pipe (vertical line) represents this type of navigation. Clicking the rewind link goes to the beginning of the set of chunks; clicking fast-forward goes to the last. If you browse to the ninth page in a set of items but want to return to the first, clicking rewind allows you to go there in one simple step.

Whitepages.com uses rewind (First) and fast-forward (Last) controls in Figure 3-3:

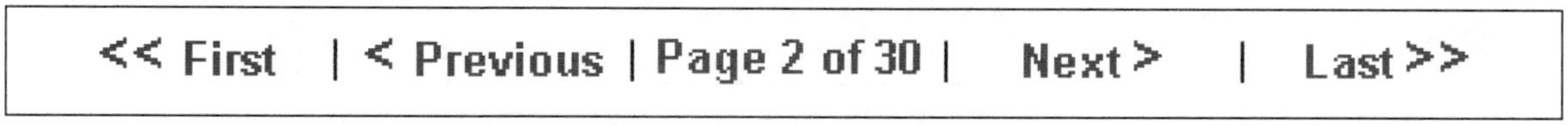

<< First | < Previous | Page 2 of 30 | Next > | Last >>

Rewind and fast-forward mechanisms are good for larger sets of things. If the list of items is alphabetical, for instance, it may be efficient to jump to the end to look for the Zs, but it also might not. Rewind and fast-forward may only add more clutter and cause potential errors. People rarely need to jump to the last chunk of a set if the results are ranked by relevance, for instance. In such a case, increasing the number of items on a given page to reduce jumping around may be better.

DIRECT ACCESS PAGING

Direct access paging is often seen at the top or bottom of search engine results. Usually a linear count of page chunks is shown (e.g., page 1, 2, 3, 4, etc.) along with step navigation controls. This allows direct access to any page in the entire set.

The REI web site (*www.rei.com*) combines simple paging navigation with random access paging at the top of search result pages. The second page is selected in Figure 3-4, indicated by an unlinked number 2 in the page count.

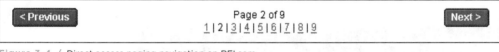

< Previous | Page 2 of 9 | 1 | 2 | 3 | 4 | 5 | 6 | 7 | 8 | 9 | Next >

Figure 3-4 / Direct access paging navigation on REI.com

The paging navigation on Amazon.com is also simple, and it gives a clearer indication of the current chunk of items. Note in Figure 3-5 that the Previous link is not present: this is the first page in the set.

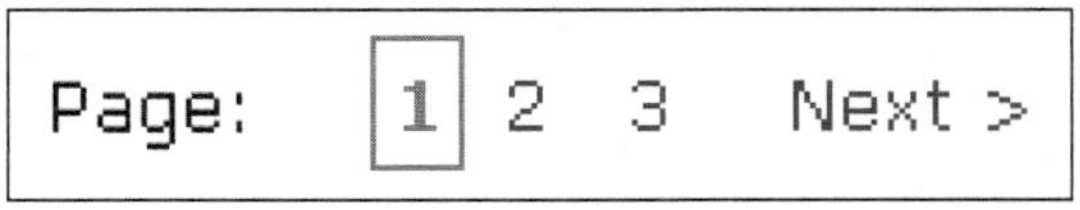

Page: 1 2 3 Next >

Figure 3-5 / The paging at the bottom of search results on Amazon.com

An alternative is to show the number of items in each chunk. For example, the navigation for the chunks of search results for the Library of Congress site (*http://catalog.loc.gov*, Figure 3-6) reflects the total number of items on each page of the set, not the page number. In this case, there are 25 hits per page. The count is therefore 1, 26, 51, 76, and so on.

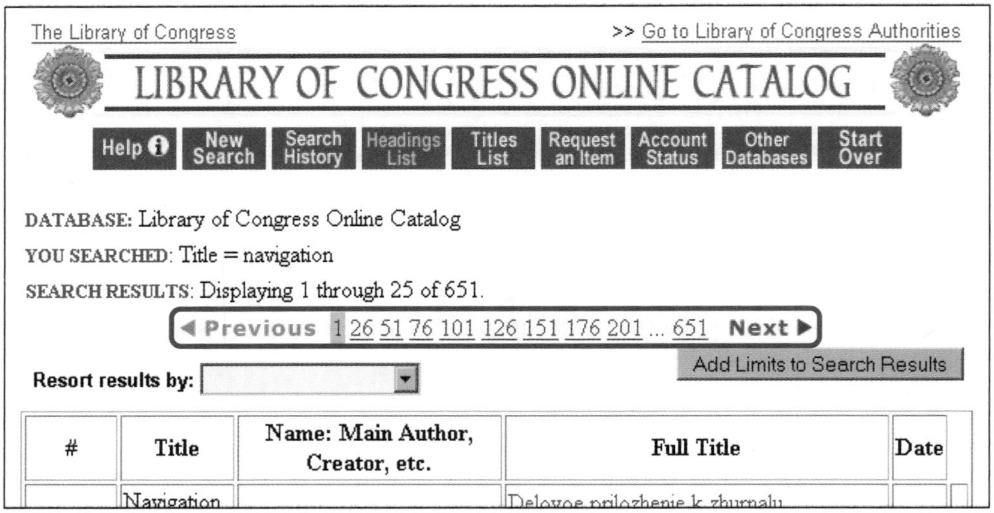

Figure 3-6 / Results list paging on the Library of Congress site

Yet another application of direct access paging is to allows users to directly enter the segment to which they want to jump. This can be done by embedding a text box within the paging arrows. The Gutenkarte web site (*www.gutenkarte.org*, Figure 3-7) employs this mechanism. Visitors can jump directly to a chapter of a book with this feature.

Figure 3-7 / Direct access to book chapters on the Gutenkarte web site

A combination of elements from the above examples is also possible. The paging mechanism for Yellowpages.com (Figure 3-8), for instance, counts chunk numbers sequentially, but also indicates which items are displayed.

Figure 3-8 / Sequential chunk numbers and an indication of the range of items on Yellowpages.com

A question for implementation is whether inactive elements are not shown at all, or shown in a grayed-out state. For instance, when the visitor is at the first chunk of items, does the display show a Previous link or icon that's inactive and gray, or does it not include such a link at all? Generally, showing the arrows in a grayed out state is best, because it provides potentially valuable information for orienting the visitor.

Finally, consider this elaborate example of paging for the online Hammacher Schlemmer catalog, which includes step navigation and random access paging, as well as a horizontal scrollbar to move ahead in the catalog (*www.hammacher.com*). Moving from one page to next simulates turning a page of real book with an animated motion. (Figure 3-9 shows the middle of a page turn.) You can also add virtual sticky notes to a page and then navigate directly to them.

Critics will quickly point out that replicating an offline catalog in this manner doesn't take advantage of the digital medium. They're right. But there is at least one advantage to this approach: it retains the native format of the catalog and captures its intended information shape. This may not increase look-up speed, but it certainly offers a unique browsing experience. And for a company with a small, specialized catalog that itself has a tradition and brand equity, it's not inappropriate.

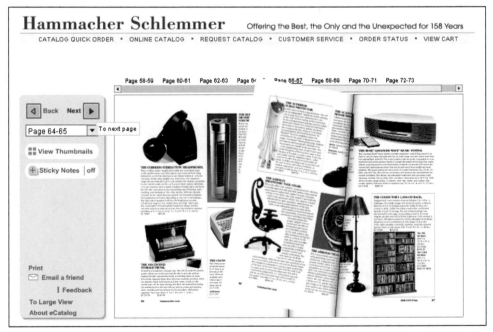

Figure 3-9 / Turning pages in the Hammacher Schlemmer catalog

BREADCRUMB TRAIL

In the fairy tale, Hansel and Gretel left a trail of breadcrumbs in the woods so they could find their way back home. The lesson for the Web is clear: people need to navigate back along a path they've already taken. Ironically, though, birds ate their breadcrumb trail in the story, and they got terribly lost. So perhaps the metaphor is not the best one. The term "breadcrumb trail" is widely used in web navigation design nonetheless.

As a navigational mechanism, the breadcrumb trail shows a person's path through a site. It consists of elements, or *nodes*, that are chained together. The nodes are linked to previously visited pages (or parent topics) and are separated with a symbol, usually a greater-than sign (>), colon (:), or pipe (|).

LOCATION BREADCRUMB TRAILS

The most common type of breadcrumb trail generally:

- Shows the current position within a site.
- Provides shortcuts to previously viewed pages and/or other areas of site.

These are called location breadcrumb trails. In essence, they are a linear representation of a site's structure, e.g., Home > Men's Clothes > Shirts > Dress Shirts. Regardless of how people arrive at Dress Shirts, the breadcrumb trail is the same.

The National Health Service (NHS) web site in the U.K. labels its location breadcrumb trail "You are here:" (*www.nhs.uk*, Figure 3-10).

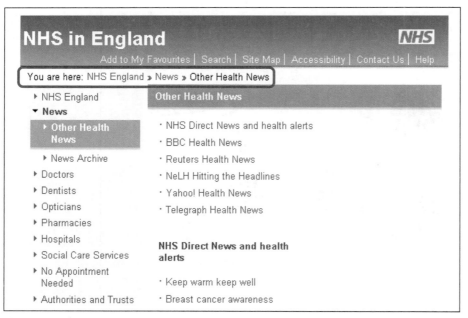

Figure 3-10 / Location breadcrumb trail on the NHS web site beginning with "You are here"

Unlike Hansel's trail, which showed his exact path (or would have, if the birds hadn't eaten it), location breadcrumb trails on the Web do not show navigation history. They show a fixed position in the overall site. On the NHS web site, regardless of how someone accessed the Other Health News page, the breadcrumb trail is the same.

Accessibility

Including the phrase "You are here:" can be helpful for users of screen readers (programs that read pages aloud to the seeing-impaired) to understand the context of the links that follow. This phrase can be hidden in the page code if desired, so sighted visitors don't see it.

There are two other types of breadcrumb trails beside location: path and attribute trails.[1]

PATH BREADCRUMB TRAILS

Path breadcrumb trails are dynamic. Any given page will show a different breadcrumb trail based on how the user reached the page.

A good example of this type of breadcrumb trail is on Epicurious, a site for recipes (*www.epicurious.com*). The browsing feature employs a type of faceted browse, discussed further in Chapter 11. The trail shows exactly what you've clicked to get to a given recipe. Compare the values in the breadcrumb trails (after "browsing by:") in Figures 3-11, 3-12, and 3-13.

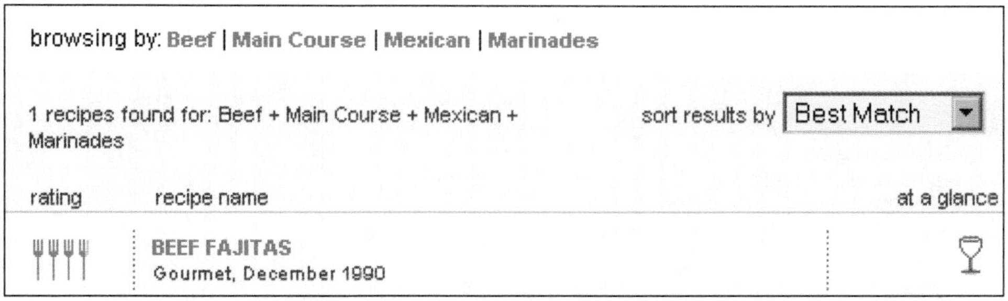

browsing by: Beef | Main Course | Mexican | Marinades

1 recipes found for: Beef + Main Course + Mexican + Marinades   sort results by Best Match ▼

rating	recipe name		at a glance
₩₩₩₩	**BEEF FAJITAS** Gourmet, December 1990		♀

Figure 3-11 / Recipe for beef fajitas reached by clicking Beef, then Main Course, Mexican, and finally, Marinades

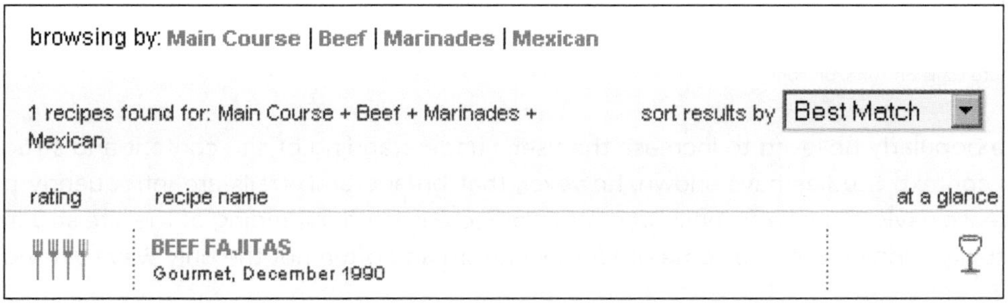

browsing by: Main Course | Beef | Marinades | Mexican

1 recipes found for: Main Course + Beef + Marinades + Mexican   sort results by Best Match ▼

rating	recipe name		at a glance
₩₩₩₩	**BEEF FAJITAS** Gourmet, December 1990		♀

Figure 3-12 / The same recipe for beef fajitas reached by clicking Main Course, then Beef, Marinades, and finally, Mexican

---

1 Keith Instone has done some of the most detailed work on breadcrumb trails. The terms in the chapter are taken from his site on the subject. See: *http://user-experience.org/uefiles/breadcrumbs/*.

browsing by: **Mexican** | **Beef** | **Main Course** | **Marinades**

1 recipes found for: Mexican + Beef + Main Course + Marinades   sort results by [Best Match ▾]

rating	recipe name	at a glance
🍴🍴🍴🍴	**BEEF FAJITAS** Gourmet, December 1990	🍷

Figure 3-13 / The same recipe for beef fajitas reached by clicking Mexican, then Beef, Main Course, and finally, Marinades

Each trail results in exactly the same content, but different paths were taken to get there. Unlike location breadcrumb trails, which are fairly static, implementing this type of trail is more difficult.

ATTRIBUTE BREADCRUMB TRAILS

Attribute breadcrumb trails describe a page in some way, rather than showing its location within a site or path to get to there. They display its position within some metadata scheme, often a topic hierarchy.

Amazon.com uses attribute trails. These show the category that books belong to, and they allow direct access to parent categories via linked category names. Showing the entire trail provides context for the elements at the lowest level, or the end nodes. For instance, the topic "General" at the end of several attribute trails for the book *Information Architecture for the World Wide Web*[2] (Figure 3-14) is fairly generic and appears in many subject categories. Only along with its parent nodes does "General" have meaning.

Look for similar items by category

Engineering
O'Reilly > Programming > General
O'Reilly > Programming > Web Programming
O'Reilly > Web Development > Web Authoring & Design
Subjects > Computers & Internet > General
Subjects > Computers & Internet > Hardware > Microprocessors & System Design > Computer Design
Subjects > Computers & Internet > Programming > General
Subjects > Computers & Internet > Programming > Software Design > Software Design
Subjects > Computers & Internet > Programming > Web Programming > General
Subjects > Computers & Internet > Web Development > Internet Commerce > Web Site Design
Subjects > Professional & Technical > Engineering
Software Books > Design & Development > Software Design

Figure 3-14 / Attribute trails on Amazon.com

Breadcrumb trails are popularly believed to increase the user's understanding of site content and structure by providing greater context. Studies have shown, however, that breadcrumb trails are infrequently used, don't necessarily increase navigational efficiency, and may not increase understanding of the site structure.[3] They are therefore usually supplemental to some other mechanism and often not the only way to navigate.

---

2   Louis Rosenfeld and Peter Morville. *Information Architecture for the World Wide Web*, Second Edition (O'Reilly, 2002).

3   See Bonnie Lida, Sping Hull, and Katie Pilcher, "Breadcrumb Navigation: An Exploratory Study of Usages," *Usability News* 5.1 (2003). *psychology.wichita.edu/surl/usabilitynews/51/breadcrumb.htm* and Bonnie Lida Rogers and Barbara Chaparro, "Breadcrumb Navigation: Further Investigation of Usage," *Usability News* 5.2 (2003). *psychology.wichita.edu/surl/usabilitynews/52/breadcrumb.htm*.

TREE NAVIGATION

Tree navigation allows for access to a hierarchical structure. This type of mechanism is commonly seen in operating systems to navigate file folders, e.g., in Microsoft Windows Explorer. It is invariably shown as a vertical arrangement of folders, terms, or nodes of some hierarchy. Often there are small plus and minus icons to open and close nodes of the hierarchy, or there may be small arrows that point right and down for closed and open, respectively.

Opening and closing the tree on the Web can be problematic if a page reload is involved. If a user has scrolled down and the page refreshes to the top after expanding a node, the open node may be located offscreen. Avoid page reloads with tree navigation on the Web if you can. If page refreshes are needed, scroll the page automatically to the position the user last left it.

Safari Books Online (*http://search.safaribooksonline.com*) uses a tree navigation to access book categories. This appears on the lower-left side of the store's main page, seen in the closeup in Figure 3-15.

This tree is simple and effective, but there is a distinct interaction problem: after opening a branch, the page reloads back to the top, not to the point where a category was opened. Trying to get to the section on the programming language C, for instance, requires scrolling several times to re-access the tree navigation after each reload.

SITE MAPS

A site map is a representation of a site's structure used for navigation.[4] This provides a top-down overview of the site's content at a glance. Using a site map, visitors can jump directly to any page listed.

| ▶ Applied Sciences |
| ▶ Artificial Intelligence |
| ▶ Business |
| ▶ Certification |
| ▶ Computer Science |
| ▶ Databases |
| ▶ Desktop Publishing |
| ▶ Desktop Applications |
| ▶ E-Business |
| ▶ E-Commerce |
| ▶ Enterprise Computing |
| ▶ Graphics |
| ▼ **Human-Computer Interaction** |
| Information Architecture |
| Interface Design |
| Online Communities |
| Usability |
| Content Generation/Writing |
| ▶ Hardware |
| ▶ Internet/Online |
| ▶ IT Management |
| ▶ Markup Languages |
| ▶ Multimedia |
| ▶ Networking |
| ▶ Operating Systems |
| ▶ Programming |
| ▶ Security |
| ▶ Software Engineering |
| View All Titles > |

Figure 3-15 / Tree navigation on Safari Books Online

A site map is often afforded its own page, but it may also appear, in part, on other pages. Site maps should therefore be fairly simple and easy to scan. It's also critical that labels used in the site map match the main navigation categories, as well as page titles.

One line of reasoning is that if your main site navigation matches user needs, a site map is not necessary. Ideally, this may be true, but it isn't always the case. Sites with a great deal of content and a wide variety of user types may not be able to predict every information need for every visitor in every situation. A site map could help.

Site maps have gone in and out of style. In the early years of e-commerce, many sites included one. But creating and maintaining a site map is not easy and sometimes costly. The investment often doesn't match the benefit.

More recently, site maps have been recognized as a means of optimizing search engine indexing. Search engines can get a better overview of your site's total content via a site map. So, although site visitors may not use them often, site maps may have other benefits. You'll need to weigh the advantages and disadvantages carefully.

---

4   This type of site map is not to be confused with the deliverable "site map" used to create sites, discussed in Chapter 8.

A fundamental question in creating a site map is that of granularity. It may not be possible, nor desirable, to list every page. But providing too little detail may also not help. The trick is achieving the right balance. Generally, site maps show two to three levels of site structure, providing access only to the main pages of a site.

For example, the web site of the French car manufacturer Renault has a simple site map (*www.renault.fr*, Figure 3-16). The main categories are listed with the key pages one level down.

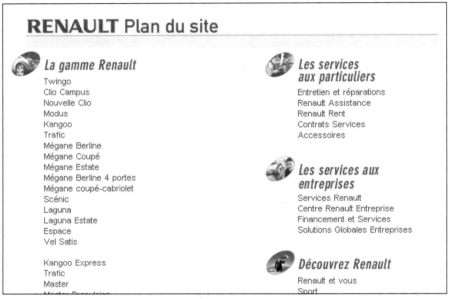

Figure 3-16 / The top half of a simple site map on Renault.fr

The Iberia web site for the national airline of Spain shows multiple levels of site structure (*www.ibaeria.es*, Figure 3-17). *Busi*ness Class is hierarchically nested within main category Viaje con Nosotros, and then under Productos y servicios > Nuestras clases. Indentation and different font sizes indicate the position of a page within this hierarchy. This takes up more vertical space, but it works well for this site, which isn't too large.

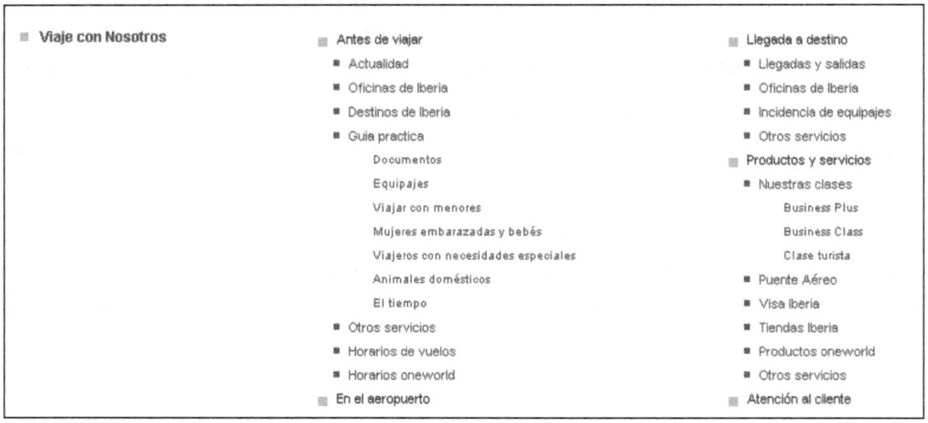

Figure 3-17 / A multilevel site map on Iberia.es

Each of the previous examples appears on a separate page. The social networking site LinkedIn, however, displays a portion of a simple site map at the bottom of each page of the site, along with a link to the entire, more-detailed site map (*www.linkedin.com*, Figure 3-18).

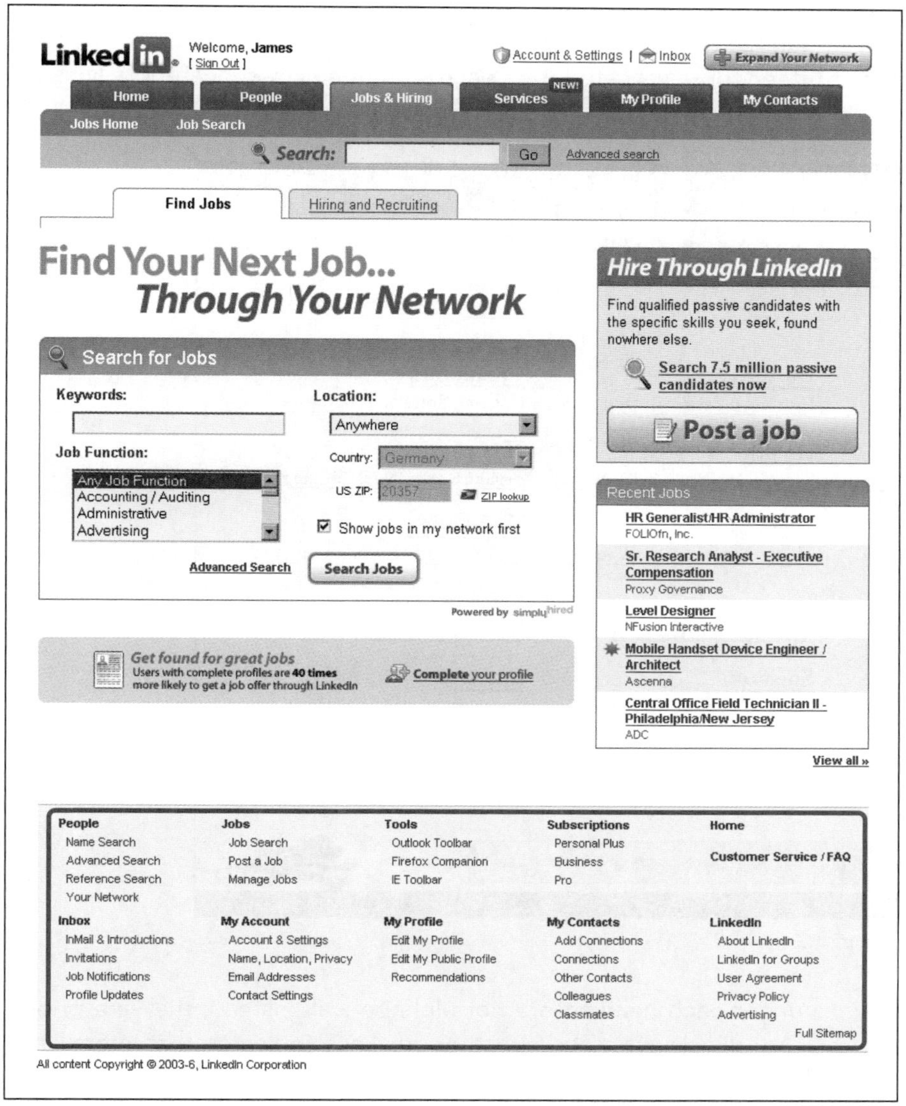

Figure 3-18 / Portion of the site map for LinkedIn.com on every page

DIRECTORIES

Directories usually provide access to pages via topics. Yahoo!, the first commercial topical directory on the Web, popularized the notion of web portals. Unlike site maps, directories may classify content by category. They are also different from indexes, which list terms alphabetically (see the next section). Directories are useful when dealing with mixed types of information without a hierarchical relationship. They are also effective for organizing and linking to external sites.

Category headings are usually arranged alphabetically, with the main topic often shown in a larger font, followed by a few key subtopic links displayed underneath. Clicking a link brings you to a page for that topic. That page displays all links under the topic. In this way, you can drill down into the categories.

DMOZ.com hosts the Open Directory Project (*www.dmoz.com*). Edited by a team of volunteers around the world, this directory seeks to categorize the Web at large. Positioned front and center on the home page, the DMOZ.com directory shows fifteen top-level categories, each with three key subcategory links (Figure 3-19).

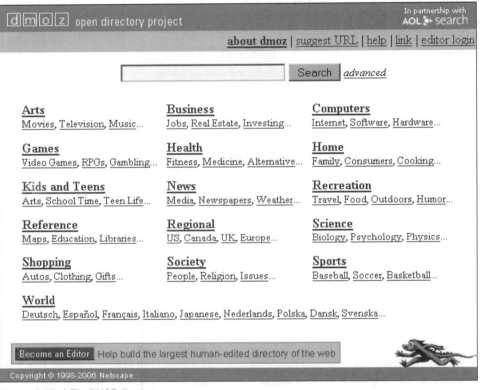

Figure 3-19 / The DMOZ directory

Note that the subcategory links under each heading are not alphabetical. Instead, they are prioritized, presumably by their usefulness. An ellipsis after the subcategory links indicates that more links are available.

TAG CLOUDS

A recent addition to navigation mechanisms is the tag cloud, which lists links alphabetically and weighted by frequency; the more frequently occurring a topic the larger it appears. This gives a snapshot into the relative significance of a topic: the larger the link, the more important it is. Although most often implemented with tags (hence the name), these mechanisms sometimes employ other types of links as well.

Tag clouds are good for dynamic content. Flickr is reported to be the first site to use the tag cloud (*www. flickr.com*, Figure 3-20).[5] Tags that are used more frequently are displayed in a larger font, so the cloud shows popularity of tags. (See Chapter 12 for more on tagging).

As a navigational mechanism, tag clouds have limited value. If a visitor has a known information need, for instance, a cloud of links isn't really efficient. They seem to be more of a novelty than an effective navigation mechanism. But the visual weighting of links provides valuable information: it shows at a glance what others are talking about or about the concerns of a community. Tag clouds reflect a certain zeitgeist for a site or topic.

Explore Flickr Through Tags

architecture art australia baby beach birthday blue bw california cameraphone canada cat chicago china christmas city dog england europe family flower flowers food france friends germany green holiday italy japan london me mexico music nature new newyork night nyc paris park party people portrait red sanfrancisco sky snow spain spring summer sunset taiwan tokyo travel trip usa vacation water wedding winter

---

Figure 3-20 / Flickr's famous tag cloud

A–Z INDEXES

An A–Z index is an alphabetical guide to topics, terms, and concepts found throughout a web site. Indexes generally supplement access to content and aren't a main point of entry. They provide a bottom-up view of a site's content and are the electronic version of the traditional back-of-the-book index. For sites with many repeat visitors, such as a company intranet, a site index can be particularly beneficial.

In a site index, each alphabetically arranged entry is linked to the page where that topic is discussed. Indexes can be quite long and are often divided into pages for each letter of the alphabet. A strip of letters is then linked, allowing users to jump to specific letter pages of the index.

Note that the body can also be a mix of links and text. Not all entries in an index are linked, particularly for "use" or "see" references. For example, if an entry for ping-pong points to table tennis via a see function, ping-pong may not be linked. Like this:

Ping-Pong

See: *Table Tennis*

The University of Auckland web site, for instance, has a simple A–Z index (*www.auckland.ac.nz*, Figure 3-21). In this case, the entire index is on one page. Clicking a letter in the alphabet jumps to the appropriate anchor. It is a simple, flat list of links with no cross references.

---

5   See "Tag cloud" on Wikipedia: *en.wikipedia.org/wiki/Tag_cloud*.

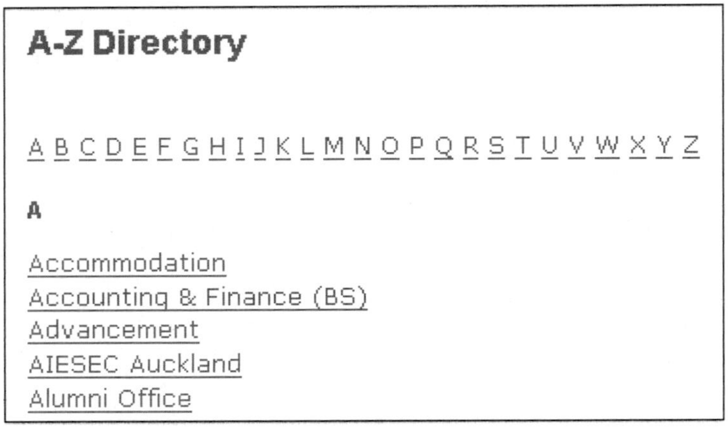

A-Z Directory

A B C D E F G H I J K L M N O P Q R S T U V W X Y Z

A

Accommodation
Accounting & Finance (BS)
Advancement
AIESEC Auckland
Alumni Office

Figure 3-21 / University of Auckland's simple index

By contrast, the BBC web site uses an extensive A–Z index[6] with each letter on a separate page. Notice the mix of links and plain text on the M page in Figure 3-22; the heading Macedonia itself is not linked, but its sub-entries are.

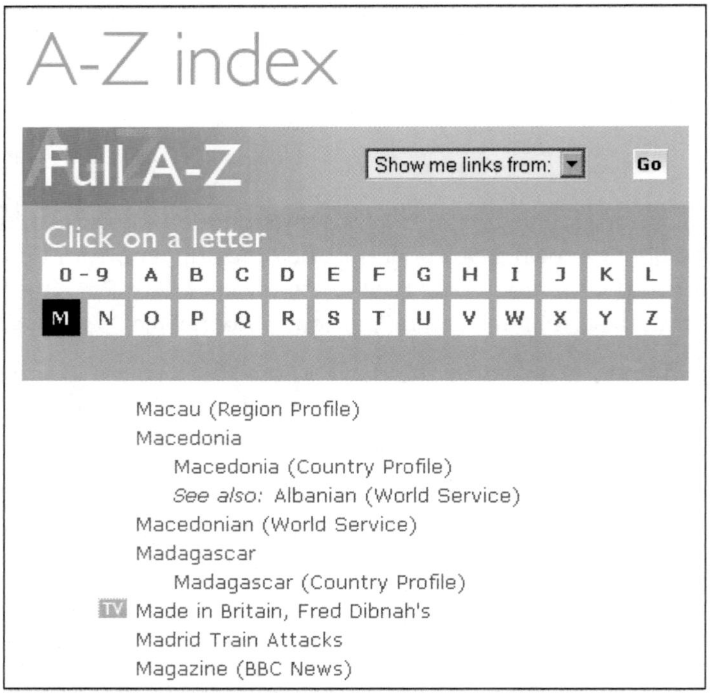

A-Z index

Full A-Z

Show me links from: [▼]   [Go]

Click on a letter

0-9	A	B	C	D	E	F	G	H	I	J	K	L
M	N	O	P	Q	R	S	T	U	V	W	X	Y	Z

Macau (Region Profile)
Macedonia
    Macedonia (Country Profile)
    See also: Albanian (World Service)
Macedonian (World Service)
Madagascar
    Madagascar (Country Profile)
TV Made in Britain, Fred Dibnah's
Madrid Train Attacks
Magazine (BBC News)

Figure 3-22 / BBC.co.uk has a very detailed site index

---

6   Helen Lippell describes BBC site index in detail in an excellent article: "The ABCs of the BBC: A Case Study and Checklist," *Boxes and Arrows* (December 2005). *www.boxesandarrows.com/view/the_abcs_of_the_bbc_a_case_study_and_checklist*.

A–Z indexes have three key advantages:

- They are familiar. The simple alphabetical structure and back-of-the-book experience means almost no learning curve for most people.

- Though indexes best support known-item searching, they can also point to relevant topics that may initially be unknown. For instance, if someone is looking for the term "information architecture," an index might also point to "wayfinding" via a "see also" reference.

- Like site maps, A–Z indexes can also enhance search engine optimization.

A–Z indexes aren't appropriate for all sites. Large, dynamic sites with thousands of content page are impossible to index by hand. A–Z indexes work best with very small sites or intranets of up to 500 pages. Alternatively, you could index part of a web site to provide access to key pages higher up in the site structure that may be more stable. Still, maintenance is difficult, costly, and time consuming.

NAVIGATION BARS AND TABS

The simplest form of a navigation bar is a horizontal chain of plain hypertext links. These are sometimes separated by a vertical line (pipe) as shown in the main navigation bar on del.icio.us (Figure 3-23).

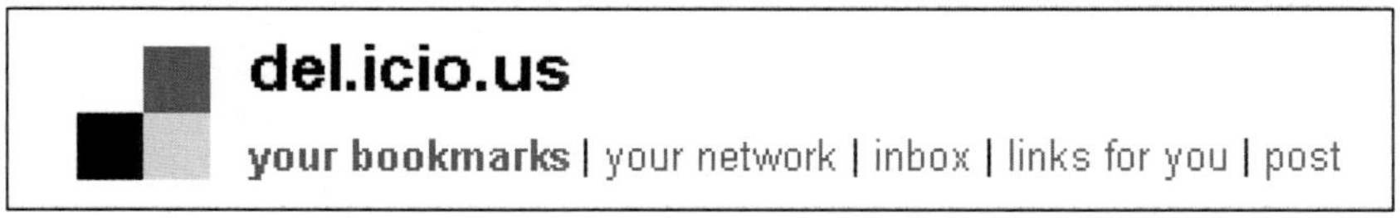

del.icio.us

your bookmarks | your network | inbox | links for you | post

Figure 3-23 / A simple navigation bar on del.icio.us with plain text links

Accessibility

The inclusion of a text-based pipe may cause accessibility issues. Screen readers will read the character aloud between each link name. Alternatively, you can represent the pipe as an image with the ALT attribute set to "" (blank quotes). This, of course, adds weight to the page—though minimal—and requires a hit on the server for the initial image.

Note that this also applies to breadcrumb trails, discussed earlier. The trail shown in Figure 3-10 might be read by a screen reader as: "You are here colon NHS England is greater than news is greater than other health news." Some screen reader users may be used to this; others may find it disorienting.

Navigation bars often have a colored background, or may use graphical images for the options. This creates a strong sense of a bar across the page. The web site for the Russian newspaper *Pravda*, for instance, uses a navigation bar with white text on a dark blue background (*www.pravda.ru*, Figure 3-24).

Figure 3-24 / The dark blue navigation bar on the Pravda site

A key advantage to navigation bars is that they don't take away from the horizontal width of the main content area. Instead they are positioned above the primary areas of the page. The content can then spread out across the entire width of the browser.

TABS

The distinction between tabs and navigation bars is their presentation. There is no real difference in function. Rather than a solid bar, tabs are like overlapping shingles, usually sticking up from the main content area. Each tab is distinct from the next, often with rounded or slanted corners.

Amazon.com was probably the first major e-commerce web site to use tabs as a primary navigation mechanism. Since then, tabs as navigation have become wildly popular. However, both tabs and navigation bars have a distinct scalability problem: there is a limited amount of horizontal space on a web page.

In addition to the number of tabs in the navigation, the length of labels will drive the use of horizontal space. Generally, tabs must necessarily have short and concise labels. One way to increase the amount of text that can fit on a tab is to allow for two lines of text. This makes the tab taller, which also increases visibility and makes it easier to click.

E*TRADE, for example, has tabs as a main navigation (*www.etrade.com*, Figure 3-25). Each can have two lines of text, which allows for at least seven very visible tabs across the page with fairly descriptive labels.

Figure 3-25 / E*TRADE's double-row tabs with longer labels on each

Amazon.com has dealt with the scalability issue of tabs in unique ways. As the company began offering more and more products and services, the tabbed navigation became strained. Their information architecture grew bigger than the navigation mechanism could accommodate. In addition to the eight main tabs, a See More Stores link to the right of the main tab navigation (Figure 3-26) was added. Clicking this presented all products and services on a single page, in a directory-style fashion.

Figure 3-26 / Early Amazon.com: the tabs couldn't show all their stores

Amazon's first solution was to change from eight or so main tabs to just two: Welcome (the home tab) and Store Directory (Figure 3-27). To the far right, the Today's Featured Stores section contained simple buttons that could rotate as needed. Detaching these buttons from the main tabs provided an opportunity to swap them more readily: they weren't part of the tab structure.

Figure 3-27 / Later Amazon.com: two tabs and Today's Featured Stores

More recently, Amazon moved to yet another model to combat the scalability limitations of tabs. It is a more compact design and makes use of a dynamic menu. The tabbed navigation has three different states:

- State 1: the permanent tabs are the Amazon logo, the My Store, and See All 35 Product Categories (Figure 3-28). This is the initial state of the navigation.

- State 2: the rightmost tab provides access to all product categories with a dynamic menu. This is fairly large with links to each department (Figure 3-29).

- State 3: selecting one of the product categories then adds a fourth tab to the main navigation for that product category. In Figure 3-30, DVD is newly added.

Figure 3-28 / State 1: the initial, compact tab structure Amazon.com with three tabs

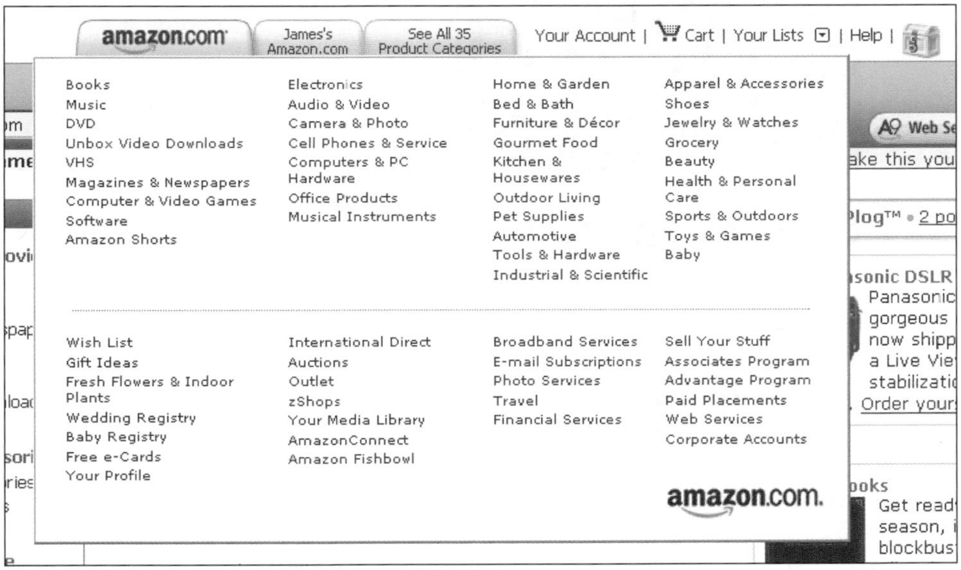

Figure 3-29 / State 2: a menu of all product categories

Figure 3-30 / State 3: the temporary tab, reflecting the selected product category (here: DVD)

With this arrangement, visitors are essentially customizing the main navigation by selecting a product category. In Figure 3-30, the tab for DVD is transient and changes with a category selection. This allows Amazon.com to keep its hallmark tab look while accommodating a growing business.

VERTICAL MENU

Jacob Nielsen claims that CNET.com was the first to make extensive, consistent use of a navigation mechanism (a stack of links on the screen's left) across an entire site. Called a vertical or left-hand menu (or right-hand menu if on the right), this vertical arrangement has become prevalent in web navigation design.

Vertical menus are generally more flexible than navigation bars or tabs. Because the mechanism can easily extend downward, adding options is usually not as problematic as adding a tab. Additionally, vertical menus generally allow for longer labels, particularly if they can wrap onto two or more lines.

The Oracle web site uses a vertical menu with long, descriptive labels on the left of its home page to provide access to the major areas of the site (*www.oracle.com*, Figure 3-31). In a horizontal navigation bar, many of these labels would have to be shortened.

Figure 3-31 / A vertical menu of the left side of Oracle.com

Vertical menus can also appear elsewhere on the page, such as for related links further down or for adaptive navigation, both discussed further in Chapter 4.

Also known as fly-out menus, pull-down menus, or pop-up menus, dynamic menus provide quick access to navigation options. They are considered "dynamic" because visitors must interact with them before they display. After the visitor selects a navigation option with a mouse rollover or click, the site presents a menu window similar to those found in software applications.

A key advantage to this mechanism is ready access to more options than could otherwise be displayed on a single page. The downside is potentially reduced visibility of these options. Visitors have to explore more before making a navigation decision.

If the dynamic menu displays with a simple mouse rollover, it's common to delay the appearance of the menu. The menu should first appear about a half-second after the mouse has rolled over the navigation point. The menu should stay open as long as the mouse is over the navigation point or within the menu area itself. After the mouse rolls out, the menu should close after about a half-second delay. Another variation is to have the menu close with a click elsewhere on the page.

Even with a delay, dynamic menus from vertical navigation menus can be problematic. Depending on the menu's placement, trying to select an option may cause people to move the mouse outside of the menu area or touch a neighboring option. Exact movement along the navigation label itself is required. Dynamic menus therefore work better with a horizontal navigation bar or with tabs: they drop down (or up) and can easily be reached with the mouse without touching other navigation options.

For example, try using the dynamic menus on the Barilla page (*www.barilla.it*), shown in Figure 3-32. If the mouse touches any of the other main options, the currently open dynamic menu closes, and the other opens. This is inefficient and annoying.

Figure 3-32 / The dynamic menus on Barilla's web site are hard to use

The main navigation for *Le Monde*, a large French newspaper, uses dynamic menus extending downward from the navigation bar, which solves this interaction problem (*www.lemonde.fr*). The menus here appear on rollover. Figure 3-33 shows a dynamic menu extending downward from the Perspectives option.

Accessibility

Screen readers have trouble with dynamic menus that activate with a rollover only. Instead, a click to reveal the menu is better. Be sure to test with screen readers before going with this solution.

Also note that visitors with motion impairments might have problems operating dynamic menus. Although they may not being using a screen reader, the menu may still prove inaccessible.

Figure 3-33 / Dynamic menus on LeMonde.fr extend downward

It's also not advisable to include dynamic menus in the middle of the page. In this case, dynamic menus may extend off the page and may not be visible. The web site for Sun Microsystems, for instance, uses dynamic menus on the home page (*www.sun.com*). Unfortunately, these can extend below the bottom edge of the browser if the page is not scrolled down (Figure 3-34).

Figure 3-34 / Cut-off dynamic menu on Sun.com

DROP-DOWN MENUS

Drop-down menus are simple HTML selection menus with options. Selecting an option brings the user to the new page. This type of navigation is often used for quick links, which jump to a new page across a site structure, for instance.

Accessibility

For accessibility reasons, do not have the new page reload just by selecting the option and releasing the mouse. This requires JavaScript (called an "onChange" event) and can cause problems with screen readers. Some screen readers will trigger the link as soon as it is read, prohibiting the user from getting to any other options it the menu.

An alternative is to activate the menu selection with an explicit button or link click just after the menu. An advanced solution might be to change the site's behavior based on whether a screen reader is used. A Go button would then appear only if needed.

A drop-down menu on the IBM web site navigates to the site in a different language and country (*www.ibm.com*, Figure 3-35) and is followed by a Go button to activate the selection.

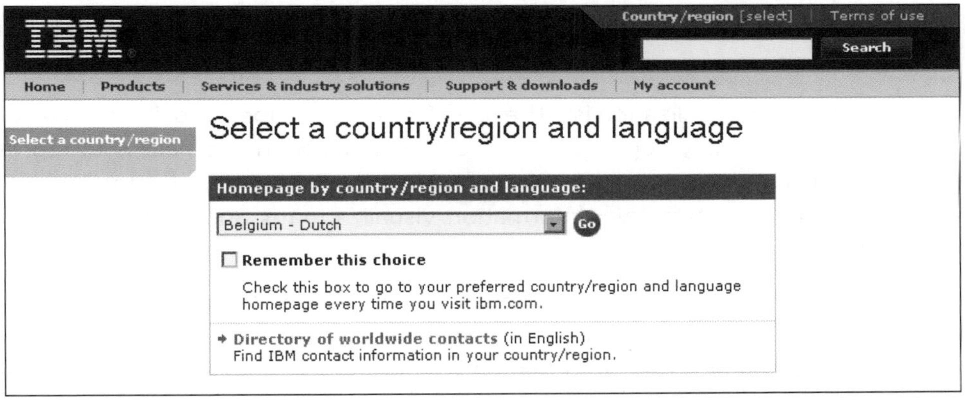

Figure 3-35 / Using a drop-down menu on IBM.com for language selection

The web site for the ASBA Group, a South African banking group (*www.absa.co.za/absacoza*), has an interesting navigation mechanism. Two drop-down menus allow visitors to first pick a verb, then an action (Figure 3-37). This is part of a sentence beginning with "I want to." A selection in the first menu updates choices in the second menu. This provides many combinations and navigation paths in a compact space.

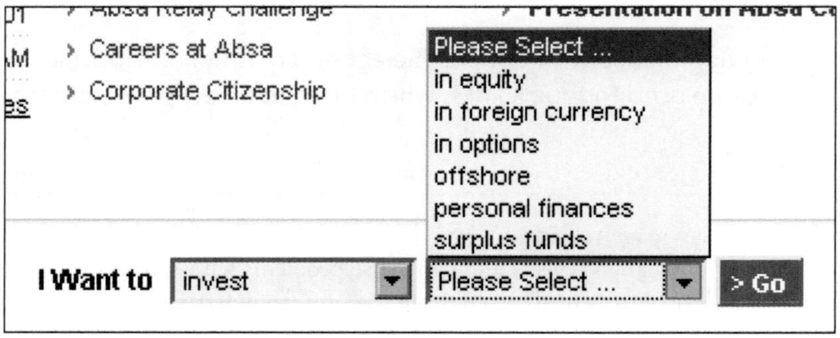

Figure 3-36 / Two drop-down menus work in tandem

Internationalization

A mechanism such as the one seen in Figure 3-36 may not translate to other languages well. If you are planning a multi-language site, it's best to avoid sentence-based navigation, such as embedding navigation within a partial sentence. Word order and word forms are different in different languages.

VISUALIZING NAVIGATION

Beyond traditional tabs, bars, and menus lies a category of mechanisms that use information visualization.

The standard definition of information visualization is: "The use of computer-supported, interactive, visual representations of abstract data to amplify cognition."[7] The common vision in this field is to represent information in spatial or visual relationships to make complex data sets clear and understandable. More importantly, these representations are interactive. Information visualization is about manipulating and navigating information, not just about how it is displayed.

Information visualization doesn't aim to replace textual displays of information. Visual representations and plain text complement each other. For instance, text doesn't scale up well. Displaying thousands of items as text can't be done on a single computer screen. Information visualization techniques, on the other hand, provide views into information on different levels. Patterns of millions of items can be shown in a chart or graph of some kind. People can then zoom in or out for more or less detail.

Visualization mechanisms tend to have limited use and should be reserved for special situations. General web users may not be accustomed to them. But, as research in information visualization mechanisms continues, their application may become more widespread. Three common mechanisms are star trees, visual thesauri, and visual clusters.

STAR TREES

Also called a radial tree layout, a star tree represents hierarchical relationships in a hub and spoke display. Large amounts of data can appear within a relatively compact space. A star tree might be an alternative to tree navigation and even a site map. Inxight offers a commercial star tree, such as the one in Figure 3-37 showing a diagram of Richard Saul Wurman's *Understanding USA* (*www.understandingusa.com*).

---

7   Stuart K. Card, Jock Mackinlay and Ben Shneiderman (Editors), *Readings in Information Visualization: Using Vision to Think* (Morgan Kaufmann, 1999): 7.

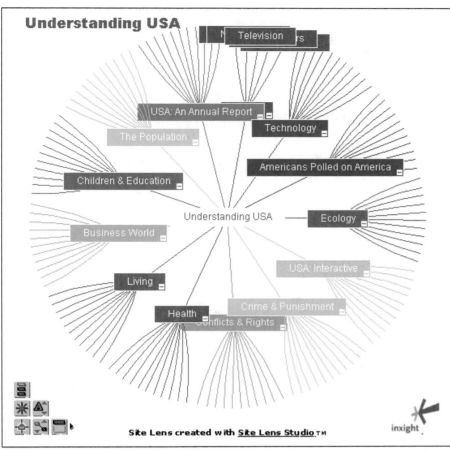

Figure 3-37 / *Understanding USA* as a star tree

Clicking on any term shifts the whole display so that term is now at the center. The categories from the selected one are then larger and easier to click. Though interesting to view and manipulate, the mechanism is generally used as supplementary navigation for special situations.

VISUAL THESAURI

The Art and Culture site (*www.artandculture.com*) employs a simple visual thesaurus as a supplemental navigation. This presents the topic of the current page in the center. Related terms then "float" around that term (Figure 3-38). Clicking any term leads to the corresponding page.

Figure 3-38 / A visual thesaurus on the Art and Culture web site

Unlike a star tree, which attempts to show a great deal of information in small space, the intent of a visual thesaurus is to encourage user exploration. It generally shows a limited set of related concepts to aid in discovery of new information. The implementation on Art and Culture works well for this reason: the site itself encourages exploration and learning.

The Visual Thesaurus from Thinkmap, Inc. is a fairly mature, commercial example of this mechanism. It shows the nodes of a thesaurus in a web-like display (Figure 3-39). Definitions of terms are shown when rolling over a node. Clicking a term makes it the new center of the display. With this tool, you can continually chain terms and explore all kinds of relationships.

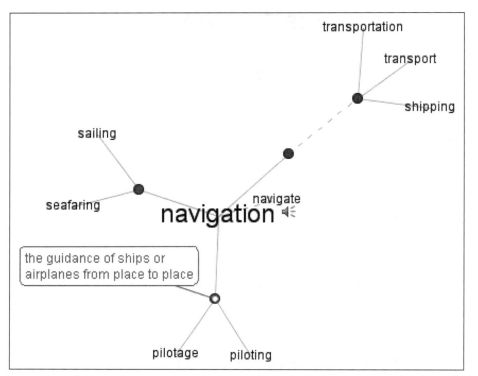

Figure 3-39 / The Visual Thesaurus with "navigation" at the center

VISUAL CLUSTERS

More advanced visualization mechanisms have been recently applied to search results. Grokker.com, for instance, displays search results in a graphical display, as shown in Figure 3-40. Results within a similar category are grouped within circles. People can then zoom in and out to explore each category circle. Web pages themselves are displayed as small page icons. Rolling over an item instantly displays more details about that item. Controls on the lower left allow users to manipulate and filter the results.

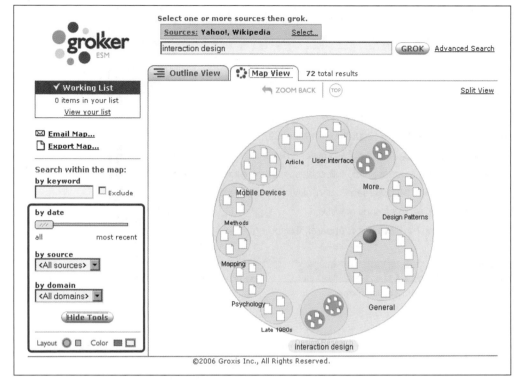

Figure 3-40 / Results clusters from the Grokker search engine

In theory, this seems quite useful. But it does take some getting used to—something people may not want to invest time in. What's more, categories that are generated on the fly are often too broad, too narrow, or just plain meaningless. The groupings for Article, General, and More... in Figure 3-40 don't help users hone in on a topic.

BROWSER MECHANISMS

Keep in mind that web browsers have built-in mechanisms of their own. Consider these while designing a site's navigation system. The most important browser mechanisms in terms of navigation include:

Back button

The most obvious and relevant browser control for navigation is the Back button. Clicking it is perhaps one of the most frequently performed actions while navigating the Web.

Forward button

The Forward button isn't used nearly as much as the Back button, but is still a way to move forward in a path.

Session history

This is a reverse chronological list of recently visited pages. Figure 3-41 shows a session history, extending down from the Back button. Session history is a good reason to supply meaningful browser titles; this is discussed further in Chapter 5.

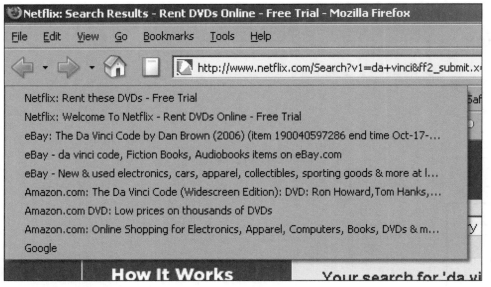

Figure 3-41 / An example of a browser's session history

Browser history

Many browsers also have a more permanent history of activity going back for weeks. This is often accessed in a left sidebar. Users can use this tool to return to sites visited in the past.

URLs

The URL itself is also a mechanism that allows for navigation. See more about URLs in Chapter 5.

Other features to consider include things such as bookmaking, page reloading, and the Home button. Make sure your site doesn't break browser navigation features. Expect people to navigate with them, especially with the Back button. However, it's generally advisable to avoid relying on browser controls as the *only* means of navigating to content. Web navigation systems are best when they don't rely on the browser as the sole means of navigation.

SUMMARY

Before beginning to design navigation, you must understand its individual components. These mechanisms are the basic building blocks for navigation systems. If web navigation were a story, mechanisms would be the sentences and paragraphs that comprise it. In the end, a blend of mechanisms comes together to form the overall construction of your site's navigation.

Each of the mechanisms you choose has a different role within the overall navigation scheme. Step navigation, paging, and breadcrumbs are a few simple examples of linear navigation mechanisms that move forward or backward, step by step. Other mechanisms show many details of an information structure at once, such as a tree navigation, site map, directory, or A–Z indexes. These are good for providing an overview to many pages at once.

Typically, however, web navigation is made up of menus, tabs, and bars. More advanced navigation mechanisms, such as star trees, visual thesauri, and clustering displays, visualize navigation spatially. These are not common mechanisms and tend to be used only in special situations in which they complement other navigation mechanisms. Finally, you must also consider that web browsers have built-in features such as Back and Forward buttons, history, and URLs, which affect web navigation.

Chapter 4, "Types of Navigation," provides more context for when and how mechanisms should appear in a site. One may be the primary navigation to access the main categories of the site, for instance. Another might provide access to related content at the bottom of page. These different functions will guide the selection and use of mechanisms in your site's navigation.

Additionally, you must consider the structure of the site and how people will move around within it. Chapter 9, "Layout," outlines how to arrange navigation on the page. Basically, it's a process of evaluating the navigation needs people will have when they are coming to and leaving from key pages in your site. As you then try to assemble the navigation around those needs, having a good understanding of possible means of access via different mechanisms is essential.

QUESTIONS

1. Think up analogies for three of the discussed navigation mechanisms. For instance, step navigation is like turning pages in a book. What does a location breadcrumb trail resemble? A directory? A dynamic menu?

2. Analyze the various navigation mechanisms on a few pages on Amazon.com (or Amazon in your country), including a search results page. Identify all the different kinds of navigation mechanisms you find.

    a) How is each used? For what types of content is each used?

    b) What are potential problems of each?

    c) What works well? What doesn't? What don't they use that they could possibly benefit from?

    d) List at the advantages and disadvantages of the three most prevalent navigation mechanisms on Amazon.

3. Compare results paging for three popular search engines. First, do a search for a common term that produces a large results set, such as "design." Then go to the twentieth page on each.

    a) How does page numbering on the twentieth page differ?

    b) What are the rules for the display of page numbers?

    c) What is good and what is bad about each?

    d) Specify the display rules for one of the paging mechanisms in words or in a flowchart using "if" statements.

4. Other than for user-created tags, what other types of navigation could be displayed as a tag cloud? List three other ways links in a tag cloud could be ranked, other than by popularity. How might a tag cloud be used for navigation on a news site, for instance? Or on a shopping site?

5. Redesign the home page of a site you are working on or that you visit frequently with the following three mechanisms only:

- Step navigation
- Breadcrumb trail
- Drop-down menus

What difficulties do you have? What is gained? What is lost?

FURTHER READING

Designing Interfaces, by Jenifer Tidwell (O'Reilly, 2006).

This book gives a broad tour of various interface elements and principles of interaction design. Discussions cover both software graphical user interfaces (GUIs) and web interfaces. Among other things, Tidwell covers many mechanisms in detail using patterns, which are a way of representing a prototypical solution to commonly encountered design problems. This book contains hands-on information and is well-suited for practitioners.

Readings in Information Visualization: Using Vision to Think, Edited by Stuart Card, Jock Mackinlay and Ben Shneiderman (Morgan Kaufmann, 1999).

This collection of classic papers has quickly become the standard volume for information visualization. It is academic in nature, but clearly written and approachable. With over 700 pages and 47 articles, it is a valuable reference source.

Types of Navigation

04

Not all navigation mechanisms on a site are equal.

Your job is to sort them out. You must determine the purpose and importance of the navigation within your site, bringing similar options together and presenting them as a cohesive unit. Of course, there are conventions to get you started—bars and tabs are commonly used for the main navigation, vertical mechanisms on the left for local navigation—but there are no set usage rules, and many variations exist.

To sort them out, try thinking like a visitor, not a designer. Take time to consider how visitors perceive the navigation mechanisms. Understanding the type of navigation a menu represents can help people predict links and reorient themselves on new pages.

But what makes a main navigation the main navigation? What makes a related link different than a local navigation? Several aspects distinguish types of navigation:

- The type of content a mechanism accesses
- Behavior of the navigational links and transition to the next page
- The tasks and modes of seeking the mechanism supports
- Visual treatment of navigational options
- The position of a navigation on a page

What's more, the type of page on which a navigational menu appears greatly determines the navigation's purpose. The navigation on home pages is usually different from the navigation on product pages, for example, and visitors expect certain navigational elements to appear on search results pages. The role the page plays in the overall site also gives purpose to different types of navigation.

All of these aspects work together to allow site visitors to recognize that the main navigation is a main navigation and that local navigation is a local navigation. This sets the stage for interacting with the navigation and the site as a whole.

To help you ensure navigational concepts are immediately clear on your sites, this chapter surveys the various navigation types and their functions, as well as key page types. As you read on, however, keep in mind that there isn't a standard language among designers. The terminology describing navigation and navigational types can vary greatly. Whenever possible, alternative names are provided with each of the descriptions. Still, you may find alternative (or even contradictory) uses of terms in your organization. In all cases, just remember that your goal remains the same: to understand the role and purpose of navigation.

CATEGORIES OF NAVIGATION

Most navigation types fall into three primary categories[1] (Figure 4-1).

Structural

>   Connects one page to another based on the hierarchy of the site; on any page you'd expect to be able to move to the page above it and pages below it.

Associative

>   Connects pages with similar topics and content, regardless of their location in the site; links tend to cross structural boundaries.

Utility

>   Connects pages and features that help people use the site itself; these may lie outside the main hierarchy of the site, and their only relationship to one another is their function.

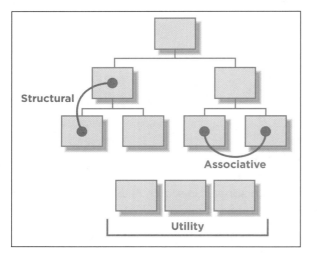

Figure 4-1 / Three primary categories of navigation (after Fiorito and Dalton)

STRUCTURAL NAVIGATION

As its name implies, structural navigation follows the structure of a web site. It allows people to move up and down the different points of a site's hierarchy. Structural navigation can be further subdivided into two types: main navigation and local navigation.

MAIN NAVIGATION

Also called: global navigation, primary navigation, main nav.

The main navigation generally represents the top-level pages of a site's structure—or the pages just below the home page. The links in the main navigation are expected to lead to pages within the site and behave in

---

1   See presentations from David Fiorito and Richard Dalton, Vanguard Group: "Creating a Consistent Enterprise Web Navigation Solution": *www.iasummit.org/2004/finalpapers/73/73_Handout_or__final__paper.ppt* and "Thinking Navigation." *www.iasummit.org/2005/finalpapers/101_Presentation.ppt* presented at the IA Summits in 2004 and 2005. These navigation types are derived directly from this work.

a very consistent way. Users don't expect to land somewhere completely unrelated when using main navigation links. Changes in navigation from page to page are usually small when using the main navigation.

Overall, a main navigation supports a variety of user tasks and modes of information seeking, including known-item seeking, exploration, and even re-finding. From a user's standpoint, the main navigation plays a critical role in using the site:

- The main navigation provides an overview and answers important questions users may have when first coming to a site, such as "does this site have what I'm looking for?"

- The main navigation aids in orientation. It is comforting to have a persistent navigation mechanism across the site, particularly for large, information-rich sites.

- It allows people to switch topics. Visitors can get to other sections of a site efficiently, or they can reset their navigation path and start over using main navigation options.

- It helps when users get interrupted while navigating and reminds visitors where they are in a site.

- Main navigation gives shape to a site. In many ways, the main navigation defines the boundaries of the site itself.

The main navigation is often presented in a global navigation area, which generally includes the site logo and utility navigation. (See the following section for more on utility navigation). As the name "global" implies, these controls generally appear in an unchanged, consistent position on all or nearly all pages of a site.

Consider the global navigation area of the University of Valencia (*www.uv.es*, Figure 4-2), for example. The six main navigation options are on the left below the logo. Some utility links are included to the right, such as a site map and link to site search. It's also typical to include a design element, such as a picture or graphic, to help create a brand image.

Figure 4-2 / The global navigation area on the University of Valencia home page

Critics of an ever-present global navigation point to its intrusion on valuable screen real estate. These concerns are entirely valid. The global navigation area in Figure 4-2 occupies a fair amount of the page, and the designers might have done a better job reducing it, particularly on content pages further down in the site. But it's not a question of including or excluding a global navigation: a global navigation area is usually a valuable navigational device. The question is how prominent and persistent it should be. The answer depends on several factors:

The size of the site

Larger sites with thousands of pages may benefit from a steady main navigational mechanism across pages. Smaller sites may be navigable with only breadcrumbs or contextual navigation.

User behavior and needs

Don't create prominent and persistent main navigation just for the sake of it. You need to understand your users and their information needs, then design accordingly.

Stakeholder objectives

Companies have goals. Inherently, some options will be promoted and highlighted over others. A visible, persistent global navigation may fulfill a stakeholder need.

Workflows that can't be interrupted

There are times when global navigation shouldn't be shown, or can vary its form. For instance, some task flows, such as a checkout process or online bank transfer, should restrain people from jumping out in the middle of a process.

Compare Figure 4-3, which shows the home page of the Opodo travel site (*www.opodo.co.uk*), to Figure 4-4, which shows first step of the site's checkout process. For checkout, the main navigation tabs were removed to provide focus during the process and avoid errors.

Figure 4-3 / The Opodo home page, with main navigation tabs highlighted

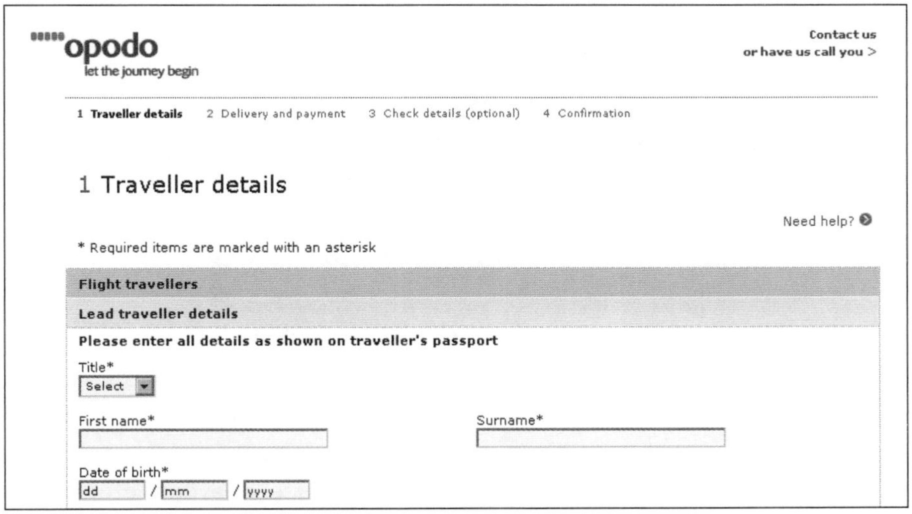

Figure 4-4 / Checking out on Opodo, without the main navigation

LOCAL NAVIGATION

Also called: sub-navigation, page-level navigation.

Local navigation is used to access lower levels in a structure, below the main navigation pages. The term "local" implies "within a given category." On a given page, local navigation generally shows other options at the same level of a hierarchy, as well as the options below the current page.

Local navigation often works in conjunction with a global navigation system and is really an extension of the main navigation. Because local navigation varies more often than main navigation, it is often treated differently.

Common arrangements of local navigation and main navigation include:

Inverted-L

It is very common to place a global navigation along the top of the page and have local navigation as a vertical link list on the left in the shape of an inverted L.

Horizontal

Local navigation might also be represented by a second row of options under a horizontal global navigation or by dynamic menus.

Embedded vertical

When the main navigation is presented in a vertical menu on the left or right, it's common to embed the local navigation between the main navigation options in a tree-like structure.

Figure 4-5 diagrams these three common arrangements. Keep in mind that other arrangements are possible, such as a right-hand local navigation, as well as combinations and hybrid arrangements.

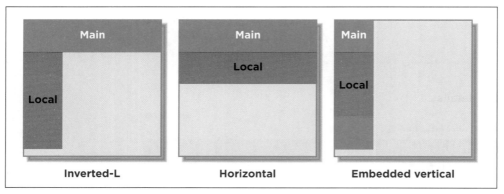

Figure 4-5 / Three common arrangements of main and local navigation

Generally transitions from page to page with a local navigation are smooth and consistent. There's likely no expectation that links in local navigation will cause the user to leave the site, or even the site category. But local navigation can be more volatile than global navigation in some instances. It may be used to link to other page types, content formats.

Overall, local navigation provides a great deal of context, such as which topics belong together, related content, and so forth. In this sense, local navigation plays a key role in indicating the "aboutness" of the site. It also gives a sense of granularity of a topic. For this reason, local navigation supports general exploration, as well as known-item seeking and re-finding. It also points to content a visitor might not have known existed.

The Dutch version of the Philips web site (*www.philips.nl*) represents the local navigation with dynamic menus, which conserve screen real estate while providing quick access to options. In Figure 4-6, a dynamic menu extends from the main navigation and displays options for Over Philips. Clicking one of these local navigation then leads to a page where the menu is repeated on the left (Figure 4-7). Pages one level down from here are then also revealed, between the grey bars in the image. Overall, this is an efficient navigation strategy that makes good use of screen real estate.

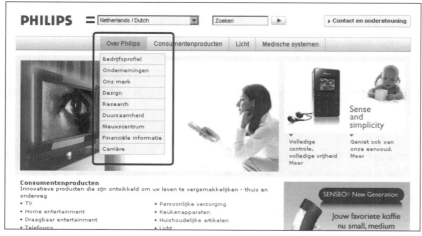

Figure 4-6 / Dynamic menus for local navigation from the Philips home page

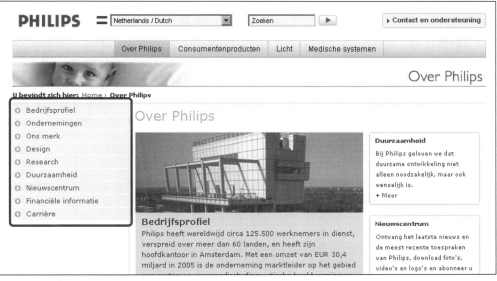

Figure 4-7 / An embedded vertical local navigation on Philips.nl

Accessibility

Skip Navigation

Persistent, global navigational elements present issues for screen reader users: people don't need every menu option read aloud on every page repeatedly. For the first page a screen reader user encounters while using a site, this may be helpful. But on subsequent pages, it's time-consuming and annoying to hear the same options read each time.

For persistent navigation with many options, place a Skip Navigation link before the navigation mechanism starts, so visitors can jump to the main content of a page, thereby skipping the navigation. Such links can be coded so that sighted users don't see them, but screen readers catch them.

Another strategy is to show navigation at the bottom of the page and to have a Skip to Navigation link at the top of the page for keyboard-based browsers. Then, at the bottom of the navigation, include a Back to Content link to bring users back to the content of the page.

ASSOCIATIVE NAVIGATION

Associative navigation makes important connections across levels of a hierarchy or site structure. While reading about one topic, the user can access to other topics. This is a key aspect of hypertext in general, but is also at the heart of the embedded digression problem mentioned in Chapter 2.

Three common types of associative navigation are: contextual navigation, quick links, and footer navigation. Take a closer look at each in turn.

CONTEXTUAL NAVIGATION

Also called: associative links, related links.

As the name implies, contextual navigation can vary. It's situational. Though links may transition to similar pages at the same level within the site, they quite frequently lead to new content areas, different page types, or even a new site.

Generally, contextual navigation is placed close to the content of a page. This creates a strong connection between the meaning of a text and the linked related pages. There are two typical arrangements of contextual navigation on the page (Figure 4-8):

Embedded navigation

Contextual navigation may be embedded within the text itself. As a result, contextual navigation is often represented as plain text links.

Related links

Contextual navigation may appear at the end or to the side of content.

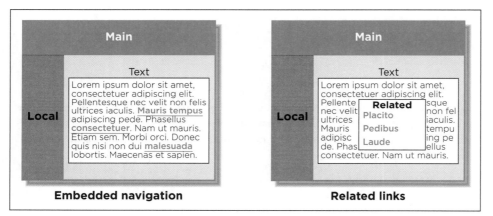

Figure 4-8 / Two types of contextual navigation: embedded links and related links

If the navigation is embedded within text, there may be an explicit indication to prepare users for more disjointed interaction, such as linking to a different content format or another site. For instance, an embedded link may be preceded or succeeded by text indicating that the linked material is on a different site or in a different format. Figure 4-9 shows the Education page on the web site of the Information Architecture Institute (*www.iainstitute.org*). Links in the text lead to other pages in the site on various levels of the structure. The first link in the last paragraph opens a PDF document, as noted in the text. The second link goes to Amazon.com.

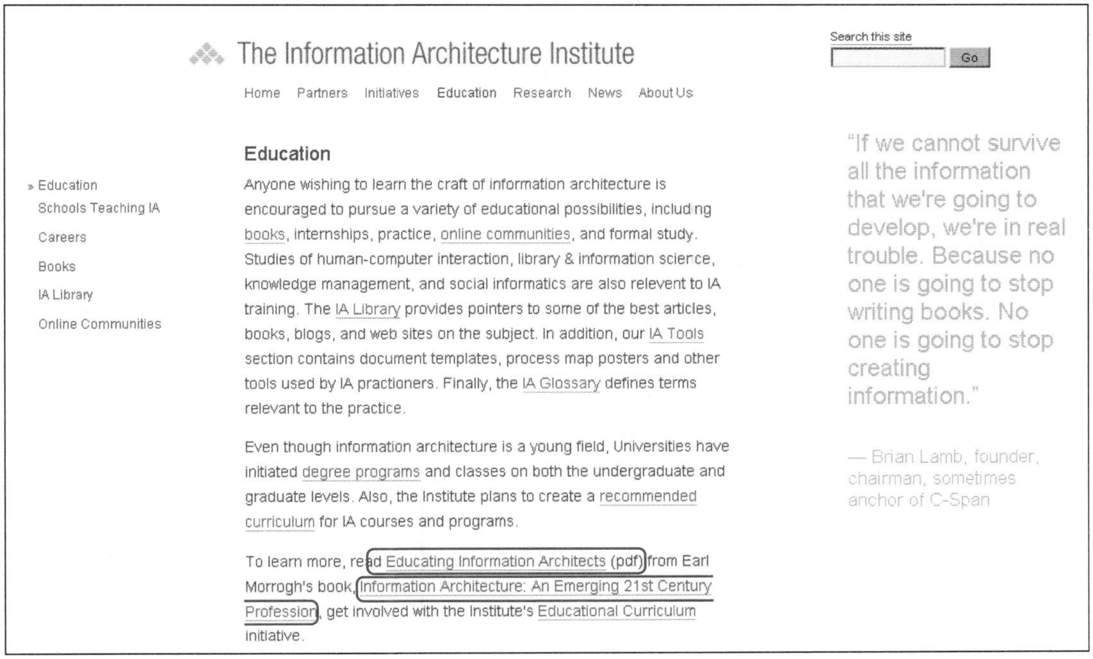

Figure 4-9 / Embedded contextual navigation on the IA Institute web site

Contextual navigation doesn't support known-item seeking well. Instead, it supports exploration and may point people to new information. From a business standpoint, contextual navigation provides opportunities for upsell. Product pages in e-commerce sites, for instance, often have links to related products and services. This is a common use of contextual navigation in e-commerce.

Accessibility

Embedded links or associative navigation must make sense when read out of context. It's common to label associative links "For more information, click here," for example, with "click here" the only linked words. When skipping from link to link on a page, a screen reader user would just hear the link text and not the preceding phrases: "click here," "click here," "click here," and so on. It's better to link the entire sentence, or at least enough so that the linked portion is understandable on its own.

Related links are also used effectively on news sites. From one article, readers can get to other related articles. For example, each story on the web site for *The Washington Post* (*www.washingtonpost.com*) ends with related links (Figure 4-10). There are two main parts:

- More stories on the same topic (Sports) as the current article. This includes a link that allows users to automatically search for even more articles on the same topic.

- Links to the most-viewed articles from the same section that the current article is in (in this case, Sports), including a link to see the top 35 most-viewed articles in that section.

Rutgers' offense couldn't control the ball, but it needed only one strike to leap back into the game. It came when Mike Teel found Kenny Britt on a post up the seam on third and seven. Britt zoomed all the way to the 4 before being caught from behind. Rice took a toss and ran for a touchdown on the next play and a two-point conversion followed, making it 25-22 with 4:42 left in the third quarter.

By the time Ito's heroics were complete, the Rutgers Stadium crowd was delirious. As the Scarlet Knights walked up a tunnel back into their locker room, a placard hung above the the entrance. In block letters, it read, "HISTORY."

Print This Article   E-Mail This Article   Permission to Republish

More on washingtonpost.com
- Three Make a Move
- National Title Race Finally Arrives
- 'The Chop' Is Secret to Rutgers Success
- » Related Topics & Web Content

powered by inform

Most Viewed Sports Articles
- Terps Hold On Against Spartans
- Getting Off the Ground Is a Problem
- Bo Schembechler, 77; Stormy Michigan Coach
- For Caps, Hurricanes, Not Much Has Changed in 8 Days
- » Top 35 Most Viewed

View all comments that have been posted about this article.

© 2006 The Washington Post Company

Figure 4-10 / Related links component for an article from *The Washington Post*

ADAPTIVE NAVIGATION

Look again at the links in the contextual navigation area of Figure 4-10, and you'll notice the Sports Articles links change based on which stories readers visit most. By observing what all site visitors do, a new type of navigation link arises: adaptive navigation.

Adaptive navigation is a special kind of a contextual navigation. Its links are generated from a process referred to as collaborative or social filtering. The process relies on an algorithmic ranking of some kind, based on user behavior. The principle is similar to a traditional best-seller list: if many people read something, it must be good. In this case, link relevance turns out to be a socially constructed phenomenon.

Adaptive navigation has been most prominently used to make recommendations on e-commerce sites. The classic example of this is the "Customers who bought this item also bought…" feature on Amazon. com. Figure 4-11 shows an example of this feature, using Jeffrey Zeldman's book *Designing with Web Standards*.[2]

---

2   Jeffrey Zeldman, *Designing with Web Standards*, Second Edition (New Riders, 2003).

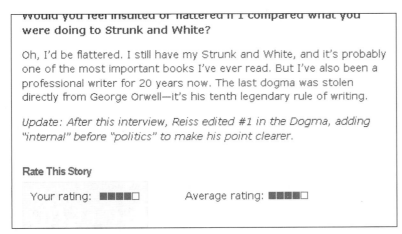

Customers who bought this item also bought

Web Standards Solutions: The Markup and Style Handbook (Pioneering Series) by Dan Cederholm

Eric Meyer on CSS: Mastering the Language of Web Design by Eric A. Meyer

Bulletproof Web Design: Improving flexibility and protecting against worst-case scenarios with XHTML and CSS by Dan Cederholm

The Zen of CSS Design: Visual Enlightenment for the Web (Voices That Matter) by Dave Shea

Don't Make Me Think: A Common Sense Approach to Web Usability (2nd Edition) by Steve Krug

▶ **Explore similar items** : Books (46)

Editorial Reviews

Amazon.com
Standards, argues Jeffrey Zeldman in *Designing With Web Standards*, are our only hope for breaking out of the endless cycle of testing that plagues designers hoping to support all possible clients. In this book, he explains how designers can best use standards--primarily XHTML and

Figure 4-11 / Adaptive navigation on Amazon.com

This is an example of passive collaborative filtering: the site automatically collects user behavior to generate the list. With active filtering, participants in the site must explicitly rate a product, person, or service. You may have seen this on web journals and other sites that have a Highest Rated Articles list or similar. *Boxes and Arrows* (*www.boxesandarrows.com*), for instance, allows readers to rate each story at the bottom of the text (Figure 4-12). Based on all ratings for all articles, visitors are then able to view the site's top-rated stories in the navigation.

Would you feel insulted or flattered if I compared what you were doing to Strunk and White?

Oh, I'd be flattered. I still have my Strunk and White, and it's probably one of the most important books I've ever read. But I've also been a professional writer for 20 years now. The last dogma was stolen directly from George Orwell—it's his tenth legendary rule of writing.

Update: After this interview, Reiss edited #1 in the Dogma, adding "internal" before "politics" to make his point clearer.

Rate This Story

Your rating: ■■■■□   Average rating: ■■■■□

Figure 4-12 / Rating articles on *Boxes and Arrows*

Lists of links produced by collaborative filtering are potentially long—virtually endless in some cases. Typically only the top items are displayed in a top-10-list fashion. If necessary, a More link might also be include to see more of the list. Because of the dynamic nature of adaptive navigation, you generally don't know how long each link may be in the mechanism. Commonly a vertical link list with ample space is used for adaptive navigation. It would be hard to imaging a horizontal arrangement of adaptive navigation options.

Digg.com has a list of top articles for each of its main categories. Because it's impossible to account for the length of article title, the design has to account for a mix of lengths (Figure 4-13).

Top 10 in Technology

2657	Ads.War: BMW started it, Audi answered...Bentley chairman had final say !!!
1244	Top 7 Freshest Designs of 2006
1106	Encode a binary file - like an image, or even an MP3! - into a text URL
945	The Five Best and Worst Things About Vista
826	Nine Amazing Future Military Technologies We Want
781	See real-time weather on a Google map
727	BBC moves to file-sharing sites
685	What happens when you take a photo at the right angle?
652	New Leopard build gallery reveals OS far from finished, but coming along
645	Ubuntu: OpenGL Login Manager? Pics/Mockups!

Figure 4-13 / Top ten stories in the Technology category on Digg.com

QUICK LINKS

Quick links provide access to important content or areas of the site that may not represented in a global navigation. Although similar to contextual navigation, quick links are contextual for the entire site, not a given page. They generally highlight frequently accessed content areas or tasks, but may also be used to promote areas deeper in the site. Marketers may see the value in quick links for an upsell effect.

Transitions from page to page using quick links may vary greatly. By definition, they tend to jump around. They may link to a related sub-site, online shop area, or even to a completely new web site.

Quick links often appear at the top or on the sides of pages. On the home page, they may be prominently positioned in component of their own, but on subsequent pages they may be reduced to a drop-down or dynamic menu.

On the Princeton University web site (*www.princeton.edu*, Figure 4-14), quick links highlight key areas that are not represented by top-level navigation options. On the home page shown here, however, it might be better to display these links directly on the page, perhaps in a site map-like arrangement. Hiding them in a menu reduces the ability to rapidly scan the options.

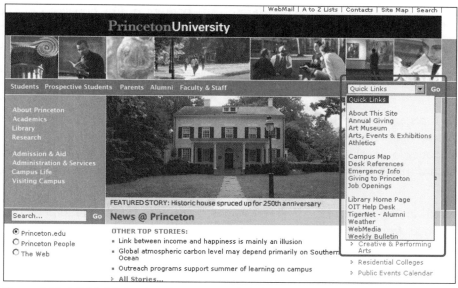

Figure 4-14 / Quick links in a drop-down menu on the Princeton University home page

FOOTER NAVIGATION

Located at the bottom of the page, footer navigation is usually represented by text links. These often access a single page with no further levels of structure below them—a deadend, so to speak.

Traditionally, footer navigation contains supplementary information not pertinent to main topic of the site, such as copyright information, terms and conditions, and site credits. In this sense, footer navigation doesn't address a specific user need, but addresses a legal requirement for site owners. Footer navigation is often used as a catch-all for various types of content and it can lack consistency in an organizational scheme.

But footer navigation doesn't have to be insignificant. For instance, part or all of a site map can be included, as mentioned in Chapter 3. Related links and logical next steps may also be included. eBay.com offers task-based options at the end of item pages (Figure 4-15). These lead to various areas of the site across the hierarchy of pages. Amazon.com even shows visitors' history for a given session at the bottom of product pages. Other elements that may appear in a footer area include a Print This Page feature, an Email a Friend link, site help, the ability to comment on a page, and page rating features, among others.

Figure 4-15 / Logical next steps in the footer navigation on eBay

The advantage of footer navigation is that it doesn't intrude on site content or functionality, potentially saving valuable real estate. Of course, links in a footer area may not be as visible as navigation elsewhere on the page. But as web users become savvier in general, scrolling longer pages becomes less problematic. Web designers can therefore make use of bottom-of-the-page navigation.[3]

UTILITY NAVIGATION

Utility navigation connects tools and features that assist visitors in using the site. These pages are generally not part of the main topic hierarchy of the site. For example, a link to a search form or help pages aren't part of the main navigation or local navigation systems. Other options may not have a page associated with them at all. Instead, they are functions of the site, such as logging out or changing the font size.

Utility navigation may lead to varying page types or site functions. Transitions from page to page may be dramatic at times. For instance, from a single mechanism there may be links to a shopping cart, to a search form, and to a page about the site owner's organization—all quite different from one another, and potentially requiring significant reorientation on each new page.

Utility navigation is generally smaller than primary navigation mechanisms and appears on the top, sides, or bottom of the page. Global utility navigation quite often appears as simple text links. In some cases, the utility navigation is very closely related to the main navigation. As mentioned, utility navigation and main navigation often appear together in a global navigation area.

Figure 4-16 shows a fairly common utility navigation grouping found on Vitaminshoppe.com just above the main navigation bar. It includes a search input field, shopping cart link, help, and contact information.

Figure 4-16 / Utility navigation on Vitaminshoppe.com

But utility options aren't necessarily insignificant. For instance, on e-commerce sites, a shopping cart may appear in the utility options. This is obviously quite important for business.

---

3   For more on using footer navigation to its fullest, see Jeff Lash, "More Than Just a Footer," *Digital Web Magazine* (February 2004).

There are many types of utility navigation, including:

- Extra-site navigation
- Toolboxes
- Linked logos
- Language and country selectors
- Internal page navigation

Each deserves a detailed look.

EXTRA-SITE NAVIGATION

Important for large corporations that may have diverse product areas or businesses, extra-site navigation links to other related sites, sub-sites, or companies. This type of meta-navigation allows people to switch to related web properties owned by a single provider.

Extra-site navigation is typically positioned at the top right of the page. Although generally quite small and represented as plain text, links in extra-site navigation may result in dramatic transitions. After all, they do lead to completely different sites. A common goal, however, is to make the navigation mechanism consistent across all sites. Unfortunately, these links are not always reciprocal, and the destination site may not link back to the originating site.

Figure 4-16 shows the extra-site navigation found on the top left of many Google.com sites, so users can move from product to product easily. Clicking the link in Figure 4-17 takes you from Google Mail to the Google Calendar and back quite easily. There is then a link to see more Google services at the end of the list.

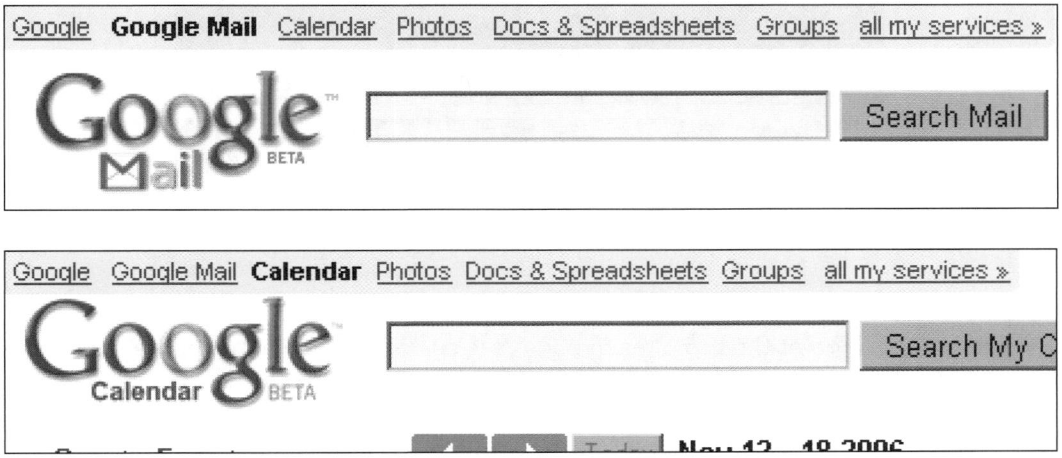

Figure 4-17 / Reciprocal extra-site navigation links from Google Mail to Google Calendar and vice versa

TOOLBOXES

Toolboxes bring together site options that perform functions—"tools" for doing things on the site. Toolboxes may include links to content or navigation pages, but often they link to functional pages. For this reason, transitions from this type of navigation may be great, even dramatic. From the home page, for instance, a toolbar may link to a search feature, contact form, and online shop. This may require more effort in reorientation.

Figure 4-18 shows the toolbox navigation component from the Toyota UK web site (*www.toyota.co.uk*). This grouping of links is not thematically related; instead, they are grouped together because each link points to an important site function or tool.

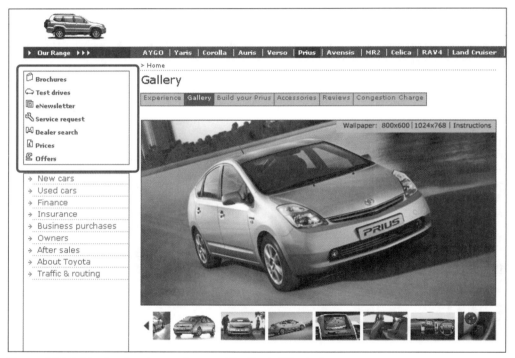

Figure 4-18 / A toolbox found on most pages of the Toyota UK web site

LINKED LOGO

Web sites very often have a logo at the top of each page. It is customary to link the entire image itself to the home page. People may or may not know of this behavior, so some sites add an explicit label underneath or to the side of the logo. In general, linking the logo provides a predictable way to return to a familiar starting point. In some ways it is like an "undo" option within for the navigation process.

Because a Home option is often included in the global navigation, some sites have combined the two: the logo is incorporated in the navigation. Apple.com was one of the first to do this (Figure 4-19). Amazon.com also includes the logo in a main navigation tab, as does Toyota.com. This is an efficient way to save space and offer persistent visual branding throughout the site.

Figure 4-19 / Logo integrated into the main navigation on Apple.com

LANGUAGE SELECTORS

For sites that have sites in multiple languages, a language selector allows people to switch between them. Most often, visitors jump to the same web site, but in a different language. Sometimes, however, the local language site is completely different. Transitions may therefore be small or large. If there are only a few languages to select from, simple links at the top or bottom of the page may suffice.

Internationalization

It's bad practice to use images of national flags to switch language. Languages are often spoken in more than one country. For a Portuguese language site, you could potentially use an image of flags for Portugal or Brazil. Or, there may be more than one official language per country, such as in Switzerland, Belgium, or Canada.

You also need to consider what language the selections appear in. Do they appear in the language of the web site you are currently viewing, or in their original languages? This will affect the order of the options. Take the English version of a multi-language site as an example. If visitors from France are looking for française, they may see and understand the nearby option for French. But would someone from Finland find the English label Finnish when looking for Suomi? Or would someone from Spain find Spanish when looking for español? It's generally better to show the selections in their original language. Be sure to include diacritics (accents, umlauts, and other special characters) if you choose this option.

Accessibility

Keep in mind that if you do have a multi-language site, you need to declare the language of each site at the very top of the HTML code for each page. The code for this might look like this, for instance:

```
<html lang="en" xml:lang="en" xmlns="http://www.w3.org/1999/xhtml">
```

Additionally, alt texts for images and all other accessibility measures built into your code, such as frame titles, need to be translated for multi-language sites.

COUNTRY OR REGION SELECTORS

In some cases, content may differ based on the country or market. A country selector allows visitors to pick their market region. Note that language selection and country selection are different activities. For instance, eBay sites in the U.S., U.K., and Australia all appear in English, but each has different products available in each version of the site. There may be legal requirements involved here as well.

Large international organizations may have dozens of localized web sites. Country selection is more complicated in these cases. Sometimes country selection is done visually with a clickable world map. This, of course, assumes that people can identify the country they want on the map. Here, unlike for language selection, it is acceptable to use images of national flags.

The country selector on the Coca-Cola site (*www.cocacola.com*, Figure 4-20) takes a two-pronged approach: The map is clickable by region, but there is also a navigation to select a country from an alphabetical list on the right.

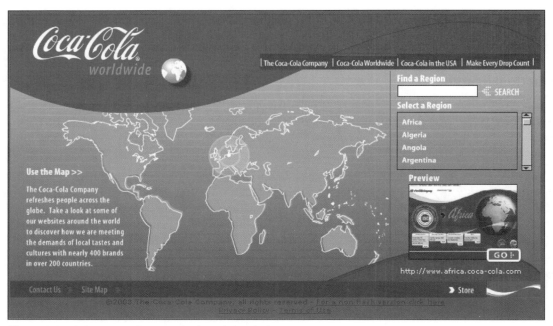

Figure 4-20 / A country selector on the Coca-Cola web site

Internationalization

Many countries speak multiple languages. If you have a multi-language site, consider breaking region selection by language as well. Figure 4-21 shows the country selection menu at the bottom of Google News (*http://news.google.com*). The labels appear in the language of the country. If a country has two languages, the country name appears in both. Compare België to Belgique, and Canada English to Canada Français. Notice also the Spanish version for the U.S. as well (Estados Unidos). Finally, countries with non-alphabetical languages are listed at the end with the original characters, such as Chinese and Arabic. The designers include the English translations in parentheses.

International versions of Google News available in:
Argentina - Australia - België - Belgique - Brasil - Canada English - Canada Français - Chile - Colombia - Cuba - Deutschland - España - Estados Unidos - France - India - Ireland - Italia - México - Nederland - New Zealand - Österreich - Perú - Portugal - Schweiz - South Africa - Suisse - U.K. - U.S. - Venezuela - 中国版 (China) - 香港版 (Hong Kong) - 日本 (Japan) - 한국 (Korea) - 台灣版 (Taiwan) - ישראל (Israel) - العالم العربى (Arabic)

Figure 4-21 / Country selections on Google News

INTERNAL PAGE NAVIGATION

Also called: anchor links, jump links.

Some web pages can be very long. In these cases, it may be advantageous to add internal page links that allow people to jump from one section of a page to another. Internal navigation links basically scroll the page up or down, providing a more efficient way of reaching sections of a longer page. It's customary to then provide a reciprocal link back to the top, so internal page navigation tends to come in pairs of links.

Beyond the quick access to content sections, internal links provide an overview of page content, much like a table of contents. It may be very difficult to get a sense of what's included on a longer page simply by scrolling and reading page headers. Sometimes a set of internal page links may even appear to be part the local navigation scheme.

Technical specifications of the World Wide Web Consortium (W3C, *www.w3c.org*) are often very long, as the table of contents for the CSS 2.1 specification shows (Figure 4-22). These internal links jump within a page with no reload.

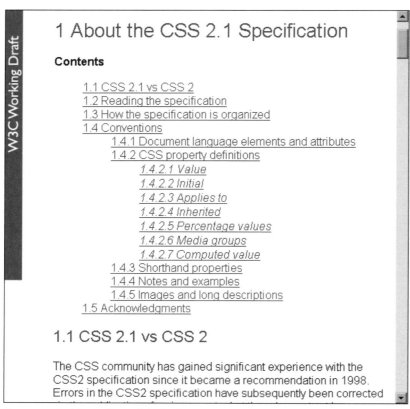

Figure 4-22 / Internal page links for the CSS 2.1 specification on the W3C site

Here are some common internal linking issues:

- Browsers don't distinguish between internal page links and external links. People may expect a transition to a new page when clicking a link, but instead, they are simply moved down on the same page.

- Internal links may or may not be shown as visited links, depending on the link construction and browser. Sometimes internal links never appear as visited links, and sometimes all internal links appear as visited.

- For consistency, all sections of a longer page may be included in jump links. This may mean, however, that the first link jumps to the first section, which may already be showing the page. You may have noticed that this happens on the W3C page shown in Figure 4-22.

- Internal links at the top of pages take up valuable screen real estate.

- Sometimes a sitewide decision is made to include "Back to Top" links on all pages. These links may then appear on pages that don't scroll.

- If the last section of content is short, an internal link to it at the top may not scroll to the proper position. Though the last section will be present, it may be shown at the top of screen.

PAGE TYPES

Navigation type and page type are closely related. A given navigational scheme may have two different purposes on different page types. For instance, visitors may expect contextual navigation on the home page to lead to pages within the site. But related links on a page deeper in the site may point to other sites or content formats. People understand navigation, in part, from the context of the page type on which it appears.

Each page in your site should have a purpose, a reason for being. It's critical to determine the purpose of each page while structuring a site. When this gets overlooked, the result may be unnecessary levels of structure. What's more, the purpose of the page should be immediately clear to visitors. People recognize different pages types quickly. This sets expectations for navigation and affects how people interact with the site.

Traditionally, there are three main categories of pages:

Navigational pages

> The purpose of navigational pages is to direct people to the content they are looking for; examples include home page, landing pages, and galleries.

Content pages

> Content pages are the substance of your site and why people are ultimately there; examples include articles and product pages.

Functional pages

> Functional pages allow people to perform a task, such as conduct a search or check email; examples include search pages, submission forms, and applications.

In practice these divisions are often blurred. Page types refer to the primary focus of the page or its primary purpose within the overall site.

NAVIGATIONAL PAGES

Navigational pages point visitors to their ultimate goal: content or functional pages. They are stepping stones in information seeking. Designers may strive to reduce these pages in order to keep visitors closer to the site's content, but navigational pages aren't just necessary evils. They play an important role in telling the story of your site. They also support a range of seeking modes, help orientation, and even affect purchasing decisions. Key navigational pages include the home page, landing pages, and galleries.

HOME PAGE

Providing a dashboard-like view into the rest of your pages, home pages direct visitors to key areas of your web site. A common strategy is to show lower levels of navigation directly on the home page. This aids in scanning and provides a path to content that may not otherwise surface immediately within the site. For example, the home page for the University of California, Berkeley (*www.berkeley.edu*, Figure 4-23) is a portal to the all of the other pages and sites maintained by the university.

Figure 4-23 / Navigation on the home page for the University of California, Berkeley

A home page may also contain text content or functionality, but usually in an abbreviated format only. News sites, for instance, may present the first lines of top stories and then link to the full story elsewhere. E-commerce sites may feature a product on the home page, but link to the full details within the site. Or, travel sites may present a range of functions that visitors can perform right from the home page.

The home page is often viewed as a chance to market products or promote a brand image. However, visitors coming to site with a specific information need want to first get to their destination directly and quickly. For this reason, Forrester Research recommends merging the site map with the home page, arguing:

" *Home pages tend to get cluttered with the latest marketing jargon from the firm, which Web users may have a hard time deciphering. Site maps, on the other hand, often organize links with simple labels like 'products,' 'services,' and 'help' — exactly the kind of language that customers understand.*[4] "

Even if you aren't willing to give up that prized home page real estate for an entire site map, consider that visitors will see it as a navigational page nonetheless. You will need to provide the guidance and navigation they expect, or risk that they go somewhere else.

---

4   Iris Cremers, "Merge Your Site Map with Your Home Page," *Forrester Report* (November 18, 2005).

LANDING PAGES

Also called: sub-section start pages, category pages, overview pages, department pages.

Landing pages provide an overview of main site categories. These often correspond to the options in a main navigation and might be departments of an online store or the main sections of an online newspaper. Similar to how a home page provides an overview of the entire site, landing pages provide an outline to the content in a given section.

Keep in mind that people arrive at sites in various ways, such as via bookmarks and search engine results. They may never see the site's home page, but instead arrive on a page somewhere in the middle. For this reason, landing pages must provide both local and global orientation.

With mechanisms such as dynamic menus, you may be tempted to omit landing pages completely. Instead, you can just bring visitors directly to the pages that correspond to the options in the menu. But if you skip landing pages, be aware of the consequences. Namely, you won't be able to link to a section overview page directly.

Gateway, a large mail-order computer distributor in the US, has a range of products on its site (*www. gateway.com*). Clicking on Computers in the main navigation brings you to the corresponding landing page (Figure 4-24). This provides an overview to the types of computers that are available.

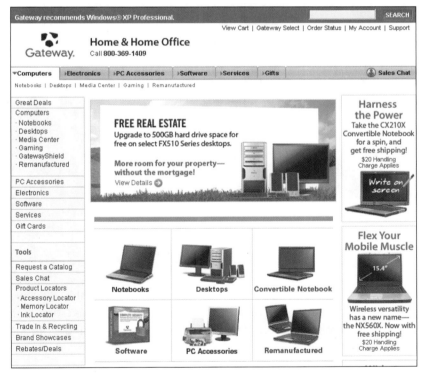

Figure 4-24 / Landing page for Computers on Gateway.com

GALLERY PAGES

Galleries are similar to landing pages, but provide an overview of a specific group of products or content instead of links to a site department or section. Gallery pages are more than just a means to navigate a product page: they contain critical shopping information and allow visitors to compare products. Shoppers may even decide to purchase from gallery page alone. They then go to the product page for more detailed information to confirm a decision.

Figure 4-25 shows a gallery page for Lands' End in the UK for women's shirts (*www.landsend.co.uk*). Although it contains thumbnail images and price information, more basic details about each shirt might help this page be more effective. On the plus side, visitors can see nearly all of the products Lands' End offers in the category at a glance. Galleries like this one are vital for e-commerce sites and the online shopping process.

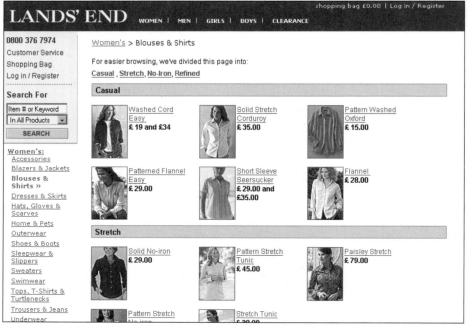

Figure 4-25 / A gallery of women's blouses and shirts on Landsend.co.uk

SEARCH RESULT PAGES

Search results pages resemble gallery pages, but are dynamically created based on user-entered keywords. The collection of resulting links doesn't necessarily have the benefit of handcrafted categories such as those found on gallery pages. Depending on the search terms, results may or may not be of a single product or content type.

For example, compare Figure 4-26, which shows the search results for the term "shirts" on the Lands' End UK site, to Figure 4-25. Note that men's shirts are also included in the results and that the display and format of each of the hits is different than the setup of the gallery page. Within the search results, more detailed information is offered, but visitors initially get less of an overview of all available shirts.

Figure 4-26 / Search results for shirts on Landsend.co.uk

For more about navigating from search results pages, see Chapter 11.

CONTENT PAGES

On information-rich web sites, content pages are ultimately what people are looking for: text, stories, articles, personal résumés, blogs, news, company histories, and how-to information are just some examples. Content pages are the fundamental currency of the Web. Accordingly, the focus of content pages should be the content. All too often, unnecessary navigation and graphics clutter the page.

For instance, the content pages on *A List Apart*, a leading online magazine for web design and development, devotes most screen real estate to article text (*www.alistapart.com*, Figure 4-27). The navigation is kept to a minimum and there are no gratuitous graphics. This allows readers to engage the text without becoming distracted.

Figure 4-27 / An article from *A List Apart*

PRODUCT PAGES

Product pages are obviously critical to e-commerce sites. There are many typical elements to product pages:

- Product pictures
- Product descriptions
- Further details
- Related products

In addition, product pages often contain several functional elements:

- Add to a shopping cart or purchase
- Save to a wish list
- View larger images or zoom in
- Change size or color
- Email this page

Figure 4-28 shows a product page for hiking books on the REI web site, a large U.S. outdoor goods retailer, as an example of an information-rich product page (*www.rei.com*). In addition to the many typical elements of a product page, note the good use of contextual navigation to point out related products in the center left of the page. Visitors can also look at products up close in a separate pop-up window, shown in Figure 4-29. This allows for examination of the hiking boot from all angles, mirroring how people scrutinize products in a brick-and-mortar store.

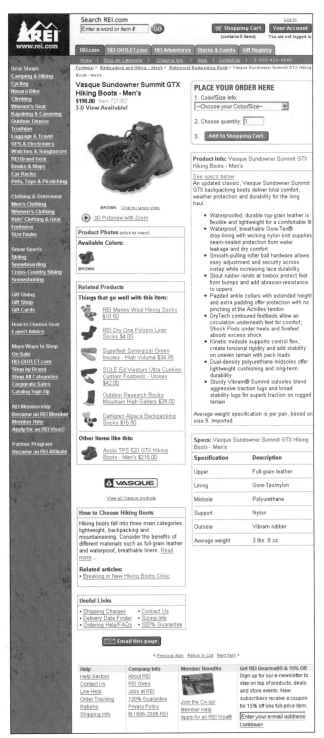

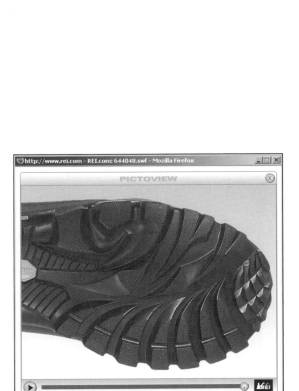

Figure 4-28 / A product page for hiking books on the REI web site

Figure 4-29 / 3-D manipulation of a product photo on the REI web site

FUNCTIONAL PAGES

Functional pages allow people to complete a task online, such as conduct a search or send an email. Like content pages, they are often the destination page that fulfills a user need.

There may be little or no text on such pages, so they often lack embedded navigation and related links. Contextual navigation and cross-structural linking can be problematic when used from functional pages. First of all, users need to focus on completing the task at hand. Additionally, linking to another page while filling out a form or finishing a process may result in loss of input. Try to protect user-entered data so that visitors don't have to fill it in again after they navigate away from the page, accidentally erase the form, or interrupt a submission process.

SEARCH FORMS

It's quite typical for the site search feature to be a small input field on the home page or on all pages of a site. Sometimes, however, a more detailed search is required, typically called an advanced search. As the name implies, this offers more control than a simple search. An advanced search interface requires more space; consequently, a separate page is usually needed.

Navigation on a search form is often quite minimal. There might be links to search tips, help, and other explanations, or links that show or hide options or clear the form. Two types of navigation that can assist searchers are scoping options and word wheels, both discussed further in Chapter 11. Otherwise, it's appropriate to reduce, or even remove, main navigation mechanisms from a search page.

Figure 4-30 shows the advanced search form for Yahoo.com, which offers many specific search options. Navigation is limited to only few links for help and tips, as well as a way back the Yahoo! home page.

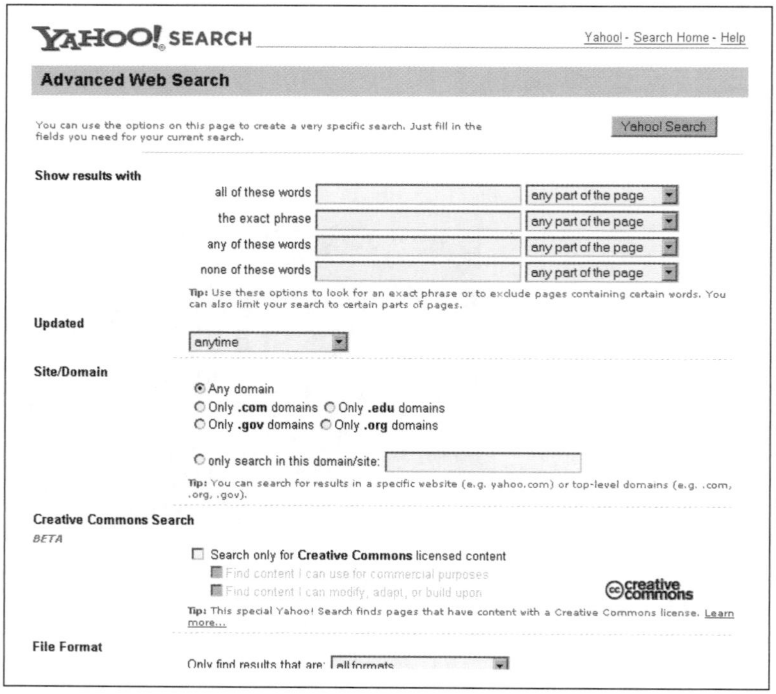

Figure 4-30 / The top portion of the advanced search form for Yahoo.com

SUBMISSION FORMS

Forms allow people to submit information. This might be to create an online account or profile, to apply for a job, or to reserve a car, for example. Forms allow for transactions on the Web. As with search pages, associative navigation on forms is discouraged. You generally don't want to interrupt the task of filling out the form—this is particularly important on the Web, because such forms require explicit action to save data. If you do allow people to navigate away from a form in the middle of filling it out, be sure to maintain user-entered information when returning. It's extremely annoying to have to fill out a form again after reviewing terms and conditions or a help tip.

Figure 4-31 shows the registration form for Facebook (*www.facebook.com*), an online social networking platform. The navigation is limited to a few links only, including help and terms of use.

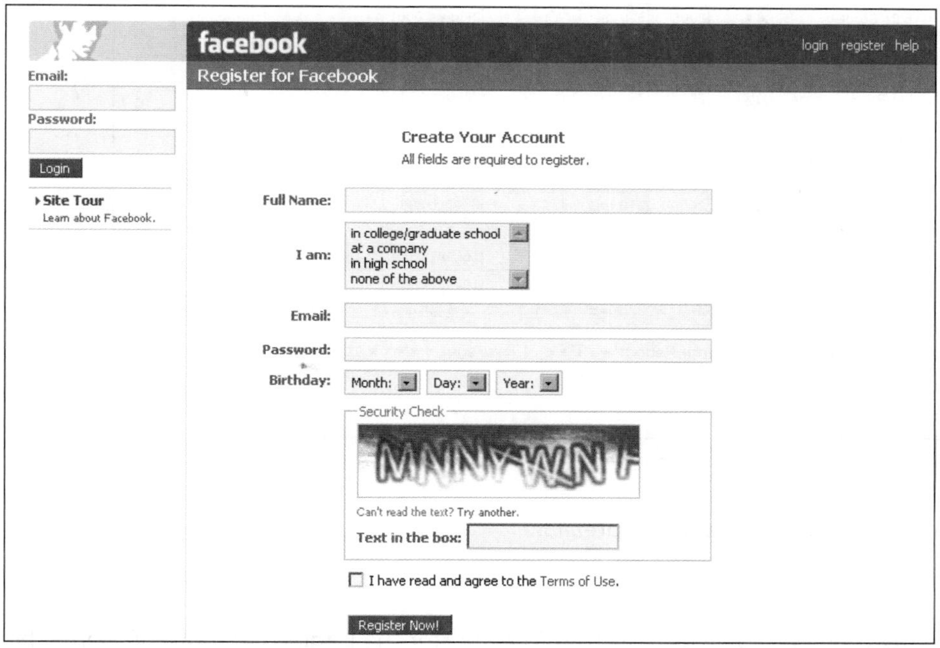

Figure 4-31 / The registration form for Facebook

WEB APPLICATIONS

Web applications refer to a range of pages that contain interactive features and functionality. People accomplish tasks on these pages: they write emails, edit spreadsheets, manage projects, and so forth. As web technologies become more and more robust, online applications will become more common.

Web mail applications are a common type of application. For instance, you may have a Hotmail, Yahoo!, or Gmail account. More advanced types of applications are becoming more and more common, mirroring desktop programs. Figure 4-32 shown an example of an online spreadsheet using NumSum, a free spreadsheet sharing service (*www.numsum.com*). The functions to manipulate the datasheet at the top closely resemble software navigation. Notice, however, that there are a few links in the upper-right and at the bottom that navigate away from the workspace. If they have not saved their work, users are warned before they are allowed to navigate away from the page.

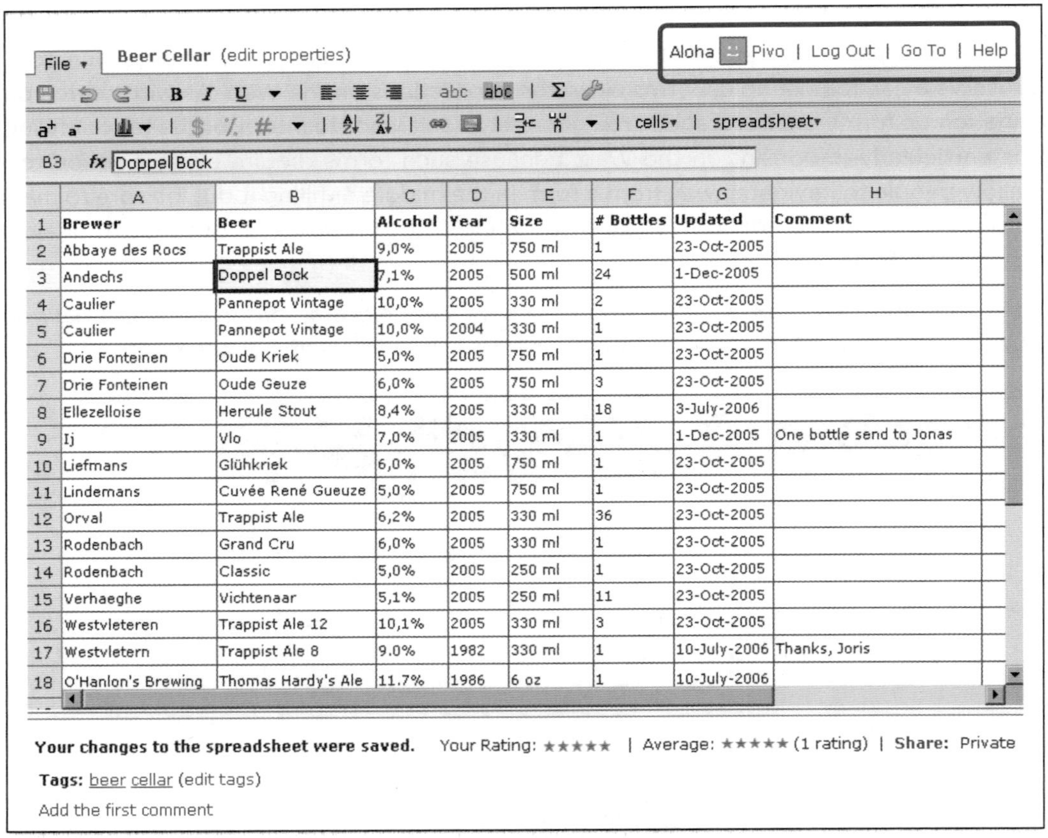

	A	B	C	D	E	F	G	H
1	Brewer	Beer	Alcohol	Year	Size	# Bottles	Updated	Comment
2	Abbaye des Rocs	Trappist Ale	9,0%	2005	750 ml	1	23-Oct-2005	
3	Andechs	Doppel Bock	7,1%	2005	500 ml	24	1-Dec-2005	
4	Caulier	Pannepot Vintage	10,0%	2005	330 ml	2	23-Oct-2005	
5	Caulier	Pannepot Vintage	10,0%	2004	330 ml	1	23-Oct-2005	
6	Drie Fonteinen	Oude Kriek	5,0%	2005	750 ml	1	23-Oct-2005	
7	Drie Fonteinen	Oude Geuze	6,0%	2005	750 ml	3	23-Oct-2005	
8	Ellezelloise	Hercule Stout	8,4%	2005	330 ml	18	3-July-2006	
9	Ij	Vlo	7,0%	2005	330 ml	1	1-Dec-2005	One bottle send to Jonas
10	Liefmans	Glühkriek	6,0%	2005	750 ml	1	23-Oct-2005	
11	Lindemans	Cuvée René Gueuze	5,0%	2005	750 ml	1	23-Oct-2005	
12	Orval	Trappist Ale	6,2%	2005	330 ml	36	23-Oct-2005	
13	Rodenbach	Grand Cru	6,0%	2005	330 ml	1	23-Oct-2005	
14	Rodenbach	Classic	5,0%	2005	250 ml	1	23-Oct-2005	
15	Verhaeghe	Vichtenaar	5,1%	2005	250 ml	11	23-Oct-2005	
16	Westvleteren	Trappist Ale 12	10,1%	2005	330 ml	3	23-Oct-2005	
17	Westvletern	Trappist Ale 8	9.0%	1982	330 ml	1	10-July-2006	Thanks, Joris
18	O'Hanlon's Brewing	Thomas Hardy's Ale	11.7%	1986	6 oz	1	10-July-2006	

Figure 4-32 / An example of an online spreadsheet application with NumSum

For more on navigation for applications, see Chapter 13.

PAGE LENGTH

When should one page become two? Will users scroll? The shorter the pages, the more of them. This will require more clicks and more page loads. The longer the pages, the fewer of them. But people then have to scroll. There is no single guideline for page length; many factors are influential:[5]

- Screen size is problematic because there is no single screen size to design to. On the Web, a wide range of browser sizes exist and vary based on monitor resolution, the number of browser toolbars or sidebars a person has, and the size of the browser window on the desktop.
- Content might not have the same impact or meaning when it's broken up into multiple smaller pages. Consider the REI example in Figure 4-28. If each element on that page—the photo, the description, the specifications, the related product, and so forth—were on a different page, the resulting experience would be quite different. Keeping things together creates a natural relationship between pieces of information.

5 Patrick Lynch and Sara Horton, *Yale Web Style Manual*, 1997. *www.info.med.yale.edu/caim/manual/contents.html*.

- People don't like to read online. For longer texts, it's safe to assume many people won't read from the computer screen. Reading longer documents offline is less problematic and preferred by most. It's acceptable to provide long text pages if people are going to print them anyway.

- It may not be efficient to require people to download pages for small bits of content. Instead, sending more information with each page (i.e., longer pages) may reduce the number of calls to the server. But there's long and then there's *long*. At a certain point it makes sense to chunk volumes of information. Presenting an entire book as a single page, for instance, would cause performance problems.

Figure 4-33 shows an example of a U.S. Supreme Court decision found on the web site for The Legal Information Institute of the Cornell Law School (*www.law.cornell.edu*). On this site, cases are generally given a single page. Note the size of the scrollbar in the upper right; this document is over 50 screens long, even at a fairly large browser size. For smaller resolutions it may occupy 100 screens. The nature of the content, however, calls for a single page. People doing legal research online need to see the entire document, even if they end up using only a single sentence from it for their own work. Additionally, it is probably safe to assume visitors will either download or print it for reading.

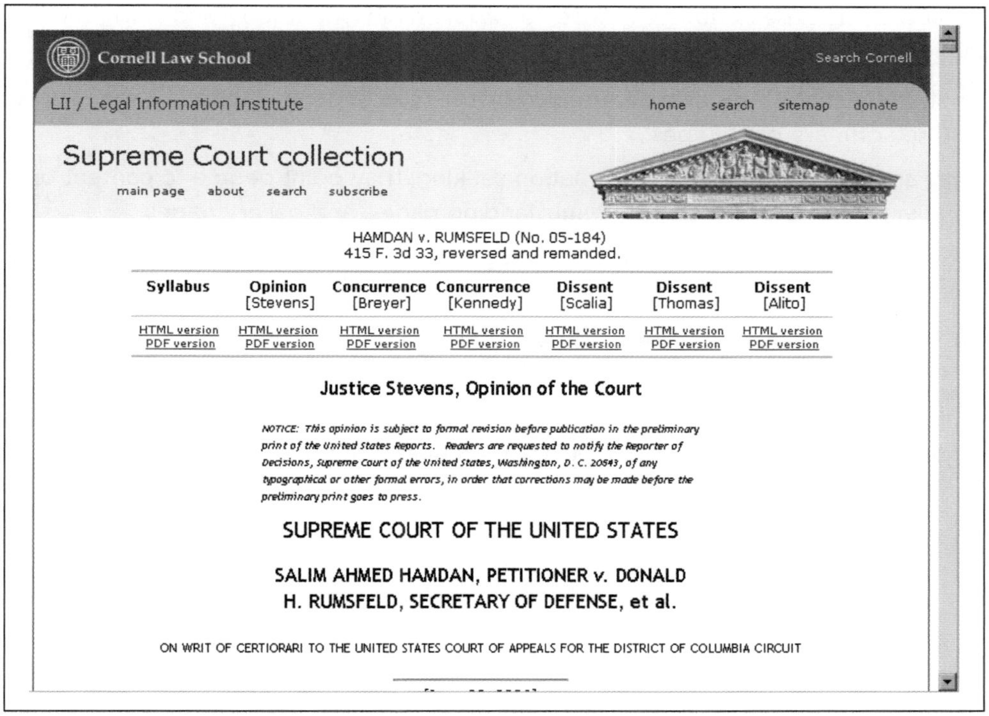

Figure 4-33 / A U.S. Supreme Court decision online

Page type is also a key factor in determining page length. Generally, it's best to use short pages when people need to browse and scan quickly, or when they are completing a task with an online application. Longer pages are good for content that is best presented together for context. For instance, visitors benefit from long product pages such as the one seen in Figure 4-28. It provides an overview and all of the context necessary to make a purchasing decision.

SUMMARY

Various mechanisms come together within a web site to form a comprehensive navigation system, with each unit in the system playing a different role. Some access the main categories of the site. Others offer links to related pages throughout a site. Some links might provide access to useful features for the site itself, such as site search and help. When designing your system, keep the three main categories of navigation in mind:

- Structural navigation provides access to content following the structure of a web site and includes the main navigation and local navigation.

- Associative navigation links across levels of a hierarchy, creating semantic relationships between related pieces of content. Contextual navigation and quick links are examples.

- Utility navigation accesses information about the site itself or site functions and may include global utility options, such as "help" and "search," as well as extra-site navigation and tools.

The way the different types of navigation are arranged on the page plays a large role in how visitors will perceive and use them. The purpose of a navigation type should be clear and obvious for a more efficient interaction. For instance, links in a navigation bar across the top are expected to lead to main category pages. Designing against such expectations can lead to problems in orientation and navigation. For a more detailed discussion of page layout, see Chapter 9.

The function of navigation mechanisms is also determined by the type of page on which it appears. As you work, remember the three primary page types:

- *Navigational pages* are stepping stones in information seeking; they point people to content or functional pages. Examples include the home page, landing pages, and gallery pages.

- *Content pages* contain text, articles, and images. Product pages on e-commerce sites, for example, are content pages.

- *Functional pages* allow visitors to complete a task of some kind online; examples of these pages include search forms, data entry forms, and web applications.

Finally, for an overall flow that makes sense within a site, each page should also have a primary purpose. You will largely be determining the purpose of pages in the Architecture phase, discussed in Chapter 8.

1. Look at the following home page for the Czech Technical University in Prague (Figure 4-34, *www. cvut.cz*). On a separate piece of paper, make a table with two columns and eight rows. Number the rows from 1 to 8. Label the columns Type and Mechanism. Then, for each circled element on the image, indicate the type of navigation and the mechanism used.

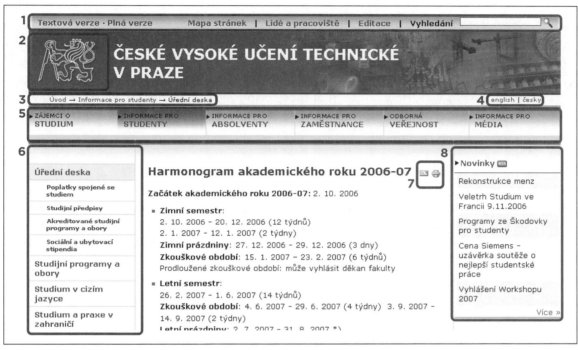

Figure 4-34 / A page from the web site for the Czech Technical University

a) Is this the home page? How do you know what type of page it might be? How would you get back to the home page?

b) If you can't read Czech, what do you think this page is about? What clues did you use to determine that?

2. Visit a popular e-commerce site and look for a product you're considering purchasing. Find that product first by browsing to it and then by doing a search.

   a) Along the way identify each of the navigation page types you encounter, including:

      - Home page
      - Galleries
      - Landing pages

      Is the purpose of each easy to recognize? What have the site designers done or not done to make the purpose of the page clear to you? What could they do better?

   b) Identify all of the types of navigation on each page. Don't forget to scroll down and look at the footer area as well. How are each of these displayed? How consistent do they stay across pages?

FURTHER READING

"Navigation Systems," Chapter 7 in *Information Architecture for the World Wide Web*, by Peter Morville and Louis Rosenfeld (O'Reilly, 2006).

This chapter details different types of navigation in the classic book on information architecture. The authors define slightly different types of navigation than those presented here, but the same principles apply. Also included in this chapter are good discussions of site maps, site indexes, visualization, and social navigation.

Labeling Navigation

If everyone always agreed on what to call things, the user's word would be the designer's word would be the system's word, and what the user typed or pointed to would be mutually understood. Unfortunately, people often disagree on the words they use for things.

—George Furnas et al.
"The Vocabulary Problem in Human-System Communciation"

05

Creating the right navigational labels for a web site is often an underestimated part of the design process. "Oh, that's just a labeling problem," some may say, brushing off the decision for "more important" design issues.

From a user's perspective, however, navigation labels *are* the site's content, functionality, and structure. If navigation has a narrative role for a web site, labels are the words that tell the story.

Critical to findability, navigation labels are the trigger words site visitors look for when they scan navigation options. The words in a label draw a person's attention to the link, or, if the words are uninteresting to them, ignore the link. Navigation labels are also key elements in predicting what's coming next, after the decision is made to click a link. They come immediately before a decisive point in navigation: the transition from one page to another. Getting navigation labels right is vital.

Information often doesn't let itself be chopped up and described neatly, however, and language gets messy, making labeling decisions difficult. This chapter provides insight on taming language and organizing information into clear and easily navigable labels that will highlight—rather than hide—your site's content.

THE VOCABULARY PROBLEM

Research shows that the chances of two people naming the same thing the same way are low. Professor George Furnas and his colleagues, then researchers at Bell Labs, explain:

> " *The fundamental observation is that people use a surprisingly great variety of words to refer to the same thing. In fact, the data show that no single access word, however well chosen, can be expected to cover more than a small proportion of user's attempts.[1]* "

In many tests with hundreds of people across different situations and subject areas, they found that a single access point (i.e., a term chosen for navigation) will at best match user's terms only 10-20 percent of the time. This would seem to make your job quite difficult. But it's not mission impossible. The best approach is to start with the user's words. You need to know what users will expect to see, or how they might describe the content you're offering. Methods such as card sorting and free listing, described in Chapter 7, seek to do just that.

Keep in mind that the Bell Labs research focused on database search systems and predated the Web. Although the basic principle of the Vocabulary Problem is still present, the context of other labels and texts on a web page, as well as the visitor's past experience, provide additional clues for the interpretation of labels.

---

1 George Furnas, T.K. Landauer, L.M. Gomez, and Susan Dumais, "The Vocabulary Problem in Human-System Communication," *Communications of the ACM* 30, 11 (1987): 964.

Jesse James Garret, author and a leader in information architecture, writes about the importance of this overall context:

> *All the information users have to go on are the language of the link, its visual treatment, and its placement on the page. Yet, despite this extreme shortage of information, they somehow develop mental images of the result they'll get when clicking a link. The mental image might not literally be a picture of the page in their minds—although if they're visual thinkers, it may take exactly that form. They may have formed a mental impression of the content and the manner of its presentation. This impression isn't derived solely from the information they have gleaned from the navigation design, though. They also take their own experience into account.*[2]

Your job, then, is to design an overall system of labels with the aim of lowering ambiguity as much as possible. This means considering a broader context of use and creating a shared reference of understanding. (See the sidebar below for more details.)

Creating a Useful Shared Reference

By Eric Reiss

It's just about dinnertime. A pot is bubbling on the top of the stove. And you're asked, "Does this need more salt?" You grab a spoon and taste, and in doing so you create a shared frame of reference with the chef.

There's no guesswork involved, no uncertainty, no doubt, no fear of doing something wrong. You and the chef have tasted the same pot and are ready to critique its contents. Simple concept—or so it would seem.

Time and time again site visitors stare at their screens trying to guess the designer's intentions: "Er...there are three pots here. Which is which?" Or visitors click aimlessly about in the hope that something will bring them closer to their goal: "One of these pots must surely contain something to eat." Other times, visitors are forced to jump back and forth between related pages to gain a more complete understanding of a concept, product, or service: "Wish I could taste the chicken and the sauce at the same time." And all too often, people end up ordering the wrong product because a label or description was misleading or left too much to the imagination: "Yikes! You call this "mildly spicy?" It's dissolving my tongue!"

Ambiguity and omission are the two great sins in the shared-reference business.

Ambiguity usually comes from being either very creative or very sloppy. For example, what does the label "Our heritage" mean on a museum web site? Who or what is represented by "our?" It could be a link to the history of the institution, but it might refer to a cultural group. And what about the word "heritage?" Does it refer to a birthright or a legacy? Whenever there's doubt, you'll always find frustration and failure lurking nearby.

---

2   Jesse James Garret, "The Psychology of Navigation," *Digital Web Magazine* (December 2002). *www.digital-web.com/articles/the_psychology_of_navigation/*.

Creating a Useful Shared Reference
(continued)

Omission rears its ugly head when time is tight and people are lazy: "Our audience doesn't really need an explanation. They understand. Who wants all these details? We don't have room for a lot of description in our layout." Well, perhaps it's all true—then again, maybe your visitors want proof that you understand, too. Maybe that obscure detail is critical to somebody. And maybe it would be possible to make room for a more descriptive label and presentation if the perils of omission were more widely recognized. Omission is one of the leading killers of customer conversion rates on the Web. Let's face it, nobody wants to buy "a pig in a poke." (Don't know the phrase? It would seem we lack a shared reference. Good thing we've got Wikipedia.)

So how do we make things better if words alone don't seem to be enough? Because labels rarely exist in isolation, designers can combine a variety of elements to create the proper context and improve the shared reference. Photos and graphics can help users with weak language skills better understand our vocabulary. A color change helps people understand that they've successfully clicked on something. Sounds can provide useful feedback, too. And the labels themselves can be grouped in understandable categories.

Is this difficult? No, but it takes a little thought. So, be on guard the next time someone tells you "Oh, it's just a label."

Eric Reiss heads FatDUX in Copenhagen and is currently the president of the Information Architecture Institute. He is the author of Practical Information Architecture *(Addison Wesley, 2000) and Web Dogma '06.*

ASPECTS OF GOOD LABELS

Ambiguous labels leave people guessing their intent. If site visitors go down the wrong path because of an unclear label, they may get lost or give up. Good labels instill confidence while navigating and help avoid frustration. The following sections detail some of the most important aspects of labels and predict how successfully they may guide users to the content they seek.

SPEAK THE LANGUAGE OF THE USER

The site should speak in terms visitors can understand naturally. It's easy, however, for site designers to assume that others know the same terms and abbreviations they do. This may not always be the case. There are several aspects of labeling that can potentially cause a mismatch in understanding. You should avoid company lingo, technical terminology, clever labels, and abbreviations, while using the appropriate tone of voice.

AVOID COMPANY LINGO

Company lingo creeps into web sites all too easily and all too often. Such jargon confuses more than it helps. In rare circumstances, in which a brand name has become a household word, for instance, marketing-speak might be acceptable. But if you are inventing new products and words, chances are the "outside world" won't understand them. And people won't click on what they don't understand.

Realistically, however, some products and services have trademarked names. Some business sites may even require that a term appear in its trademarked form. In these cases, qualifying and enhancing a label with explanatory text is helpful. Include the jargon if you have to, but explain it for better understanding.

AVOID TECHNICAL TERMINOLOGY

Most visitors to a given site are not as web savvy as those who created it. Not everyone knows what a plug-in is, what a secure server refers to, or even what they can do with a site map. If visitors have to choose a bandwidth to view a video clip, will they know how many megabits their Internet connection is? Perhaps not. It's best to use everyday language for clarity.

Be sure to consider the subject knowledge of your site's target visitors; technical terminology can be precise and specific to those who do understand it.

For example, internal intranets or B2B sites may assume prerequisite knowledge of the domain; therefore, technical terms will not cause problems. Or, a web site for programmers to share and exchange knowledge may require a deep understanding of the subject. On general web sites, however, subject-specific language and technical terminology may confuse. Be sure to clarify any uses with simple text as well.

AVOID CLEVER LABELS

Clever, cool, or cute labels are usually self-defeating. It may be more interesting to come up with labels that play on words while designing a site, but it's not fun for people trying to navigate by them later.

For example, consider Health.com, a women's health magazine site. The offline version of this publication has five different sections: Looks, Living, Motion, Feeling, and Flavor (Figure 5-1). These are mirrored as the main categories on the web site. Flavor is a clever label for the section on food and eating well. Living could be about anything, really, and the local navigation options in this category are Retail Rx, Room Doctor, and Ask Us Anything. For an outsider, these labels are cryptic. In Figure 5-1, Retail Rx is selected, revealing an article about accessories for pets.

As categories for an offline publication, these groupings are less problematic. Everyone knows how to navigate a magazine: you turn the pages between the front and back covers. But these clever labels don't suit an interactive medium well. As web navigation, they don't help predict what comes next. As a result, visitors to the web site who aren't familiar with the offline magazine may be put off. Assuming one of the site's goals is to gain new readership, these labels harm more than they help.

Figure 5-1 / Cryptic navigation labels on Health.com mirror categories from the offline publication

If you feel compelled to use a witty or playful label, be sure to explain it such a way that it is understandable. Provide context or other cues as to what the label should convey. Don't assume that people will be curious or will explore the category to figure out what a label means.

Internationalization

Both clever labels and abbreviations present particular problems for non-native speakers of the site's language. Labels that play on words, use slang, or refer to idioms may be completely meaningless to a non-native speaker. Abbreviations may also require prior knowledge and can be confusing. If your site has an international reach, be particular careful about the labels you choose in these respects.

AVOID ABBREVIATIONS

Abbreviations save space, but can prevent people from scanning for the right keywords quickly. Some visitors may not even understand certain abbreviations at all. Not everyone knows what FAQ, PDF, or RSS mean, for instance.

If you use abbreviations, make sure that visitors will understand them. Intranets and business-to-business sites may be able to use abbreviations without problem if users are domain experts. But on the open Web, abbreviations can stop people in their tracks.

Even so, there may be situations where common abbreviations are OK. The abbreviation "IRS," for the Internal Revenue Service in the U.S., is so pervasive in America that it would be difficult to find an American visiting the site who doesn't know what IRS stands for. There is a clear shared reference among American taxpayers. Links such as Contact IRS and About IRS are fine in this situation. Even the URL uses the common abbreviation: *www.irs.gov*.

_____ **Accessibility** _____

Note that screen readers often have a hard time with abbreviations. The vocalization software tries to make words out abbreviations. Abbreviations for U.S. state names, for example, may sound like ahhk for AK (Alaska) or wah for WA (Washington). You can use an abbreviation tag to correlate abbreviations with their full meaning:

```
<abbr title="Frequently Asked Questions">FAQs</abbr>
```

With this, screen readers will sound the full text and not the abbreviation. Most browsers also display the full text of the abbreviation when the mouse hovers over it with the abbr tag.

_____

USE APPROPRIATE TONE OF VOICE

Labels on an investment banking site generally have a different tone of voice than those on a teen music site. The one is formal and business-like; the other young and modern. It's important to understand the appropriate tone a certain target audience expects.

Tone of voice also supports brand. Whether slang or popular terms are used, for instance, can reflect the values of the organization. How visitors are addressed is also important. Whether you call personal profile My Stuff or Your Personal Information makes a difference. A mismatch in tone of voice to brand may negatively affect credibility as well.

Kidshealth.com, for example, goes a long way to match the language of target audiences. They effectively have three different sites that share some of the same content. Upon arriving at the site, users must first choose the site they want to enter: for parents, for kids, or for teens. The navigation within each site has different main categories, tones of voice, reading levels, and general presentations (Figure 5-2).

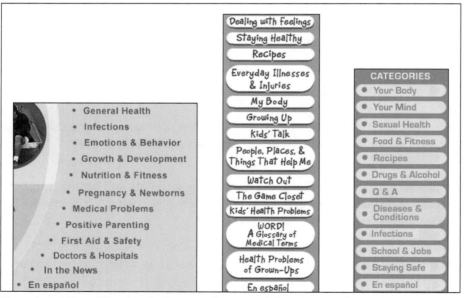

Figure 5-2 / Three different navigation menus for parents, kids, and teens (left to right) on Kidshealth.com

For instance, Emotions & Behavior on the parents' site corresponds to Dealing with Feelings and Your Mind on the kids' and teens' sites, respectively. Or, My Body on the kids' site is expressed as Your Body on the teens' site. There are also audience-specific categories, e.g., Positive Parenting, Kids' Talk, and Drugs & Alcohol. Of course, the visual appearance of the three navigation mechanisms is also tailored to the target audiences.

For some reason, however, the site designers felt it appropriate to devise clever labels for the kids' site, for instance, Kids' Talk and Watch Out. There is really no reason to assume the children will not have the same problems with labels adults do.

DESCRIPTIVE LABELS

When faced with a great deal of unorganized content, it can be tempting to create categories that serve as a catch-all. Navigation options such as Information or Details are generally meaningless. It's all information. It's all detail. These and similar labels often serve the convenience of the navigation designer more than the end user—they are trash cans for content that couldn't be sorted elsewhere. You might as well label them Miscellaneous, which offers no description.

Of course this has as much to do with the categorization as with labeling. But the two are closely related. What you call a group of things affects the meaning of the category and what can go into it. Classification and labeling go hand in hand. Meaningful labels clearly communicate the intent of the category.

Try to make labels as descriptive as possible. Provide clues as to the content they represent. If you need a broader, vague label, try to qualify it in some way. For instance, Information for Buyers and Site Details are better than just Information and Details.

MUTUALLY EXCLUSIVE LABELS

Labels often appear as a group in a given menu. The meaning of one might affect the interpretation of the others in a series. Good labels are mutual exclusive: the clearer the distinction between categories, the better. Differentiate labels as much as possible to help with navigation decisions.

In some domains, this may be more obvious than in others. Auction sites, for instance, commonly have options for buying and selling. The difference couldn't be clearer.

In other situations, it's not so apparent. Figure 5-3 shows a close-up of the main options on the University of Oxford main home page (*www.ox.ac.uk*). Some of them overlap. If, for example, you were looking for information on research in enterprise innovations at the Oxford's Saïd Business School, it might not be clear where to start. You could look in Research, Innovation, or Divisions & Departments. Luckily, there are cross references from one category to the other with this section's pages.

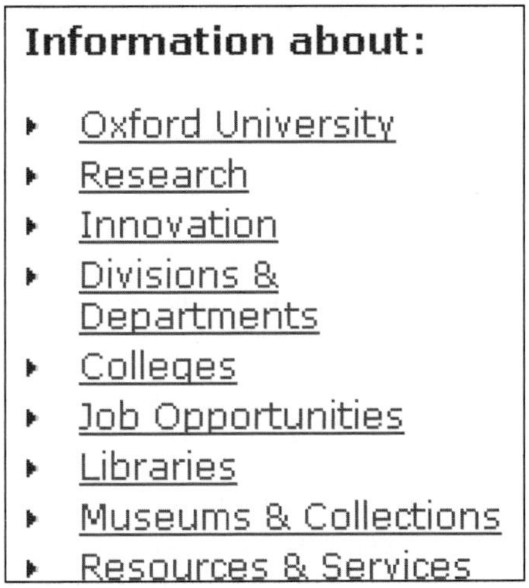

Information about:
- Oxford University
- Research
- Innovation
- Divisions & Departments
- Colleges
- Job Opportunities
- Libraries
- Museums & Collections
- Resources & Services

Figure 5-3 / Overlapping labels on the University of Oxford home page

FOCUSED LABELS

In traditional indexing and cataloging, *specificity* refers to how subject terms are assigned to a book or work. Cutter's rule of specificity, named after the famous American librarian Charles Ammi Cutter, recommends using the most specific term that applies. For example, a book about protecting woodland areas should be placed under the subject Forestry (if that's available) and not under the parent class Agriculture. You also shouldn't apply both terms. Assign only the most specific topic.

Likewise, navigation labels are more successful when they are narrow as possible without being too specific. For example, don't label a category for cats, dogs, and hamsters as Animals when Pets is also a possibility. On the other hand, Felines & Canines would be too specific, as it excludes hamsters. Focused labels are more predictable and increase confidence while navigating.

CONSISTENT LABELS

Consistency can help reduce ambiguity. There are several types of consistency to consider with navigation labels:

Granularity

> Granularity refers to the relative detail or breadth of a topic. Pages lower in a site structure are usually more granular in meaning than higher pages. Navigation options at the same level of site structure should reflect more or less the same breadth of content.
>
> For instance, consider how these options reflect different levels of granularity: white roses, red roses, flowers, bouquets, and sunflowers. The mind might try to make sense of the series itself: white roses are to red roses as red roses are to flowers. In this case, the mix of granularity doesn't add up.
>
> Of course, in some disciplines, there may be a narrow focus on a specific area which receives disproportional weight when compared to other topics. A flux in granularity may be natural in these cases.

Syntax

> Labels of a given navigation type should have a similar grammatical formation. Strive to use the same part of speech. For instance, if one navigation label in a mechanism starts with a verb, start them all as verbs if possible. This gives a nice rhythm to a series of labels in a given mechanism.

Presentation

> Consistent fonts, sizes, and styles are important for creating a sense of unity. Displaying labels consistently also aids in scanning. Note that a change in presentation can intentionally call attention to a navigation option. A break in consistency can therefore add necessary contrast. Even so, the presentation of labels should communicate that the options belong together.

Usage

> Use the same labels in different places or on different pages when referring to the same thing. For example, avoid labeling a link to your service center Hot Line in one place and Contact Us or Customer Support Center in others. This type of consistency should also apply to other media channels as well, such as print. You're not helping people understand your business by using three different labels for the same thing, regardless of medium.

It can be difficult to describe diverse content or abstract concepts with just one or two short words. Screen real estate may limit label length. Horizontal mechanisms, for instance, place restrictions on the number of words a navigation option can have.

Many navigation designers strive for an economy of label length implicitly. However, Jared Spool and colleagues correlated link length with navigation success.[3] They looked at hundreds of navigation paths people took through sites. They broke these paths into two groups: those where people failed to find what they wanted, and those where people succeeded. A pattern emerged, showing that the best links were between 7 and 12 words long.

The reason is clear: longer labels are more likely to contain the trigger words people are looking for. Said another way, short labels block information scent. Longer labels also help people better predict what will come next.

The popular travel site Expedia.com, for instance, is at times very generous with labels. Figure 5-4 shows a long link at during the booking process. It takes up more space, but at the same time brings clarity at critical point in the process: committing to a purchase or reservation.

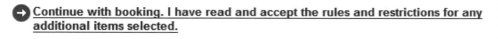

Continue with booking. I have read and accept the rules and restrictions for any additional items selected.

View this itinerary

Figure 5-4 / A long label on Expedia.com

However, there are limits to label length. Spool also found that links with 13 words and above started to perform poorly. There's threshold to the amount that people can comprehend at once.

This isn't to say that a single-word label can't provide good information scent. Sometimes a single word is just the right label. Ultimately there is no hard-and-fast rule on how many words are needed for a label. It could be one, or it could be ten. There are design trade-offs either way. You must consider these carefully, but it's better to err on the side of clarity and being more specific, even at the expense of screen real estate.

One technique to bring clarity is to use a short link label with accompanying instructional text. This may be easier to read than a long, underlined link. This approach layers the label—a short link plus a longer description—to address different expectations while providing a better chance of trigger words appearing on the page.

Note that extended explanations in so-called tool tips may not help much. These are small bits of text that appear in a dialog window (usually yellow) when you roll your mouse over an option. You can't count on people using these as help in making navigation decisions, however. People tend to decide which options to select before they move their mouse toward the navigation.[4] By the time they see the tool tip, they've already decided what to click.

---

3   Jared Spool, Christine Perfetti, and David Brittan, "Design for the Scent of Information," *UIE Fundamentals* (User Interface Engineering, 2004).

4   Erik Ojakaar, "Users Decide First; Move Second," *UIE Tips* (October, 2001). *www.uie.com/articles/users_decide_first/*.

Internationalization

Some combinations of terms are culture-specific. Be conscious of meanings in different countries if the site will be localized. For instance, conceptually combining Home and Office may not be universal. Some cultures clearly separate the two. Dell.com uses different labels on versions of their web site for the U.S. and for France. On the U.S. site, there is a Home & Home Office category, shown in Figure 5-5. On the Dell France site the same category appears as Grand Public (General Public) in Figure 5-6.

Figure 5-5 / The compound label Home & Home Office on Dell.com

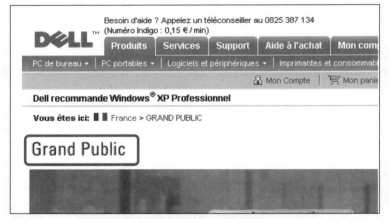

Figure 5-6 / Home & Home Office as Grand Public on Dell.fr

LABELING SYSTEMS

Navigation labels don't exist on their own: they are part of a system of headers, titles, and texts that direct people to the information they want. The design of navigation labels must fit within the overall system. Often there is a tendency to focus on one element or the other. In many cases, the people creating the navigation labels are different from those writing page titles. You job is to bring these together to make a cohesive system. In addition to navigation options, key elements to consider are browser titles, URLs, and page titles.

BROWSER TITLES

Most browsers have a title in a bar at the very top of the application. Figure 5-7 shows the browser title for The New York Times (*www.nytimes.com*) as an example.

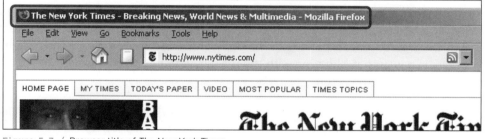

Figure 5-7 / Browser title of *The New York Times*

People don't pay attention to browser titles while surfing the Web. As a result, site designers can overlook them. But browser titles are important for many reasons:

Bookmarking

When people bookmark a page, most browsers use the browser title as the default label for the bookmark name. Most people don't manually change these. If you want site visitors to be able to bookmark pages and get back to them, design good browser titles.

Tabbed browsing

Popular browsers such as Firefox offer tabbed browsing. The label displayed in the tab is usually the browser title for a given page. This also applies when people open multiple windows on their computer desktop: the label displayed for each instance is the browser title.

Printing

When printing, the browser title is may appear at the top of the printed page. This becomes an important part of the printed document.

Search results links

Browser titles are frequently the linked element in the results of a site search or web search. This might be the only information people have to determine whether the page fits their needs when searching. Further, if browser titles contain topic information, this also appears in search results. For instance, browser titles for a page may be structured: topic > sub-topic > page name. If this matches the site's main navigation, scanning a list of search results will also give clues as to which category a given page belongs.

People may rely on URLs as a navigation mechanism in many ways:

Starting

> People enter URLs directly into browsers to navigate to a web site initially. Sometimes they have it written down, sometimes they do it from memory, or some people may just guess. For instance, you might expect the URL for The New York Times to be *www.thenewyorktimes.com* or just *www. newyorktimes.com*. Both redirect you to *www.nytimes.com*, the actual URL for the home page. Redirects, then, allow you to catch variants of terms and get people to your site. They are also good for marketing. For a temporary online contest that actually is hosted on another domain, URLs such as *www.yoursite.com/contest* are possible, for instance.

Orientation

> URLs can show location. First and foremost, they generally reflect the company or site owner's name. Being able to glance at a URL and confirm where you are helps orientation. Second, the directory structure of URLs can show location of a page within a site. Simple URLs will indicate the category a page belongs to, usually in a way that is in sync with the main navigation mechanisms.

Destination

> Most web browsers reveal the destination of a link in the lower left of the screen when hovering over it. This provides valuable clues about the following page and may aid in navigation.

URL Manipulation

> More advanced web users may manipulate URLs directly to navigate. Deleting directories and parameters from the end of the URL, for instance, may bring people back to the home page or a key landing page.

URLs often get overlooked by site creators. And content management systems and other server-side scripts tend to generate incomprehensible strings. Instead of this:

> *http://www.someonlineshop.com/home_electronics/stereos*

People very often see something more like this:

> *http://www.someonlineshop.com/gp/product/102378/ref=s9_asin_image/7670835-5884863?n=2831 55prel80HDUS/EN_US/_main/pg_diy.jsp?TYPE=PROD&pos=n11&MID=9876& session.new=Yes&N=29 84+9147&CNTKEY=misc%2homeel_main.jsp*

But this doesn't have to happen. Even the longest URLs with strings of parameters can easily be converted to meaningful, user-readable URLs.[5] Designing URLs that fit with other mechanisms and page content is part creating an overall coherent navigation system.

Note also that a human-readable URL can potentially help search engines find your site. If someone searches for the exact words found in a URL, the page's ranking could go up in search results.

---

5   See, for instance, Till Quack, "How to Succeed with URLs," *A List Apart* (October, 2001). *www.alistapart.com/articles/succeed*.

It's common to have a title on each page within the main content area. The coordination of navigation labels and page titles is important in the reorientation process. If someone clicks on a link for Company History, the following page should reflect and confirm that it is the Company History page. This is often done in the page title.

Within a page there may be section headers as well. These should make sense in relation both to navigation link labels and page titles. A hierarchy of headings must be clear.

CREATING A FLEXIBLE SCHEME

Creating a logical scheme for labeling is practical for managing a large amount of pages. It would be very difficult, for instance, to handcraft the navigation, page titles, and other elements on each page for a site with 10,000 pages. Instead, it's more efficient to establish rules and patterns of labeling. Content management systems are often set up to work with such rules. For instance, the nodes of breadcrumb trail may be taken from the same source as the page title. This eases maintenance and updates: a change in one causes a change in the other.

However, inflexible schemes can produce outcomes that appear mechanical. They don't reflect the subtleties of a desired information experience. Redundancy, for instance, is a primary concern. Although links and page titles, browser titles and URLs should match, all may not be needed on every page in every instance. Or, they may need to vary to avoid strict repetition of labels.

REDUNDANT SCHEMES

Consider an example from the Finnish version of the Nokia web site (*www.nokia.fi*) in Figure 5-8. The main navigation option (Lisälaitteet) and page title match, as does the header for the local navigation on the left. The browser title and URL also reflect this category. Technically, this is a good scheme. But the end result is that all instances of Lisälaitteet appear very close to one another on the page.

Figure 5-8 / Redundant labels on Nokia.fi

Are all three needed? Perhaps it doesn't hurt. But you should also strive to reduce unnecessary elements that may add to clutter. In this example from Nokia, moving the page title over to the left would label both the page and the navigation options with one element.

In another example, the United Nations Framework Convention on Climate Change (UNFCCC) supports discussion and debate on climate change between participating countries. It is the body that administers the Kyoto Protocol, among other things. Their web site primarily serves the members of the convention.

On the UNFCCC web site (*www.unfccc.int*), the browser title, URL, navigation options, and page title are synched up to form a consistent system across pages. In Figure 5-9, each element is labeled Document Lists. Though redundant, the position and visual treatment of each separates them on the page. There is no immediate sense of repetition.

However, some of the labels are not very distinct. The page shown in image below has the breadcrumb trail Home > Documentation > Documents > Document Lists. (What part of "document" didn't you understand?)

Note also that site is riddled with jargon and abbreviations. For example, labels include CDM, JI, GHG, CC:iNet, and TT:Clear. Without prior knowledge of this alphabet soup, these tabs are meaningless. Navigating this site is left to insiders.

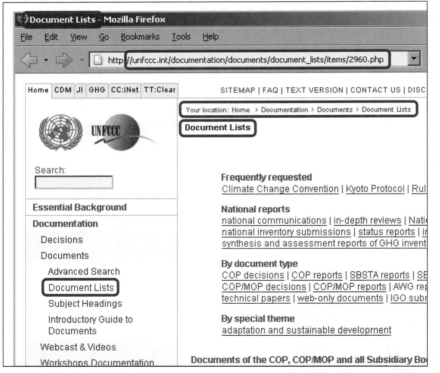

Figure 5-9 / Redundant browser titles, URLs, navigation options, and page titles on the UNFCCC web site

ADDRESSING REDUNDANCY

Symantec is a leading internet security and antivirus protection software provider. Their main web site (*www.symantec.com*) offers a good, predictable navigation experience overall. There is a well thought-out system of labels for the entire site. For instance, link labels are coordinated with the page titles on destination pages to help in orientation. Even the URLs are human-readable and synchronize with the main navigation of the site.

Symantec has distinct sub-sites for different target audiences: Home & Home Office, Small Business, and Enterprise. Each of these is branded with a prominent label toward the top of the page. Below that is the site breadcrumb trail, and below that, the page title. The rules of the scheme are clear: label the sub-site, and coordinate the breadcrumb trail with the page title. But the end result is, at times, perhaps too rigid.

Figure 5-10 shows one version of the page for Home & Home Office Products. This label appears three times within a very small area. This doesn't present any immediate problem, but perhaps visitors could do without one or two instances of the label.

Figure 5-10 / Repetition of Home & Home Office on the Symantec site within a small region of the page (Image from July 23, 2006)

Further, there may be a missed opportunity to provide a better narrative through the site. For the most part, labels of the inbound links already indicate Home & Home Office on this site. With the same language in the site title, breadcrumb trail, and page title, there is no forward motion in the site's flow. Flexibility might enhance the user experience here.

In an updated version of the site (Figure 5-11), the designers at Symantec changed the page title. It now begins with the last word of the breadcrumb trail and then extends it: Products by Category. This better explains the page and continues the flow of the navigation. There is something more active about the new title as well: it suggests that the visitor should browse the categories below.

Figure 5-11 / Better page explanation with an updated page title on Symantec (image from August 9, 2006)

Another approach to reducing the redundancy of a labeling system is to combine the breadcrumb trail (if present) with the page title. The last node of the trail is either presented in a larger font or in a different color to make it stand out as a title. Alternatively, the page title could appear on the next line below the clickable trail.

Figure 5-12 shows a section of a page from the MSN shopping site (*http://shopping.msn.com*). Within the Cutlery category, selecting Knives places that label just below the breadcrumb trail. It is both the page title and the last position of the breadcrumb.

Figure 5-12 / The MSN shopping site merges page titles with the breadcrumb trail to reduce redundancy

PERSUASIVE LABELS

As mentioned in Chapter 1, persuasion doesn't mean tricking people. It refers to encouraging people to take a certain action or have a certain belief. This isn't a bad thing. Site owners generally want to motivate visitors to view some specific content or take some action.

Bryan and Jeffrey Eisenberg have done some of the most extensive work in persuasion in online retailing. They show that persuasion takes place both on the macro-level and the micro-level. The macro-level is trying to get people to take action. On the micro-level, however, it's about links and navigation:

> *Every click represents a question your customer is asking. It represents your customer's willingness to stay engaged with you. It represents a unique point of conversion. It represents continue persuasive momentum.*
>
> *If you customers don't click, communication ceases and persuasive momentum evaporates. If you can't help people get to the information they require to satisfy their questions, why should they bother doing business with you?[6]*

On the micro-level, labels to be critical in the process. In his article "Persuasive Navigation," Jeff Lash points out the difference between call to action and persuasive labels.[7] A call to action is an imperative to the visitor, e.g., Sign up Now and Apply Today. Persuasive navigation, however, provides benefits to visitors: "Sign up and get exclusive content" and "Receive discounts if you apply today." Call to action becomes *persuade to action*. The goal is to entice or encourage people to do something. Providing clues about benefits to the user helps.

Even stronger persuasion occurs when speaking directly to user needs. This is often difficult, but can be effective. It's a matter of aligning people's desires and needs with business goals and reflecting this in labels.

Consider the web sites of the World Wildlife Fund (WWF), a global environmental conservation organization. It relies on donations and support from individuals. Naturally, the main navigation has an option for offering support. The approach to labeling this option on the various sites around the world differs, however, reflecting different levels of persuasion. There are examples of descriptive labels, calls to action, and persuasive labels.

Descriptive label

The navigation option for member donations and support on some sites has a simple, descriptive label. This is neither a call to action nor persuasive. For example, the German web site of the WWF has a menu point that translates as Donating & Helping (*www.wwf.de*). In Figure 5-13, see the second option from left labeled Spenden & Helfen. This is prominent in the navigation and may be effective, but the label is rather passive.

Figure 5-13 / The German localization of the WWF web site with a simple, descriptive label (here: Spenden & Helfen in German)

---

6   Bryan Eisenberg and Jeffrey Eisenberg, *Waiting for Your Cat to Bark?* (Nelson Business: 2006).

7   Jeff Lash, "Persuasive Navigation," *Digital Web Magazine* (December 2002). *http://digital-web.com/articles/persuasive_navigation*.

Other web sites for the WWF have an explicit call to action in the main navigation. These use imperatives: Take Action, Donate Now, or Get Involved, for example. These are active and directed toward visitors, involving them closer: "You there, donate now." Figure 5-14 shows a close-up on the navigation on the WWF site in Canada (*www.wwf.ca*) with labels Take Action and Donate Now. Figure 5-15 shows the label Get Involved on the WWF site in Japan (*www.wwf.or.jp*).

Figure 5-14 / Calls to action on the WWF site in Canada: Take Action and Donate Now

Figure 5-15 / Call to action on the WWF web site with Get Involved as a label

Persuasive label

Persuasive labels speak to people's needs and desires. Visitors to the WWF international site (*www.panda.org*, Figure 5-16), may be predisposed to support their cause. They might have a visceral need to sustain the organization or even to save the planet. Arriving at the site, target audiences may have the question "how can I help?" in mind. The How You Can Help option in the main navigation answers that question directly. In doing so, it is persuasive.

Figure 5-16 / The label How You Can Help on the international web site for the WWF is a persuasive label that potentially speaks to visitors' deeper needs

The distinction between these verbal cues is small, but important. Of course, there are other factors in persuasion. The visual design and the site architecture also play key roles. But labeling is important part of encouraging a certain behavior.

TRANSLATING LABELS

The World Wide Web is just that: worldwide. Many international companies have web presences in various market countries based on a common web interface. This usually means the same page layout appears in different languages. In translating navigation labels from one language to another there are several aspects to look out for:

Label length

Words in one language may require significantly more real estate than in another. All navigation mechanisms have limits, some more than others. If flexibility for various label lengths is not built into the interface, translated labels may not fit.

Additionally, some languages have compound words that don't separate and wrap easily on the screen. A four-word label in French may actually be as long as a German translation of the same term, but the German label may appear as one long term without break. The French label would wrap normally, while a single German would not. Consider these three terms for the same concept, here in English, French, and German:

> Job Creation Scheme
> Programme de création d'emplois
> Arbeitsbeschäftigungsmaßnahmen

As a general rule of thumb, translated labels may require up to fifty percent more space than the original language. Where this is not possible, be sure to account for the longest term possible in the page design.

Grammar

Navigation labels that rely on a specific syntax or grammatical construction may present problems in translation. The labeling system must account for this. There are several differences in the grammar of languages that could potentially cause problems:

- Sentence structure is different across languages. Embedding navigation elements within a sentence may not result in the same order of links as desired when translated.

- Some grammatical constructions and devices don't exist in other languages. German doesn't make use of gerunds, for instance. These are verbs ending in the suffix "ing" and used as a noun, as in the phrase "designing web navigation." If your navigation scheme relies on a specific part of speech, be sure that makes sense in other languages.

- Some languages associate gender with words. For instance, Spanish nouns are either masculine or feminine. El dia (day) is masculine, and la noche (night) is feminine, reflected in this case by the definite article (el or la). Furthermore, word forms may change case with prepositions or function in a sentence. Consider the adjective bueno/-a in Spanish. In one case you say "qué tenga un buen día" (have a great day); in another you say "qué tenga una buena noche" (have a good night).

- The rules of capitalization are different across languages. English capitalizes proper nouns, French doesn't. German capitalizes all nouns. Additionally, in some languages, sentence case is common; in others, capitalizing all words in a label is the norm.

Literal translations of labels can have different meanings than originally intended. Port authority translates easily to French and German as autorité portuaire and Hafenbehörde. But the meanings are different. In English, port authority also refers to bus and train terminals. In French and German it is limited to sea ports only. Be careful that translations capture the intended meaning of the category and are not just translations of the words in the label.

The above examples focus on three common Western languages. Asian and Arabic languages complicate the situation even further. When designing web navigation that is to be translated, plan ahead. Try to identify the worse-case examples and build around those. Make sure grammatical constructions work in other languages. Also allow for local variation as needed.

SOURCES OF LABELS

Where do good labels come from? First and foremost, learn from your users. Attempt to match your labeling system to user expectations. Chapter 7 outlines some research techniques for doing so, including methods such as card sorting. But, as previously noted, there will never be a single, perfect system that meets all of your visitors' needs. The goal, then, is to optimize as best you can.

And, of course, an important resource is your own creativity. No amount of user research is going to give you the absolute correct answer. There is no silver bullet. Your intuition plays a big role in navigation design. From time to time, you may need inspiration, however. Here are some places to get ideas and a broader perspective on labels:

Thesauri and word generators

If you get stuck, brainstorm as many alternatives as possible. Look to dictionaries and thesauri for synonyms and alternative word forms. Or, you can consult keyword suggestion tools. These have emerged as a tool for search engine optimization to track keyword usage. These show frequency of search queries that contain any word or phrase you enter. Google's AdWords suggestion tool (*https://adwords.google.com/select/KeywordToolExternal*) and Overture's keyword selector (*http://inventory.overture.com/d/searchinventory/suggestion*) are two examples.

Competitor sites

Patterns in labeling emerge across sites in a similar business and market. Look at how competitors are labeling their navigation and site features. It may to your advantage to use these terms. If a visitor comes to your site from a competitor site, for instance, they may have gotten used to a certain pattern of labels. Or, you may want to explicitly be different from competitors to set yourself apart. Either way, looking at labels on competing sites is a good place to start.

Search logs

If your site has a search engine, you should be able to see the queries people are submitting. These are essentially the trigger words they didn't find on the site before turning to the search box. They represent the labels people expected to see but didn't. This is a primary source of labels for your navigation. Look for patterns in the language used and word forms for describing content on your site.

Free tagging sites, such as *http://del.icio.us*, have become increasingly popular. Such sites allow people to bookmark pages with any label they'd like so that they can return to them later. Corporate intranets and other applications of free tagging have also emerged and continue to gain use.

For you, this is a potential source of labels. Techniques for analyzing tags for the purpose of creating labels and taxonomies haven't yet matured, but this will become increasingly more interesting. As with word generators, you can search for a term or phrase and see related tags for items that are tagged with that term. Then find the users who tagged that item to see their tags.

Some have suggested creating a separate list of your preferred labels and managing this as a so-called authority file. This seems impractical. Creating a labeling system is an ongoing process that gets captured in many deliverables and activities. For instance, the labels in the site map deliverable, discussed in Chapter 8, can serve as the authoritative list of labels. These then get reflected in wireframes and screen designs, where they can be reviewed for consistency.

SUMMARY

Getting the right labels is critical to navigation. The Vocabulary Problem, proposed by Professor George Furnas and his colleagues, is an important concept. Their research shows that the likelihood of two people using the same term to describe an object is very low. On the Web, however, navigation labels don't appear out of context. When creating labels, consider the context of the site, page, and user expectations and experiences. Create a meaningful shared reference of understanding.

A primary quality of good navigation labels is speaking the user's language; avoid company lingo, technical terms, clever labels, and abbreviations. Try to make labels as descriptive as possible. Good labels are also mutually exclusive and focused. Finally, labels should be consistent in granularity, syntax, presentation, and usage.

Longer labels tend to be more successful than short ones. Research shows that links that are between 7 and 12 words long perform the best. If a link label is too long, however, it becomes too much for people to read. Trigger words are less likely to be present in shorter labels. There is no rule with label length, but try to clarify labels appropriately.

Labels are part of a larger system of elements that all contribute to navigation. Menu items, browser titles, URLs, and page titles, for instance, are best when coordinated into a unified scheme. However, flexibility needs to be accounted for to avoid issues of redundancy and unnecessary navigation elements.

Persuasive labels encourage a certain behavior. Descriptive labels tend to be passive, whereas calls to action speak directly to users. Persuasion is best when verbal cues match the needs, questions, and desires of site visitors. On a micro-level, persuasive labels are critical for achieving overall business goals.

Finally, when translating labels, pay attention to label length, grammar, and the intended meaning of the original terms. Identify worse-case translation situations and plan for them.

QUESTIONS

1. The following concepts influence label selection. Define each term and provide examples for each:

   a) Homonym

   b) Synonym

   c) Antonym

   d) Polysem

   e) Paronym

   f) Hypernym

   g) Hyponym

2. In their article "The Vocabulary Problem in Human-System Communication," George Furnas and his colleagues propose a simple exercise to demonstrate the chance of two people naming that same object the same way. Try this exercise with several people:

   " *On a piece of paper, write the name you would give to a program that tells about interesting activities occurring in some major metropolitan area (e.g., this program would tell you what is interesting to do on Friday or Saturday night). Make the name 10 characters or less. Try to think of a name that will be as obvious as possible, one that other people would think of.*[8] "

8   George Furnas, T.K. Landauer, L.M. Gomez, and Susan Dumais, "The Vocabulary Problem in Human-System Communication," *Communications of the ACM* 30, 11 (1987): 964.

3. Visit three or four pages on popular e-commerce sites by browsing categories to find a particular product (i.e., don't perform a search). In the table below, record the label used for each element indicated on each page. How do the terms align? What is good about the system? What can be improved? How can the entire system provide a meaningful user experience?

	Page 1	Page 2	Page 3	Page 4
Browse title (at the top of the browser)				
URL				
Selected navigation				
Breadcrumb trail (if present)				
Page title (within the main area of the page)				

FURTHER READING

Waiting for Your Cat to Bark?: Persuading Customers When They Ignore Marketing, by Bryan Eisenberg and Jeffrey Eisenberg, with Lisa T. Davis (Nelson Business, 2006).

This book presents an end-to-end process for creating web sites that persuade. It deviates from traditional marketing techniques and instead focuses on creating valuable user experiences for visitors. The method relies on personas and scenarios—cornerstones of user-centered design. This book is easy to read and understand, and offers some unique perspectives on persuasion.

"Labels," Chapter 4 in *Information Architecture for the World Wide Web*, by Louis Rosenfeld and Peter Morville (O'Reilly, 2002).

This is a brief chapter about labels and labeling in the classic book on information architecture. Examples of good and bad labeling systems are reviewed in detail. Practical information about creating labeling systems and sources of appropriate labels is offered.

Part II

A Framework for Navigation Design

Part 2 presents design phases that together form a framework, or a set of practices for solving the problems of navigation design. Though these phases suggest a linear approach, in practice, the actual steps of navigation design are rarely continuous. Instead, you'll move back and forth between them.

Consider the phases as presented in Part 2 to be modes of thinking, rather than blocks of time on a project plan. The progression of activities moves from abstract to concrete. This suggests that you should try to keep your work at the relative same state of completeness. For instance, it's generally not advisable to develop icons before an analysis of the business or before information architecture has been determined.

Part 2 begins with a chapter on evaluating navigation (Chapter 6) prior to actual design work for a reason: you must know how navigation will be measured for success before you begin designing. The remaining four chapters reflect a progression of thought in designing navigation:

- Phase 1, Analysis (Chapter 7): The goal in this phase is to understand the problem you're trying to solve before setting out to design.

- Phase 2, Architecture (Chapter 8): The purpose here is to determine how to best structure the site. Even if the site's architecture already exists, you'll still need to understand basic principles of organization and categorization to design an appropriate navigation.

- Phase 3, Layout (Chapter 9): In this phase, you define how the navigation system will work at the page level.

- Phase 4, Presentation (Chapter 10): The culmination of all your plans, this phase is when you create final designs for your navigation.

Finally, note that this framework is agnostic to specific development methods, and it does not suggest an old-fashioned "waterfall" approach to development. Even within so-called agile development methods, where little or no documentation is required, these patterns of thought about the navigation design are still present. Within each agile iteration you will still see the progression of conceptual design activities to tangible results, as represented by the phases presented here.

Evaluation

06

IN THIS CHAPTER

- Qualities of successful navigation
- Aligning navigation to site purpose and user needs
- Evaluation methods
- Heuristic evaluations and checklist reviews
- Navigation stress tests
- Usability testing
- Metric analysis

A common goal in navigation design is to create effortless interaction with information. Navigation should be "invisible" to the user. Measuring its effectiveness is therefore problematic: it's difficult to demonstrate the value of something that's at its best when you don't notice it.

At the same time, navigation is deceptively complex. The thousands of pages you've provided access to, the numerous relationships you've established between different pieces of content, and the smooth interaction detailed in countless flowcharts all get reduced to a handful of links. The navigation on any one page is just a small portion of a larger system, which is sometimes hard to grasp.

What's more, many variables—from technical performance to graphic design—potentially affect the success of navigation. Showing cause and effect is sometimes difficult. For example, if visitors don't use a navigation option that could potentially help them, is it because they didn't see it or because they didn't understand the label? Making that option bigger won't help if the label is wrong.

Ultimately, the success of navigation is relative: what's good for one site might be catastrophic for another. Nonetheless, there are overarching guidelines that hold true across most situations. This chapter reviews them and introduces methods for evaluating whether your site hits the mark.

QUALITIES OF SUCCESSFUL NAVIGATION

The following sections outline some of the more important qualities of successful navigation. These are not rules. They don't prescribe how to design navigation. But understanding them can guide your thought process while designing. Overall, these aspects predict the effectiveness of a navigation:

- Balance
- Ease of learning
- Consistency (and inconsistency)
- Feedback
- Efficiency
- Clear labels
- Visual clarity
- Appropriateness for the site type
- Aligning with user goals

Now take a look at each aspect in more detail.

BALANCE

Breadth versus depth refers to the balance between the number of visible menu items on a page (breadth) and the number of hierarchical levels in a structure (depth). There is a clear trade-off: the fewer the navigational items, the deeper the structure; and, the more navigation items at once, the fewer levels of hierarchy (Figure 6-1).

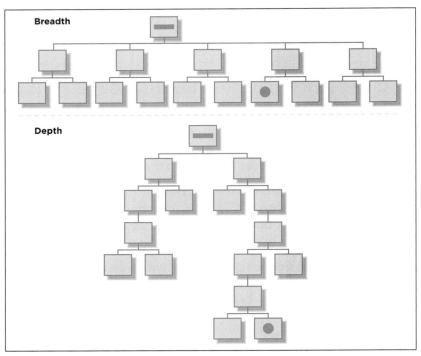

Figure 6-1 / The same number of pages arranged to demonstrate breadth versus depth

On web sites, breadth and depth is a function of both the information structure and the navigation. Directories, for instance, often show options to two levels of the hierarchy on one page, thereby reducing the number of clicks to get to a second-level page. Dynamic menus have a similar effect in that they can access deeper pages in a site directly from a top-level page.

Generally, broader structures work better than deeper ones. The effort it takes to continually choose categories across many levels of a deep structure outweighs the effort to scan many items in a broad navigation. The eye is much faster than a mouse click (and page load). Although users tend to become disoriented (and possibly lost) quicker in deeper structures, don't swing too far toward breadth. Showing all links at all times can be overwhelming and make choices harder. Visitors may just take the first option that appears to fit their need, or simply give up.

A common tactic in navigation design is to cluster options, grouping like items together to provide layers of focus. Users then don't have to scan every link on the page; they can look at component headings. From there they can focus on the links in that area. It's a two-stage scanning process: first find the right group, then zoom in on the individual links.

EASE OF LEARNING

People don't expect that they'll need to learn how to use a web site. There is no training period or expectation of having to study a manual or set of instructions first. On the open web, the duration of time spent on a single page is typically measured in seconds. The intent and function of the navigation must be immediately clear, particularly for information-rich sites with business goals, but also for any type of web navigation.

"Mystery Meat Navigation,"[1] or frivolously concealing navigation options through rollovers and other tricks, lowers the ease of learning for a site. Although concealed navigation is fine for situations in which the target audiences may already be looking for entertainment, such gimmicks can be a usability catastrophe for e-commerce sites, corporate portals, and other information-rich sites. Increasing the time it takes to learn a navigation for a site will generally lower its success. Luckily, mainstream web designers are steering away from this approach.

CONSISTENCY AND INCONSISTENCY

"Be consistent" is a primary guideline of interface design. In terms of navigation, this usually refers to the mechanisms and links that appear in a steady location on the page, behave predictably, have standardized labels, and look the same across the site. Generally, this is good approach and something you should strive for.

But keep in mind that consistency does not equal uniformity; inconsistency is just as important in navigation design. Things that work in different ways should also differ in appearance. The real rule when people say to "be consistent" is: "balance consistency with inconsistency." Some inconsistency is critical to navigation. Varying the position, color, labels, or general layout of a mechanism creates a sense of progress through a site.

In evaluating navigation, it's more revealing to analyze the use of inconsistency than merely identifying that something is not consistent. You have to consider *why* an inconsistency exists and the potential role it plays in navigation.

Random inconsistencies reflect haphazard design and tend to cause problems. Inconsistency used wisely, on the other hand, can be powerful. A change in page layout from the home page to a landing page may engage visitors. A warning message that fills an entire page might be inconsistent with the rest of the site, but communicates critical information. Making one navigation option stand out from the rest (by highlighting it or making it bigger) is the type of inconsistency that can be beneficial to navigation.

What is the right balance between consistency and inconsistency? It depends, naturally. This is where your judgment comes into play. And, of course, testing with real users always helps.

Consistency is ultimately a perceived quality. Users may not have a problem with a change in navigation options if they can still accomplish their goals. People may perceive a technically inconsistent navigation as being consistent if it's intuitive to use. If there is a good reason for an inconsistency and users don't perceive it as such, is the interface inconsistent? The only consistency that counts is consistency with user expectations.

FEEDBACK

When navigating your site, visitors should be informed about what's going on. The navigation system you design gives them cues as to how to navigate through the site. Text and labels are the primary way people will know which option is which or what the title of the current page is. But beyond this, feedback in navigation can be considered in two ways: with rollovers before selecting a navigation option, and by showing location after transitioning to a new page.

---

1   Vincent Flanders, "Mystery Meat Navigation," *Web Pages That Suck*. *www.webpagesthatsuck.com/mysterymeatnavigation.html*.

A rollover is a technique that highlights an option when users hover over it with the mouse. Whether by changing color, size, or something more, rollovers aid in clearly marking the option a person is about to click. This is particularly helpful with smaller elements, such as arrows in paging mechanisms or the numbers in a small calendar.

Showing the position of a page within a site by highlighting its category in the navigation helps orient visitors to their location. On large information-rich sites, this is valuable to orientation. Showing location also helps if someone gets interrupted and needs to resume their session later.

For example, the web site for the Association for the Advancement of Retired People (AARP, *www.aarp. org*) clearly shows location in the navigation in many ways. As seen in Figure 6-2, the selected option in the main navigation is highlighted with a background color. The categories are color-coded, and the local navigation on the left shows the selected option.

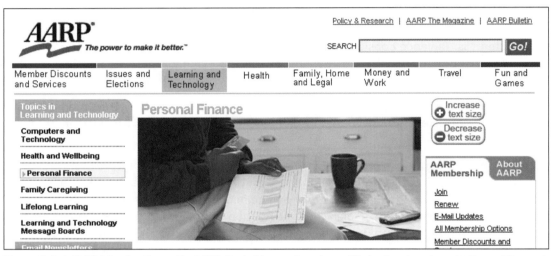

Figure 6-2 / Highlighting location on the AARP site; in this case, Learning and Technology in main navigation and Personal Finance for local navigation

EFFICIENCY

The paths to information should be efficient. Strive to create navigational links, tabs, and icons that are easy to see and easy to click. For instance, dynamic menus that require hand-eye coordination just to reach the options will slow users down. Interacting with the link, buttons, tabs, and menus you create should require minimum effort.

Unnecessary clicks with accompanying page reloads are annoying. Avoid them. Good navigation minimizes the effort to get to content. For larger sites, you can improve efficiency in several ways:

Duplicate access points

Provide multiple links on a page to the same destination. While reading an article, for instance, it may be quicker for the visitor to click on a link at the end, rather than scroll back up to the main navigation. Or, an advertisement on a home page may simply lead to the product landing page for one of the main navigation options.

Shortcuts

Associative links create shortcuts to content. Instead of having to navigate up one branch of a structure and back down another, a cross link can bring users directly from one page to the next.

Escape hatches

People often follow a hub and spoke pattern of navigating. They return to the home page or landing page to restart their information-seeking strategy. Navigation should provide a quick way to "reset" a search and go back to a common starting point.

Be careful when providing duplicate access points and shortcuts, however: too many options can create more confusion than efficiency.

Beyond efficiency in the paths to get to content, good navigation should also have an efficiency of interaction. Navigation links, tabs, and icons should be easy to see and easy to click. For instance, dynamic menus that require hand-eye coordination just to reach the options slow people down. Interaction with the links, buttons, tabs, and menus you create should require minimum effort.

CLEAR LABELS

Link labels are absolutely critical for creating a strong information scent, as mentioned in Chapter 2. Avoid jargon, brand names, abbreviations, and the overly cute or clever. Aim for:

- Meaningful categories that are mutually exclusive
- Consistent forms of labels
- A coordination of navigation labels with other text elements, such as titles

Keep in mind that label ambiguity and breadth versus depth are related. The optimal balance of a site's structure is related to the clarity of labels. Research shows that the quality of link labels affects how well people can navigate structures of different depths and breadths.[2] Though broader structures tend to work better in general, deeper structures may also be just as efficient in navigation if the link labels are unambiguous.

See more about labeling in Chapter 5.

VISUAL CLARITY

Color, font, and layout all contribute to a richer information experience. Visual design isn't just about making things look nice: it creates a better sense of orientation and to the usability of navigation. Clarity, prominence, and visibility can be the difference between finding information and getting lost in hyperspace.

Some important visual aspects of navigation that contribute to its success are:

Visual logic

When designed well, the layout and visual treatment of navigation can guide people through the site. A clear visual hierarchy of options will communicate "click here first, then here," virtually instructing users as to which steps to take, and when to take them.

---

2 Craig S. Miller and Roger W. Remington, "Modeling Information Navigation: Implications for Information Architecture," *Human-Computer Interaction* 19, 3 (2004): 225-271.

Remember that people tend to read pages quickly as they look for trigger words. Good navigation menus foster scanning and make skimming options as easy as possible. See Chapter 10 for tips on improving your navigation for users who are in a hurry.

Clickability

Buttons and links should look clickable. Navigation is best when people aren't left guessing "is this text clickable?" Visual distinctions, such as underlining links, can be important for ease of navigation.

The Creative Commons[3] web site (*http://creativecommons.org*) has a wealth of information, with many navigation options and many levels of site hierarchy. The home page, however, unmistakably communicates two key tasks on the site: finding works and publishing. Figure 6-3 shows these options prominently positioned in the center of the screen. The visual design is quite clear.

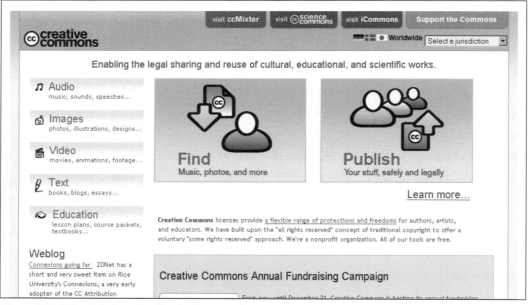

Figure 6-3 / Visual clarity on the Creative Commons home page

APPROPRIATENESS FOR TYPE OF SITE

The success of navigation is relative to the kind of site in appears on. Generic rules and guidelines for web design often miss this critical aspect and attempt to make blanket statements that apply to all situations. They treat all sites the same, as if their intent were uniform. When evaluating navigation, consider the site type:

---

3   Creative Commons is a nonprofit organization that allows copyright holders to grant some of their rights to the public, while retaining other rights. This fills a gap between full copyright, in which no use is permitted without permission, and public domain, where permission is never required. The intent is to encourage the sharing of information while protecting copyright holders' rights.

Information sites

News sites such as Wikipedia, C|Net, and so forth, are in the business of providing information. Navigation is critical for success. Broad navigation displays give a better overview of this type of site. With diverse target groups, following common design practices reduces the learning curve and better meets user expectations.

E-commerce sites

People can't buy what they can't find. Not following common practice in navigation design can cost money. Visibility of options is critical, as is associative linking: suggest related products where appropriate.

Corporate intranets

Intranets are a tool for communicating and sharing information within an organization. The time employees spend looking for information on an intranet takes away from work time. Efficiency is important. But intranets enjoy repeat traffic, so features with a longer learning curve may be acceptable. Jargon and abbreviations may also be appropriate, or even desirable, to increase efficiency.

Community sites

Online communities are places for people to exchange ideas and discuss topics. The navigation for community sites must support these activities. There may be many "insider" labels and terminology used in navigation, including abbreviations.

Entertainment sites

Experimentation with navigation may be completely acceptable with entertainment sites. Visitors to online gaming sites may be more tolerant of playful navigation than visitors to a news site.

Learning sites

Distance education and online training programs are more and more common. Generally, navigation should be simple and clear on these types of sites. While taking an online test, for example, the instructions and mechanisms for moving forward are critical. Here, navigation may even affect performance on the test.

Identity sites

Sometimes a web site's main purpose is to support a company image. For example, the main site for Unilever (*www.unilever.com*), a global manufacturer of food and hygiene products, features its various brands in a scrolling selection menu of logos, shown in Figure 6-4. Though the interaction of this menu is tricky at first, it seems appropriate for an identity site. It allows visitors to explore and interact with the various brands of the company. Note that there are other ways to get to information on brands as well; this isn't the only access point.

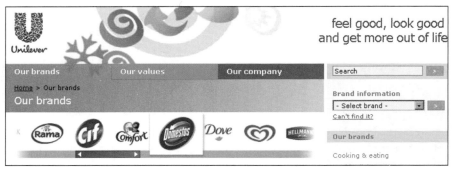

Figure 6-4 / Selecting a brand product from the global portal for Unilever

ALIGNING WITH USER NEEDS

Navigation success is relative to the target groups and their information needs. But identifying information needs isn't easy. For one, target groups can be large and disparate on the open Web. And information needs change, even for a single person in the middle of a single search.

First, define your target group. "Everyone who uses the site" is not a good answer, but one that is often heard. Narrow the group down to a few key user types and capture these personas. See Chapter 7 for more on this.

Second, identify the key information needs of each group. Look beyond the basic questions of Where am I?, What's here?, and Where can I go next? Effective navigation is aligned with deeper user goals and expectations, such as:

- How can I quickly find specific information or products I want?
- How do I know that information is up-to-date?
- Is the site's content trustworthy?
- How can I contact the site owner?
- How can I send information I find to people I know?

This list should focus on a limited set of user needs. Trying to satisfy all people all the time is problematic, and, in the end, the site may end up serving no one's needs. Focus on the primary goals of your primary target groups.

Understanding modes of searching (discussed in Chapter 2) can also be useful in evaluating navigation. Do people tend to have known-item searches, or are they repeat visitors trying to re-find content? Answering such questions can help determine the effectiveness of a particular site's navigation.

EVALUATION METHODS

Evaluating navigation can take place throughout the lifecycle of a web site.

When relaunching or enhancing a web site, it's imperative to first determine the problems of the old one. At the beginning of a project, review the current site's navigation. This will also familiarize you with the site in general. Evaluating navigation of competitors can also reveal best practices and show how to effectively position your site in the marketplace.

During the research and design phases of new sites, try to identify potential issues on an ongoing basis and address them before it's too late. Peer reviews of navigation can detect potential problems early in the process.

Finally, evaluations of a site after it is launched can point to actual issues visitors have. This feedback can flow into enhancements during the maintenance phases of a web site.

The following sections introduce some common methods for evaluating navigation. Those that don't involve users are referred to as inspection methods. Though outcomes of these can be subjective, their more structured approach to site inspection yields valuable feedback. Usability tests and web metric analysis, on the other hand, focus on data about real user behavior. They can point to actual problems that users have while using your site. You can use the methods listed in Table 6-1 as a guide.

No single evaluation will give you a complete picture of navigation success. Findings and conclusions are strongest when they are validated by a combination of techniques. For instance, you can't conclude from inspection methods that people will have problems navigating. Instead, you can only claim that it is likely for them to have problems. Follow up with a usability test to confirm your suspicions.

Finally, in reality, evaluations are rarely limited to navigation alone. The techniques listed in this section focus on navigation evaluation, but have a broader context as well.

Table 6-1 / Some methods particularly suited for evaluating web navigation

Method	Pros	Cons
Heuristic evaluation	Inexpensive Quick to conduct, often within a day or two	Results are subjective Requires an experienced reviewer
Checklist review	Inexpensive Quick to conduct Doesn't necessarily have to be done by an expert	Findings may not give the "big picture" on potential navigation problems Conclusions can be subjective
Navigation stress test	Inexpensive Extremely quick to conduct Do not need experts	Limited in generalizations that can be made across the entire site
Usability testing	Puts navigation in context with other aspects of the site Provides richer data that can be used for broad conclusions	Can be costly and time-consuming Requires experienced test interviewers; best done by usability professionals
Metric analysis	For existing sites, reflects actual navigation behavior and patterns Yields hard numbers and percentages that management tends to like	Data may be unreliable (e.g., logfiles) Hard to show cause and effect relationships

A popular, low-budget analytical usability method, heuristic evaluations are qualitative and rely on subjective inferences made by the person doing the evaluation. The evaluator makes judgments as to the compliance with recognized principles, or heuristics. Heuristics generally apply across situations and are used to predict potential problems with the navigation. Potential problems are identified and rated for severity; for example:

0—No problem at all

1—Cosmetic issues only

2—Minor problems present for some users

3—Major problems are present

4—Catastrophe and unusable for nearly all users

The knowledge and experience of the reviewers greatly influences the results, so two or more evaluators from the design team should systematically inspect site navigation. They should then compare notes and discuss the findings after a review is complete.

The steps in a heuristic evaluation are:

1. Prepare

    a) Agree on who will do the review.

    b) Become familiar with key pages of the site.

    c) Determine the principles for evaluation. Standard heuristics are available (see the next page), but these can be tailored. Consider the site purpose and the context of use in determining heuristics. Have stakeholders approve your evaluation process.

    d) Agree on the key content areas and features to review. It's generally impossible to review all pages of a large site. Select a diverse set of pages that cover a wide range of navigation types. Align pages to review with key user tasks and needs.

2. Execute

    a) Go through the site, focusing on one principle at a time. Alternatively, you can also review each page once for all the heuristics before moving on to the next. Make notes and take screen shots as you go along—you'll need to support your conclusions when presenting to others later on.

    b) For each heuristic, provide a severity rating from 0 to 4; use a table of graphics (such as stars or partially filed circles) for quick comparison.

3. Consolidate

    a) Discuss your findings with other reviewers. Agree on the potential problem areas and on the interpretation of issues.

    b) Look for patterns across your notes and between reviewers. Summarize these.

    c) Determine appropriate recommendations for addressing the identified issues.

    d) Create a presentation for the project team and stakeholders.

    e) Develop a plan for addressing the identified issues.

SUGGESTED HEURISTICS

The following heuristics are based on principles of information seeking and web navigation. They focus on navigation and general information-seeking patterns:

- *Balance*. The number of navigation options presented is balanced with the depth of the site's structure.
- *Ease of Learning*. Using navigation is intuitive and easily learned.
- *Efficiency*. Findings and using navigation options is easy. Paths to information are short.
- *Consistency*. The presentation and interaction of navigation options is consistent and predictable. Inconsistency is appropriately used to show contrast and priority.
- *Clear Labels*. Navigation labels are unambiguous and predictable. Categories are meaningful and mutually exclusive.
- *Orientation*. It is clear where you are within the site on each page.
- *Exploration*. The navigation promotes free exploration and information discovery.
- *Differentiation*. The site facilitates scanning and browsing. It also allows people to quickly differentiate relevant information from non-relevant information.
- *Information Use*. After finding relevant information, people can use it appropriately. They can capture content for integration into personal information sources.
- *Modes of Searching*. The navigation supports multiple modes of seeking (known-item, exploration, don't-know-what-you-need-to-know, re-finding) that are appropriate to the site.

___ **Note** _____

For more suggestions, see Jakob Nielsen's "Ten Usability Heuristics" at *www.useit.com/papers/heuristic/heuristic_list.html*.

Evaluating navigation with checklists is similar to a heuristic evaluation. Instead of overarching principles, concrete test statements (such as those in Table 6-2) are the basis for the review. Your responses to each statement may be yes or no, or you could use a severity scale, as with a heuristic evaluation.

Similar to a heuristic evaluation, it's best to conduct the review with more than one person. Generally, you should involve several members of the design team. Compare notes and discuss the issues afterward. The basic steps include:

1. Prepare

    a) Agree on who will be doing the review.

    b) Become familiar with key pages of the site.

    c) Determine the checklist items to be used in the evaluation.

    d) Agree on the areas of the site that will be considered for the evaluation.

2. Execute

    a) Review pages with a group of test statements in mind. (See the categories in Table 6-1 for some examples).

    b) Rate how well each checkpoint is met.

3. Consolidate

    a) Look for patterns across the findings. Summarize these. How does the navigation work as a total system or not? What's good and what's bad?

    b) Determine appropriate recommendations for addressing the identified issues. Try to answer broader questions: Is the navigation is appropriate for the type of site? Is the navigation is appropriate for the business goals? Will the navigation likely support users' primary information needs?

    c) Create a presentation for stakeholders.

Table 6-2 / A checklist designed specifically for web navigation

Test statement	Rating	Comment
Orientation		
The scope of the products and services is visible from the home page		
The function of main navigation mechanisms is clear at a glance		
Location within the site is shown on each page		
Global navigation appears consistently throughout the site		

Table 6-2 / A checklist designed specifically for web navigation

Test statement	Rating	Comment
Navigating		
All major parts of the site are accessible from the home page		
Critical content is located high in the structure of the site		
Content is within three clicks of the home page		
Alternative navigation mechanisms are available		
An exit point appears on every page		
Further navigation suggestions on every page apart from a global navigation		
Related information is linked together		
Navigation links behave consistently and predictably		
Labeling System		
Links are labeled accurately with mutually exclusive terms		
The language used is simple and in terms that site visitors can understand		
The meaning of navigation options is clear, consistent, and useful		
The destination of navigation links is predictable		
Abbreviations are not used; or, when used they are clear and obvious to target audiences		
Each page has a browser title that is coordinated with the navigation and page title		
Each page has a clear page title related to other labels around it		
If the site supports multiple languages, the navigation is flexible to accommodate translations		
Visual Design		
Navigation options are clear and visible		
Navigation options are readable and quickly scannable		
There is a clear visual hierarchy of options, labels, and headers on each page		
The navigation mechanisms are pleasing and attractive		
The layout is clear with a sufficient amount of white space		
Colors are used effectively to prioritize and organize navigation		

Table 6-2 / A checklist designed specifically for web navigation

Test statement	Rating	Comment
Browser		
Back buttons and other assumed browser functions are operable		
Each page has a human-readable URL		
The URL is related to the name of the company and shows a predictable structure within the site via its directory structure		
There are no broken navigation links		

NAVIGATION STRESS TEST

Keith Instone developed what he calls the "navigation stress test"[4] around the three basic questions of navigation:

- Where am I?
- What's here?
- Where can I go?

Table 6-2 demonstrates how these can be expanded to include more detailed questions about navigation.

The stress test method is simple:

1. Pick a page or pages randomly from deep within the site. Don't use the home page.

2. Print the page or pages in black and white. Remove the URL from the printed page.

3. Assume that you are a first-time visitor to the site and have arrived from a search engine results list. Alternatively, you could ask someone else who has never seen the site before to participate in the test, such as someone in your office or even a friend or family member.

4. Mark up the printed page with the symbols for each test question in Table 6-3. You may also add or delete from this list, depending on the type of site or user needs.

5. For questions that can't be answered, determine the cause. Is this a problem with this page only or with the navigation system as a whole?

6. Draw up recommendations for improving the navigation based on your findings.

---

4   Instone, Keith. "Navigation Stress Test." *http://user-experience.org/uefiles/navstress*.

Table 6-3 / Navigation stress test questions and mark-up[5]

Navigation question	Mark up on the paper
What is this page about?	Draw a rectangle around the title of the page or write it on the paper yourself
What site is this?	Circle the site name, or write it on the paper yourself
What are the major sections of this site?	Label with X
What major section is this page in?	Draw a triangle around the X
What is one level up from here?	Label with U
How do I get to the home page?	Label with H
How do I get to the top of this section of the site?	Label with T
What does each group of links represent?	Circle the major groups of links and label: D: More details, sub-pages of this one N: Nearby pages, within same section as this page S: Pages on same site, but not as near O: Off-site pages

Figure 6-5 shows a random page from deep within the web site of the World Bank (*http://econ.worldbank.org*). The markings reflect the results of a navigation stress test using the questions in Table 6-3. In this case, the navigation passes the test questions for the most part. Note that this is just one measure of a good navigation system and doesn't mean that there is no room for improvement.

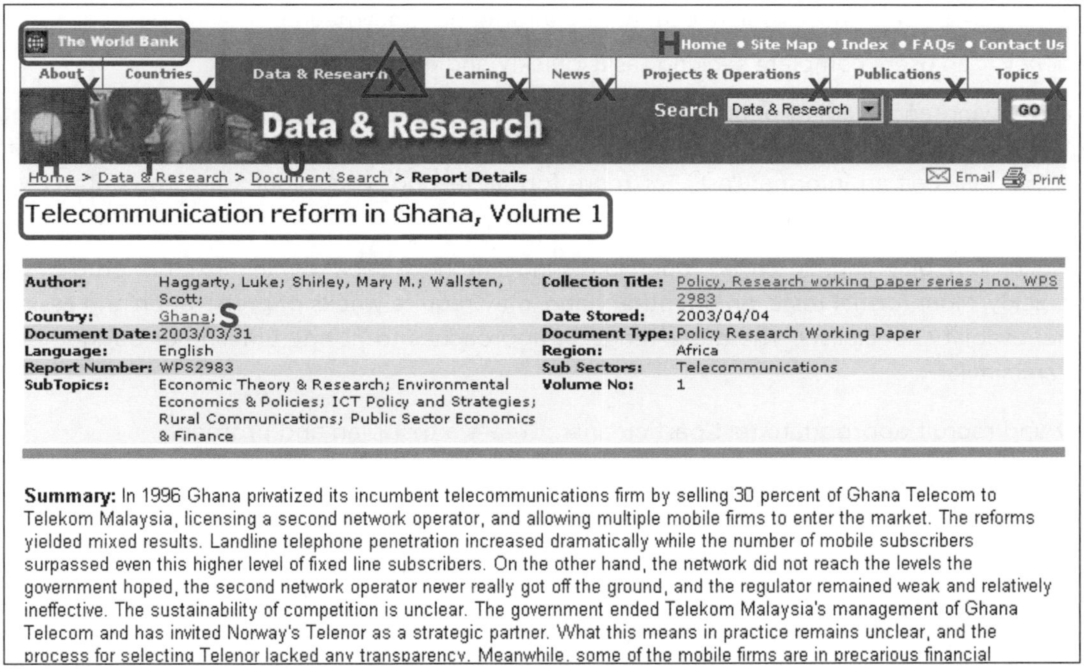

Figure 6-5 / Example of a stress test for a page on the World Bank web site

---

5   Adapted from "Navigation Stress Test" by Keith Instone: *http://user-experience.org/uefiles/navstress*.

Usability tests are often structured as laboratory-based trials in which test users perform tasks that represent the way they might interact with a web site. While completing these tasks, they are asked to "think aloud" and describe what they see, do, and feel. Your job is to watch, listen, and take notes while they navigate. Then identify areas where users struggle with the site and then to make recommendations for improvement.

The number of people tested is a key cost-driver and is highly debated in usability circles. Some feel that several, iterative tests with only a few people is better than a single test with twelve or more. Others feel that, in order to identify all problems, a larger sample size is needed. You'll have to determine the purpose of the test and the audience of the results before answering this question.

Remote testing is also possible with a live site. With this method, participants use their own computers as they normally would to browse the web site. Software then tracks where they clicked and how they navigated. Participants can even give feedback on each page via text input fields. Remote usability testing is a good way to test geographically dispersed user groups.

You can explicitly test the navigation with targeted tasks. For instance, have participants find a specific article or products and then return to gallery page. Observe the following aspects:

- *Visibility*. Do users see key navigation elements on the page?
- *Labels*. Are labels clear and understandable?
- *Orientation*. Do users get lost moving back and forth in a site?
- *Findability*. Are users successful in locating the information they need?
- *Efficiency*. Can users complete seeking tasks quickly and efficiently?

Because interviewing and guiding people through the test scenario is an art, conducting tests requires some practice. Gain experience by first watching others, then grab someone in the office and have them perform sample tasks as an informal test. For more formal testing, you might want to contract with a usability professional.

Usability tests require planning. So-called "guerilla testing" methods seek to minimize the setup overhead by testing quickly. More formal tests, on the other hand, may require weeks of preparation and assistance from external usability specialists. There is a range of approaches to fit any timeline or budget, but the basic steps are similar:

1. Identify and recruit appropriate test participants. Create a test plan and protocol.

2. Set up a laboratory for observation and data collection.

3. Conduct the test. Analyze findings.

4. Present final recommendations.

METRIC ANALYSIS

A good way to learn whether your web site is achieving its goals is to gather traffic data. Traditionally, collecting site metrics is the job of the webmaster, who uses them to monitor performance. Marketers also pay close attention to statistics in terms of sales, conversion rates, and advertising volume. However, usage data is valuable for web designers as well,

It's difficult to show cause and effect with web metrics. Site statistics are great at showing detailed traffic patterns, but don't explain why people act the way the do. Metrics are often used to identify places in which to dig deeper, using other methods of analysis.

Logfiles are the most common way to measure site traffic. But be careful of this data. Due to client-side caching, conclusions about actual navigation patterns cannot be made. Statistics such as popular pages, frequent paths, exit pages, and so forth are generally unreliable when looking at the logfile data. Reviewing logfiles is useful in getting a rough picture of site use, but it's risky to make concrete conclusions from them.

Modern web measurement tools, on the other hand, better capture the paths people take through a site. The data is also reliable. Further, many important business-specific metrics are also captured, such as:

- Conversion ratios
- Customer-acquisition costs
- Order size
- Overall sales

Your goal is to tie an improvement in the navigation to an improvement in business. Before a relaunch, get a baseline measure of a key statistics important to stakeholders. Then take the same readings after the site is live and compare them. The steps break down this way:

1. Prepare
    a) Agree on the metrics to measure success, such as conversion rate or revenue.
    b) Get a baseline reading on this criteria before making improvements to a site.

2. Execute
    a) Conduct heuristic evaluations of the current site, as well as usability tests, to arrive at a list of improvements.
    b) Implement design changes.

3. Consolidate
    a) After a period of use, compare the agreed-upon metrics to the baselined values.
    b) Calculate the increase or decrease in the figures. Note other possible factors that could potentially influence the findings (marketing campaigns, promotions, etc.) and include these in your conclusions.

Evaluating Accessibility

Checking for accessibility of navigation can be complicated and detailed. Simple inspection methods, however, may help in taking the first step. A range of techniques exists, and typically you'll rely on more than one. The three main approaches are:

Automated Evaluation

Consider one of the several programs and services that run automated accessibility checks across a site. These tools crawl through your code and compare it to known standards guidelines and then highlight potential problems. For example, if all images don't have `alt` attributes, the software will flag it. Free tools include WebXACT (*http://webxact.watchfire.com*) and Wave (*http://wave.webaim.org*). Fee-based tools include InFocus (*www.ssbtechnologies.com/products/infocus*) and AccVerify (*www.hisoftware.com/access/newvIndex.html*).

Inspection

A great deal about accessibility can be learned by looking at the web site with different browser and computer settings:

- Turn off images to see if `alt` attributes are used consistently.
- Change font sizes to see if pages are still usable with larger texts.
- View the site at different screen resolutions to verify that horizontal scrolling is not required.
- Turn off the colors or print the page to determine is color contrast is sufficient.
- Unplug the mouse and navigate through the site with the keyboard only.
- Verify that information is generally presented is a logical order.

Browser toolbars, such as the Web Developer Toolbar for FireFox (*http://chrispederick.com/work/webdeveloper*) and the Web Accessibility Toolbar (*www.visionaustralia.org.au/info.aspx?page=614*), greatly help this process. They are ease to install and use. Fangs, an extension for Firefox (*www.standards-schmandards.com/projects/fangs*), and aDesigner from IBM (*www.alphaworks.ibm.com/tech/adesigner*) simulate screen readers and are also recommended.

User Testing

There is a difference between being compliant with guidelines and being truly accessible. You could fulfill all guidelines of a given standard, but your pages may still present hurdles for seeing-impaired users. Further, different types of disabilities require focus on different aspects of accessibility techniques. Sometimes these contradict each other. Testing a site with disabled users can uncover real issues they may have with the navigation.

SUMMARY

The definition of successful navigation is relative to the site type, business objectives, and user goals. Still, there are basic qualities of navigation and evaluation tools that predict its effectiveness across situations.

A good navigation structure is balanced between breadth and depth. It doesn't require unnecessary clicks or pages to reach target content in the site. Generally, but not always, broader structures work better than deeper ones. Chapter 8 contains more detail on structuring information to help you decide which approach is best for your site.

On the Web, it's safe to assume that people won't want to spend a great deal of time learning how to use a navigation system. Don't leave visitors guessing what to do with overly clever mechanisms or ambiguous labels. As discussed in Chapter 5, clear labeling is essential to the success of navigation.

Be reasonable—not rigid—about consistency. You need to vary the position, color, labeling, and the amount of navigation presented to create a sense of movement through a site. In evaluating navigation, focus on how inconsistencies are used, and determine if they help or hurt the navigation experience.

Clarity and visual logic is important for effective navigation. Provide clear feedback as to location within the site and provide effects such as rollovers to help users select and click navigation. People will make out the intent of mechanisms quickly and automatically. The visual hierarchy you create then guides them on how to use the navigation For more details about the layout and visual design of navigation, see Chapters 9 and 10.

To check your work, perform a user-based usability test or try one of the structured evaluation techniques, such as a heuristic evaluation, checklist review, or navigation stress test. In addition, web metrics are important in determining navigation success after a site is live. Compare readings for such things as conversion rates or revenue before and after to measure improvement.

Finally, be certain that your site complies with accessibility guidelines. Ideally, you'll be considering accessibility issues throughout the design process. Don't wait until the end to retrofit accessibility measures. Inspect and test the site for accessibility as soon as possible to avoid unnecessary rework.

QUESTIONS

1. Review the navigation of a local online newspaper in your area. Take notes on the following aspects:

    *   *Balance*: is the site balanced without unnecessary levels?
    *   *Efficiency*: is the navigation efficient to use?
    *   *Feedback*: is it clear where you are in the site?
    *   *Labeling*: are navigation labels clear and understandable?
    *   *Consistency and inconsistency*: is inconsistency used wisely?
    *   *Visual design*: does the visual design of the navigation enhance its use?
    *   *Appropriateness*: is the navigation appropriate for an online newspaper? Does it help you find what you need?

    Pick the one you like best and compare it to the web site for your favorite band or movie. What are the differences?

2. Together with a friend or someone you know, conduct an informal checklist review and a navigation stress test on your favorite e-commerce site. Compare notes and discuss. Where do the findings overlap between a checklist review and the stress text? What differed between the two? Which was more telling about the overall navigation system?

FURTHER READING

"Heuristic Evaluation," by Jakob Nielsen in *Usability Inspection Methods*, ed. Jakob Nielsen and Robert L. Mack (John Wiley & Sons, 1994).

> This chapter is a comprehensive discussion of heuristic evaluations. Nielsen was an early advocate of heuristic evaluations and brought the technique to the attention of the web design community. This text is also available online at *www.useit.com/papers/heuristic/heuristic_evaluation.html*.

A Practical Guide to Usability Testing, By Joseph Dumas and Janice Redish (Intellect, Ltd, 1999).

> This book is an excellent guide to usability testing with a wealth of practical information. It focuses on formal usability testing methods with laboratory settings and multiple experimenters.

Usability Engineering, by Jakob Nielsen (Morgan Kaufmann, 1993).

> Traditionally usability tests are done in a controlled laboratory by trained psychologist. This is intimidating to many designers and developers. Nielsen advocates discount usability engineering approaches, also called "guerrilla" methods. He proposes simplified "think aloud" tests with a small number of users. Also see his essay online: *www.useit.com/papers/guerrilla_hci.html*.

Web Accessibility Initiative (WAI), *http://www.w3.org/WAI*.

> The guidelines from the World Wide Web Consortium (W3C) are regarded the standard for web accessibility. This site has many valuable resources. The accessibility checklist is a must for developers: *www.w3.org/TR/WCAG10/full-checklist.html*. There is also detailed information on evaluating accessibility: *www.w3.org/WAI/eval/Overview.html*.

Web Site Measurement Hacks, by Eric T. Peterson (O'Reilly, 2005).

> This is a well-written, well-structured book from an authority in the field. Discussions assume some of technical understanding, but are approachable by novices to the field. With 430 pages, this is a comprehensive book that digs deep into topics such implementation of web measurement tools and reporting issues. Chapter 4 specifically looks at how web metrics can inform usability testing.

Analysis

" People don't want to buy a quarter-inch drill. They want a quarter-inch hole! "

—Professor Theodore Levitt,
Harvard University

07

IN THIS CHAPTER

- Reflecting on business goals, strategy, and brand
- Analyzing your content
- Understanding technology concerns
- User intelligence and methods of user research
- Personas and scenarios

It's tempting to dive into the details of a design as soon as the project starts. People will start talking about button placement, labels, and even color as soon as a project begins. Resist this urge. Understand the problem first. The amount and type of analysis you perform at the outset will influence navigation design throughout the project. It's like hitting a golf ball: the slightest deviation up front has a huge effect on the final trajectory.

Having a clear and early understanding of the problem generally saves time and money in the long run. A common vision can short-circuit unnecessary debates or avoid major changes later on. When you hear the term "analysis," you may envision an unnecessarily long "discovery" phase. Don't be put off. Analysis need not be time-consuming or costly, and documentation doesn't have to be overwhelming. Focus on the key points:

- Business goals
- Content
- Technology
- Users

Good navigation design is not just about providing links to pages. It's about coordinating goals, content, technology, and user needs into a cohesive user experience. This chapter examines each area and offers some advice to help you analyze the broader context that will frame your entire approach to navigation design.

BUSINESS GOALS

Commercial businesses ultimately want to be profitable, of course, but even nonprofit organizations, governmental bodies, and the smallest volunteer groups have goals. They want to sell ideas or grow their cause. "Business goals" is used here broadly to refer to the goals of any organization.

Apart from increasing profits, common goals are usually variations on:

- Winning new customers or members
- Increasing customer loyalty
- Strengthening the brand or core message
- Improving operational efficiency
- Reducing customer support costs
- Managing corporate knowledge effectively

Beyond identifying the concrete goals of a business, there are many other aspects to consider, including the vision, mission, brand, and strategy of the organization. Navigation proves to be a crucial aspect of web design in meeting all of these objectives. Mapping stakeholder concerns to navigation at an early stage makes certain that the two are aligned.

Table 7-1 defines some important goal-related aspects of design using a hypothetical financial services company for illustration. The rightmost column of the table demonstrates how each of these can influence navigation, resulting in a broad set of guidelines for design.

Table 7-1 / Mapping business goals to navigation design

	Definition	Example for a financial services company	Navigation guidelines
Vision	The underling reason for the company's existence; a concise description of the overall company ethos.	We help our customers to get the most out of their finances to realize their dreams.	Ensure primary navigation is directly relevant to customer's needs and desires.
Mission	The concrete goal the company as a whole is headed toward; a statement that looks to the future.	We will become the most trusted financial consulting and solutions provider in the nation. We will be seen as the benchmark for customer-oriented, innovative financial services.	Clearly organized menus with a credible navigation structure.
Core Promises	The commitment an organization shows to customers during each interaction.	We offer uncomplicated, comprehensive, and professional financial consulting and solutions tailored to your individual needs.	Provide clear and simple menu options in the main navigation. Allow for customization and include personalization.
Brand Personality	The character of the brand, reflected in how an organization creates and expresses its products and services.	Reliable Unconventional Open minded Serious Independent	Create task-based navigation that addresses visitors directly. Set navigation apart from competitors.
Brand Values	The guiding principles for fulfilling the brand vision; they describe how the organization responds to customers.	Collaboration Transparency Flexibility Proactiveness	"Remember" user navigation activity to support re-visitation. Show recent activity with each visit.
Strategy	A plan to realize the vision and mission; provides guidance for specific actions that accomplish an organization's goals.	Increase online transactions to improve availability and ease of customer services. Improve brand image. Increase network of affiliates by 30 percent in 5 years.	Create flexible menus to allow for growth. Plan for a extra-site navigation mechanisms. Avoid jargon, keep labels clear or explained by context.

Though some of the guidelines you generate may seem obvious, making them explicit gives you an underlying rationale for future design decisions. They can also draw a clear picture of how the navigation should be created for the entire development team. More importantly, rooting your overall approach in the goals and strategy of an organization makes them a central force in navigation design, and ensures that you'll meet stakeholder expectations.

This type of mapping exercise can be applied to other aspects of the site design as well, such as visual design and content. The key is to get agreement from stakeholders at the outset and coordinate these with the design of the site, regardless of the size of your project or site. This is important when architecting the site as well, discussed in Chapter 8.

Internationalization

How far will your web site reach? Though you may be targeting markets in a single country, people around the world may end up using your online service. If you don't want to or can't allow for international customers, make sure this is clear at the beginning.

COMPETITORS

Knowing your competitors is critical for an effective online strategy. By definition, *strategic* design intentionally positions a web site in relationship to its competitors. In other words, to be unique and to differentiate your service, you necessarily need to be aware of what others are doing in your market. And because navigation plays an important part of an online strategy, looking at competitor sites can help you position your designs deliberately and effectively.

One way to formally analyze the design of competitor sites is with an heuristic evaluation (see Chapter 6). For a good overview at a glance, rate your findings with stars or partially shaded circles (Table 7-2).

Table 7-2 / Chart summarizing competitor site evaluations

	Us	Competitor 1	Competitor 2	Competitor 3
Balance breadth and depth	●	◕	○	◐
Design for learnability	◔	●	◐	◕
Strive for efficiency	◔	●	○	●
Use inconsistency wisely	●	◕	◐	◔
Speak the language of the user	●	◕	◔	◐
Provide feedback and orientation	◔	◐	◐	◐
Enable free exploration	◕	◕	◐	◕

Table 7-2 / Chart summarizing competitor site evaluations

	Us	Competitor 1	Competitor 2	Competitor 3
Anticipate what the user wants	◑	◕	◔	◔
Support different modes of seeking	◔	●	◔	◑
Provide usable displays of information	◔	◑	◔	◔
Provide help documentation	◔	●	◑	◔
Build trust and credibility	◔	◑	◔	◑
Create an aesthetically pleasing design	◔	◑	○	◔

The goal is to see how your web site compares with competitors when it comes to interface design. Identify common patterns and practices in navigation, such as common navigation elements for a given genre of sites or standard layouts for navigation. Then determine how your navigation fits into this landscape. Will it be similar to or contrast with competitors' sites? Does it improve on what the competition offers?

SITE GOALS

Many organizations ask the wrong questions at the outset of web project. They may be convinced that they need a complete relaunch or an expensive content management system. They see what competitors have done and think "we have to have that too." Then, with little or no analysis, a large-scale project may get underway. Needless to say, such projects often fail.

Stop and ask "why is *this* organization starting *this* web project at *this* time?" Find the root cause of the motivation for starting a project. Find the problem behind the problem and record the site goals. These form the basis for measuring the ultimate success of the site later on and will steer your overall approach.

A technique to get at the underlying intent of a project is fishbone diagramming, also known as a cause-and-effect diagram. With this, you iteratively break down problems into smaller causes until you get to the root causes. Do this as a group with a variety of stakeholders and project team members. The steps are:

1. Write the main problem or objective at the head of the "fish," to the far right (Figure 7-1).

2. Identify and list the causes of the problem along the "bones" of the fish, being as complete as possible.

3. Take the most important causes listed in Step 2 and make each the head of a new diagram

4. Repeat breaking down the causes until it is no longer useful to ask "why is that a problem?"

5. Look for patterns and recurring themes, which are likely to be the problems behind the problem.

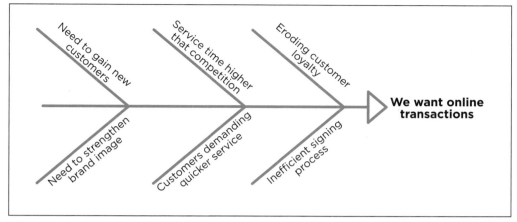

Need to gain new customers

Service time higher that competition

Eroding customer loyalty

Need to strengthen brand image

Customers demanding quicker service

Inefficient signing process

We want online transactions

Figure 7-1 / An example of a fishbone diagram for a loan and insurance company that wants to provide transactions online

Keep in mind that complete web site relaunches can be very disruptive on many levels. They change patterns of site maintenance and content production, as well as how visitors interact with the site. Instead of going for a relaunch, consider a more evolutionary approach by making smaller, incremental enhancements over time. Be certain about the implications of a complete relaunch if the idea is suggested.

Accessibility

In addition to defining business goals and site goals, it's important to record accessibility objectives at the start of a project. If an organization doesn't have a formalized accessibility policy, you may want to formulate one. Define the scope of the policy, include background information, and describe how it will be enforced. Consider making this public on the site.

UNDERSTANDING CONTENT

You can't effectively design navigation without knowing what it is you're providing access to. Understanding your content is critical to creating an effective navigation system. Content analysis is a technique that looks at the type, structure, and general nature of information. This will, in part, determine the types of categories and labels you create for navigation, as well as how content will be organized.

There are three levels of detail at which you can analyze content[1]:

*   A *content survey* is a high-level analysis of existing sites and content, requiring a *sample* of different types of information.

*   With a *content inventory*, you account for *all* pages of site, but you don't look at every piece of content in detail.

*   A *content audit* implies that every page, document, and other piece of content is recorded and examined. This can be very painstaking and may not be possible for large sites.

Regardless of the approach you take, a content analysis can be very tedious. You'll have to systematically track various aspects of each page in a spreadsheet (Figure 7-2). Record information that will help you

---

1   These terms may vary. One person's content survey is another person's content audit.

find patterns in the information. Although your list might change or evolve as you encounter more content, start by tracking things such as:

- Page number or ID
- Page name
- Page type, such as those presented in Chapter 4
- Source and content owner
- Discards or content that should not be included in a new site
- Subject
- Notes or any other comments about the content

ID	Name	Page Type	Source	Discard?	Subject	Notes
00	Home	Home	Current site		Site overview	Static page; Suggest dynamic, changing content for enhancement.
A1.0	Products	Gallery	Current site		Products	
-	Standard Edition Manual	PDF (36 pp)	Offline		Customer support, Manuals	Manuals are currently not available for download; Currently 10 mb - needs to be reduced in file size.
-	Professional Edition Manual	PDF (41 pp)	Offline		Customer support, Manuals	Manuals are currently not available for download; Currently 12 mb - needs to be reduced in file size.
A1.1	Standard Edition	Product page	Current site		Products, Standard Edition	Do we need this page and an overview page? Can they be combined?
A1.1.1	Overview	Content 1	Current site		Products, Standard Edition	
A1.1.2	Features	Content 2	Current site		Products, Standard Edition	
A1.1.3	Specifications	Content 2	Current site		Products, Standard Edition	
A1.1.4	Demo	Content 2	Current site		Products, Standard Edition	Also includes screens shots for download
A1.1.4.1	Play Demo	Popup	Current site		Products, Standard Edition	In popup window; Flash movie; Need to make Flash accessible with alt. Text
A1.1.5	Trail Version	Form	Current site		Downloads	Download functionality; File size = 2.3 mb.
A1.1	Professional Edition	Product page	Current site		Products, Standard Edition	
A1.2.1	Overview	Content 1	Current site		Products, Standard Edition	
A1.2.2	Features	Content 2	Current site		Products, Standard Edition	
A1.2.3	Specifications	Content 2	Current site		Products, Standard Edition	
A1.2.4	Demo	Content 2	Current site		Products, Standard Edition	Includes static screenshots as well.
A1.1.5.1	Play Demo	Popup	Current site		Products, Standard Edition	In popup window; Flash movie; Need to make Flash accessible with alt. Text
A1.2.5	Trial Version	Form	Current site	?	Downloads	Check if trial version for Pro Ed still in scope
A1.3	Bug Logging	Form	Current site	Yes	Customer support, Open source community	Includes functionality; Site metrics show this page is hardly used.
A1.4	Updates	List	Current site		Downloads	
A1.5	Custom Solutions	Content 1	Current site		Custom solutions	
B1.0	Customer Support	Content 1	Current site		Customer support	

Figure 7-2 / A sample content analysis spreadsheet

The key is to find common themes in the content—how it's created, stored, categorized, and used. In terms of navigation, you want to look for logical groupings of content and learn how people are likely to find information on your site. Then consolidate your findings so that you can make overall recommendations:

- Extract a complete list of all material formats.
- List the content types that will be considered in the future.
- Indicate required technologies for content, such as plug-ins or players.
- Show where gaps in content lie.
- Identify content that should not be maintained and discarded.

Note that the column for ID on the left of Figure 7-2 reflects the position of each page in the existing hierarchy, assuming there is an existing site. Capturing this information is important for modeling a new navigation. It allows you to map current page location to future page location and can help identify gaps before reworking a navigation system.

Becoming familiar with the subject area is not just a side benefit of content analysis. You also want to understand how information is generated and how knowledge is created for the field in which you're working. Some common aspects to look for while analyzing a given domain are:

Frequency

How often is new content generated in a given field? In some, information is produced rapidly. In others, information accumulates much more slowly. Navigation for information that updates frequently is generally more dynamic, such as with adaptive navigation mechanisms, and needs to be highly flexible.

Longevity

How long does information remain valid? Information in computer science goes out of date extremely fast. In philosophy, a text that is over 100 years old may still be wholly relevant today. Planning navigation for content that is more permanent is generally easier than for information that is outdated quickly.

Quantity

What are average document lengths? How much information is typically produced by any one author in the field? This has to do with both the volume of overall publication as well as the length of typical documents or resources. The volume and length of typical documents will determine page length and how you chunk content.

Linking and cross-referencing

What roles do citation and referencing play in the domain? How is information inherently linked? In scholarly works, citations acknowledge previous works on a similar topic, providing evidence to make a point. In popular essay writing or in news articles, referencing other works may not occur at all. Knowing this may suggest whether you'll need associative navigation types, for instance.

Authority

Are there names that are authoritative? Is there an authoritative methodology? For instance, science tends to place authority on methodology, while arts and humanities recognize well-known figures in the field. The organization of navigation menus could reflect and support the different patterns of authority in different domains.

Genres

Does information in a given domain have standard genres? Identifying common document forms may influence everything from page length to your navigation concept (Chapter 8).

How information is created and used, in general, influences its organization and access. Domain-specific aspects of information, in turn, inform navigation design. For example, the navigation for large amounts of short texts that update very quickly (such as classified ads), will be different than the navigation for long documents that remain static for long periods of time (such as a company history or legal documents). An awareness of such aspects can help you align content with user and business expectations, set priorities, and create a natural browsing experience.

UNDERSTANDING TECHNOLOGY

Just as an architect understands the properties of the construction materials used to build a house and an artist understands the qualities of paint and color, you need a fundamental comprehension of how web sites are put together. You may not be a programmer, nor aspire to become one. Still, it's critical to understand the basic capabilities and limitations of web technologies. The underlying technology of the site will constrain or enable the types of navigation solutions you can come up with.

For example, you may intend to support re-finding in your navigation system with features like saved items and favorites lists. However, if your site doesn't have the ability to set up user profiles and store account information, this may not be technically possible. Suggesting products via collaborative filtering in an adaptive navigation mechanism is convenient for the user, but the process is not simple to implement—the site technology may not even support such an option.

During the Analysis phase, there are three levels of technology to consider:

- Platforms
- Back-end technologies
- Front-end technologies

PLATFORM

With ubiquitous computing on the rise, organizations often don't want to limit themselves to delivery on just one "information appliance." The web site content and navigation system you design might eventually be destined for reuse on a mobile device, for interactive TV, or even on a refrigerator with a computer display. Find out what devices your design will ultimately be targeting; understanding the distribution to different devices allows you to design more flexible and effective navigation.

Consider, for example, the rapid increase of content delivery to all things mobile—cell phones, personal digital assistants (PDAs), pocket PCs, and even car navigation systems. Targeting both the Web and mobile platforms is difficult and changes how you approach creating navigation. Don't count on a site designed for web-only use to be effective on all mobile devices.

Content adaptation refers to the process of transforming a site for use on mobile devices. Standard, off-the-shelf content adaptation products that automatically convert web sites into a format for mobile devices generally do a poor job, in terms of usability. For instance, some of these programs might transform your carefully thought-out navigation options to plain numbers or generic labels such as "menu 1" and "menu 2." Instead of solely relying on these applications, you must plan the content, information architecture, and navigation to scale appropriately from the very beginning.

Your job is to understand the constraints of each medium you're ultimately designing for. The differences in platform give rise to different design considerations, including:

Display size

Screen size is one of the most obvious differences across platforms, and it's also one of the most critical, particularly with mobile technologies. A smaller display is the primary reason why you can't just easily redisplay a web site on a mobile phone.

Interaction

Different hardware and software across platforms results in dramatically different ways of interacting with a site or application. Clicking a link on a PDA or tablet with a stylus represents a different type of interaction than using a mouse to click a navigation option on the Web, for instance.

Usage contexts

The device used creates different usage contexts. Because mobile devices tend to be slow and expensive for web access when compared to using a desktop computer, they are rarely used passively. People often have specific targets in mind when they are seeking with mobile devices.

Development differences

The way that content is created, stored, and displayed on various platforms requires different technologies and development. Each browser on each phone model renders content differently. Additionally, the range of available fonts, colors, and styles may vary greatly across platforms.

Connection rates

Downloading large files to a mobile phone can take a long time, while interacting with a locally stored document on a PDA has no connection issues. Connection speed affects how an application is designed.

Note that navigation is a key element that carries across different platforms. It may appear different, but most information platforms have some kind of navigation. Compare a movie finder service for the Web and for a mobile phone. The web site may have color images, logos, animations, and even video clips; the mobile service may have no color or images. Nonetheless, navigation is a common element in both that creates cross-channel consistency.

But it's not as simple as pushing a button to get content from one platform onto another. The information system has to be designed to accommodate multiple platforms from the beginning. Following these guiding principles will help:

Separate content from presentation

Do not mark up documents in such a way that they contain information about how they are to be displayed. Format documents semantically. For example, in HTML, use the <h1>...<h6> tags for headers, and apply style sheets for different devices. The same header can then appear more appropriately on different devices.

Plan for alternative display formats in your content model

Because of varying amounts of screen real estate, text length becomes a critical factor. When developing for both the Web and mobile devices, label length, title length, and even article length may have to be formatted differently. News articles may need a long title and a short title, for instance. Your content management system must be able to serve up different page titles.

Don't rely on device-dependent navigation mechanisms

Dynamic menus found on the Web don't work well on mobile phones. Also, long lists of links, such as an A–Z index, are also cumbersome on small screens. Instead, use fewer options with a deeper hierarchy when designing for mobile devices.

Don't use plug-ins and scripting languages

At this writing, for example, Flash is not yet widespread on mobile devices, and JavaScript generally doesn't work on a mobile phone display. To be cross-platform compatible, the content and navigation you design has to work if scripting languages are turned off and plug-ins are absent.

For more information, see the World Wide Web Consortium's Guidelines for Mobile Access: *www.w3.org/TR/NOTE-html40-mobile*. Although fairly technical, this is a good set of recommendations for developing mobile-ready HTML.

BACK-END TECHNOLOGIES

Also called server-side technology, the back-end of a web site is what makes it operate. Issues include the database structure, password protected areas, firewalls, personalization, and user profiles. When analyzing this level of technology, focus on how the back-end might enable or constrain what you can design. Is personalization or customization possible? Will user accounts and profiles be possible? Can you technically integrate content from different sites and databases seamlessly? These are all questions you should ask up front so there are no surprises.

Pay particular attention as well to your site's Content Management System (CMS). A CMS manages digital information throughout its lifecycle on the Web—from authoring to publishing. Even the smallest of sites employs a CMS, and it's safe to assume you'll be working with one, if you haven't already. In general, a CMS does two key things:

- Provides storage and retrieval of content
- Manages the workflow to create and maintain content on a site

A CMS is essentially a brain, or central coordinating unit, which takes content from various sources and publishes it through different channels (Figure 7-3).

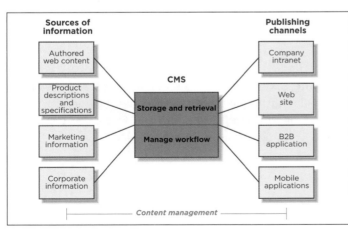

Figure 7-3 / A CMS: the central coordinating unit for content

In creating site navigation, you are developing many of rules the CMS follows to be able to display content. Not only does a CMS affect navigation design, navigation design also has a huge impact on the structure of a CMS. For instance, the templates you create (Chapter 9) influence how the CMS system is configured at a fundamental level.

For more on content management, see the many web sites on the subject such as CMS Watch (*www. cmswatch.com*) or articles on Wikipedia. Two very good books on the subject are:

> *The Content Management Bible (2nd Ed.)*, by Bob Boiko (Wiley, 2004).
> *Content Management for Dynamic Web Delivery*, by JoAnn Hackos (Wiley, 2002).

FRONT-END TECHNOLOGIES

Also called client-side technologies, front-end technologies represent all the code that gets sent from a server to a person's browser. The browser then interprets this code and renders it on the screen. The foundation of all web sites, HTML (and its stricter cousin XHTML) are the basic programming languages for creating a web site's navigation mechanisms and structure. The W3C is the standards body charged with overseeing the languages. For more information, consult its web site: *www.w3.org/MarkUp*.

Because front-end technologies can directly impact navigation, you should become familiar with their capabilities:

Cascading Style Sheets (CSS)

CSS enables the separation of page content from its presentation. With CSS, style information for the entire site—colors, fonts, layout, and more—can be created and maintained in a single file. This provides flexibility and consistency in making changes across the site. For instance, if you change the size of a font once in the CSS, it will cascade to all other pages where that font appears. What's more, end users can also use a different style sheet to view a site. Browsers combine the HTML code and the CSS file to render the page as intended.

For a demonstration of the power of CSS, visit the CSS Zen Garden (*www.csszengarden.com*).

JavaScript

JavaScript is a programming language that can be embedded into a web page to add interactive functions. Some common navigation actions that rely on JavaScript are:

- Opening a pop-up window or a new browser window with control over its size, position, and inclusion of browser controls or not.

- Displaying rollover effects, or swapping one image for another when the cursor rolls over it.

- Automatic linking from drop-down menus without an explicit click on a button, technically referred to as onChange event.

Frames

Frames allow a Web page to be displayed in a separate scrollable pane on screen. One of the first uses of frames on the Web was to fix a vertical navigation on the left while allowing the main content to scroll. The prevailing recommendation is to avoid their use and explore alternative solutions instead.

If you use frames, they must be titled with meaningful labels, using the `title` attribute. The code for adding titles to a page with two frames might look something like this:

```
<frame src="navigation.html" name="navlinks" title="Navigational Links">
<frame src="content.html" name="maincontent" title="Main Page Content">
```

As with other labels on your site (see Chapter 5), make sure you use a clear system of naming conventions for your frames.

Flash

Created by Macromedia and now owned by Adobe, Flash is a graphics animation program that allows for dynamic menus and other animated features to appear on web pages. It can be embedded in to a normal HTML page so that only parts of the page are Flash. Its small file size has made it a popular way to animate web pages and make them more interactive. Flash can also be used to display images and videos quite effectively.

Visitors need a Flash player plug-in to see Flash animations, but modern browsers generally come with the Flash plug-in already installed. This means the penetration of Flash worldwide is generally very high—around 97% for older versions.[2]

Asynchronous JavaScript and XML (Ajax)[3]

Ajax itself is not a programming language, but a combination of technologies. It allows you to create interactive web applications. The intent is to make web pages feel more responsive by exchanging small amounts of data with the server behind the scenes, so that the entire web page does not have to reload each time the user makes a change. This can increase the web page's interactivity, speed, and usability. See Chapter 13 for more on rich web applications in general.

XForms

Normal HTML Forms make it possible to accept input from users on pages like search engines, surveys, e-commerce forms, and so forth. They are commonly used throughout the Web. XForms are the next generation of these forms, allowing for a richer, more secure, and device-independent way to handle input.

XForms also allow for dynamic replacement of the data, replacing the need for JavaScript for Ajax-style applications in many situations. You can use them to show and hide parts of the page without refreshing the page or resorting to JavaScript. Entire interactive web applications can be constructed with XForms—even as complex as Google Maps—without the use of JavaScript.

At the time of printing this book, no common browser supports XForms, although the standard has been made an official W3C Recommendation in March of 2006. If XForms catch on, they promise to increase the interactivity of page and ease implementation. See *XForm Essentials*, by Micah Dubinko (O'Reilly, 2003) for more details.

---

2 See *www.adobe.com/products/player_census/flashplayer/version_penetration.html*.

3 Jesse James Garrett coined the term "Ajax." See his original article on the topic: "Ajax: A New Approach to Web Applications," *Adaptive Path Essays* (February, 2005). *www.adaptivepath.com/publications/essays/archives/index.php*.

USER INTELLIGENCE

The final variable in the analysis equation is also the most important: the user. Navigation design is really about predicting the types of questions people will have when they come to your site, then matching the navigation to user expectations. But as with any prediction, there is the risk of being wrong. User intelligence is the practice of understanding how people use your site in order to reduce this risk.

Keep in mind that the outcome of user intelligence doesn't replace your judgment—it informs your judgment. User research does not mean "do what users say." Instead, it's about detaching yourself from your own perspective and focusing on user goals. In the end, your intuition is still very important to the design process.

User intelligence generally requires a range of techniques, including:

- Reviewing secondary literature on a given topic or in a given field
- Analyzing existing user data
- Performing primary user research

There is no silver bullet. User intelligence activities are part of an ongoing design process. Figure 7-4 shows an approximate timeline for how activities described in this chapter (as well as in other chapters) can be used to complement one another. Realistically, you may only perform a few of these on a given project, and the order may be different than suggested here.

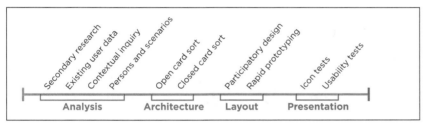

Figure 7-4 / An approximate timeline for user intelligence activities

REVIEWING SECONDARY LITERATURE

Before conducting primary user research, consult reports and articles about trends in the field your site covers. You may not find a single, focused discussion of navigation design, but instead discover relevant comments scattered throughout your reading material. Zero in on these details, and bring them together to inform your research and design efforts. Here are some places to start looking on the Web:

Web design journals and magazines

Digital Web Magazine (*www.digital-web.com*), UX Matters (*www.uxmatters.com*), and *Boxes and Arrows* (*www.boxesandarrows.com*) are great sources of practical information about a range of web design issues (Figure 7-5).

Academic search engines

Google Scholar (*http://scholar.google.com*) is a free service from Google that targets scholarly works. CiteSeer (*http://citeseer.ist.psu.edu*) is a specialty search engine for scientific and academic literature that focuses on computer and information science.

One of the largest collections of computing literature available, the ACM Digital Library (*http://portal. acm.org*) is a fee-based service, available either with a subscription or on a per-article basis. The fee-based ASIST Digital Library (*www3.interscience.wiley.com*) also has a wealth of articles on information and library science topics.

Market reports and whitepapers

Companies such as Forrester (*www.forrester.com*) and Jupiter Research (*www.jupiterresearch.com*) regularly produce reports on market verticals, technology, and, more recently, specific web design techniques. These may be very expensive to purchase, but contain a wealth of accurate data in a clear report.

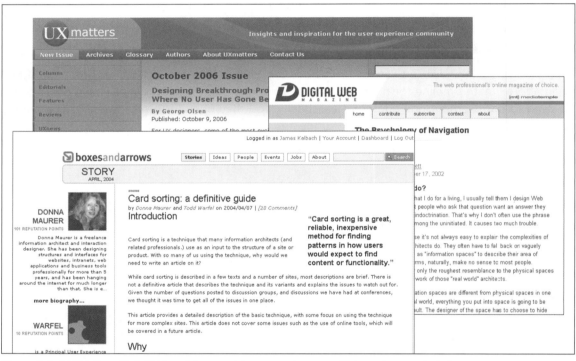

Figure 7-5 / UXMatters, *Digital Web*, and *Boxes and Arrows*: good sources of information on web design

Don't let secondary research limit your creativity, however. Just because something tests well in other places doesn't mean it will work in your context. In the end you'll need to do you own research to validate and expand on what others may have written. Also keep in mind that reviewing existing literature is no substitute for conducting primary research. But secondary literature can inform user research and guide your line of inquiry in understanding users better.

ANALYZING EXISTING USER DATA

If you're redesigning navigation for an existing site, take advantage of the fact that many organizations already have rich data on site usage. This can help you gain a broader understanding of the site. Specifically, look at things such as:

Email feedback

If a web site has a contact email address, find out where that email ends up. Analyze it for issues visitors have while using the site. But keep in mind that customer emails may not reflect a representative sample of your target groups. Emails tend to come more often when users have complaints. Still, many visitors with the same problem can point to an area that needs improvement.

Prior marketing studies

Some companies spend a lot of money on marketing efforts, which can generate a lot of customer information. Details about navigation and site usage may be hidden, but contained throughout such reports.

Site metrics

Traditional log file analysis is problematic for many reasons. First, the statistics are so skewed by such issues as client-side caching and other technical difficulties that the numbers are unreliable. Second, log analysis doesn't explain *why* people did what they did. Still, you may find some important clues in log files about how people are using a site.

Search logs or records of the search terms people enter on a site in particular are very helpful for navigation design. Analyze the search terms people are using on your site to gain a better understanding of the labels they expect to see.

PERFORMING PRIMARY USER RESEARCH

Primary user research is the most important part of a user intelligence effort. There is no substitute for doing your own research. Important detail can get lost in a report. You need to see users' frustrations first hand or experience their delight when they find something new to truly understand their needs.

Although user research is usually done with broader considerations in mind, this section focuses on some of the methods that are most relevant to navigation design. No matter what your goal, planning a strategy before you begin will make your research far more effective.

PLANNING RESEARCH

First and foremost, establish what you'd like to get out of the research before you begin. Ask the wrong questions, and you'll get the wrong answers. Consider these questions in determining your research goals:

- Why is the organization undertaking user research?
- What questions would you like answered?
- When will research take place?
- Who is the audience for research findings?

After setting your goals, choose a research method. Don't make the mistake of doing this the other way around. Fit the method to the research questions. Secondary research and existing user data greatly shape the open questions you may still have. They point to the gaps in knowledge and to larger issues that require further investigation. The various methods are covered in detail in the next sections; for now, just consider the two fundamental approaches:

- *Qualitative methods* tend to be exploratory in nature with no hypothesis to prove or disprove. Instead, qualitative methods seek to gain rich descriptions of user behavior. The data that is collected and analyzed is generally text, or what people say and do. For this reason, qualitative methods can often explain why people behave in a certain way, as well as uncover previously unexpressed needs. In general, qualitative research requires one-on-one sessions and targets a much smaller sample size than quantitative methods.

- *Quantitative methods* yield hard numbers, which can confirm or disprove a hypothesis. You'll be able to stand up in a meeting and say "72 percent of users could successfully navigate to our product pages." Quantitative methods tend to involve larger sample sizes, however, and produce a depth of understanding that is usually not as rich as with qualitative methods. You may know *that* people do certain tasks on your site, for instance, but quantitative data often doesn't explain *why*.

Quantitative and qualitative methods are not mutually exclusive. You may focus on collecting quantitative data from a card sorting exercise, but at the same time interview people with open questioning during the session (qualitative data). In the end, select a method based on the depth of understanding you need.

Whether your chosen method requires a large or small group of study participants, finding the right people to research is critical. Ideally you'd like to a get a random sample of participants from a target segment. If you're developing a business-to-business site for niche market, for instance, you don't want to study people from one firm only. Strive to get a mix of participants from different groups.

Ideally, you'll employ a mix of methods for user intelligence to validate findings. While the sections that follow describe the most salient methods for navigation design in detail, Table 7-3 provides a quick comparison. These center on techniques that are more specific than typical user interviews and questionnaires. What's more, this list focuses on activities that take place in the formative stages of the Design phase, when you are generating ideas. Other methods for evaluation are detailed in Chapter 6.

Table 7-3 / Some user research methods relevant to navigation design

Method	Description	Strengths	Weaknesses
Contextual inquiry	Interviewing and observing users in their context of use Qualitative	Generates very rich data on actual use in context	Identifies unexpressed needs Can be time intensive
Card sorting	Create categories and groupings of cards Variations include open sorts and closed sorts Quantitative, qualitative, or both	Cheap Straightforward method Focused on categories and their meaning	Assumes correlation between card groupings and navigation Doesn't consider tasks in context Results often vary Separates labels from content

Table 7-3 / Some user research methods relevant to navigation design

Method	Description	Strengths	Weaknesses
Participatory design	Workshop with users to design a page or navigation Qualitative	Focuses on design solutions Interactive and engaging for participants	Subjective results Outcomes may vary greatly
Rapid Prototyping	Prototype of navigation menus tested and discussed with users Qualitative	Interaction with concrete designs and situates navigation use in context Can determine actually usability issues	Significant preparation time required

CONTEXTUAL INQUIRY

Contextual inquiry seeks to understand people in their natural setting. This means you must necessarily go to the user's home, workplace, or wherever they come into contact with the site. Interviewing and observation are the key ways to collect data. The method is best used toward the beginning of projects to gain a deep understanding of users and of user behavior. It can also inform your development of personas and scenarios greatly.

There are traditionally four main phases in conducting contextual inquiry:

1. Up-front interview

   Start by interviewing participants to get an overview of their work and their setting.

2. Master-apprentice teaching and demonstration

   In general, people don't consciously consider their own work habits when they've become second nature. A key aim of contextual inquiry is to uncover these internalized processes. To do this, have participants show and explain in detail how they work, as if you were their apprentice learning their job. Don't skip steps or gloss over seemingly unimportant tasks. You want all the detail you can get.

3. Observation

   After you've learned what participants do, watch them do it. Just let them carry out their normal business and observe them in action. Focus on their surroundings as well as what they say. Look for the things that are potentially missing from your site. For instance, you may find a notepad next to the computer used to make quick calculations. This may be an opportunity to better fit into a user's workflow by offering online calculators to fill this gap. Intervene and seek explanation at convenient points.

4. Summarize and follow-up

   Close the session by confirming with the participant what you believe you saw them do. Ask any open questions you have at this time.

Such sessions can take some time, perhaps as much as two hours per person. Because of this, your sample size may be small. Still, this method generates a great deal of rich data in different forms, including:

- Firsthand observations
- Field notes
- Audio recordings of each session and text transcriptions
- Photographs

While performing contextual inquiry, don't just focus on how people use your site. Instead, try to uncover how they surf the Web and what they do in general. The challenge of navigation design is trying to fit it into the normal activities of your site's visitors. Understanding what it is people are doing in the context in which they do it can greatly inform all of your design decisions.

ANALYSIS

You need to convert the information you've collected to actionable design input. Start by looking for common themes in the data. Focus on the actions people perform by picking out verbs in the session transcripts. Also look at the information that people need to complete those actions and how they make decisions. For instance, don't merely indicate that people scan a list of products on a gallery page and select the appropriate one. Indicate the criteria used to make that decision. Was it the label, the product details, the price, or the photo that got them? Was it a specific combination of elements?

Aggregate this information across users to build the big picture of user activity and information needs. This can be done with sticky notes or a deck of cards. Cluster activities and tasks into meaning groups. You may also use a spreadsheet to break down observations and categorize them. Looking at a single row in the table gives you a picture of what people are doing for a given task across participants. Use this to find patterns and draw conclusions.

Later in the design process, you can use the findings from contextual inquiry to model user behavior. A particular approach for this is called User Environment Design (UED) as developed by Hugh Beyer and Karen Holtzblatt. Like the floor plan of a building, the UED seeks to partition tasks into discrete groups, called *focus areas*. Each focus area is a bucket of activity that points to a group of tasks or content types, which in turn can directly inform the appropriate navigation for your site. For more on the UED methodology, see their book *Contextual Design: A Customer-Centered Approach to Systems Designs* (Morgan Kaufmann, 1997).

As the Web becomes increasingly interactive and more dynamic in general, methods such as contextual inquiry become vital to good navigation design.

CARD SORTING

Card sorting is a popular evaluation performed at the beginning of the Architecture phase in order to help create and refine navigation. Basically, you give participants a stack of cards, each labeled to correspond to a page or function in the site. You then ask the participants to sort these cards into categories.[4] There are two basic variations:

---

4   For detailed information about planning and conducting card sorting exercises, see this excellent article on the subject: Donna Maurer and Todd Warfel, "Card sorting: a definitive guide," *Boxes and Arrows* (April 2004). *www.boxesandarrows.com/view/card_sorting_a_definitive_guide.*

- Open Card Sort, in which participants have no initial categories to work with and must create their own groupings
- Closed Card Sort, where top-level categories are predetermined and participants must then order the cards within these

Using a stack of plain cards and sorting them on a tabletop is quite common and very effective. But to remove some of the burden of card preparation and analysis, you might try a computer-based card sorting programs, such as:

- MindCanvas (*www.themindcanvas.com*)
- CardZort (*http://condor.depaul.edu/~jtoro/cardzort*)
- CardSort (*www.cardsort.net*, Figure 7-6)
- CardSword (*http://cardsword.sourceforge.net*)
- WebSort (*www.websort.net*)

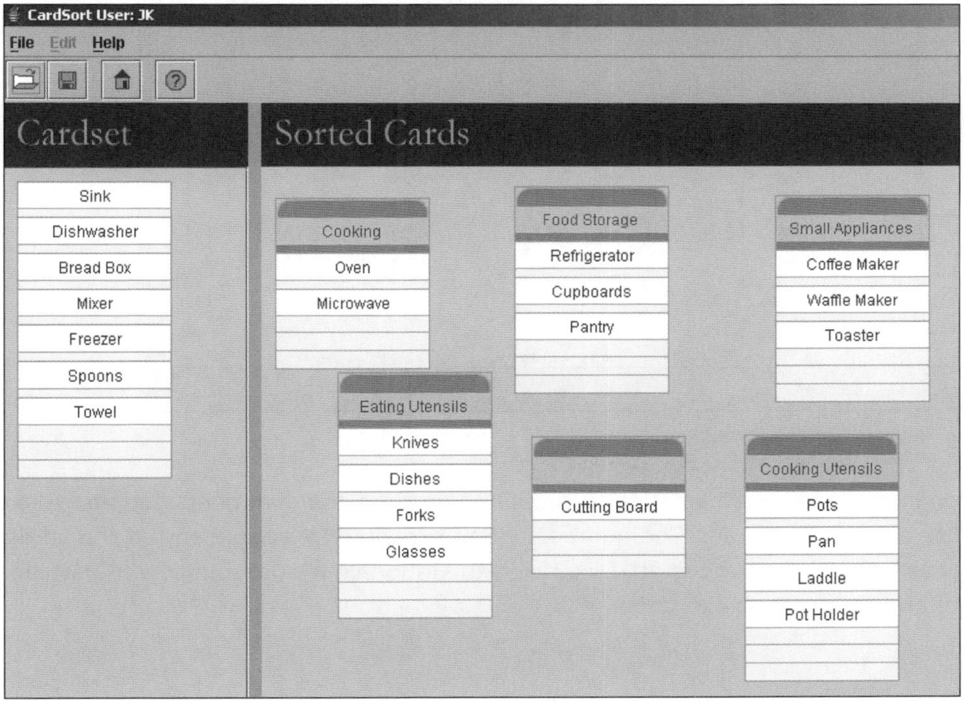

Figure 7-6 / CardSort, a computer-based card sorting tool

ANALYSIS

The ultimate goal of card sorting is to find patterns in categories, as well as the types of labels people come up with. One simple approach to analysis is to visually inspect the groupings. Though simple and fast, this type of casual eyeballing tends to be fairly subjective.

A more rigorous approach uses a spreadsheet to break down the data and provide percentages and distributions of categories in detail.[5] If you want to get truly scientific, you can apply clustering algorithms to statistically compare groupings. Essentially, clusters show the perceived relationships between the topics and categories sorted and are usually represented in a graph, chart, or spatial diagram.

CardZort can perform simple clustering for you. Figure 7-7, for example, shows a simple cluster analysis of likely top-level category labels for terms or groups of terms.

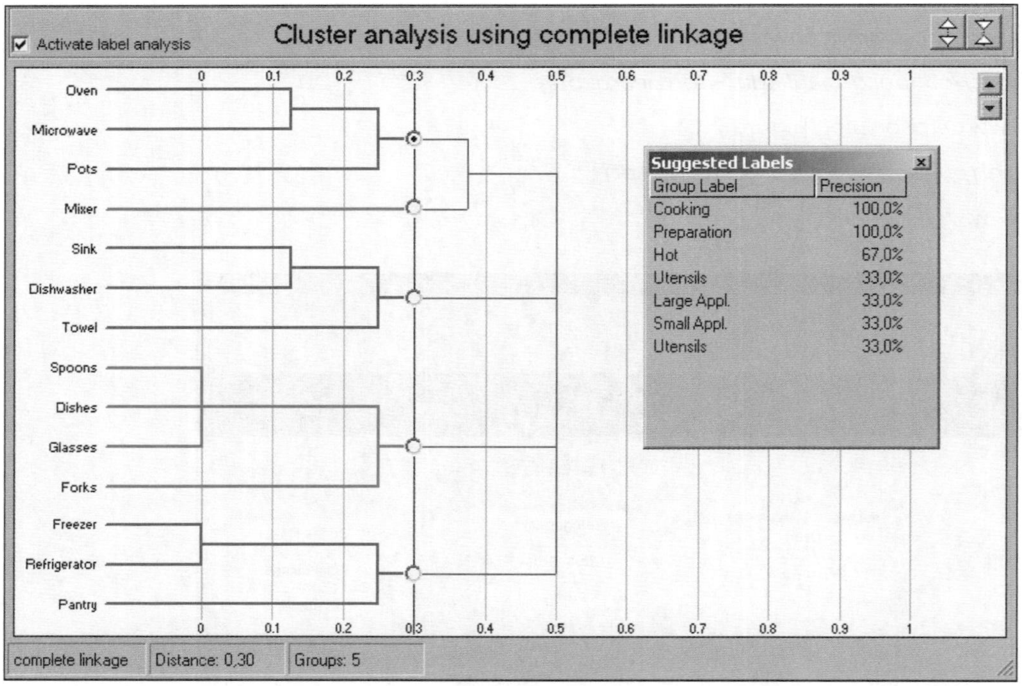

Figure 7-7 / Example cluster analysis from CardZort

Keep in mind that even if you take a mathematical approach to analysis, the comments people make during the sorting exercise are still important. The numbers won't explain why people sorted the cards the way they did or the alternatives they suggested. Discussing the rationale for groupings with participants is an important part of any card sorting exercise.

---

5   Joe Lamantia's excellent card sort spreadsheet template is available online: Joe Lamantia, "Analyzing Card Sort Results with a Spreadsheet Template," *Boxes and Arrows* (August 26, 2003). *www.boxesandarrows.com/view/analyzing_card_sort_results_with_a_spreadsheet_template*.

How Card Sorting Can Inform Web Navigation

By Donna Maurer

Card sorting is a user research technique focused specifically on learning how users think about information groupings. The way users think may be quite different to how designers or business people think. For example, a business owner may think about grocery items terms of brand, but users may think in terms of an existing store layout, packaging types (all the canned food together), or recipes.

One of the most interesting things about card sorts is to realize that everyone groups a set of information differently. Sometimes people put slightly different cards together, sometimes they make groups according to entirely different criteria. A card sort activity helps you identify these similarities and differences and create groupings that make sense for your users, allowing them to find information easily.

Card sorting helps with many navigational decisions:

- *Groups of content*. A card sort provides information about cards consistently placed together and cards grouped differently. With this information you can identify content that belongs together and content that may be difficult to organize into natural categories.

- *Audiences*. Card sorting helps you learn whether there are audiences who think differently about content groupings and whether one navigational approach suits everyone.

- *Classification schemes*. People may organize the cards in different ways, such as by topic, task, or document type. Based on this information, you may create your main navigation using a main classification scheme (e.g., topic) and use other classification schemes for alternate navigation approaches (document type, task).

- *Navigation labels*. The descriptions provided by users can be used as ideas for navigation labels.

The main disadvantage of card sorting is that it does not provide a full answer. It focuses solely on content organization and it does not consider users' tasks, priorities or information needs. The output from a card sort should be analyzed together with other user research findings when designing a navigation system.

Donna Maurer is an Australian freelance information architect who works with a wide range of government and private organizations. She is a board member for the Information Architecture Institute and is the author of Card Sorting: The Book (www.rosenfeldmedia.com/books/ cardsorting).

PARTICIPATORY DESIGN

As the name implies, *participatory design* methods allow potential users to take part in the design process. This technique is helpful when starting to develop page layout and design. There are many variations of this technique, but they all have one thing in common: stepping back and watching what people make. It is a good precursor to creating the layout of the navigation, discussed in Chapter 9.

Give participants a simple task, such as "design your ideal home page for our site." Or, you could give a richer scenario, such as "you'd like to purchase a book as a gift for your mother. Design the ideal system to do that online." The more context you can give, the easier it may be for the participant to begin designing.

Then, let people create what they want using props and materials you supply. This is best done with physical artifacts—usually paper. You may supply predesigned components that are available as a palette of tools to arrange on a page. Or, you can ask participants to draw on a flipchart or piece of paper from scratch. Participatory design can be done with individuals, or as a group.

ANALYSIS

As with other user research techniques, look for patterns. A simple visual inspection of all of the designs side-by-side may reveal similarities. Be sure to consider what participants said about their designs and thought processes that went into creating them.

To be more systematic, you could try to quantify common elements and attributes across participants, as well as the position of elements on the page. For instance, measure the regularity with which the navigation appears on the top, left, or right.

If multiple teams are working simultaneously in a group session, have them present their creations to the whole group after completion. Ask them to explain why they did what they did. Listening carefully: their thoughts can help you interpret their designs.

RAPID PROTOTYPING

It's easier to change a prototype than the final web site. As your layout begins to take shape, show a prototype of it to potential users for feedback. *Rapid prototyping* refers to an iterative testing process. With it, you show a version of the prototype to a few potential site visitors, make changes based on their feedback, and then test the new design with a few more people. The goal is to quickly identify potential problems and make adjustments iteratively. This allows you to not only find issues in the navigation, but also have a chance to test the solutions.

Low-fidelity prototypes are easier and faster to produce. There may be no color or graphic elements in this incomplete version of site pages, and content may consist of placeholder information only. Paper prototypes can be created very rapidly, and they are quite disposable. Carolyn Snyder, an independent usability consultant and author, advocates this technique in her book *Paper Prototyping* (Morgan Kaufmann, 2003) as a valuable for method for testing navigation and labels, among other things.[6]

Although more time consuming, *high-fidelity prototypes* more closely resemble the final intended look and feel of the pages, simulating content, navigation, and even functionality. Showing screenshots on a

---

6   Carolyn Snyder, *Paper Prototyping: The Fast and Easy Way to Design and Refine User Interfaces* (Morgan Kaufmann, 2003).

computer closely simulates how a page will look. You can also link the images together so clicking on one leads to the next, which can give a sense of the transition between pages—something critical to navigation design. An HTML prototype requires know-how, planning, and time to build, but active hyperlinks allow people to interact with navigation directly. If built correctly, the prototype can be used as a code base for the final product.

Researching with prototypes relies on usability test techniques, described in Chapter 6. This generally involves giving participants representative tasks and observing how they solve them. Direct discussion of the designs with participants is also important. By studying reactions to prototypes, you can better understand where potential difficulties may lie and make adjustments accordingly. Rapid prototyping is a good way to compare alternatives early on.

ANALYSIS

The outcome of prototyping will vary depending on the approach you take and formality of the tests. Generally, prototyping in early stages of development doesn't need elaborate documentation. Focus on observing users and improving the design, not creating a report.

In particular, look for the moments where confidence in navigation diminishes. Ask participants about their expectations before and after clicking navigation options. If there is a mismatch, the labeling and/or scent of information may be off.

CONSOLIDATING RESEARCH FINDINGS

After conducting research, you'll have to make sense of what you've found. Be careful that research findings don't get misinterpreted. There are several potential pitfalls to avoid:

Don't make quantitative conclusions for qualitative studies

A common mistake is to make quantitative conclusions from a qualitative study. If you interview five people and two make negative comments, for instance, you can't make reliable conclusions such as 40 percent of participants dislike the web site. Instead, with qualitative methods, focus on the things people do and say that explain their behavior, not the numbers.

Refrain from treating design research as if were science

Though many of the techniques may be similar, design research has a different purpose than scientific research. Design research methods are solution-oriented, with a focus on creating innovative artifacts, e.g., a usable navigation. Scientific methods generally result in abstract models and theories that apply across situations. This is an important distinction—one that you should be clear about up front.

Avoid mixing interpretation with personal preference

Conclusions from design research, though not scientific, are not mere guesses based on opinion either. An interpretation implies there is evidence to support a conclusion and it is more than just a hunch or best guess.

Try not to overgeneralize

Don't overgeneralize your interpretations and conclusions. If one person mentions disliking the Top New Stories feature on your home page, this doesn't mean that everyone dislikes it. Try to validate your conclusions. A mix of methods provides different perspectives and can indicate if your conclusions are on track.

A systematic approach helps you consolidate your findings and avoid some of these pitfalls, particularly when dealing with data from a variety of sources. First, compile individual, detailed findings in a common format. Then group them into larger topics and patterns that feed in to more general recommendations and guidelines for design. Overall, this type of consolidation represents a bottom-up approach and ensures your conclusions are grounded in actual user behaviors and are not based on hearsay or assumptions (Figure 7-8).

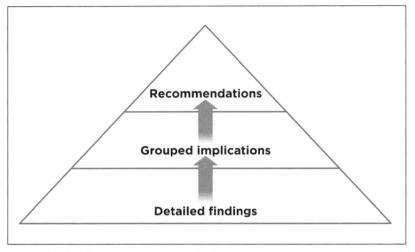

Figure 7-8 / Bottom-up process of consolidating findings

RECORD DETAILED FINDINGS

A commonly used pattern for systematically organizing user research findings consists of three elements: *observation*, *interpretation*, and *implication for design*. This generic pattern allows you to capture insight from different activities into a common format.

Observation

Note your observations without any judgment or interpretation attached to them. Consider both negative and positive observations. Include quotes from users or bits of evidence to illustrate the observation. Don't forget to include aspects of user emotions and feelings. If people reveal that they are sometimes frustrated or uncertain and sometimes happy and relieved, record that information too.

Interpretation

Explain the cause and reason behind the observation. Support any contentions you make with data, comments, or quotes you've gathered. Note any limitations of the test setting here as well, and show the strength of your interpretation with qualifying phrases. For instance, the sentence "in most cases people are likely to have a problem with the navigation" is stronger than "a few people might have problems sometimes." Avoid absolute claims unless you can support them. What's more, be certain to consider *all* possible explanations of the observed behavior. An interpretation shouldn't be the first explanation you can think of, but the best and most viable explanation that takes a range of possibilities into account.

Finally, determine what the findings mean for your web site in particular. Focus on the issue outlined in the observation and interpretation, and keep the scope of the implication within those boundaries. The implication also shouldn't propose a specific design solution, such as "put the main navigation on the left." Instead, describe the type of solution that is needed, such as "the main navigation should be in a visible location."

To consolidate findings using this technique, create a table with three columns. Table 7-4 illustrates this technique using fictitious quotes and findings from employee interviews about their company intranet.

Table 7-4 / Example consolidation table for user research findings

Observation	Interpretation	Implication
Employees often mentioned that information isn't always current. They expressed frustration over this. *"I don't know about changes to policies that affect my work until it's too late."*	Employees will likely need up-to-date information on a regular basis in order for the intranet to be of use. Note also that the nature of the business relies on changes to processes and policies being communicated effectively.	Intranet and extranets should provide up-to-date information.
Some staff commented that the intranet has no information about their projects. *"The intranet doesn't have any information related to what I'm specifically working on."*	The amount of project-specific information seems to be disproportional. For those that don't have project information readily available, the intranet seems to be less valuable.	Consider organizing the content of intranet primarily by project.
When suggested, most employees liked the idea of organizing the intranet by project instead of department. Some were very enthusiastic about this idea.	It seems that most employees are focused on their project work and would benefit greatly from access to project information on the intranet.	Consider organizing the content of the intranet primarily by project.
The employee contact feature on the home page is well-liked and reportedly used often. *"That's one of the few things I use the intranet for regularly."*	Contact with co-workers seems to be very important for most of the people interviewed.	Keep the employee contact feature prominent on the intranet.

Create a table like Table 7-4 for each of the studies or sources of information you examine, including existing data and even secondary research. This standardizes all the information you come across so you can make comparisons.

GROUP IMPLICATIONS

Next, collect all the implications from all of the user intelligence you've gathered in a separate list. Eliminate duplicate implications and merge similar ones together. Then group these by topic. For example, typical categories include the primary elements of interface design, such as structure, navigation, content, and visual design. Or, group the implications by the behaviors or phases in an information-seeking process, such as those described in Chapter 2.

Under each of your categories you'll have a list of implications for the design of the web site. Each of these can be tied back to a specific data point in the user research. This is important for making sound recommendations that aren't based on assumptions or anecdotal evidence.

MAKE RECOMMENDATIONS

Ultimately, you want to be able to describe the ideal information experience for your site, which should in turn drive the site's requirements. Your recommendations are not just suggestions for the layout and color of the site. They should steer the types of feature and functionality that gets included in the first place. Illustrate the recommendations with quotes to further tie your conclusions back to things you observed.

For instance, from Table 7-4, you may arrive at the following recommendation:

Recommendation: organize intranet content by project

The current organization of the intranet by department doesn't seem to support how people work. While there are departmental concerns, most people have local sources for that information. The primary organization of content should instead be by project. Each project should have a "hub" within the intranet, around which all other information is organized.

"I know what's going on in my department already. It's right there on the bulletin board."
(Interview)

"To get an update about a current project, I have to visit many department sections first."
(Comment from Participatory Design)

A substantial number of participants arrived at the top-level category "Projects."
(Card Sort)

PERSONAS

Personas are narrative descriptions of user archetypes reflecting patterns of needs and behavior discovered during user intelligence. They are a way of capturing details about visitors in format that is tangible and accessible to a larger team. Personas are then used to guide design decisions. They are generally short—no longer than a page or two each—and usually include a photo. Multiple formats of a persona might be created as well, such as short form (e.g., bullets of the highlights only) and poster size personas.

Personas aren't new. Alan Cooper introduced them to the design community back in 1999 in his book *The Inmates Are Running the Asylum* (Sams). They have since become a mainstream design tool.

Accessibility

When creating segments and personas, create a separate persona to represent target groups with accessibility needs. Or, consider making one of your personas have poor eyesight. This will serve as a reminder that not all visitors are of the same able body and mind, and you must account for all user groups.

CREATING PERSONAS[7]

Creating a persona is not creative writing. You don't simply make up information based on anecdotes, or worse invent it all. Instead, to be truly useful, personas must be based actual data. The process is not at all easy and requires detailed research and validation.

Briefly, creating personas consists of the following steps:

1. Identify the most salient attributes that distinguish one segment of users from another.[8] This may include demographic details, but probably focuses on more such important attributes as online purchasing behavior and domain knowledge. What are typical patterns of information seeking? What mode of seeking are people generally in, e.g., is re-finding important? What are their typical gaps in knowledge? What do people do, think, and feel will finding information?

2. For each of the attribute determine the minimum number of personas that you need to represent the range of your target groups. For instance, if experience shopping online is an important attribute, you may need a persona with little experience and one expert to represent your intended users. Base this on user research findings.

3. Write the personas. Start with the list of attributes as a kind of outline for your text. Use evidence from user research to support everything you include. Keep extraneous details low, but do add a small amount of colorful details to make them come alive.

4. Validate the personas. This can be done with stakeholders and team members to check if the target personas are aligned with business and project goals.

5. Make the personas visible. Hang them up in brainstorming sessions and include them in project documents. Don't expect others to actively read and then remember the details of a several page personas. It's your job to make them come alive.

There are many good sources of information on creating personas. In addition to articles and sites on the topic, you can start with these two excellent books:

The User Is Always Right: A Practical Guide to Creating and Using Personas for the Web, by Steve Mulder with Ziv Yaar (Berkeley, CA: New Riders, 2006).

The Persona Lifecycle: Keeping People in Mind Throughout Product Design, by John Pruitt and Tamara Adlin (Morgan Kaufmann, 2006).

---

7   There are many good sources of information on creating personas. See the following and other resources available on the Web for details about getting started on your own persona: Steve Mulder and Ziv Yaar, *The User Is Always Right: A Practical Guide to Creating and Using Personas for the Web* (New Riders, 2006). John Pruitt and Tamara Adlin, *The Persona Lifecycle: Keeping People in Mind Throughout Product Design* (Morgan Kaufmann, 2006).

8   George Olsen, a leading design consultant in the San Francisco area, provides an excellent toolkit to help you get started in his article "Making Personas More Powerful: Details to Drive Strategic and Tactical Design" (*Boxes and Arrows*, September 2004). *http://www.boxesandarrows.com/view/making_personas_more_powerful_details_to_drive_strategic_and_tactical_design*.

SCENARIOS

Another efficient and effective way to reflect a great deal of information uncovered from user intelligence activities, scenarios are detailed descriptions of what the site should do from the user's perspective. They are important in describing the user experience. Scenarios can quickly communicate your vision of how the site will be used to a development team and stakeholders

Consider this example of a scenario from the beginning of the landmark article "The Semantic Web" by Tim Berners-Lee, inventor of the World Wide Web, and his colleagues.[9] This scenario sets the stage for a broader, more technical discussion later on in the text:

> " *The entertainment system was belting out the Beatles' 'We Can Work It Out' when the phone rang. When Pete answered, his phone turned the sound down by sending a message to all the other local devices that had a volume control. His sister, Lucy, was on the line from the doctor's office: 'Mom needs to see a specialist and then has to have a series of physical therapy sessions. Biweekly or something. I'm going to have my agent set up the appointments.' Pete immediately agreed to share the chauffeuring.*
>
> *At the doctor's office, Lucy instructed her Semantic Web agent through her handheld Web browser. The agent promptly retrieved information about Mom's prescribed treatment from the doctor's agent, looked up several lists of providers, and checked for the ones in-plan for Mom's insurance within a 20-mile radius of her home and with a rating of excellent or very good on trusted rating services. It then began trying to find a match between available appointment times (supplied by the agents of individual providers through their Web sites) and Pete and Lucy's busy schedules. (The emphasized keywords indicate terms whose semantics, or meaning, were defined for the agent through the Semantic Web.)*
>
> *In a few minutes the agent presented them with a plan. Pete didn't like it—University Hospital was all the way across town from Mom's place, and he'd be driving back in the middle of rush hour. He set his own agent to redo the search with stricter preferences about location and time. Lucy's agent, having complete trust in Pete's agent in the context of the present task, automatically assisted by supplying access certificates and shortcuts to the data it had already sorted through.*
>
> *Almost instantly, the new plan was presented: a much closer clinic and earlier times—but there were two warning notes. First, Pete would have to reschedule a couple of his less important appointments. He checked what they were— not a problem. The other was something about the insurance company's list failing to include this provider under physical therapists: 'Service type and insurance plan status securely verified by other means,' the agent reassured him. '(Details?)'* "

This example has many qualities of a well-written scenario:

Easy to understand

There is no technical language. Just about anyone can approach it.

Enjoyable to read

There is a limited amount of extraneous detail in the scenario. That "We Can Work It Out" was playing isn't important. But in small doses, such detail makes a story that people can related to.

---

9   Berners-Lee, Tim, James Hendler, and Ora Lassila, "The Semantic Web," *Scientific American* (2001). *http://www.sciam.com/article. cfm?articleID=00048144-10D2-1C70-84A9809EC588EF21&sc=I100322.*

The scenario shows the impact the semantic web could have on everyday lives.

Clear vision

Without describing how the "agent" works in detail, it is clear what it's supposed to do and the impact it could potentially have.

Scenarios ultimately describe the ideal the user experience in an abstract way, which can guide concept development (Chapter 8) and page layout (Chapter 9).

TASK ANALYSIS

Notice that in order to create the flow of a scenario, you'll first have to understand the broader goals and tasks of your site's visitors. Goals are why people are coming to the site in the first place. They may be looking for information on getting a house mortgage or want to buy a pair of earrings. Tasks are the concrete steps people have to take to get to their goal.

Start by modeling the overall seeking process in steps or phases. Rely on existing models of information seeking to get started, such as the Information Search Process (ISP) discussed in Chapter 2. Tailor these phases to the specific needs and goals your visitors have. This provides a good framework for understanding how people will approach your site. The aim is to understand an overall activity cycle for your target audience. This may extend beyond just their interaction with your site and describe what they are doing in general.

Then, within each step or phase of your model, break the down the behaviors into specific workflows, or definable tasks. For instance, buying earrings online could be described as:

1. Access site
   - Search with search engine
   - Select site from results list

2. Find earrings
   - Choose category for earrings
   - Browse catalog pages
   - Compare prices, styles, and size

3. Checkout
   - Place earring in shopping cart
   - Enter address and credit card information
   - Print confirmation screen

You can even go down to the mouse movement or keystroke level of detail if needed. There is no hard and fast rule about the granularity of a task breakdown. It depends on the project and your needs. You can then represent a task flow with a diagram. Use a parallelogram for overall start and end points, squares for actions, and diamonds for decision points. Figure 7-9 shows a simple task flow diagram for buying earrings online.

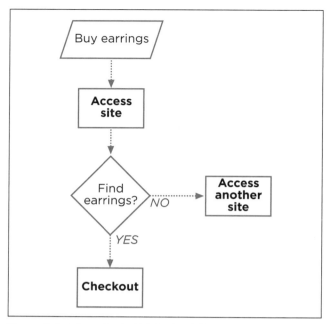

Figure 7-9 / Example of a high-level task flow diagram

For more on task analysis, see *User and Task Analysis for Interface Design,* by JoAnn Hackos and Janice Redish (John Wiley & Sons, 1998). Mark Edwards' sidebar in Chapter 13 includes further details about creating screen flows based on task analysis later in the design process.

SUMMARY

Abraham Lincoln is reported to have once said, "Give me six hours to chop down a tree, and I will spend the first four sharpening the axe." Preparation is clearly as important—if not more important—than execution. But when projects begin, people tend to grab the closest implement, no matter how dull, and jump right into the detail.

Good planning ultimately saves time by focusing design decisions later on in the project. Web navigation design does not take place independent of project goals. You must at least be aware of key elements of project background.

For example, consider the stakeholders, the overall goals of the business (such as revenue targets and operational cost goals), and the site's goals. Understanding the vision, mission, strategy, and brand is also important. And in order to create a unique position in a market, it's necessary to examine competitor products and services. Finally, ask why *this* company is embarking on *this* web project at *this* time: Find the problem behind the problem.

Remember, you can't design effective navigation without understanding what it is you're providing access to. Gather existing content for analysis and use a survey to get an overview of the major content types, formats, and structures. Or, develop a detailed content inventory or audit in which every page is systematically reviewed and tracked. You need to become fluent in the language of the information you will be organizing and understand the general subject matter.

Likewise, understand the technology of the medium you are designing for. This doesn't mean you have to become a programmer, but you should become familiar with how the relevant platforms and back-end and front-end technologies work. Developing a navigation for a mobile phone presents different constraints than developing one for a web site.

Finally, and most important, pay attention to your users. User intelligence is a series of ongoing activities to reduce the risk that people won't be able to use your site navigation properly. This isn't a discrete task that can be easily crossed-off a project plan, and no single method will give you all the answers you are looking for. Instead, you'll have to blend a range of techniques that complement one another. The goal of user intelligence is to uncover user needs and expectations, which in turn inform navigation design.

The outcome of user intelligence should ultimately drive the project requirements. Communicating findings to others is therefore critical. Summarize your conclusions in a concise set of design recommendations. Personas and scenarios are a good way to consolidate and present research data. Both are important for developing a site's architecture (Chapter 8) and arranging navigation on the page (Chapter 9).

QUESTIONS

1. Compare at least two of the computer-based card sort programs mentioned in this chapter. (Note that installation and setup of these programs is generally very quick and easy. You can start using each within 10 minutes).

   a) What the advantages and disadvantages of each program?

   b) What are the major limitations?

   c) Other than facilitating statistical analysis, what are other general advantages of computer-based sorting programs?

2. Interviewing is a good way to understand more about your target population. Using the Web, find out the differences between *directed interviewing* and *nondirected interviewing* techniques. What are the advantages and disadvantages of each?

3. Create a task flow for performing a search on Google. Pick something you're looking for on the Web and try to find it using Google. Be as detailed as you can, down to the individual action. What happens after you type the first letter into the input field? What are the various conditions that can occur (e.g., no results, etc.)? What do you do on the results page? Represent the task flow first as an outline, then as a diagram.

FURTHER READING

Elements of the User Experience, by Jesse James Garret (New Riders, 2003).

This is a slim volume breaks down and explains the author's famous diagram of user experience design (*www.jjg.net/elements/pdf/elements.pdf*). Two elements of his diagram—Strategy and Scope—are of particular interest in relation to analysis as outlined in this chapter. This is a must-have book for any web designer.

Observing the User Experience: A Practitioner's Guide to User Research, by Mike Kuniavsky (Morgan Kaufmann, 2003).

This is a hands-on book full of practical information about conducting user research. There is detailed information on planning user research and participant recruiting. Most of the book focuses on user research methods, including card sorting. The text is clear and accessible, appealing to a wide range of readers.

Rapid Contextual Design: A How-to Guide to Key Techniques for User-Centered Design, by Karen Holtzblatt, Jessamyn Burns Wendell, and Shelley Wood (Morgan Kaufmann, 2004).

This book offers step-by-step instructions and detailed research tools for conducting contextual inquiries during fast-paced projects. It includes techniques for storyboarding, creating personas, and prototyping, among other things.

Strategy Safari: A Guided Tour Through the Wilds of Strategic Management, by Henry Mintzberg, Bruce Ahlstrand, and Joseph Lampel (Free Press, 1998).

In this comprehensive book on corporate strategies the authors survey ten schools of thought on strategy, bringing many different perspectives to the table. *Strategy Safari* is well-written with many examples to illustrate concepts. It is a good starting place for anyone interested in the subject.

Architecture

"Every link in hypertext creates a category. That is, it reflects some judgment about two or more objects: they are the same, or alike, or functionally linked, or lined as part of an unfolding series."

—Geoffrey C. Bowker & Susan Leigh Star
Sorting Things Out: Classification and Its Consequences

08

IN THIS CHAPTER

- Persuasive architecture
- Creating a navigation concept and concept diagrams
- Linear structures, webs, hierarchies, facets, and emergent structures
- Organizational schemes and categories
- Creating site maps and detailed site plans

Imagine you're planning a trip to Paris in the spring and coincidentally see an online advertisement for what looks like a good package price—better than what you've been able to find so far. You click on the ad and land on the home page of a travel service you've never heard of, but that appears reputable nonetheless. A quick scan of the teasers in the middle of page reveals that none of them are for the Paris trip you want. One of them is for something called Europe Tours, but that doesn't seem right and sounds like a group thing.

Still curious, you scan the main navigation options on the site: Flights, Hotels, Rental Cars—those are clear. But then you see options called Top Deals, Package Specials, and something ambiguous called Boarding Pass. Unsure, you click on Specials. Here, you see an offer for a flight to Paris, but without a hotel, as listed in the advertisement. You then convince yourself it must be under Top Deals. This, however, reveals a form where you can search for last minute deals, which also isn't what you want.

By now, the offer in the advertisement isn't looking so good, and the site's credibility is quickly diminishing. But you give it one last chance and click the Back button until you get to the home page. You then select Europe Tours option from the home page. To your surprise, this opens a new browser window to reveal what appears to be a separate service from the travel company. There is nothing there to indicate they have super deal for a Paris trip, and you quickly close that browser and get back to what you were doing.

What has happened here? You wanted to purchase a trip, and the travel service surely wants to sell it to you. But you couldn't. The individual steps to get to your ultimate goal prevented you from reaching it.

On the one hand, visitors to a site usually have a goal in mind. In this scenario, you want to buy a trip to Paris. But do so you must perform a series of individual steps. These activities can be considered on two levels:

- *Macro-level actions* related to the larger objective (booking that Paris trip)
- *Micro-level actions*, the individual steps taken to reach the goal (the clicks required to accomplish the purchase)

Navigation design concerns both levels: the individual clicks to get from one page to the next, as well as how those single actions add up to meet a larger goal (Figure 8-1).

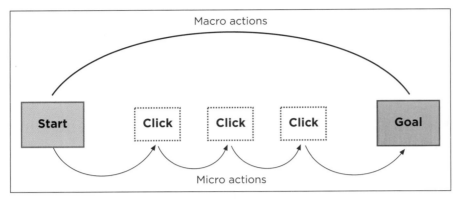

Figure 8-1 / Micro and macro actions to reach the same goal

What's more, if any of these steps fail, neither user goals nor business goals are reached. Navigation design is a critical part of the overall chain of activities that comprise an online strategy. In the Architecture phase, your task is to structure pages in such a way that the macro and micro actions achieve the same goal for both users and for the business.

PERSUASIVE ARCHITECTURE

It's no secret that brick-and-mortar stores are laid out to promote the sale of products. The candy bars, magazines, and other small items aren't placed at the checkout register by accident. And someone made a conscious decision to put the milk in all the way in the back. Promoting products and optimizing sales is a normal part of any business.

Bryan and Jeffrey Eisenberg, leading online marketing experts, detail a method for planning sites they call persuasive architecture.[1] In optimizing a site to sell things better, the Eisenbergs point to three critical questions to ask from the beginning:

- What is the action you want someone to take?
- Who are you trying to persuade to take the action?
- What does that person need in order to feel confident taking that action?

Personas and scenarios stand at the center of their persuasive architecture method. Together, they represent how visitors make decisions and reflect the process for buying online. The choices customers make that are captured in your personas and scenarios need to match how you sell products and ideas on your site. Bryan Eisenberg explains:

" When a customer makes a decision, that decision represents the culmination of a cognitive process. It may take place almost instantaneously or stretch out over a long period of time, but it's a process, not an event. Persuasive architecture weaves the buying process into the selling process.[2] "

1   Bryan Eisenberg and Jeffrey Eisenberg, *Waiting for Your Cat to Bark?: Persuading Customers When They Ignore Marketing* (Nelson Business, 2006).

2   Brian Eisenberg, "Do You Want to Inform or Persuade?" *ClickZ Network* (October, 2002). *www.clickz.com/showPage.html?page=1474771*.

Web navigation plays a central role in persuasion architecture and in aligning user goals with business goals. Note that even if you're not creating an e-commerce site, you are still selling ideas and communicating a message. Persuasion architecture plays part in these cases too.

This chapter investigates the three key aspects of this process:

Navigation concept

>A concept is an abstract model of how the navigation works. It not only guides the team though development, but can also give users a clear pattern to follow when using the site.

Site structure

>The structure of a web site is how pages are arranged in relationship to one another or how the site is constructed.

Organization of navigation

>Organizational schemes group navigation options together in a logical way, providing context for understanding navigation as a whole.

Even if you are not creating a new site architecture from scratch, you'll still have to be aware of your overall navigation concept, structure, and organization. Understanding these three aspects of site architecture is important for both site redesigns and when adding enhancements to existing sites.

NAVIGATION CONCEPT

A navigation concept is a model of how people will navigate the site. It doesn't specify a solution, but instead provides the vision for how the solution should be created. A concept guides design and development for the entire team. In terms of persuasive architecture, a navigation concept represents how the site will encourage users to take certain actions. Two common ways of describing a site concept are by genre or metaphor.

GENRE AS CONCEPT

As discussed in Chapter 2, recognizable forms or genres of information potentially improve visitor orientation and give a sense of context. You can also use them as the basis of a navigation concept. For instance, newspapers have a recognizable form: there is a front page, headlines, a lead story, and topical sections. Online newspapers typically retain some of these common genre-defining aspects of offline newspapers. But new elements are brought in as well, including links to blog postings, the ability to comment on articles directly online, and the inclusion of video footage. The basic concept of a newspaper—which we are all familiar with—is not lost online and serves as an underlying concept for news sites.

Figure 8-2 shows the home page of *The Los Angeles Times* (*www.latimes.com*). The lead story, other headlines, and various sections are familiar within the newspaper genre. But some online-only aspects can be found, such as Most Viewed Stories, Blogs, and Videos. By treating these areas as further sections of the newspaper, the result is an online experience that borrows from traditional formats and extends them online.

Figure 8-2 / *The Los Angeles Times* home page

Genre is important for navigation and for the overall usability of the site. Visitors can recognize the intent of the site easily and quickly based on existing knowledge and expectations. A recent study compared a genre-conforming news site with a genre-violating news site with the same content.[3] The findings showed that following conventions and matching user expectations significantly improved performance, particularly when navigating the sites. The study also found, however, a consistent internal site structure allowed people to build a mental representation of a site, even the genre-violating version of the newspaper.

In creating a navigation concept, consider the genre your site will represent and the conventions you will follow. This may include offline and online genres, or a mix of both. If you are planning not to follow standard conventions in your navigation, regularity and predictability are still important. Starting the architecture of a site with a clear concept is the first step in creating this consistency.

METAPHORS AS CONCEPT

Metaphors, which describe something abstract in terms of something that is more commonplace, can be used as a concept for your site as well. For instance, the classic Google search page uses the Swiss army knife metaphor for its well-known search engine page. Marissa Mayer, Google product manager responsible for user experience, explains:

---

3   Misha Vaughan and Andrew Dillon, "Why Structure and Genre Matter for Users of Digital Information: A Longitudinal Experiment with Readers of a web-based Newspaper," *International Journal of Human-Computer Studies* 64 (2006): 502-526.

> " *I think Google should be like a Swiss Army knife: clean, simple, the tool you want to take everywhere. When you need a certain tool, you can pull these lovely doodads out of it and get what you want. So on Google, rather than showing you upfront that we can do all these things, we give you tips to encourage you to do things these ways.* [4] "

This does not mean that the web site should look like the metaphor. Rather, it's intended to elicit a common understanding across a team. It potentially communicates a wealth of ideas efficiently and provides a starting point for addressing design issues or conflicts that may arise. Suppose someone asks "should we advertise all of our products on the home page?" With the Swiss army knife metaphor in place, the first answer would be "No—a Swiss army knife would open only one thing at a time."

Some possible metaphors for a navigation concept include such things as a:

- Dashboard
- Library
- Marketplace
- Storefront
- Showroom

The Pottery Barn web site makes use of what they call "shop rooms" as a concept for online shopping (*www.potterybarn.com*; Figure 8-3). This leverages a showroom metaphor common to furniture stores in which products are initially presented together by purpose instead of by type.

Figure 8-3 / A showroom concept on the Pottery Barn web site, called "Shop Rooms"

---

4   Mark Hurst, "Interview with Marissa Mayer, Product Manager, Google," October, 2002. *www.goodexperience.com/blog/archives/000066.php*.

Through metaphor exploration, you can create a conceptual underpinning to the site that guides its development. The goal is to represent your navigation in a single, easy-to-remember model that others can quickly comprehend. This will aid in buy-in to your approach and potentially guide the design team through all other design decisions later.

CONCEPT DIAGRAM

A helpful tool to capture a navigation concept is a concept diagram, which graphically illustrates the key elements and ideas involved in a navigation system. Figure 8-4 shows an example of a concept diagram, in this case for the redesign of the web site for the Information Architecture Institute (*www.iainstitute.org*). This diagram was used to organize and document the various elements of the site and how they relate to one another. Wolf Nöding, a German information architect and creator of this particular diagram, explains:

> *With its molecule-like appearance, this model presents the main user tasks of the web site arranged around a circle. The interests of the organization are shown on the two poles: from the top down (management) and from the bottom up (members). The weight of the arrows reflects the relative importance of a given relationship. Input was gathered from surveys and interviews with members of the institute and from many discussions with stakeholders. Overall, this concept diagram helped define a global scenario for the site from different points of view and was then used to guide further development.*

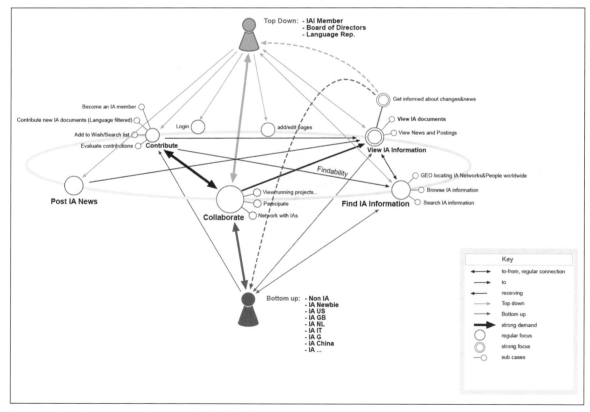

Figure 8-4 / A concept model diagram for the IA Institute web site[5]

Note that the act of creating a concept diagram is as valuable—if not more so—than the deliverable document itself. Though it is interesting to look at, you may find Figure 8-4 hard to understand at first. But for Wolf and the redesign team it served as an important means for envisioning the architecture of the site. Such a diagram allows designers to conceive both macro-level and micro-level actions of the site.

Dan Brown, author of *Communicating Design: Developing Web Site Documentation for Design and Planning* (New Riders Press, 2006), explains the value of concept diagrams, which he calls a concept model:

> *What's most important about a concept model, however, is that unlike other documents, it's as much about facilitating the thought process as it is about communicating ideas. It's as much for the creator of the document as it is for the consumers; an opportunity to wrap your head around complex ideas and relationships that, until you were hired by your client, you never had occasion to think about. The utility of the concept model is not so much in the output as it is in the getting there. It is very much a Zen deliverable.*[6]

Chapter 6 of *Communicating Design* is a good resource for more specific information creating diagrams.

CREATING A NAVIGATION CONCEPT

The concept is a fusion of various elements, many of which have been identified during the Analysis phase (Chapter 7):

* Business goals
* Site goals
* Competitors
* Brand
* User types
* User goals and scenarios

Very often, projects form navigation concepts tacitly, not explicitly. Teams make assumptions about the conceptual direction of the site. On smaller projects this might be fine. But with larger, complex sites it's better to make the concept explicit. This means that creating a concept should be a collaborative exercise. Involve development team members as well as stakeholders in brainstorming sessions and storyboarding meetings. A concept conceived at a single person's desk has little chance of surviving.

Qualities of a good concept include:

* Easy to remember
* All encompassing, covering macro- and micro-level navigation and future design decisions
* Aligned with stakeholder goals
* Meets user expectations

---

5   Used by permission from the Information Architecture Institute and from Wolf Nöding.

6   Dan Brown, *Communicating Design: Developing Web Site Documentation for Design and Planning* (New Riders, 2006): 138.

Overall, creating a navigation concept involves the following steps:

1. Review the information collected during Analysis, including vision, brand, competitors, goals, and of course users.

2. Describe the desired actions people need to take to meet their goals and the business goals in a scenario. Rely on the personas and scenarios you've created.

3. Brainstorm and explore different possible models of navigation. Get all the key decision makers together in the same room. Use genre and metaphors to guide your concept.

4. Develop a concept diagram showing the relationships between site features and content.

5. Describe the concept in words. This should be simple and memorable.

With your navigation concept defined, you're ready to consider the structure of the information in your site. Whereas a concept reflects an abstract model of the site, the structure captures the specific arrangement of pages and content in a concrete manner.

INFORMATION STRUCTURES

The *information structure* refers the plan or map of pages in your site. It is the skeleton of the site that you'll be filling out with page layouts and final designs, discussed in the following two chapters. As you investigate how to construct the navigation, keep the different types of structure in mind, including:

- Linear structures
- Webs
- Hierarchies
- Facets
- Emergent structures

Of course, hybrids of these are not only possible, but common. A web navigation system may make use of any or all of these basic structures simultaneously.

LINEAR STRUCTURES

In a simple *linear structure*, pages are arranged in a sequence, as shown in Figure 8-5. Linear structures occur when people can't get to one page without having first seen a previous page. A site search is an example of a natural linear structure: you can't see a results page without entering a search on the search form. Wizards and online tests are other common examples of linear structures.

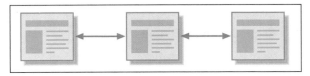

Figure 8-5 / A simple linear structure

Or consider Figure 8-6. This is the second step in setting up an account on Apple's .Mac service. To get here, visitors must first enter their personal details. These are validated by the system for format. On this screen, credit card details must be entered before proceeding to the third and final step. A simple Continue button moves the user through this structure one step at a time.

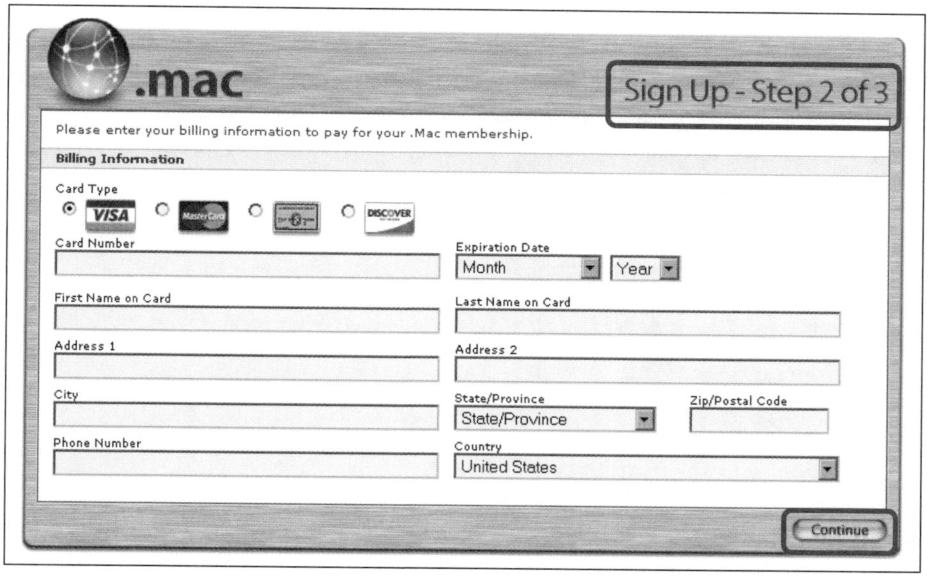

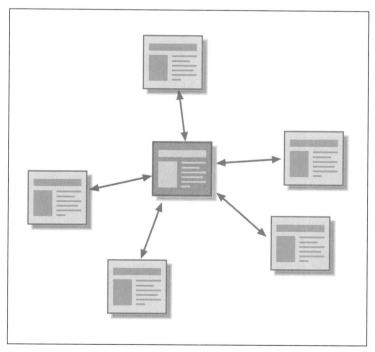

Figure 8-6 / A simple linear structure

A *hub and spoke structure* can be considered an extension of a linear arrangement of pages. This is essentially a collection of linear structures from the same starting point (Figure 8-7). You start out on a key landing page and navigate to other pages individually. From there, your main navigation path is back to the hub.

Figure 8-7 / A hub and spoke: an extension of linear structures

A *web structure* has many nodes that are linked together without levels or sequence. Information is cross referenced and linked such that there is no real start or end. Each page is a potential hub in a hub and spoke structure that webs yield (Figure 8-8). Associative navigation works like a web structure, with multiple pages and cross linking. Web-like structures also occur naturally on sites like MySpace (*www.myspace. com*), for instance, where users freely create links between pieces of content and other people themselves.

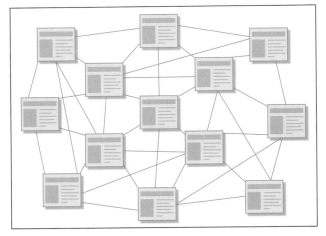

Figure 8-8 / A web-like structure

HIERARCHICAL STRUCTURES

Hierarchies show levels of nodes that are arranged in parent-child relationship, also called a tree structure (Figure 8-9). There is a top-level node, or the highest level of the hierarchy, usually the home page. Nodes in the hierarchy can have parents (a level up) and children (a level down). All levels below inherit the level designation from the parent level and extend it to the next level. This allows you to note that item 1.2, for example, is below item 1, but above 1.2.1 and 1.2.2.

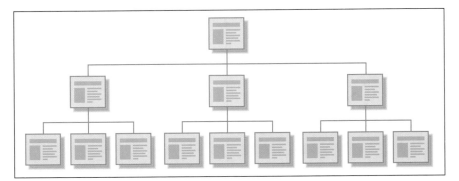

Figure 8-9 / A hierarchical structure

Most web sites have some kind of hierarchy. The home page > landing pages (or gallery) > product pages structure is common for most e-commerce sites. Even a simple personal web site with only a few levels represents a hierarchical structure.

Polyhierarchy is a special term that refers to the condition when a page has more than one parent (Figure 8-10).

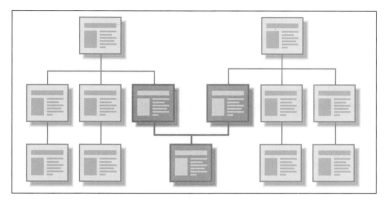

Figure 8-10 / A polyhierarchical structure

Polyhierarchy is an important construction for reusing pages and content, or having them appear under two categories. For instance, two different areas of a given site may have a shared page for common contact information. This contact page has two parents.

Note that polyhierarchy can present problems in displaying certain types of navigation. If you have a breadcrumb trail, does it reflect where the user came from or the location of the page within the site? If you have color-coded sections of the site, what color does a child page with two parents inherit? If your site has polyhierarchy, identify it early on and plan accordingly.

FACETS

Facets offer an alternative to hierarchies. In hierarchies, the location of a given item is determined by its position in a tree-like structure. Strict hierarchical organization is also limiting: there is only one way to locate a piece of information. People are shunted into that path to find information.

With facets, the location of an item is given by the categories that it belongs to: item 1 belongs to categories A, B, and C, but not D. This offers multiple points of access. Faceted systems address the fact that information seekers might seek a resource from any number of angles. This provides greater flexibility in locating information.

Both hierarchies and facets make use of *categories*, leading to confusion in understanding them. You can have hierarchical categories or facet categories. The difference is in how the categories are arranged and their relationship to one another. Think of facets as mutually exclusive categories that describe the properties or dimensions of an item. Each facet category then has *values* that further describe an object.

The difference between hierarchies and facets is illustrated in Figure 8-11. In a hierarchy, the position of a page is given by its parents, siblings, and children. The highlighted object belongs to its parent category, and in turn it is a category for its children. To contrast, the position of an object using facets is given by the categories of values it belongs to. The highlighted object represents the intersection of value categories that describe it.

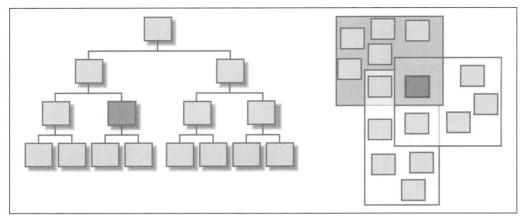

Figure 8-11 / Classification of an item in a hierarchy (left) versus with facets (right)

Consider an example: Compare how the music albums in online store for MP3s might be structured hierarchically and then structured by facets. First, here's how you might arrange them hierarchically:

Rock
    New Releases
    Classic Rock
        Beatles
                Abbey Road
                Sgt. Pepper's Lonely Hearts Club Band
        Pink Floyd
                Dark Side of the Moon
    Experimental Rock
        Frank Zappa
                We're Only in It for the Money
                London Symphony Orchestra, Vol 1
                Jazz from Hell

Jazz
    Essential Jazz
    Bebop
        Miles Davis
                E.S.P
                Kind of Blue
    Vocal Jazz
        Ella Fitzgerald
                Best of Ella Fitzgerald & Louis Armstrong
Classical
    Johann Sebastian Bach
        Goldberg Variations
    Igor Stravinsky
        The Firebird
        Petrushka

With facets, you need to look at the characteristics and properties important to users. These might be style, artist, title, release date, price, and mood. Table 8-1 structures the same music offerings with a faceted classification.

Table 8-1 / An example of facets and values

Facet	Values
Style	Rock Classical Rock Experimental Rock Jazz Bebop Vocal Jazz Classical
Artist	Louis Armstrong Johann Sebastian Bach Beatles Miles Davis Ella Fitzgerald Pink Floyd Igor Stravinsky Frank Zappa John Zorn
Title	*Abbey Road* *Best of Ella Fitzgerald & Louis Armstrong* *Dark Side of the Moon* *E.S.P* *The Firebird* *Goldberg Variations* *Jazz From Hell* *London Symphony Orchestra, Vol. 1* *Petrushka* *Sgt. Pepper's Lonely Hearts Club Band* *We're Only in It for the Money*
Price	Under $10 $10-15 Over $15
Mood	Upbeat Laid-back Agitated Sad Romantic

When it comes to navigation, each album can be found by starting with any facet. The path Mood: Upbeat > Price: $10-15 could lead to *Abbey Road* as could Style: Classic Rock > Artist: Beatles. What's more, multiple values from a given facet can be assigned to a single item. The three Frank Zappa albums in this example could belong to multiple style categories as needed. *Jazz from Hell* could be found under both Experimental Rock and Jazz categories, and *London Symphony Orchestra, Vol. 1* could also be found under Classical.

Beyond offering multiple entry points to information, facets are scalable. A key principle of faceted classification is that the categories are mutually exclusive. Therefore, a change to a value in one set doesn't necessarily affect values in others. In a hierarchy, a change to one level may disrupt the entire structure. For instance, the facets Topic and Price may be used to describe products on an e-commerce site. Changing the available values for the Topic facet won't affect those under Price.

For more on navigating facets, including examples from the Web, see the section "Faceted Browse" in Chapter 11.

EMERGENT STRUCTURES

Emergent structures are not planned in advance, but materialize spontaneously. They are not created by a single person or event, but instead develop incrementally. Instead of a top-down process, where a designer plans and determines a structure to ensure it's balanced and efficient, emergent architectures are formed from the bottom up. Individual elements—pages and content on the Web—come together and build up in a self-organizing system. In this sense, emergent structures describe how the site's architecture is created, rather than the relationship of its pages to one another.

The classic example of an emergent structure is a *wiki*, a web site that allows visitors to edit, add, and remove content and pages. Figure 8-12 shows the Recent Changes page for Wikipedia (*www.wikipedia.com*), the largest wiki on the Web. Toward the bottom of the page you'll see a list of the changes to the site for the given point in time. On Wikipedia, visitors are constantly changing content and adding new topics. The site structure itself grows organically as more and more information is added.

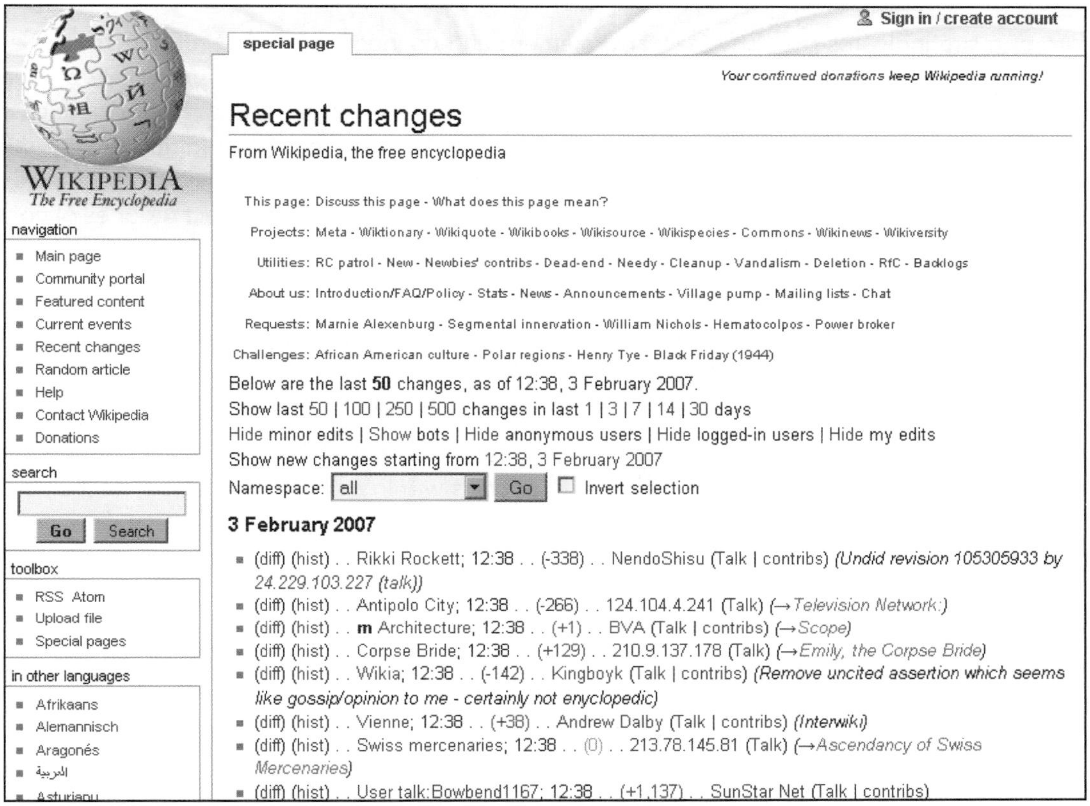

Figure 8-12 / Recent changes page on Wikipedia

In this example, the individual contributors determine the size, direction, and growth of the architecture. They co-create their information environments online. It would be impossible to have a preconceived, monolithic, top-down structure for Wikipedia: it expands too fast to control centrally. Instead, the site structure is based on rules that allow it to grow as members contribute to the community.

But this does not mean that there is no structure. Most emergent structures are web-like or hierarchical. Note that Wikipedia has a very traditional left-hand navigation, as well as a tabs, a footer navigation, related links, language selectors, internal page anchors, and lots and lots of embedded links. There is a clear system of the navigation that provides a framework for an emergent structure that was conceived by the site owners. Not all wikis or sites with emergent structures have such regular means of navigation, but in the case of Wikipedia, relying on familiar mechanisms and conventions eases the overall navigation of the site in general.

ORGANIZATIONAL SCHEMES

The structure of a site indicates the "physical" arrangement and connection of pages. It doesn't, however, determine how pages and content is thematically related. A hierarchy—which you'll most likely be dealing with—is agnostic to the categories of pages that comprise the structure. Regardless, if the navigation is categorized by subject, by date, or by audience, the structure will still be hierarchical. In addition to determining the site structure, the next step in navigation design is to consider the types of categories and topics that will be used to organize information. But note that defining a structure and organizing categories of content go hand in hand. One may not precede the other.

The organization of a site's navigation itself can be instructional, potentially helping visitors better understand the topic at hand. Providing a logical categorization of options and grouping them by a consistent scheme increases the ease with which people can comprehend and use a navigation menu. This in turn adds to the predictability of navigational links, potentially bringing visitors closer to their ultimate goal.

The general recommendation for navigation design is to create menus that share a common organization. For instance, it might be confusing to see the following options within a single navigation mechanism:

* Kitchen Appliances
* Search
* About us
* Download PDF Catalog
* International Sites
* Jobs

Instead, navigation design seeks to create menus out of a similar links. This also helps create a sense of purpose for a type of navigation, as discussed in Chapter 4.

Navigation is largely about creating relationships between content on your site. But keep in mind that ultimately there is no right or wrong way to design categories and organize your information. The objective is to organize navigation in a way that makes sense to users and achieves your business goals. To do this, you must explore alternatives and find what works best. Many different organizational schemes exist. Keep these in mind as you categorize content on your site and develop navigation options.

OBJECTIVE AND SUBJECTIVE SCHEMES

Classification is the act of organizing items into groups based on some common aspects. It draws a line between items that belong together and those that don't. Categories, organizational schemes, and labels are closely related, and it's hard to talk about one without discussing the other. Still, we can identify several common kinds of classification schemes, divided into two types: objective or exact schemes, and subjective or ambiguous schemes.

Objective schemes organize information into well-defined categories.

Alphabetical schemes

> Although very familiar, alphabetical schemes don't communicate anything about the relationship of the objects to one another in a meaningful way. They are most useful only when visitors know the exact wording of the desired item.

Chronological schemes

News sites frequently make use of chronological organization, and company histories fit neatly in timeline representations. The History Channel web site offers visitors an interactive timeline for specific periods in history (to try it go to *www.history.com* and choose Exploration, Figure 8-13).

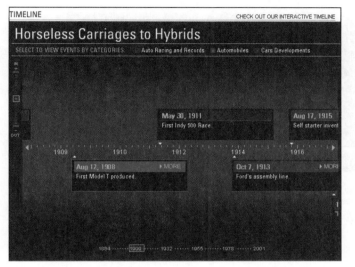

Figure 8-13 / Chronological timeline on the History Channel web site

Geographical scheme

Location is the basis for organization with geographical schemes: global or national, city or state, region or country.

When creating site navigation, you'll be dealing primarily with *subjective schemes*.

By topic or subject

On large, information-rich sites it's very common to group products, services, or site content by topic. The navigation to the main areas of the page often reflects the topics of the site. People like to look for information by topic, particularly if they don't know exactly what it is they searching for. Directories are good mechanisms for displaying many topics at once. Tree structures are also good. Of course, for a limited set of topics, just about any menu will do, including tabs, bars, and vertical menus.

By audience group

Here the navigation options speak to different user groups. For instance, the NASA web site (*www.nasa.gov*) includes separate navigation for audience-based options, seen in red on the left side of Figure 8-14. Visitors can then self-identify with one group or the other.

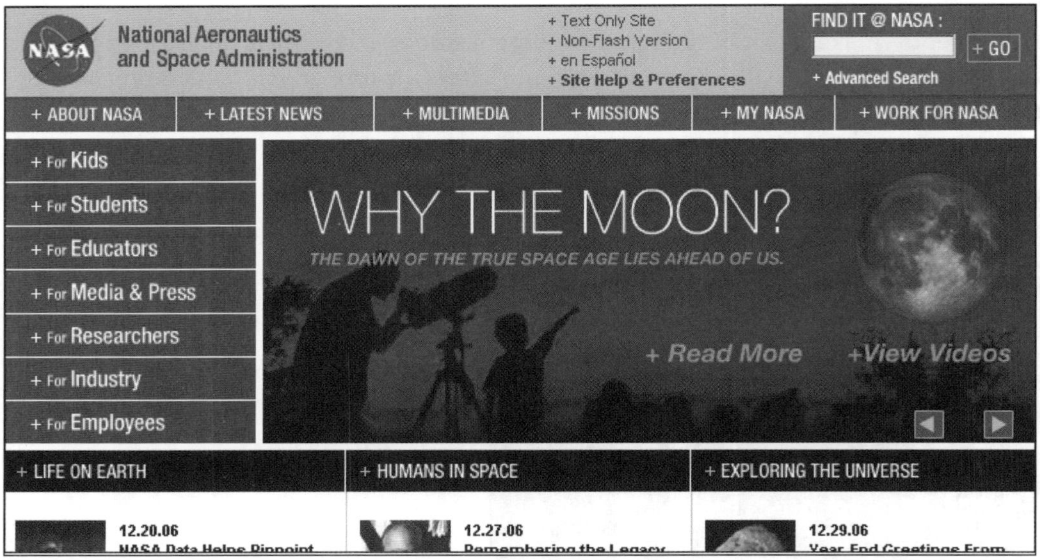

Figure 8-14 / Audience-based navigation on the NASA web site

By Task

Sites that are more interactive and call for user input can benefit from a task-based organization scheme of navigation options. The main navigation for the Princess Cruises web site (*www.princess. com*, Figure 8-15) is task-based. Notice that the labels also form a process from left to right—one that mirrors planning, booking, and taking a cruise.

Figure 8-15 / Task-based navigation for Princess Cruises

Internationalization

The notion of categorization seems to be universal. All cultures engage in some level of categorizing of things in the world. Creating categories is a fundamental act of humans. But specific categories themselves aren't natural or universal. They are learned and culture-dependent.

For example, George Lakoff, professor of linguistics at the University of California, Berkeley, begins his book *Women, Fire, and Dangerous Things* with a description of a complex category from the Australian aboriginal language Dyirbal called *balan*. This actually describes women, fire, and dangerous things as a single category. It also includes birds and exceptional animals, such as the platypus, bandicoot, and echidna.[7]

Is *balan* a good or bad category? Neither. Ultimately, there are no right or wrong categories, only useful ones. When designing categories for web navigation, the usefulness of categories is ultimately determined by users. To arrive at the most useful categories for your site, you must find the shared references that make sense to your target audience and base your organization scheme on them. If you are dealing with international visitors, your assumptions about categorizations may not always hold true.

MISCELLANEOUS SCHEMES

People like information to be organized consistently. But information doesn't always let itself be categorized neatly and evenly. The content and functionality of a site might not allow for a purely topical or geographical organization, for instance, even though that's the scheme which works best for visitors. You can almost expect to end up with a mixed bag of content to organize when dealing with large bodies of information.

Consider the main navigation of Marks & Spencer, a large retailer in the U.K. (*www.marksandspencer.com*, Figure 8-16). What is the basis for this classification? What is the principle for the order of the options? The organization of the main navigation options communicates "here's the stuff we have to sell" without an apparent underlying scheme.

Figure 8-16 / Miscellaneous scheme for the main navigation on Marks & Spencers

---

7   George Lakoff, *Women, Fire, and Dangerous Things: What Categories Reveal About the Mind*, (University of Chicago Press, 1987).

Is this bad? Is this compromising traditional schemes? Technically, yes, but practically, no. Classification is messier than we'd sometimes like or care to admit. Although the main navigation for the Marks & Spencer site doesn't hold together thematically, there are still other factors that create a sense of cohesion in this menu of options:

- The behavior of the navigational links is consistent and predictable
- Visual treatment of mechanism and options is consistent
- The position of a navigation menu on the page clearly communicates its purpose as a main navigation.

Strive to find logical groupings of navigation options, but be prepared to not always succeed. More times than not, you may be faced with a "miscellaneous scheme." By applying other principles of good navigation design, however, such as proper labeling, a consistent visual treatment, and a predictable position on the page, you can still create a navigation system that works.

SITE MAPS

A site map is a document that demonstrates the relationships between content and functionality in the site's architecture.[8] It captures the site's concept, informational structure, and organizational scheme in a visual representation. A site map is a key deliverable in designing a web site, and it's useful to many project team members:

- Stakeholders use site maps to see how the site will impact their business.
- Visual designers identify page types and page layout needs from site maps.
- Programmers visualize the scope and extent of the site from site maps.

ELEMENTS OF A SITE MAP

There are many variations of site maps: the amount of detail shown, arrangement of boxes, use of color and shapes, and so forth can vary from designer to designer. However, the main purpose is the same: to effectively communicate your architecture to others. There are no hard and fast rules on how a site map should appear, but there are common elements of site maps, including:

Nodes

Pages in your site are the basic nodes in the site map, typically shown as squares.

Connectors

Nodes are connected to show relationships. Site maps generally don't show all of the associative links, but instead show structural and utility navigation.

---

8   Note that the term site map can have different meaning to different people in different contexts. The three types of site maps are: a navigation mechanism used by site visitors (as discussed in Chapter 3); site maps derived from the web site, typically by a web site crawling robot; and a deliverable that documents the architecture of a site by use from developers, designers, and stakeholders. This section deals with the last one: the deliverable.

Business Priorities and Navigation

By Victor Lombardi

Modern business operations and strategy are often inextricably tied up with the design of products, including navigation. Here's a simple example of how navigation changes to suit different strategies.

Let's say you are designing an e-commerce web site for a company called Firm that sells building materials. Firm has several distribution centers around the world and each center carries the same selection of products. For every geographical location shown on Firm's web site you might create a navigation bar listing the products in consistent, alphabetized categories:

Doors   Hardware   Insulation   Lumber   Roofing   Siding   Windows

That might work fine from a usability standpoint. But let's say that each of Firm's distribution centers stock the products differently depending on popularity and profit margin. Moscow sells a lot of roofing and insulation, both high margin items. The navigation bar could change to match the merchandising decisions in this location, helping the customer find products they buy more often and helping the company increase profits. The navigation bar for web site visitors in Moscow might list:

Insulation   Roofing
[Blanket | Fiberglass | Foam] [Metal | Shingle | Tile] Doors Hardware Lumber Siding Windows

Factoring strategic and financial priorities into the navigation is one way designers can contribute to business results.

Because navigation can be an element that connects a customer directly to the company, the process for designing navigation needs to carefully factor in business priorities. In traditional business planning, product development was a two-phase process:

Strategy: find a business opportunity through marketing and financial analysis

Product Development: design a product or service to realize the opportunity

But if making a change to navigation can influence which products get sold or which markets get emphasized, then the design of the navigation and the design of the business plans need to be more closely aligned. In a case like Firm's, the first phase of development could be just long enough to hypothesize what online shopping opportunities are possible from a business standpoint. In the second phase, a designer can iteratively create drafts of the navigation and collaborate with business managers to ensure it reflects the differences in each region.

Victor Lombardi is a designer and business consultant living in New York City. He co-founded and served as past president of the Information Architecture Institute and teaches at the Pratt Institute of Design.

Numbering scheme

To avoid confusion, it helps to give each page a unique identifier. Often, site sections are given a letter, perhaps starting with A and going alphabetically from there. Then, a hierarchical numbering scheme is appended to each letter. You'll end up with page numbers like A1.1 and F3.4.1.

Labels

Each node in site map needs a title, which corresponds to the navigation label for that page. Use this opportunity to work out the final wording you want to use. Don't just use working titles with the intent to get back to them later if you can avoid it.

Page attributes

Beyond the page title, you also want to indicate some characteristics about each page:

- Content formats other than HTML, such as PDF
- Pages that are to appear in a pop-up window
- Dynamic content that changes on the fly
- Access rights, e.g., if a login is required to access the content
- The page type and page template (see Chapter 9 for more on page templates)
- Functionality and special features

Indicate these attributes with symbols and abbreviations on or near the nodes that they apply to. Color-coding or shading may also be applied.

Notes and annotations

Site maps aren't always able to communicate everything visually. Exceptions or special conditions often need an accompanying note in the site map.

Scope

Show pages that are in scope and out of scope for the current project. This helps plan for changes later and ensures that the architecture is scalable.

Title and key

As with all of your project documentation, title the site map along with a version number and/or the date. Create a key to explain the different shapes and symbols used.

Figure 8-17 reflects how these elements might appear in a classic site map with a hierarchical structure.

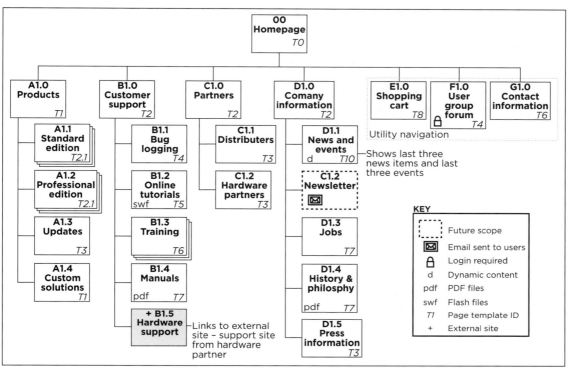

Figure 8-17 / An example site map showing some basic elements

HIGH-LEVEL SITE MAP

Also called a blueprint, a high-level site map shows how the main sections of a site or of multiple sites fit together. It doesn't show all pages, but instead attempts to define relationships between content and functionality. High-level site maps allow you to explore alternative directions before you get into the detail of all the pages—an important part of designing navigation. Visualizing the site graphically can facilitate planning the navigation in later stages.

The high-level site map is critical in getting the right concept for the site and for coordinating the macro actions needed to reach a goal both from the user's perspective and the business perspective. It also may serve as the basis for project organization. For instance, different people may be assigned to different sections of the site based on the divisions set out in the high-level site map. The basic technical architecture may also be based on the high-level site map early on in order to structure databases and back-end systems.

Figure 8-18 shows an example high-level site map of global car manufacturer. This site map actually spans three different types of sites the company is looking to enhance in this fictitious scenario:

The global portal

The main purpose of this site is to support the brand image and present information about the manufacturer. Visitors are directed to country sites for more detailed information about the products.

Each country where the manufacturer sells cars has its own site in the local language. Here, visitors can interact with the products, such as configuring their own car, comparing models, or viewing cars from inside and out with a 360 degree viewer. They are directed toward the dealer sites.

The dealer web sites

The dealer sites are the storefront for making transitions such as contacting a dealer, setting up an appointment for a test drive, or scheduling maintenance.

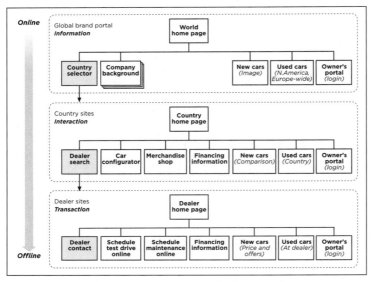

Figure 8-18 / An example high-level site map for a car manufacturer

Because most car buying takes place offline, the overall architecture encourages new car buyers to move toward the dealer sites. The desired persuasive architecture seeks to move people from a virtual, online space to an offline contact with a dealer. In this example, the country selector is critical to moving people to their local site, the dealer search is vital in finding the right dealer, and contact information for that dealer must be prominent at the lowest level of this architecture. This overall intent is captured in the high-level site map, which allows you to work out the relationships and communicate it to others.

DETAILED SITE MAP

Detailed site maps break down the site to its most granular level and document it. This is important in determining the micro-level actions from a structural standpoint needed to reach a goal. You want the paths to information to be as short and efficient as possible. The detailed site map gives you the opportunity to work those paths out.

From a documentation standpoint, it becomes impractical to diagram hundreds of pages in a single site map. Instead, multiple detailed site maps are usually the way to go. To do this, set up a separate document for a section of the site and zoom in on it in detail. Alternatively, use a spreadsheet to list the pages in a tree-like structure to reflect hierarchy (Figure 8-19). This can include many of the same bits of information normally reflected in a visual site map.

	A	B	C	D	E	F	G	H	I
1	Page						Template	URL	Notes
2	00	HOMEPAGE					T0	/home	May include news and rotating ads
3		A1.0	Products				T1	/products	
4			A1.1	Standard Edition			T2.1	/products/standard	
5				A1.1.2	Overview		T2	/products/standard/overview	
6				A1.1.3	Features		T2	/products/standard/features	
7				A1.1.4	Specifications		T11	/products/standard/specifications	
8				A1.1.5	Demo		T2.1	/products/standard/demo	
9					A1.1.5.1	Play Demo	T13	/products/standard/demo/play	In popup window; Flash movie
10				A1.1.6	Trial Version		T2	/products/standard/trial_version	
11			A1.2	Professional Edition			T2.1	/products/professional	
12				A1.2.1	Overview		T2	/products/professional/overview	
13				A1.2.2	Features		T2	/products/professional/features	
14				A1.2.3	Specifications		T11	/products/professional/specifications	
15				A1.2.4	Demo		T2.1	/products/professional/demo	
16					A1.1.5.1	Play Demo	T13	/products/professional/demo/play	In popup window; Flash movie
17				A1.2.5	Trial Version		T2	/products/professional/trial_version	
18			A1.3	Updates			T3	/products/updates	
19			A1.4	Custom Solutions			T5	/products/custom_solutions	
20		B1.0	Customer Support				T2	/support	
21			B1.1	Bug Logging			T4	/support/bug_logging	
22			B1.2	Online Tutorials			T5	/support/tutorials	
23			B1.3	Training			T6	/support/training	
24			B1.4	Manuals			T7	/support/manuals	Links to PDF documents
25				B1.4.1	Standard Edition Manual		T7.1	/support/standard_manual	in PDF format; 1.7 mb
26				B1.4.2	Professional Edition Manual		T7.1	/support/professional_manual	in PDF format; 2.3 mb
27			B1.5	Hardware Support			-	-	Links to external site

Figure 8-19 / Detailed page list

Visual Vocabulary

Jesse James Garrett, author and web design expert, developed a visual vocabulary for diagramming sites. It is designed to be whiteboard-compatible, tool-independent, and is small and self-contained. Some basic elements of the visual vocabulary to get you started are:

- *Page*. This is the basic node in a site map, representing pages in your site.

- *Page Stack*. Often groups of pages have the identical layout and navigation. Only the content differs. Use a page stack to show multiple pages of the same kind.

- *Continuation*. This figure allows you to stop a diagram of one section of a site and continue it on another page.

- *Areas*. These are used to group pages of a similar type. Enclose as many pages as needed within these shapes. Label the group with text.

- *Connectors*. These link elements of the site map together. The connector with the small bar means that upstream navigation is not possible.

- *Decision point*. This is the standard symbol for a decision point in flow charts. With this, one action generates two or more results

For a complete list of elements and thorough description, see: Jesse James Garrett, "Visual Vocabulary" (v1.1b) www.jjg.net/ia/visvocab.

Creating a site map is about immersing yourself in the content of the site and figuring out the details. The goal is to take what you've learned from card sorting, contextual inquiry, participatory design, and any other user intelligence activity (see Chapter 7) and organize the site's content accordingly. Site maps potentially communicate a lot of information in a short space and are therefore good for reducing documentation on a project.

CONSOLIDATE THE ARCHITECTURE

Creating a site map doesn't start out with some diagramming tool. Instead, you'll be better off using sticky notes. Start by recording everything you know that has to be included in the site or sites. Go for quantity, even for features and aspects of the site that are planned for future releases. On a whiteboard, start grouping and clustering things in such a way that your concept and architecture are apparent. Do this collaboratively and involve everyone from stakeholders to programmers.

The outcome of this activity forms the basis for the site map document. Transcribe the diagrams and groups of sticky notes to an electronic format. Note that there are many tools for making site maps. Microsoft Visio, Omni's OmniGraffle, ConceptDraw WebWave, Mindjet MindManager, and Inspiration from Inspiration Software, Inc. are popular programs, but many others will get the job done. Don't focus on the tool itself. As long as you can convey your architecture to others, the tool used to do it is unimportant.

ARRANGE PAGES ON THE SITE MAP

The layout of the nodes and elements on the site map should demonstrate relationships. For instance, Figure 8-17 shows a traditional site map reflecting the categories of the main navigation a basis for organization. It's clear that the pages under "A1.0 Products" belong to that category.

Other arrangements are also possible. You might want keep all pages on the same horizontal line. This makes for a very wide site map, but shows the pages on similar levels well. Or, a star map may be used. This makes a good use of space and eases drawing connections across levels of a hierarchy as well as showing polyhierarchy. Figure 8-20 shows some possible arrangements of nodes to highlight different relationships.[9]

---

9   These types of site map arrangements are identified by Christina Wodtke in *Information Architecture: Blueprints for the Web* (New Riders, 2003).

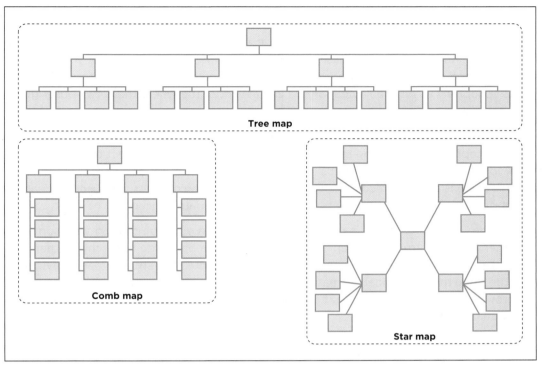

Figure 8-20 / An example of a high-level site map for a car manufacturer

ADD DETAILS

Next, include the annotations and symbols that will make the site map come to life. Keep in mind, however, that web projects change as they progress—almost without exception. As you are setting up the document, plan on having to update the site map and make it easy to change. For instance, take advantage of glue dot connectors and other diagramming features in many site mapping tools to facilitate moving nodes around.

What's more, traceability and synchronization of deliverables become more problematic as the project progresses. Seek to reduce your documentation overhead as much as possible and avoid duplication. You don't want a simple label change to cause you to update five documents. The site map is a good document in which to combine a great deal of information into a single overview. Use it to capture and reflect as much information as possible, thus reducing the need for long documentation.

PRESENT YOUR SITE MAP

Ideally, a site map communicates everything as a standalone document. This is often not the case however, particularly when explaining the more abstract concepts that underlie the basic architecture. To avoid misinterpretation, you'll need to present the site map to stakeholders and development team members.

Keep site maps visible. Post them in common project areas for others to see. They are also a reminder to you as to how the site is organized and put to together.

SUMMARY

A site's architecture is the plan or blueprint showing how visitors will reach their goals on both the macro level of initial goals and micro level of individual actions. It also reflects how the site will encourage them to take a certain action. Referred to as persuasive architecture, your job is to align what you leaned about the business, content, and technology during Analysis with what you learned about visitors with user intelligence activities (Chapter 7). The site navigation is a key aspect of the where these two—user goals and business goals—are played out.

Architecture starts with a navigation concept, which underlies the physical structure of a site. When creating a navigation concept, you are building perhaps the single most important aspect that impacts a user's experience with your site. Keep in mind that it's hard to change a concept once a site is live, so exploring alternatives at this stage is critical. I recommended testing alternative concepts with users for early feedback. No amount of post-launch enhancements can fix an inappropriate concept.

The structure of a site represents how it's put together. Most often you'll be dealing with some kind of hierarchy. But other types of structures supplement and enhance a basic site hierarchy so that a mix of structures is usually present in any given site. It's important to note that structure and navigation are related, but not the same thing. The goal in creating navigation menus isn't to represent the structure one-to-one, but to provide only the navigation that is needed to access relevant areas of the site. This is discussed further in Chapter 9.

Traditional organizational schemes, such as by user type, by topic, or by task, can help increase the ease of understanding navigation menus. But there is no one correct way to group things together. It's only in terms of user goals and business goals that you can judge the appropriateness of an organizational scheme. Further, categorizing navigation options isn't always straightforward. Often you end up with miscellaneous schemes that defy a traditional scheme. In these cases, you can still create a cohesive navigation through page layout and visual cues.

Because the navigation stands at the center of developing a web site in many ways, ensure that others are aware of your plan as early as possible. Site maps are a classic way to explore alternative structures and communicate the architecture to others.

QUESTIONS

1. The organization of information can get messy, even with simple schemes that we are all familiar with. This exercise begins with a simple task. On a separate piece of paper, arrange the following list in alphabetical order. Then answer the questions below:

El Paso, Texas	Saint Nicholas, Belgium
The Lord of the Rings	Newark, New Jersey
XVIIme siècle	*.38 Special*
St. Louis, Missouri	New York, New York
1001 Arabian Nights	*The 1-2-3 of Magic*
Albany, New York	*#!%&: Creating Comic Books*
The Hague, Netherlands	*$35 a Day Through Europe*
H2O: The Beauty of Water	Plzen, Czech Republic

   a) Did you put The Hague under T or H? Did you put El Paso under E or P?

   b) Which came first in your list, Newark or New York?

   c) Does St. Louis come before or after Saint Nicholas?

   d) How did you handle numbers, punctuation, and special characters?

   e) Now, assuming the italicized terms are book titles, what might be a more useful way to organize this list?

   f) If the cities represent places you've visited and the book titles are ones you've read, how could chronology be used to order the list in a more meaningful way?

2. This quick exercise has two parts. First, organize all the things on your desk or in your desk drawer into piles or groups any way that seems natural to you.

   a) What schemes did you use?

   b) Why?

Now organize those same things in the following ways:

   a) By size

   b) By material type

What are the differences to the first way you organized them? Which way was better or worse?

3. Shiyali Ramamrita Ranganathan, the famous Indian librarian, developed the basic theory of facets around 1933. He believed that any object or concept could be classified by five fundamental facets. Use the Web, find Ranganathan's five fundamental facets. How can they be used to help organize navigation?

4. Using the Web, define the following terms:

   a) Enumerative classification

   b) Analytico-synthetic classification

   c) Colon classification

   How are they different or similar?

FURTHER READING

Information Architecture: Blueprints for the Web, by Christina Wodtke (New Riders, 2002).

This book covers a range of core concepts in the field of information architecture. It's packed with practical advice and is downright fun to read.

Practical Information Architecture, by Eric L. Reiss (Addison-Wesley, 2000).

This is a concise book filled with timeless, practical tips for structuring web sites. Starting off with solid discussions of site goals, target audiences, and measuring success, among other things, Reiss never looses sight of the bigger picture of creating a successful site architecture.

"A Simplified Model for Facet Analysis: Ranganathan 101," *Canadian Journal of Information and Library Science*, by Louise Spiteri (v. 23, April-July 1998): 1-30. *http://iainstitute.org/pg/a_simplified_model_for_ facet_analysis.php.*

The technical literature on faceted classification is dense, long, and intimidating even to those interested in the field. Louise Spiteri, professor at Dalhousie University, provides a "boiled down" version of the key principles in this article. But make no doubt: Spiteri's article itself is not light reading. Still, it is an interesting place to get detailed information on facets.

Sorting Things Out: Classification and Its Consequences, by Geoffrey C. Bowker and Susan Leigh Star (The MIT Press, 2000).

This book tackles Classification Theory head on. Though dry and academic, the authors liven up the subject with many examples. They successfully demonstrate the potential political and ethical consequences categories can have.

Layout

" Less isn't more; just enough is more. "

—Milton Glaser

09

Navigation provides the narrative through your site. It's the story people follow to get the information they want. If the navigation concept is your premise and the site structure is your plot, you start telling the story with page layout. Some of the same principles of writing a good story hold true in designing navigation:

- Focus on one idea per web page.
- Keep extra details to a minimum.
- Hold the user's attention.
- Use visuals to enhance.

Ultimately, you want to create a flow in navigating through the entire site. In terms of page layout, this means you have to consider how your system of pages varies the position of navigation, labels, and function from page to page. A significant part of orientation while navigating is about how pages change from one to another, referred to as transitional volatility (see Chapter 2). Layout plays a large role in creating this desired sense of movement through a site, in addition to a page's labels and text.

Within the overall site development process, laying out pages proves to be a critical phase. It's at this point that people react to the design—more so than at previous stages. When the page layouts start to appear, conflicting perspectives from various project members become apparent. A systematic approach helps avoid unnecessary debates based on personal opinion and keeps your story on track.

There are three main areas of concern in the layout process:

Determining navigation paths

In selecting the menus and mechanisms for your navigation, it's usually not necessary to reproduce the entire site structure so that you can get anywhere in the site from every page. Instead, identify the *optimal routes* people will likely travel to reach your key content and model the navigation around those. Use personas and scenarios to inform the choice of mechanisms to avoid over-designing the navigation system.

Designing a visual logic

Once you know how much navigation is needed and the different mechanisms involved, you can then start arranging these on the page. Traditional principles of layout and Gestalt Theory can guide you here. The goal is to create a recognizable pattern of elements that facilitates navigating the site.

Creating page templates

A system of navigation templates is important for consistency in design, as well as for efficiency in implementation. Page templates capture your layouts and show a progression of changes from page to page.

The following sections examine each phase in further detail.

DETERMINING NAVIGATION PATHS

Site structure and navigation are related, but not the same thing. A detailed site map shows all pages of a site, but the navigation system is a limited view into that structure. From any given page in the site, navigation is a constrained window of all available pages.

Figure 9-1 illustrates possible navigation paths from a given page. Main navigation may provide access to the top-level pages in the site (thick red lines pointing up); a local navigation allows people to navigate further down (blue lines); and associative links traverse the structure as need to bring together related content (thin red lines).

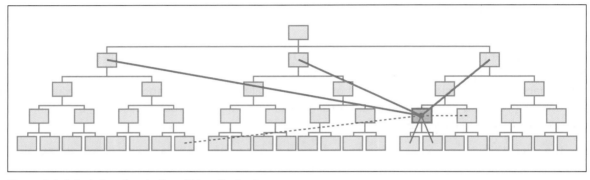

Figure 9-1 / A window of navigation within a site structure

To create this window of navigation, you must first recognize the nature of your site's structure, even if you're not the one who designed it. You'll most often deal with hierarchies, but elements of linear structures and web-like structures may also be involved. A navigation system is ultimately a mix of different types of access to information within a given structure. To determine the most effective mix, begin by identifying the optimal paths through your site.

START WITH THE END GOAL

A site's navigation is often created from the top down. The designer starts with the home page and determines all the ways to reach various parts of the site, level by level. By the time the content pages deep within the site are reached, the system is more or less fleshed out and the routes to those pages are already locked into place.

From a user's standpoint, however, the home page may be the least interesting page on the site. It's usually a mere stop on their way to where they are going. They care much more about the information and services your site has to offer. Of course, the home page often plays a key role in giving an overview, such as with intranets and news sites, but it's usually not the *target page* visitors are seeking.

Further, people may not enter the site on the home page. They may follow a link from a search engine, an online advertisement, or from another site. They may not have the chance to retrace those top-down routes to content pages you've carefully planned out. Therefore, you also need consider how people will get to your content from locations other than the home page. This leads to a simple but important piece of advice:

> *Don't start by designing the navigation on the home page.*

Instead, begin designing the navigation from the pages that are most important to visitors: content pages. For a retail site, these are product pages; for a corporate intranet, it may be a departmental page, human resources information, or a functional page for a web application.

Start by identifying a crucial page or page type, and then consider its purpose. What is its main focus? Is it an article, a product photo, or just simple text? Whatever this may be, it should grab the user's attention. In laying out the page, prominently feature the main subject of the page.

DETERMINE NAVIGATION NEEDS

After you've identified key pages and given their content a clear focus, determine the gaps in knowledge your visitors have on each of them.[1] Anticipate the types of questions people have to ask in order to fill this gap by asking those same questions yourself at various points in the site. In her book *Web Navigation: Designing the User Experience*, Jennifer Fleming points to three tiers of questions that a navigation system should answer:[2]

Tier one: general navigation questions

These are high-level questions such as Where am I?, Where did I come from?, What can I do here?, and Where can I go?

Tier two: purpose-oriented questions

These questions are specific to different types of sites. For instance, visitors to a university's web site may want to know how to use the library or view admission requirements. For an e-commerce site, people will want to see product information and learn how to contact customer service.

Tier three: product or audience specific questions

These are the most specific and have to do specifically with your target users: How do I get the manual to the product I just purchased? How do I contact customer service in my region? Where do I find products related to the one I just found?

The task isn't to come up with all possible questions, however, nor is it meant to exhaust all navigation paths. Instead, you need to determine the most important information needs for your target users and focus on these. After all, design is about making trade-offs. This is where your user research and analysis come into play. In particular, personas and scenarios prove to be vital. As Steve Mulder, web consultant and personas expert, puts it:

" Figure out where each persona needs to go from each page. After you've done this, create the system of rules that defines which navigation links are available from each type of page on the site. Are your personas likely to travel from one section to an entirely different section at any point? If so, make sure links to top-level sections are always available.[3] "

---

1   See also Brenda Dervin's Sense-Making Model, mentioned in Chapter 2 (see Figure 2-1). This model looks at the user's situation, gaps in knowledge, and how found information gets used.

2   Jennifer Fleming, *Web Navigation: Designing the User Experience* (O'Reilly, 1998): xiii.

3   Steve Mulder, *The User Is Always Right: A Practical Guide to Creating and Using Personas for the Web* (New Riders, 2007).

For instance, travel sites often have options for Flights, Hotels, and Rental Cars. Using personas, it may become clear to you that it's entirely possible for someone using such a site to switch between these while planning a trip. It makes sense, then, to provide these options globally. On the other hand, it may be unlikely for someone to switch from Private Homes to Commercial Property on a real estate site. If people aren't likely to cross sections from any point, top-level sections may not need to be present on all pages at all times. Base your assumptions on the evidence gathered during user research and use personas to guide and focus your navigation design.

Perhaps more important, consider the ways in which people will navigate *to* those important content pages in your site (Figure 9-2). This could very well be via main navigation links on the home page. But it could also be that other routes are more helpful and more likely to be traveled, such as from related content menus or even from site search results. While focusing on a single destination page or page type, plant the various links and means of navigating to get to it on other pages. When determining the window of navigation in your site's structure, this approach ensures that you won't overlook primary navigational paths that lead visitors to your valuable information.

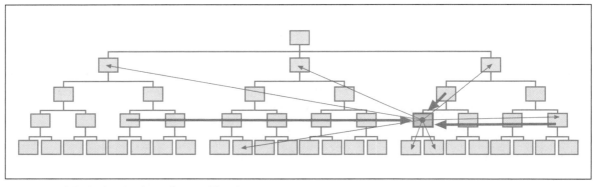

Figure 9-2 / Optimal navigation paths to and from key content pages

CHOOSE APPROPRIATE MECHANISMS

Once you've identified key paths to and from content pages, consider the specific options and menus that people need to accomplish their goals. Start by looking at the minimum number of navigation options needed, and ask: what is the easiest and simplest navigation mechanism to support the desired navigation? This may be a mere link at the end of a text. Or it may be a more elaborate menu structure, such as one of the many mechanisms discussed in Chapter 3.

Your focus should be on users and their goals, but you must also balance other considerations:

Page type

> The type of page you're designing might suggest the amount and kind of navigation you choose. For instance, the amount of navigation needed on a landing page is usually more than on a page at the lowest level of a site structure.

Content attributes

An analysis of content provides clues into things such as the quantity of content involved, the priority of certain content types, and the various formats used. If you're linking to video clips or PDF files, for instance, you'll need to consider how the navigation will handle this media. You also need to be aware of the frequency with which content will be updated, how volatile it is, and the nature of embedded linking. Navigation menus for small bits of content that are outdated within a day or two, such as classified ads, will be different than for long chunks of unchanging information, such as a company history.

Business goals

Include navigation that will also meet business needs. On Amazon.com, for instance, you can get to the shopping cart and checkout screens from any point in the site, which supports the goal of making a sale.

Scalability

Consider how the site will grow in the future. If it will expand, plan for this in the navigation layout. A row of 10 tabs probably won't give you much room to add more later, but vertical link list might.

Brand

How can the brand be reflected in the navigation? Apart from graphic design elements and color, the type of navigation menus you create should be in synch with the brand values.

While navigating, orientation is influenced by things such as page titles, page text, browser titles, and URLs. If showing location in a site turns out to be important, how will this be accomplished? Will you highlight the active navigation option or show location only with the page title? Consider the other elements of the navigation system and how they work together.

REPEAT THE PROCESS

Moving up the structure of the site, repeat these three steps with other key pages:

1. Start with the end goal.

2. Determine navigation needs.

3. Choose appropriate mechanisms.

When you complete a representative sample of pages, consolidate the results into a system of navigation that makes sense for the whole site. Keep in mind that this will require making adjustments, compromises, and exploring alternatives along the way.

VISUAL LOGIC

People make sense of web pages very quickly based on layout, even before they start reading any text. Consider, for instance, the recent practice of providing thumbnail images of home pages in search results, such as with the Alexa search engine (*www.alexa.com*, Figure 9-3). And technologies such as the Snap preview plug-in for Firefox allow site owners to give a page preview for any external link on a site (*www. snap.com*, Figure 9-4).

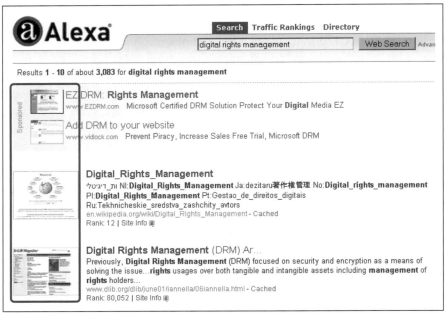

Figure 9-3 / Thumbnail images of web pages in Alexa search results

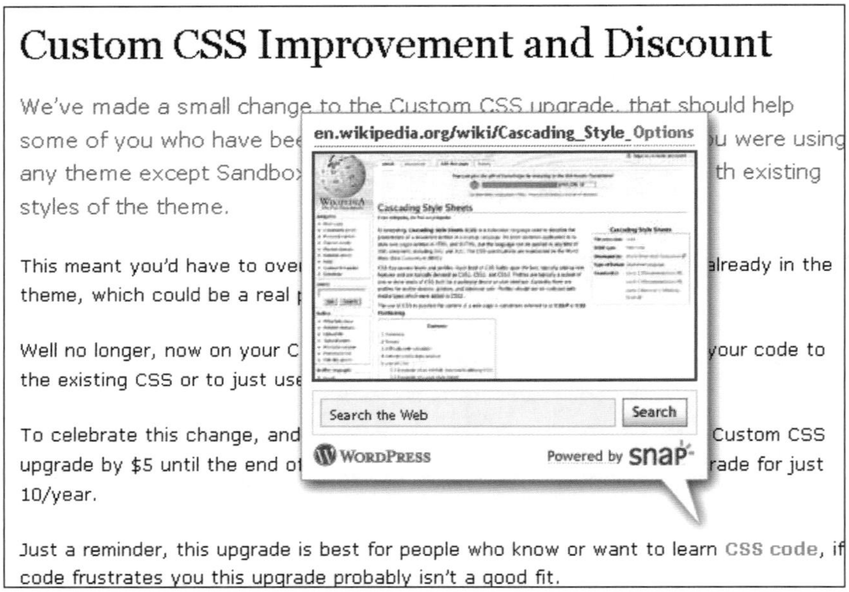

Custom CSS Improvement and Discount

We've made a small change to the Custom CSS upgrade, that should help some of you who have bee[...] you were using any theme except Sandbox[...] th existing styles of the theme.

This meant you'd have to over[...] already in the theme, which could be a real [...]

Well no longer, now on your C[...] your code to the existing CSS or to just use[...]

To celebrate this change, and[...] Custom CSS upgrade by $5 until the end of[...] rade for just 10/year.

Just a reminder, this upgrade is best for people who know or want to learn CSS code, if code frustrates you this upgrade probably isn't a good fit.

Figure 9-4 / The Snap preview plug-in for Firefox

Such small images provide little or no textual information themselves. Yet, visitors can identify a great deal about a site just from its basic layout—even in miniature form. People are able to recognize sites they already know immediately. With unknown sites, people may be able to deduce the genre (e.g., this is a news site, that's a blog) from just the thumbnail image. This provides additional cues that help with orientation.

When it comes to navigation, where it's located on the page and how it appears indicates its function. Navigation mechanisms should therefore work together as a logical visual system, along with all of the other page elements. Creating a consistent visual system aids in predictability and eases reorientation when navigating, providing a broader context for understanding content.

As you probably already noticed, page layout proves has many interdependencies. For instance, the number of options depends on the length of labels and vice versa. It's difficult to separate all of the elements that comprise navigation layout into discrete elements. Fields and disciplines overlap—a key reason why conflicting opinions are often heard at the point. This often requires revision and compromises in the design of the navigation system.

To prepare for change, start with a format that is easy to manipulate, such as with sticky notes or whiteboards. Try different arrangements of the mechanisms and navigation menus you'll need, and discuss these as a group. Explore alternatives, and weigh the trade-offs inherent in the design process.

STUDIES IN WEB PAGE LAYOUT

Unfortunately, there are no hard rules or industry standards for the layout of navigation to help you in this process. But, for better or for worse, researchers have attempted to uncover conventions in web design. Most notably, in 2001, Michael Bernard looked at where people expect common elements to appear on a page.[4] The 364 study participants indicated where they would normally find five common objects on a grid about the size of a web page. This test was repeated in 2005 for comparison over time.[5] The results of both tests are summarized in Table 9-1.

Table 9-1 / Comparison of study results for the location of common web objects, 2001 and 2005

Navigation element	Expected position, 2001	Expected position, 2005
Main navigation	Upper left side	Left side or along the top
Back to Home (i.e., linked logo)	Top left corner	Top left corner
Site Search (input field)	Upper center	Upper right or upper left
Advertisements	Top center	Top center or right side
External links	Right side or lower left	Not tested
About Us link	Not tested	In footer

As you can see, there is some consistency in expectations for the location of elements between these two studies. But there are also differences, bringing up an important wag-the-dog-type of question: should people's expectations guide design, or does web page design create the expectations? For instance, vertical advertisements started to appear right side of pages in the time between the two studies. Not surprisingly, people in the 2005 test expect ads to be located on the right.

---

4   Michael Bernard, "Developing Schemas for the Location of Common Web Objects," *Usability News* 3.1 (2001). *http://psychology.wichita.edu/surl/usabilitynews/3W/web_object.htm*.

5   A. Dawn Shaikh and Kelsi Lenz, "Where's the Search? Re-examining User Expectations of Web Objects," *Usability News* 8.1 (2006). *http://psychology.wichita.edu/surl/usabilitynews/81/webobjects.htm*.

Alternative locations of screen elements are not only possible, but quite common. In fact, Jared Spool found that the so-called "expected locations" of page elements had no effect on success in online shopping.[6] He tested 44 users on 13 sites in more than 1000 shopping expeditions. Participants had enough money to buy an item they wanted, and they were directed to sites where those items were available. The need to purchase a product and the means to do so were there, so any failure was due to problems in site design. Spool found no connection between sites that comply with Bernard's suggested schema and increased sales.

In the end, the position of navigation elements is situational. It's determined by the context you determined in the Analysis and Architecture phases. Conventions can be a useful starting point, but they don't dictate design.

Left- Versus Right-Side Navigation

If the main navigation is in the form of a vertical link list, popular practice strongly recommends placing it on the left side of the page. In redesigning the Audi web sites in 2002 (*www.audi.com* and *www.audi.de*), Razorfish Germany challenged the dominance of a left-hand navigation and placed the main navigation on the right (Figure 9-5). The key motivation was to distinguish the Audi sites from its competitors. They also wanted the core brand value of "innovation" to ring true to all parts of the site, including the navigation.

Figure 9-5 / The right-side navigation on the Audi.de site

---

6   Jared Spool, "Evolution trumps usability," *UIEtips* (September 2002). *www.uie.com/Articles/evolution_trumps_usability.htm*.

Before launching this nonstandard layout, we conducted extensive testing with 64 users. The tests compared a version of the site with left-side navigation to one with right-side navigation. Each test session consisted of three parts.

In Part 1, completion times for five tasks using the navigation were timed with a stopwatch. We believed there would be a significant difference in task completion time for the first task in the two versions of the site, but that by the last task there would be no significant difference. The expectation was that people would need to use the navigation a couple of times to learn how to use the right-side navigation, but the learning curve would be quick.

What we observed was surprising: there was no significant difference in completion times between the two navigation types for any task, including the first task. The right-side navigation actually performed better than the left in latter tasks.

In Part 2, we studied where participants focused their attention on the screen. We found that people tended to look at the content side of the page more with right navigation than with left navigation.

In Part 3, we showed both versions of the site to each participant and directly asked them what they thought of right-side navigation. Seven out of the sixty-four people tested actually preferred the right navigation to the left navigation, while only two disliked it. But a majority of participants were indifferent: they didn't seem to care one way or the other. In fact, most didn't seem to notice that the navigation was on the right or the left; they were focused the task at hand.

Subsequent usability tests and post-launch user feedback corroborate these findings: There is no apparent difficulty using a right-side menu to navigate the Audi.com and Audi.de sites. From the layout of the page itself, it is clear what is navigation and what is not. With a specific goal in mind, the position of the main navigation on the right—though technically non-standard—poses no problem.

This does not mean that all sites should have right-side navigation, however. A left navigation may work best in many cases. If a situation can benefit from a right navigation, it is entirely possible to design a site that utilizes one without sacrificing usability. Many weblogs, for instance, do well with a right-side navigation. More importantly, we were able to leverage a deviation in so-called standards to set Audi apart from its competitors and project an innovative brand image.

For more details on Parts 1 and 3 of this study see: James Kalbach and Tim Bosenick, "Web Page Layout: A Comparison Between Left- and Right-Justified Site Navigation Menus," Journal of Digital Information 4, 1 (April 2003). *http://jodi.ecs.soton.ac.uk/Articles/v04/i01/Kalbach*. *Results from Part 2 of the study have not been published elsewhere.*

The human eye naturally groups objects together. Called the Gestalt Effect, this phenomenon was first studied and documented by psychologists in Berlin around the beginning of the 20th century. It refers to processes by which people perceive combined forms and shapes from individual elements.

For example, Figure 9-6 shows four circles, each with the right angle removed. If you focus on just one by covering the others up with your hand, you just see the individual shape. However, when viewed together, a fifth shape emerges—a square nested between the circles.

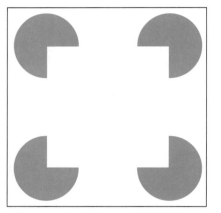

Figure 9-6 / An example of the Gestalt Effect

There are several causes of this effect, many of which are relevant to web page layout, including:

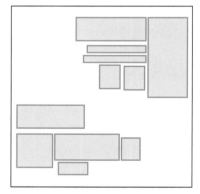

Figure 9-7 / Proximity

Proximity

Objects that are closer to one another than other objects form a shape for the group. By clustering elements together in Figure 9-7, two larger regions of page elements emerge.

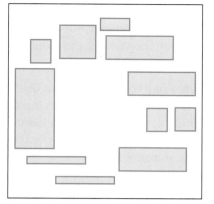

Figure 9-8 / Closure

Closure

The human eye will add missing elements to complete a shape or layout. The objects in Figure 9-8, for instance, suggest a ring, though none of them actually touch one another.

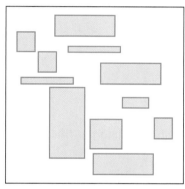

Figure 9-9 / Continuity

Continuity

A pattern can appear to extend even after it stops. In Figure 9-9, diagonal lines seem to continue across the page based on the pattern set up by the arrangement of shapes.

Figure 9-10 / Similarity

Similarity

People associate elements that have similar properties. In Figure 9-10, the different orange shapes appear to be related and share a commonality.

ALIGNMENT

Combining these principles of Gestalt Theory can have a very powerful effect on page layout. For instance, if you place similar elements close together in a way that gives them closure and continuity, the resulting visual display can be clear and strong.

Figure 9-11 illustrates how the arrangement of elements creates recognizable patterns, in this case using the same component shapes as in Figures 9-7 through 9-10. If this were a web page, the dark green boxes on the right might resemble a vertical navigation menu, and the blue elements at the top might be identified as main navigation elements. The orange figures on the left suggest text content with small photos. Each of these three areas reflects principles of proximity, closure, continuity, and similarity.

Figure 9-11 / Aligning page elements to create visual relationships

The placement of navigation menus and options on the page should convey an overall logic. This greatly adds to intuitiveness and understanding of the system in general.

BALANCE

When laying out navigation, you must also consider the balance of all elements on the page. This is often an asymmetrical balance, with the largest portion of the screen devoted to the main topic or idea of the page. For navigational pages, the attention should be navigation options, such as a directory or site map that fills most of the page. For content and functional pages, focus on content and functionality respectively.

Consider the page from the Toyota web site (*www.toyota.com*) shown in Figure 9-12. The main navigation across the top and local navigation on the left are minimal. This page has a fairly good balance: About 75 percent of the page is devoted to content, indicated by the light blue area. The navigation occupies only about 25 percent of the screen, shown in orange in Figure 9-12. This creates a clear focus on the main purpose of the page—the product details—while providing sufficient navigation to meet user and business needs.

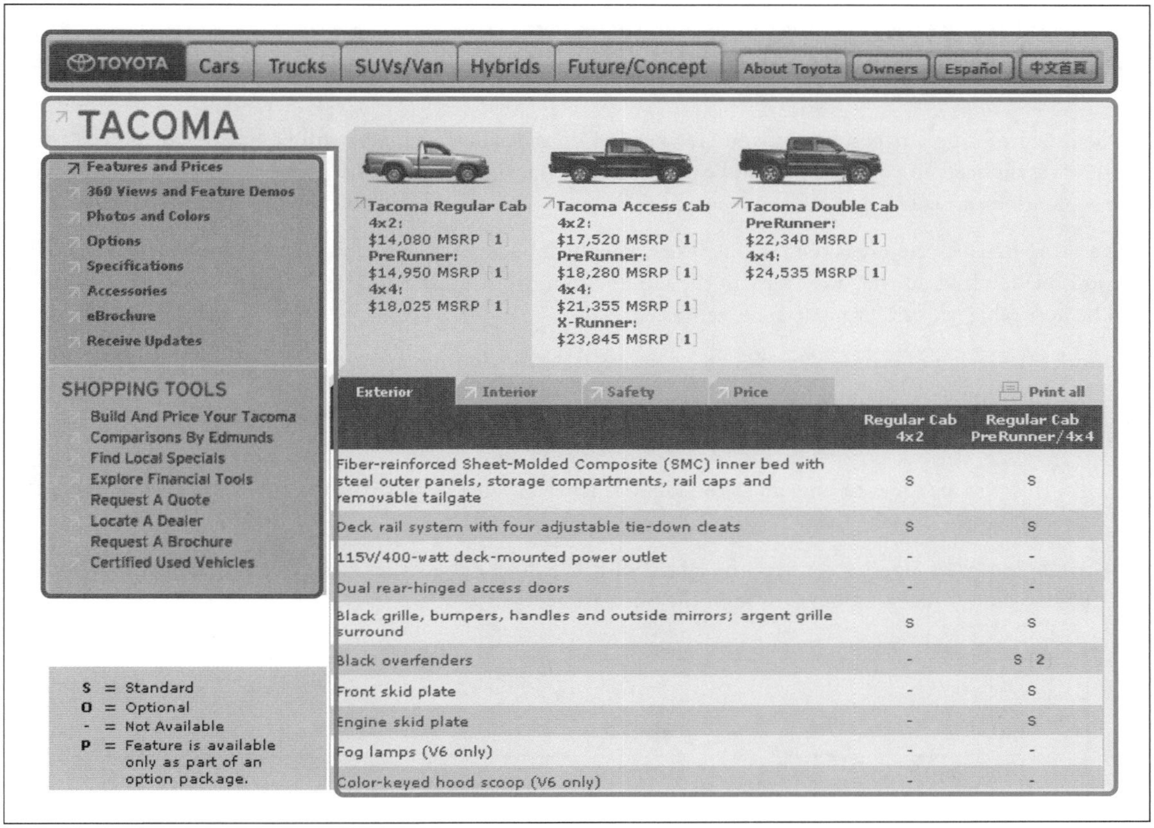

A web page screenshot showing a Toyota Tacoma configurator interface.

TOYOTA | Cars | Trucks | SUVs/Van | Hybrids | Future/Concept | About Toyota | Owners | Español | 中文首页

↗ TACOMA

↗ **Features and Prices**
↗ 360 Views and Feature Demos
↗ Photos and Colors
↗ Options
↗ Specifications
↗ Accessories
↗ eBrochure
↗ Receive Updates

SHOPPING TOOLS
Build And Price Your Tacoma
Comparisons By Edmunds
Find Local Specials
Explore Financial Tools
Request A Quote
Locate A Dealer
Request A Brochure
Certified Used Vehicles

↗ **Tacoma Regular Cab**
4x2:
$14,080 MSRP [1]
PreRunner:
$14,950 MSRP [1]
4x4:
$18,025 MSRP [1]

↗ **Tacoma Access Cab**
4x2:
$17,520 MSRP [1]
PreRunner:
$18,280 MSRP [1]
4x4:
$21,355 MSRP [1]
X-Runner:
$23,845 MSRP [1]

↗ **Tacoma Double Cab**
PreRunner:
$22,340 MSRP [1]
4x4:
$24,535 MSRP [1]

S = Standard
O = Optional
- = Not Available
P = Feature is available only as part of an option package.

Exterior	↗ Interior	↗ Safety	↗ Price	🖶 Print all	
				Regular Cab 4x2	Regular Cab PreRunner/4x4
Fiber-reinforced Sheet-Molded Composite (SMC) inner bed with steel outer panels, storage compartments, rail caps and removable tailgate				S	S
Deck rail system with four adjustable tie-down cleats				S	S
115V/400-watt deck-mounted power outlet				-	-
Dual rear-hinged access doors				-	-
Black grille, bumpers, handles and outside mirrors; argent grille surround				S	S
Black overfenders				-	S [2]
Front skid plate				-	S
Engine skid plate				-	S
Fog lamps (V6 only)				-	-
Color-keyed hood scoop (V6 only)				-	-

Figure 9-12 / Balancing content with navigation

Accessibility

Screen readers don't read web pages in the same order as the elements are displayed on screen. Instead, they read pages in the order that the code is written. This is referred to as *linearization*, or making out the page code from top to bottom in sequential order.

When determining a page's layout, you also need to consider how the page will be linearized. To test this, turn off stylesheets in your browser and check to see if the page still makes sense. Also be sure to run pages through a screen reader to check that the audio "layout" is as comprehensible as the visual layout.

One thing to check closely is the tabbing order. People not using a mouse don't have random access to navigation menus. Instead they may rely on the tab key to move from one link to the next in sequential order. To be accessible, this order must make sense.

Consider the layout of drop-downs shown in Figure 9-13. Depending on how the page is programmed, there might be two possible tabbing orders.

- The correct order would be "label 1 > dropdown 1," "label 2 > dropdown 2," and "label 3 > dropdown 3."

- But it's also possible to end up with "label 1, label 2, label 3" and then "dropdown 1, dropdown 2, dropdown 3."

If the tabbing order doesn't connect the labels with the drop-downs they describe, the navigation may be completely useless when tabbing through the navigation.

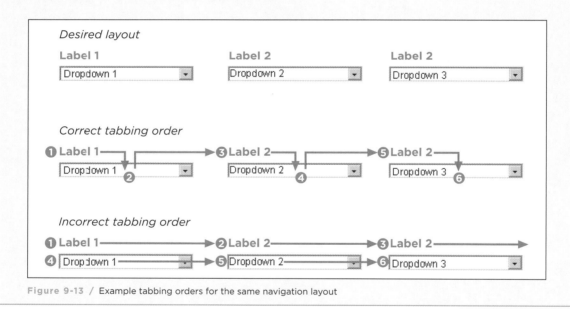

Figure 9-13 / Example tabbing orders for the same navigation layout

PAGE TEMPLATES

When dealing with large web sites, it's quite impossible to hand-design the layout of thousands of pages, nor is this desirable. Instead, rules are put in place to govern the display of navigation and content. These rules are captured in what are called page templates.

Templates are predefined collections and arrangements of navigation mechanisms. Note that two or more mechanisms may come together to form a larger navigational module. For instance, the global navigation area may consist of a linked logo, the main navigation tabs, and utility links. Within the template scheme, this may be represented as a single element, rather than three separate mechanisms. Your template design can then refer to the global navigation module as a single unit rather than three separate mechanisms.

A template-based approach is important for consistency: it ensures that a related links module, for instance, will always appear the same way across pages of the site. Templates also allow for reuse of modules, facilitating implementation. It may not be necessary to redesign and reprogram common modules, but instead you can use them again as needed. This approach requires a modular concept to the layout: you must be able to abstract navigation rules across pages.

NAVIGATION RULES

Navigation design for large sites is really about creating a formula for which navigation options appear on pages. It is a mapping of navigation mechanisms, types, and modules to form the overall navigation system. In creating this system you need to consider such things as:

Display of navigation modules

> A template definition indicates all of the modules that could possibly appear on a page. You need to indicate which are mandatory and which are not.

Position of navigation mechanisms

> Navigation modules tend to stay in a constant position on the page. But you need to account for how the layout will adjust if a given module is not present. And occasionally, a module may have variable positions. For instance, a related links component may appear on the left or right side of the page, depending on the page type and its location in the site.

Limits

> The rules of navigation templates also need to account for upper and lower limits. For instance, you may have associative navigation that usually shows three to four related links. But what happens if there are ten? You may need to include a "See more related content..." link at the bottom of the mechanism to expand it and reveal more options.

Figure 9-14 shows a rudimentary definition of a template for a product page on an e-commerce site. This reflects some of the elements that define a template. Modules are numbered throughout the site, beginning with the letter "M." Each module is then indicated as mandatory or optional. Also indicated are some simple display rules for handling a shift in layout due to an optional module not appearing.

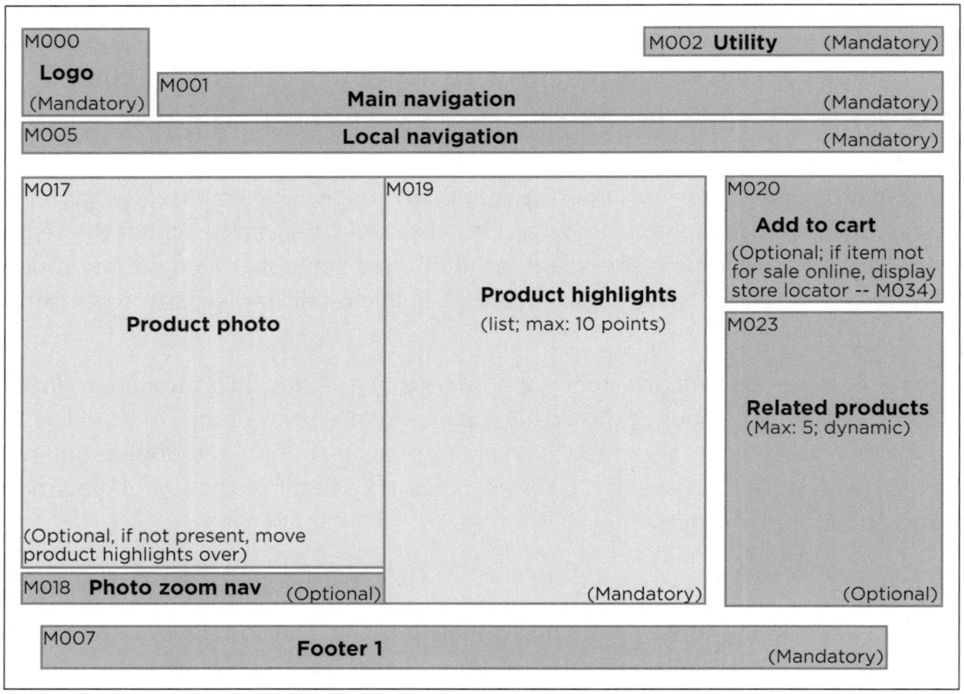

Figure 9-14 / A simple page template showing navigation rules

Note that the rules for navigation apply only to this template. For instance, here the main navigation is mandatory. During the checkout process, however, it may not be mandatory for those screens, as seen on Amazon.com and other e-commerce sites.

Content management systems (CMS), mentioned briefly in Chapter 7, generally require such an approach to page layout. If you are working with a CMS, you'll be dealing with templates on some level. But keep in mind that templates bring a certain boxed-in consistency that may be too rigorous for situations in which variation is needed. Sometimes one size doesn't fit all, particularly when dealing with navigating information. You may need to make exceptions that strict rule-based systems won't allow for. Therefore, strive to account for as much flexibility as you need from the very beginning.

VARYING NAVIGATION

Consistent page templates are critical for predictability in navigation. But too much consistency can also be detrimental. If the navigation areas look and behave exactly the same on every page, visitors may actually become more disoriented than with a navigation system that varies subtly. Changing navigation menus provides a sense of progression through the site, and in terms of layout, this is largely determined by the system of page templates you create.

A common technique is to vary the balance of navigation to content the deeper you go in site. For example, compare the three pages from the U.S. National Park Service (NPS) web site (*www.nps.gov*) shown in Figures 9-15 through 9-17.

Figure 9-15 shows the NPS home page. The navigational elements include a main navigation as a vertical menu on the left and a utility navigation below that. In the center is a park finder tool—the primary feature of the page. A simple search field then appears in the middle.

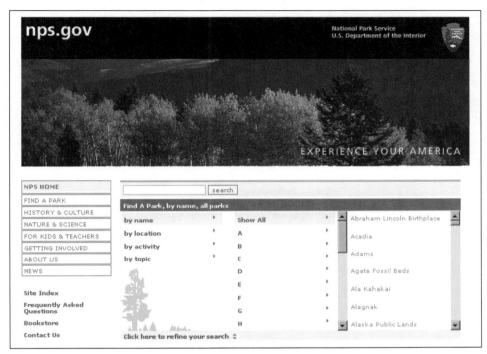

Figure 9-15 / The U.S. National Park Service home page

Figure 9-16 shows the main page for Yosemite National Park, one level down from the home page. The layout has changed in important ways from the home page. The first thing you may notice is that the banner across the top now includes an image from Yosemite, in the area where a large image was displayed on the home page. In terms of navigation, the NPS site name in the upper left is now linked to the home page. The search feature has wandered up to the left a little and includes additional options to search within this park or across the whole site. And the main navigation on the left has now become the local navigation for this park.

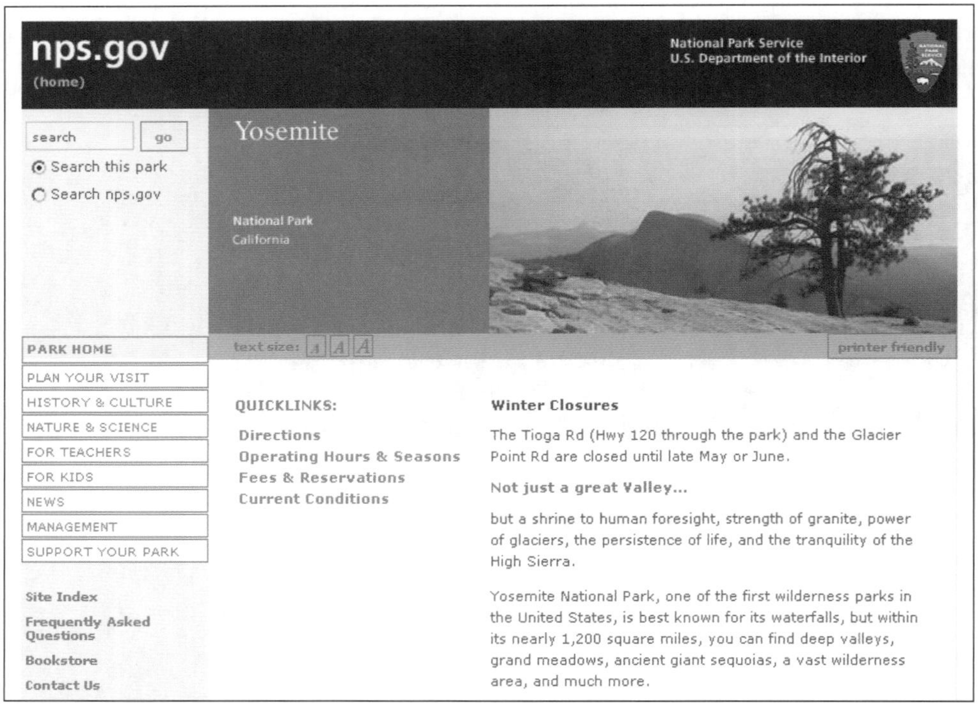

Figure 9-16 / The main page for Yosemite National Park

Moving deeper into the site structure, Figure 9-17 shows the Directions page for Yosemite, one level down from the park's main page. Here, the size of the photo is yet smaller, allowing more room for page content. The local navigation on the left is expanded to reveal the sub-categories within this section. Links within the select sub-category are repeated at the top of the content on the right.

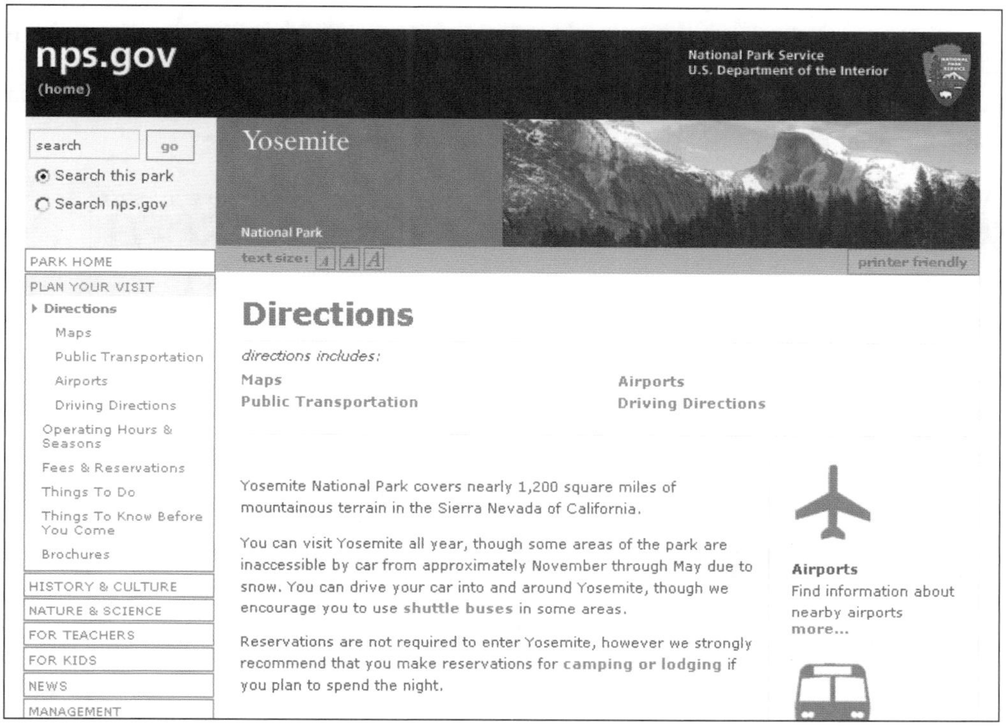

Figure 9-17 / The page for Directions within the Yosemite section of the NPS web site

SHOWING PROGRESSION

This example is just part of a pattern of page templates that pervade the entire NPS site. Each national park uses essentially the same template, so the navigation is consistent throughout the site. But at the same time, the templates vary within the site to show different navigation options or to put more emphasis on page content, as needed. Figure 9-18 illustrates this progression of change in the basic template from the three previous NPS pages.

Figure 9-18 / Changes in navigation and layout create a sense of progression

The NPS reflects a typical approach, but other approaches are possible. It's quite common, for instance, for home pages to have a completely different layout than other pages of the site, sometimes without a main navigation bar. Instead, the main categories of the site are accessed through the embedded links and associative navigation in the body of the page itself.

For example, Figure 9-19 shows the home page of Ma.gnolia.com, an online tagging service. There is no main navigation bar on this page. Instead, all of the options to other areas of the site are content in the body of the page. Clicking the word "discuss" in the first sentence, for instance, leads to the page shown in Figure 9-20. Here, there is a main navigation bar with "Discussions" highlighted in a different color in the main navigation. The other areas of the site are accessible from these links as well.

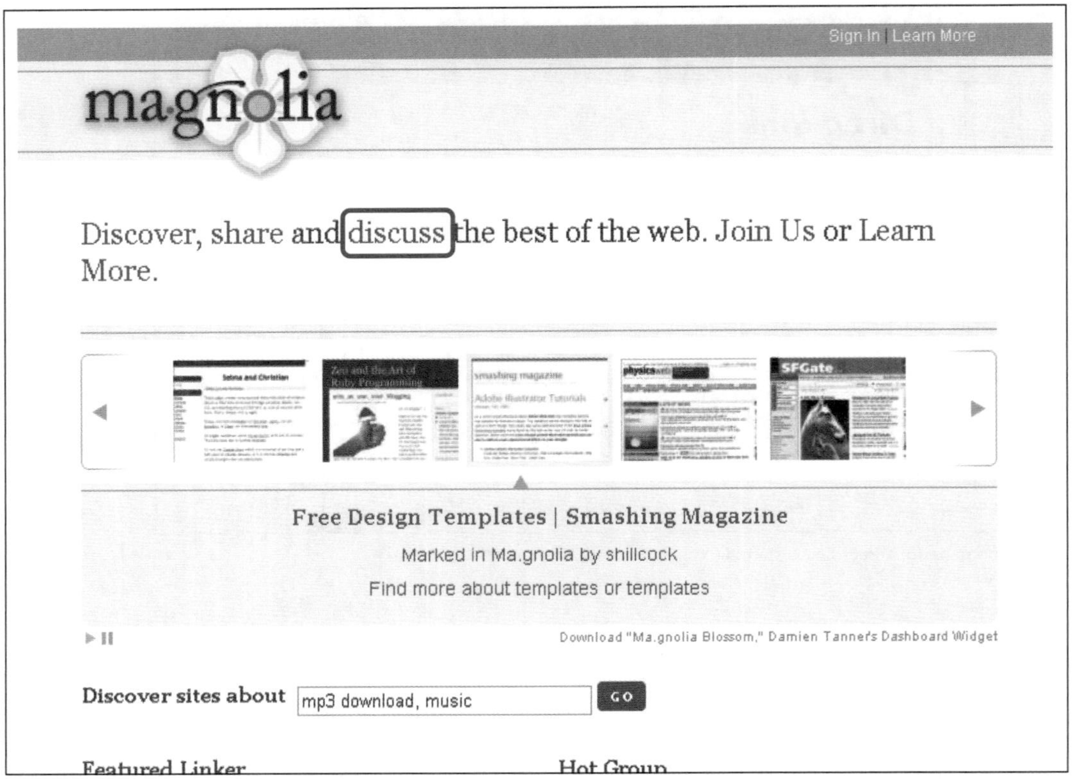

Figure 9-19 / The home page for Ma.gnolia.com without a main navigation

Figure 9-20 / A main navigation appears on pages below the home page on Ma.gnolia.com

This approach creates a natural focus on the content of the home page: to navigate further, visitors must initially engage with the home page text. This may overcome navigation blindness on the home page because no navigation area is visually isolated from the body of the page. This also mirrors how people tend to encounter new pages: they focus on the content first. By merging the navigation with the content, navigating this site may come more naturally to visitors. Then, once visitors are pages one level below the home page, a main navigation is offered to allow for movement across the areas of the site.

Note that these types of layout techniques may never be consciously recognized by visitors. But their value is still important to the overall navigation system. If used effectively, such variations in the position, balance, and appearance of navigation menus and navigation areas can guide users through the site naturally.

What's more, other techniques for showing progression and a change in navigation can also be applied to support template variations. Color and color-coding can reflect changes in navigation, discussed in the next chapter. Or, photos used throughout a site can move from wide-angle shots to close-ups the deeper you navigate in a site. Again, the boundaries of navigation design extend into other design disciplines and reveal many interdependencies.

WIREFRAMES

In the broadest sense of the word, *wireframes* are preliminary sketches of pages. They show the skeleton of the navigation system independent of the final visual design, or the primary layer of basic information needed on each page. Wireframes are a visual tool for working out how you will progress from the requirements, concept, and site map to designed pages. They allow you to deconstruct the problem and propose appropriate solutions. A primary function of wireframes is to capture your page template layouts.

There are different approaches to creating wireframes. Some aspects you should consider are:

Fidelity

As with prototypes, there are high-fidelity and low-fidelity wireframes. Low-fidelity wireframes may not even show layout. Instead they may just be a list of navigation types, content, and the functionality needed for each page. High-fidelity wireframes might clearly suggest a final design, including the size and position of navigational elements. Most web designers create wireframes that fall somewhere in between high- and low-fidelity wireframes.

Display of labels and text

One school of thought suggests using dummy text for wireframes. This is often referred to as "Greeked" text. The advantage to this approach is that other team members won't focus on the content, just the structure of the pages themselves. The other school seeks to reflect representative content in the wireframes. This can catch layout issues caused by long labels and dynamic texts before you implement the site. This is good for user testing or presenting to stakeholders. If you use this approach, don't include temporary working labels for the navigation. Show the navigation texts as they should appear in the final site as early as you can.

Format

There is a range of formats for creating wireframes—everything from using paper to a high-end graphics program. Frequently you'll have a mix of both: at first you might sketch pages on paper, and then later capture these with a program. HTML wireframes are also possible and offer the advantage of linking pages together. This allows you to check how pages transition from one to another, or to check the "feel" of the site without the "look."

Figure 9-21 shows an example a typical wireframe, in this case the gallery page for an online shop. Created in Microsoft Visio, it includes a mix of navigation labels: some are specific, while others are generic. The generic labels change from page to page. The specific labels, such as those in the utility navigation in the top right, are constant throughout the site.

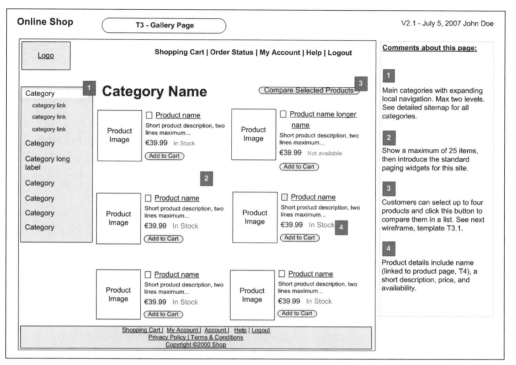

Figure 9-21 / A typical wireframe created in Microsoft Visio

Wireframes precede final page designs, but they don't dictate every aspect of the page layout. Visual designers still have the flexibility to alter the page layout to a degree. The exact alignment or placement of elements can vary depending the content, requirements, and design elements. Just as moving from a site's architecture to a layout might require negotiation between the two, moving from wireframes to the final presentation also calls for give and take.

CREATING WIREFRAMES

Wireframes bring many pieces of the site together and present them visually. This is a vital step in the design process, representing a significant move from the abstract to the concrete. In creating wireframes, you need to coordinate three primary sources of information:

Site map

The site map will show a great deal about the navigation on each page, particularly structural navigation. This is usually a key starting point when plotting out the navigation in wireframes.

Requirements

Identify the requirements that affect the screen designs of the site. For instance, there may be a branding requirement that the logo appear on all pages. There may be a legal requirement to have terms and conditions throughout the site. Requirements about functionality must also be considered, such as an ever-present search feature or shopping cart, and so forth. These must be captured in wireframes. Of course, if the requirements have been informed by user research, the needs of your site visitors should also be represented.

During the content analysis, various aspects of the content you are organizing were identified. You may know about page metadata that needs to be exposed, as well as special content formats. For instance, if there is an embedded video or link to a PDF file on a page or page template, you need to reflect that in the wireframe. A good content analysis will also give you a much better sense of issues such as title lengths, text lengths, and simply the amount of information that needs to go on any one page.

Of course, discussions with stakeholders, business goals, vision, brand, and user needs should be considered as well. Creating wireframes consolidates many types of information and activities conducted up to this point. To summarize, the following sections outline the steps in the process of creating wireframes.

START WITH THE GOAL

To better align the navigation with how people will be using your site, again, start designing with content pages. For each page type, position the main feature of the page prominently. Using personas and scenarios, work out the primary navigation needs and design the mechanisms based on that.

As you move on to the next page type, build off of what you've already established. This may mean going back and changing your initial system of navigation, as well as changing your site map. As you learn more and more about how the system fits together, you must adjust accordingly. The goal is to weave all of these bits into a consistent navigation system.

EXPLORE ALTERNATIVES

Wireframes are a design tool. They allow you to explore different directions without much penalty. Take advantage of their changeability and don't be afraid to take a completely different approach for an alternative design. Creating good navigation doesn't just happen all at once in a linear fashion. Instead, it's the sum of exploring lots of ideas—including some bad ones—before you reach a final design.

Creating wireframes isn't a solitary activity either. Rely on the creativity of your whole team to explore alternatives as much as possible. Brainstorm different navigation models as a group. It's a process of going back and forth—revising wireframes, comparing them to project requirements, and then checking them with others as you go.

For these reasons, wireframes often begin with a pen and paper. Start sketching pages freely, combining all that you know on the page. Sticky notes on a whiteboard work well too, allowing for collaboration with others. Of course, you can capture initial alternatives electronically, but that can take more time and might feel less changeable than paper.

PRESENT WIREFRAMES

Wireframes are a communication tool. They facilitate conversation with the client and translate the requirements back to the team. Graphic designers can refer to wireframes to see all the screen elements for each page and the relative importance of each. Programmers can also use them for data modeling and functional requirements. Also consider offering alternative designs when you present, and then discuss the pros and cons of each.

Whether you develop high-fidelity or low-fidelity wireframes depends on your audience. External clients may expect more detailed, polished designs. This requires more effort on your part, of course, and can lead to more attention paid to the appearance of wireframes rather than the ideas they are trying to communicate. On the other hand, internal teams may be fine with rough, low-fidelity sketches. Identify the target audience for your wireframes before you begin and create them accordingly. In any event, wireframes should suggest unfinished designs.

REFINE AND UPDATE

Wireframes should be kept fairly flexible, since you need to plan for change. Things will shift around as you come across new information, constraints, and requirements. Suddenly, there may be a new requirement to promote new products on content pages. Or, it may not be technically possible to implement a feature as initially planned. You need to be able to react without creating extra rework for yourself.

What's more, wireframes are often superseded by other project deliverables. Screen designs or an HTML prototype may be created in later phases. As with all project documentation, you don't want to update many documents just to make a small change. Instead, you may even plan for wireframes to be frozen at a certain point in the project. It depends on your situation and how all the deliverables are interrelated, but be clear about the role of wireframes within the overall project before you begin. Don't spend more time on them than you have to.

SUMMARY

Laying out pages is a critical point in the design process when many pieces come together. Abstract aspects of the site design, such as business goals or site structure, become more tangible once navigation menus and content appear on pages. This is often when potentially conflicting opinions from the development team come out. To steer discussions toward a common goal, a systematic approach to laying out the navigation options can help.

Site navigation provides a narrative for people to follow to get to the content they are looking for. Though labels and text clearly play a role in guiding people through your site, the layout of navigation communicates a great deal about its purpose and function.

In laying out web navigation, begin with end pages that people are searching for, not with the home page. Using personas and scenarios, determine the navigation your target groups will need to get to and from key pages. Don't try to reproduce the entire site structure. Instead, include only the key navigational elements. Provide enough information scent so that your visitors can navigate effectively without overwhelming them. Also consider how people will get to your important content pages, and plan ahead on other pages.

The visual logic of the page must consider all design elements, of course, including text and graphic elements. But the visual relationships you create are critical for navigation. People can make out the function and role of page elements instantly. Further, the final presentation of the site navigation also communicates a great deal about the role and purpose it plays, discussed further in the next chapter (Chapter 10).

Page templates capture your navigation system and the rules by which it appears and behaves. Templates are advantageous for consistency, but can also lead to inflexibility when variation is called for. Ultimately, the design of templates should vary the position, labels, and behavior of navigation areas in a way that creates a flow and sense of movement through the site.

Wireframes are key deliverables in creating page layouts. They reflect much of the project requirements and other information gathered to date, and they show how you will coordinate the macro and micro actions of a persuasive architecture (Chapter 8). Wireframes are a key tool in navigation design that allow you to explore alternatives. Judicious use of them will make implementing your design much smoother.

QUESTIONS

1. Visit any well-known online shopping or auction site, such as Amazon or eBay, and navigate to a product you're interested in purchasing. You don't have to actually buy the product, but from the home page, sketch the approximate layout of the pages you encounter as rough wireframes using simple shapes. Then answer the following questions:

   a) What are the different page types you come across? (See Chapter 4 for a list of page types.)

   b) How do the elements vary and move position from page to page?

   c) How does variation in page templates help or hurt navigation?

2. Find the web site of your local newspaper. Select any article that interests you. Without scrolling down, answer the following questions:

   a) What percentage of screen is devoted to navigation? To the newspaper article? To other elements?

   b) Is this a balanced layout? What could be better?

3. Study the two images of CNN (Figures 9-22 and 9-23). The first is the home page; the second is the technology section page, which is reached by clicking Technology. How does the main navigation transition from one page to the other? What are the differences and similarities between the navigation on both pages? What are the advantages and disadvantages of such a transition?

Figure 9-22 / The CNN.com home page

Figure 9-23 / The Technology section of CNN, one level down from the home page

FURTHER READING

Communicating Design: Developing Web Site Documentation for Design and Planning, by Dan M. Brown (New Riders, 2006).

This is a practical book with a clear focus: creating design documentation. Brown covers ten design deliverables in detail, including site maps, flowcharts, wireframes, and screen designs. This is a very hands-on book that goes into great detail of creating design deliverables with many good examples. It's highly recommended.

Homepage Usability: 50 Websites Deconstructed, by Jakob Nielsen and Marie Tahir (New Riders, 2000).

Based on analysis of home pages from 50 different sites, this book presents guidelines for creating home pages. The authors first present the guidelines, and then a detailed analysis of each home page analyzed. In doing so, they illustrate many principles of page layout, particularly balancing content, navigation, and other elements.

Information Architecture for Designers: Structuring Websites for Business Success, by Peter Van Dijck (RotoVision, 2003).

This is a very visual book with many images and diagrams. It covers a gamut of topics surrounding information architecture in general. There is a brief, but very good section on wireframes. Many case studies throughout this book bring the theoretical and procedural explanations to life.

Presentation

IN THIS CHAPTER

- Information and graphic design
- Visual hierarchy and text as an interface
- Sizing navigation elements
- Underlined links and rollovers
- Color coding navigation
- Designing and using icons
- Communicating navigation designs to other team members

People like context-rich information. How we find, organize, and even understand information is influenced by how it's displayed. Content that is presented with color, texture, and style has relevance to our work and to our lives. The visual treatment of navigation is not merely a "nice-to-have," but crucial to its perception and use. It can be the difference between usable and not usable, between credible and not credible, or between found and not-found.

In determining how to present navigation, the design process once again proves to be multidisciplinary. You must bring together divergent perspectives from team members and reconcile differences. Clear goals and a solid navigation concept help build a common understanding, but you can still expect conflicting opinions at this stage.

The visual presentation of navigation is also interdependent on other aspects of its design, such as navigation types, labels, and page layout. This means going back and forth between elements of your navigation and making compromises as needed. The maximum number of horizontal tabs, for instance, depends on the font size, labeling, position, and spacing of options. This, in turn, must synch up with the architecture of the site. Navigation design is never a linear process from beginning to end.

The overall aim of the Presentation phase is to visually guide visitors through the navigation system and to enhance the overall information experience. This involves three larger areas of concern, each discussed separately in this chapter:

- Information design
- Interacting with navigation
- Graphic design

INFORMATION DESIGN

Broadly defined, *information design* deals with the display of information to make it easier to use and understand by humans. The field draws on graphic design, typography, linguistics, psychology, ergonomics, computing, and other related areas. Information design is a wide-ranging discipline that considers both offline and online media. In terms of web design, it is concerned with the clarity information and with enhancing the understanding of your site's navigation and content.

Edward Tufte, professor emeritus at Yale University, has done some of the most important work in information design. He is best known for his three books: *The Visual Display of Quantitative Information*, *Envisioning Information,* and *Visual Explanations*. Above all else, Tufte teaches that content should be allowed to speak for itself, with as little ornamentation as possible.

A few principles of information design espoused by Tufte are particularly relevant to navigation design:

Negative space

Areas on the page that contain links, text, and images are called positive spaces. Negative spaces are the areas in between. These two work together visually. Areas of positive space that are near each other, but not touching, can give the illusion of a third shape between them. Such negative space adds to the clutter effect of a page and may be detrimental to your design. The example in Figure 10-1 demonstrates that the proximity of the three black bars gives the illusion that two white bars exist between them. Use the white space in your layout to your advantage and avoid creating the perception of unnecessary elements on the page.

Figure 10-1 / Negative space between the bars

Chartjunk

Chartjunk, a term Tufte coined, refers to anything unnecessary in an information display. Often people think they are enhancing information with added graphics and lines, when their additions only detract from it. A simple example of chartjunk is a table with dark grid lines. Unless the reader's focus should be on the table itself, lighter lines allow the information on the page to be scanned and read more quickly.

The navigation in the travel section of Otto.de, Germany's largest catalogue retailer, has issues with both chartjunk and negative space (Figure 10-2). Lines between the navigation options on the left are chartjunk: they appear even darker than the text labels, acting as visual "speed bumps" when scanning the menu. On the right side, negative space between the components adds to the visual complexity of the page. Together, these two problems detract from the navigation of the site, instead of enhancing it.

Figure 10-2 / Chartjunk in the form of extra lines between navigation options (left) and negative space between components (center) on Otto.de

Layering

An information display, like web navigation, can have visual depth. Some elements may stand more in the foreground than others. If used effectively, layering navigation is important to show the priority of options and guide visitors through the site. You can achieve layering by using different sized headlines and through the use of color or background shading, among other things. The goal is to create a visual hierarchy of elements on the page.

Layering can help when scanning many navigation options at once. For example, Figure 10-3 shows the site map that appears on the bottom of most pages on the Skype web site (*www.skype.com*). On one level, it's clear that this is a site map and if you don't need it, you can skip over the whole thing. Category headers then allow you scan and zoom in on options within a given topic. In this image, the Download section is highlighted and darker than the other areas of the site map, providing yet another visual layer of options. Finally, underlining the link directly under the cursor reveals another, more granular layer of focus (i.e., the link to be clicked). Layering allows users to view this on different levels: the site map as a whole, just the individual sections, and then the individual links.

Download	Call phones	Share	Shop	Help	Skype in your country and language
Skype	SkypeOut	Skype stories	Headsets	FAQs	Български
Skype Mobile	SkypeIn	Skype buttons	Starter kits	User guides	Česky
Skype Web Toolbar	Skype Voicemail	Tell a friend	Phones	Announcements	Dansk
Skype Email Toolbar	Skype SMS	Gifts	Webcams	Support requests	Deutsch
	Skype Zones	Extras	Merchandise	Ways to pay	Eesti
	Personalise Skype	Skypecasts Beta	Accessories guide	Pricing overview	English
	Gift Certificates				Español
	Skype Control panel				Français
					Italiano
					Latviešu
About us	Partners	Blogs	Forums	Business	Lietuvių
Skype news	Affiliates	Skype Beta	Forum overview	Skype for Business	Magyar
Security	Developers	Life at Skype	Support	Skype Control panel	Nederlands
Jobs	Online	Around the World	Suggestions	Business Blog	Norsk
Contact us	Hardware	Developer Zone	General discussion	Extras for Business	Polski
	Retail	Partners	Stories		Português (BR)
	Access		Skype Me!		Português (PT)
					Русский
					Suomi
					Svenska
					Türkçe
					日本語
					한국어
					中文（简体）
					中文（繁体）
					All languages...

Figure 10-3 / Layering of navigation on the Skype site

TYPOGRAPHY AND TEXT DESIGN

Typography refers to the selection of letter forms and the general design of text.

A key issue to consider when designing online typography is that reading from a computer screen is difficult, due to low resolution. Text in print media can be rendered at 1200 dots per inch (dpi) or higher. Computer screens generally don't show more than 85 dpi. This is a primary reason why people prefer to print out pages when they need to read longer passages. Eye fatigue is a major contributor to poor readability from computers as well. Reading text on a screen is simply more difficult than reading from paper.

But not only is reading from a computer screen harder, people also tend to skim web pages quickly. The typography of your web navigation should therefore facilitate scanning and generally improve legibility as much as possible. There are several aspects to consider here:

Font

There are two major types of fonts: serif and sans serif (Figure 10-4). Serifs are those short lines at the end of a main character stroke. Serif typefaces are popularly considered better for print media. But because of the low resolution of computer screens, serifs may produce jagged-looking edges leading to an unclear appearance. Sans serif fonts, on the other hand, lend themselves better to computer screens and are generally recommended for text on the Web.

Studies of online fonts at the Software Usability Research Laboratory and Wichita State University in Kansas show that Arial and Verdana are the preferred fonts for online text.[1] The researchers also found that people associate different "moods" with certain fonts. Courier and Times appear businesslike, for instance. Match the appropriate font to the type of site you're dealing with and use it to reinforce the brand.

The quick brown fox jumps over the lazy dog. (Times New Roman)
The quick brown fox jumps over the lazy dog. (Georgia)
The quick brown fox jumps over the lazy dog. (Courier)

The quick brown fox jumps over the lazy dog. (Arial)
The quick brown fox jumps over the lazy dog. (Verdana)
The quick brown fox jumps over the lazy dog. (Trebuchet)

Figure 10-4 / Examples of common serif fonts (top) and sans serif fonts (bottom)

Case

Generally, text written in all capital letters is harder to read than mixed-case text.[2] People perceive the shapes of words as a whole when reading, not each individual letter. The physical profile of mixed-cased words is important for perceiving words as units. In certain instances, however, using all capital letters is acceptable, particularly for individual words or phrases that have sufficient background contrast. It's therefore debatable whether all caps is appropriate for single-word labels of a navigation menu.

If you suspect that capitalizing all the letters of navigation labels might make scanning them more difficult, use mixed case. And don't assume that capitalizing all the letters in navigation labels will always draw more attention to them. Just the opposite may be true; because all caps can be harder to read, people may overlook them.

Size

With limited screen real estate, it's often tempting to choose a small font size for your navigation labels. This might allow you to fit more options in a horizontal navigation bar, for instance. But if text is too small, reading and scanning is impeded. Anything smaller than 10 points or equivalent may be too small to read effectively by many people, and 12-point fonts are generally preferred.[3]

Varying font sizes is also vital to creating a visual hierarchy within the navigation. The main navigation is typically larger than local navigation, and footer navigation and utility navigation may be smaller than local navigation, for instance. Contrasts in font size can instill a sense of relative importance to navigation mechanisms, giving them a clearer function.

1   Bernard, Michael, Melissa Mills, Michelle Peterson, and Kelsey Storrer. "A Comparison of Popular Online Fonts: Which is Best and When?" *Usability News*, 3.2 (2001). *http://psychology.wichita.edu/surl/usabilitynews/3S/font.htm*.

2   Patrick Lynch and Sarah Horton, Web Style Guide, Second Edition (Yale University Press, March 2002). *www.webstyleguide.com/type/case.html*.

3   Bernard, Michael, Shannon Riley, Telia Hackler, and Karen Janzen. "A Comparison of Popular Online Fonts: Which Size and Type is Best?" *Usability News* 4.1 (2002). *http://psychology.wichita.edu/surl/usabilitynews/41/onlinetext.htm*.

Bolding and italicizing can also give text extra emphasis. Bold text works well online, but due to poor screen resolution, italicized fonts are generally rendered badly, can be extremely difficult to read, and should be avoided.

Alignment

For vertical navigation menus, left-justified text is generally easier to read. This provides a clean edge to scan. Vertical menus with right-justified text leave a ragged edge to the left and make it more difficult to browse a list of items quickly. Additionally, right-justified navigation labels may wrap unexpectedly.

Consider the vertical navigation menu on the left of the Martha Stewart web site (*www.marthastewart. com*, Figure 10-5). The options are much more difficult to read than a left-justified version would be, and line wrapping causes confusion. The words "show" and "radio" in the lower left of the image appear to be their own options, but they are actually part of a longer label that wraps. As a result this menu is hard to scan.

Figure 10-5 / Right-justified text on the Martha Stewart site is difficult to scan

Most browsers have the ability to increase or decrease the size of the text on a given page. Programmers can override this function in the page code on some browsers by using pixel fonts, however. To make your site more accessible, design the text and the pages in such a way that they still work with larger or smaller text, and allow users to change text size as needed. This may mean allowing text to wrap onto two lines, for instance, and creating pages with flexible layouts.

VISUAL HIERARCHY

When designing text, strive to provide a clear distinction between what's important and what's not. By showing relationships between navigation options you can guide a visitor through the page. Contrast in typography is a key in achieving this effect.

The home page of *Sports Illustrated* (*www.sportsillustrated.com*, Figure 10-6) lacks an overall visual hierarchy, for example. It's hard to tell where to begin looking and it's unclear where the navigation begins and the text and advertisements end. The amount of text and navigation isn't overwhelming here; it's the presentation that causes confusion.

Figure 10-6 / Lack of focus of navigation and text on the Sports Illustrated site

Compare this to *Gain* (*http://gain.aiga.org*, Figure 10-7), a journal for business and design published by the American Institute of Graphic Arts (AIGA). There are many navigation options on this page, but you don't get overwhelmed. It's fairly clear what's going on, and the focus is on the main content of the page.

Figure 10-7 / Clear visual hierarchy of text and links on Gain

To provide sufficient contrast, *Gain*'s designers used two fonts, as well as upper- and lowercase navigation labels. But this is a very controlled and deliberate contrast that forms a logical whole. Just consider some of the different types of treatment that appear:

- The name of the journal appears in a very large sans serif font in all capitalized letters at the top (GAIN).
- The lead article has a large serif font in title case in black. (Which Came First: The Packaging or the Advertising?) Other articles toward to bottom of the image have smaller headlines. Each is linked to the full text of the article.
- The article categories appear in all caps and are linked to more on that topic (e.g., CUSTOMER-CENTERED DESIGN).
- The byline is also lighter in color, but mixed case. If available, these link to author biographies.
- The link to comments is bold and colored (5 comments).
- The text of the article summary is a serif font and dark gray.

TEXT AS INTERFACE

People spend most of their time on the Web engaging with text: reading articles, scanning menu options, and browsing product descriptions, among other things. The design of text is therefore a critical part of the web interface. You could even say that text *is* the interface on the Web. If you look at some of the most-visited web sites—Google, Yahoo!, Amazon, and eBay—the user experience is primarily driven by the design of the text.

Consider why a web site such as craigslist (Figure 10-8, *www.craigslist.org*), a free classified advertisements service and one of most visited sites on the Web, is so popular.[4] Mind you, this isn't necessarily a good example of typography or information design, and some people are quick to point out potential usability issues with craigslist. The point is that text *is* the interface—raw, unornamented, and direct. Or more specifically, in this case, the navigation is the interface.

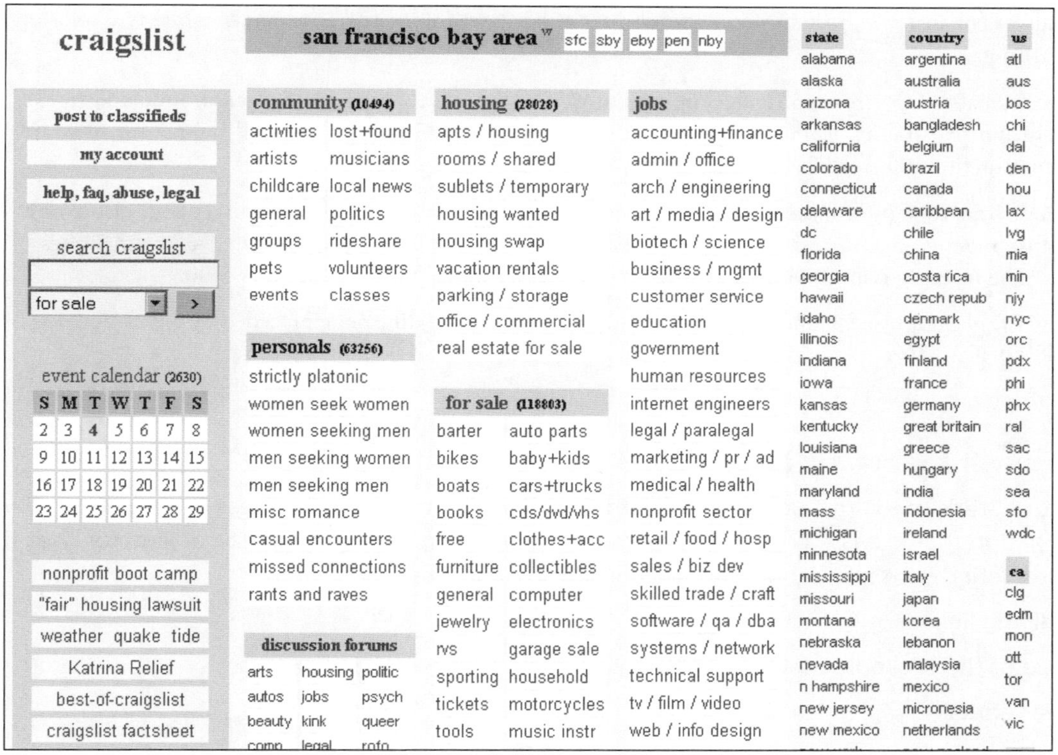

Figure 10-8 / The home page of craigslist

Furthermore, text design plays important role in branding on the Web. In the craigslist example, you'll notice there is little visual branding with logos, mottos, color, and image. Yet craigslist has a distinct and recognizable character. When the brand definition goes beyond traditional trade dress (e.g., logo, colors, etc.), it can also be expressed through other means, such as information design.

But text design is often neglected or considered an afterthought on many projects. Instead, designers spend much more time designing graphics, icons, and logos than the text. While these aspects are important in their own right, don't overlook the design of text on your site. For an optimal information experience, consider how you are presenting text on your site very carefully.

---

4 As of May 2007, Alexa's (*www.alexa.com*) traffic ranking for *www.craigslist.org* was 40. At this time, *yahoo.com* was number one in the traffic rankings.

Below are some general principles for displaying information for use by international viewers. There may be exceptions, but these guidelines generally hold true and can help you plan for potential communication problems in an international setting:

- Avoid using pictures, symbols, and icons that might have different meanings in different cultures. If you must use such elements, make sure they are neutral and universal. When in doubt, label them with text.

- Avoid religious symbols in general.

- Do not communicate meaning with color alone, as it can have different connotations in different cultures. For instance, in China the bride wears red at a wedding, and at funerals, white is a color of mourning.

- Date formats vary across cultures. The format *day-month-year* is used most often around the world, but in North America *month-day-year* is standard. Is 5/4/2007 the 5th of April or the 4th of May? Formatting it as 05 April 2007 (with the month written out) is clearer.

- Include time zone information or name a location when showing times. Using military time also avoids confusion between a.m. and p.m., which are not used in all cultures. Indicating an event with a phrase like "The meeting is at 20:00 New York Time" is clearer than "The meeting is at 8:00."

- Show the geography of phone numbers by indicating country dialing code preceded by a plus sign, e.g., +1 (800) 123-4567.

INTERACTING WITH NAVIGATION

The Web is not a static medium. People click, search, browse, and explore an endless chain of links. Beyond creating navigation that is easy to read and aesthetically pleasing, you also have to design for use. Three aspects of interacting with navigation that are particularly important are:

- Underlining links
- The size of the clickable navigation options
- Rollover effects

Each is discussed in turn in the following sections.

UNDERLINING LINKS

To distinguish them from normal text, the default style that most browsers apply to hyperlinks is blue and underlined. Although there is nothing inherent in links to suggest this styling and it is somewhat arbitrary, web users have come to learn this convention very quickly. And the double coding of links—blue and underlined—means that people who are color blind or who have black-and-white monitors can still identify them.

But underlining text can add to the overall visual complexity of web pages. Stacks of underlined links are generally harder to read than the same links would be without the underlines, for instance. And because underlining indicates clickable navigation, that means using underlining in place of italics for a book title or for emphasis may cause confusion.

To avoid the potential negative effects of underlines, some designers remove them. In many cases this can improve readability and lead to a cleaner design overall. Take the Yahoo! home page, for example (Figure 10-9). Practically everything on this page is clickable, but no links are underlined. Links are only slightly distinguishable from text by their color (dark blue). If every link were underlined, this page would seem considerably busier and less readable. The longer text links in the In the News area in the lower left in, particular, are easier to scan without the underlines.

Figure 10-9 / Links without underlines on Yahoo.com

If the standard convention is blue and underlined, why does this treatment of links on the Yahoo! home page work? Some experts in the field caution against deviating from the norm, as it may lower the overall usability of the site. But it turns out that there are other aspects of navigation design that can also indicate a clickable element, including the function of a link, the purpose of a navigation mechanism, and the position of links on the page. This is particularly important for navigation menus. Links in visually separated navigation areas, such as the vertical menu on the left of Figure 10-9, generally don't need underlining, nor must they be blue to be recognized as a link. The tabs and buttons on this page are also clearly clickable.

Accessibility

Keep in mind some people are color blind. About one in ten males have some kind of color blindness. This number is much smaller for women: less than one percent. Furthermore, as the eye ages, it is less able to differentiate color in general. Relying on color alone to communicate navigation or any other information about your site is not a good idea. Accessibility guidelines prohibit using color alone to communicate information not found elsewhere (*www.w3.org/TR/WAI-WEBCONTENT/#gl-color*).

Removing underlines from links embedded within the body of text passages is more problematic, however. There, underlining is a surefire way to distinguish links from plain text. An alternative is to use a light color and texture for the underlines. Rollyo, a customizable search engine service (*www.rollyo.com*), styles its link underlines as light gray and dotted to make their appearance less obtrusive. In Figure 10-10, notice the word "searchrolls" is underlined, indicating that it is a link, but without interrupting the visual flow of the text.

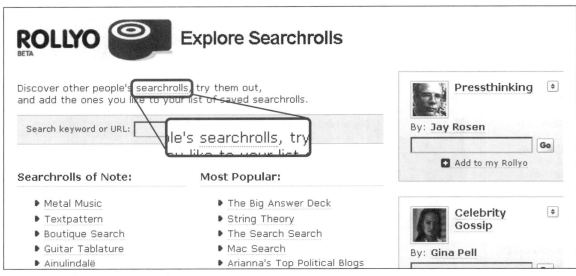

Figure 10-10 / Lighter underlining for links on the Rollyo site

In any event, if you deviate from the default of blue underlined links, be sure to rely on other means of indicating links, and create a consistent pattern across the site. Mixing and matching visual styles may cause problems.

TARGET SIZE

Fitts' Law is a model of human psychomotor behavior developed by psychologist Paul Fitts.[5] It predicts movement and motion based on rapid, aimed gestures using a computer mouse. For all intents and purposes, Fitts' Law simply means that bigger elements that are close to your mouse are easier to reach and click. In general, shorter mouse movements and larger targets contribute to "ease of click," according to Fitts' law.

For instance, paging navigation (discussed in Chapter 3) is often quite small. For someone with a motor impairment, or even arthritis, hitting a small arrow or a single linked number to move to the next page of results may be difficult.

---

5   See Paul M. Fitts, "The information capacity of the human motor system in controlling amplitude and movement," *Journal of Experimental Psychology*, 47 (1954): 381-391; Paul M. Fitts and J. Peterson, "Information capacity of discrete motor responses," *Journal of Experimental Psychology*, 67 (1964):103-112; and "Fitts' Law," Wikipedia. *http://en.wikipedia.org/wiki/Fitts'_law*.

Compare the paging mechanisms in the search results from FindLaw, an online resource for free legal information (*www.findlaw.com*, Figure 10-11), to the results on YouTube (*www.youtube.com*, Figure 10-12). In the YouTube example, the individual page numbers are clearly separated and contained in discrete boxes that make the target for each page number larger. Clicking to page 3 on the FindLaw site is decidedly harder than on YouTube.

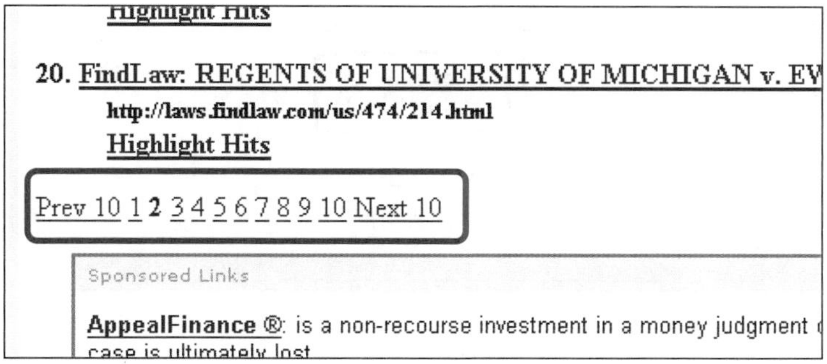

Figure 10-11 / Paging numbers on the FindLaw web site: small targets

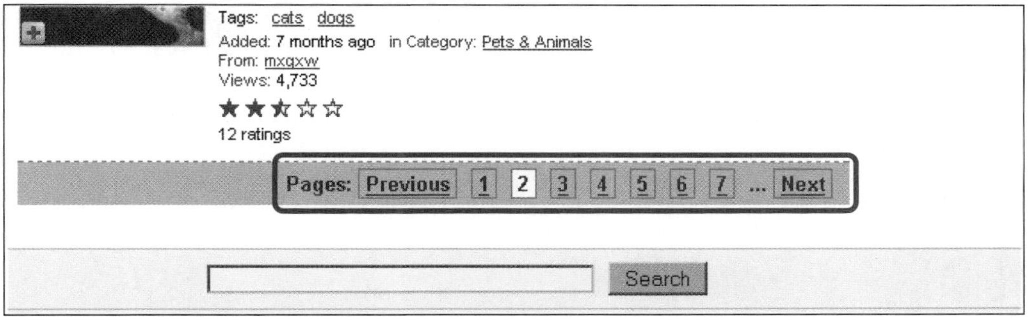

Figure 10-12 / Paging on YouTube: larger, clearer targets

A common technique to improve the "ease of click" is to make the surface of clickable elements larger, where possible. If a linked text is accompanied by an icon or even a photo, make both clickable. Or, make the clickable region for a link or icon larger than the visible region.

For example, the *Sydney Morning Herald* (*www.smh.com.au*) has options for printing, emailing, and changing the text size on its online articles (Figure 10-13). The clickable region of each option is larger than the visible icon itself. This is indicated with a blue box extending well beyond the boundaries of the icon, which appears only after rolling over the option with the mouse (see the print icon in Figure 10-13). Visually, the icons are small and out of the way when inactive, but large and more obvious when a user is attempting to click them.

Figure 10-13 / Extended clickable areas for icons on the *Sydney Morning Herald* web site

ROLLOVERS

A *rollover* refers to a change that occurs to a link or navigation option when the mouse cursor moves over it. There are then two states to consider: the inactive or normal state of a link; and the active state when the mouse moves over it. For smaller navigational elements, rollovers help indicate which option will be clicked and may create a larger clickable target. This provides useful feedback while navigating.

This simplest type of rollover is changing the color and underlining of a link. For an example, see the Babel Fish Translation link on the AltaVista start page in Figure 10-14 (*www.altavista.com*). The inactive rollover state is a simple blue link without an underline. When the mouse hovers over the link, it becomes maroon and underlined.

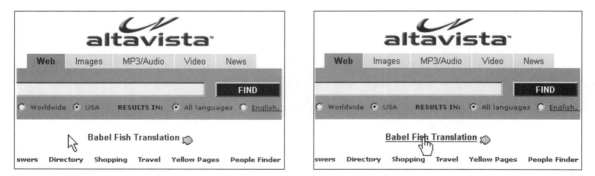

Figure 10-14 / Link rollovers on AltaVista.com (Babel Fish Translation, active state on right)

For navigation bars and tabs that use graphics, it quite common to provide a rollover effect by swapping out images when rolled over. This allows you to change the appearance and even the size of the navigation option in the active rollover state. The main navigation for the Zipcar web site (*www.zipcar.com*), a car-sharing service in the U.S. and U.K., presents three options in a vertical arrangement (Figure 10-15). Rolling over one of the orange balls changes it to green. This provides simple feedback to the user as to the option they are about to select.

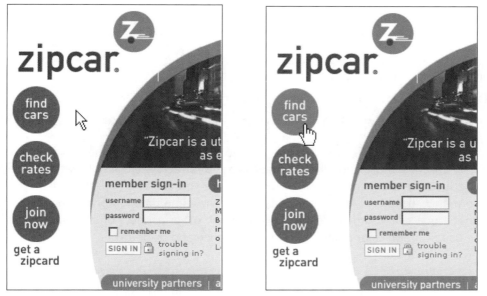

Figure 10-15 / Inactive rollover (left) and active rollover (right; green circle) for the main options on the Zipcar web site

Note, however, that the contrast between the green and orange in this example is not strong enough for people with color blindness to detect a change. If you are using color as a rollover effect, use sufficient contrast as well.

GRAPHIC DESIGN

The appearance of navigation plays a critical role in its perception and use. Background color, size, image positioning, and alignment can either cause or alleviate banner blindness, for instance. In turn, the visibility of navigation options can be the tipping point between meeting business goals and not. The graphic design of a site goes a long way in creating and reinforcing an online brand image, as well as the overall character of the site. Research shows that the single biggest factor influencing the credibility of a site is its visual appearance.[6]

In terms of navigation, a primary consideration is whether to use plain HTML text or graphic images for menu options. Text-based links have many advantages over graphics because they:

- Load faster than graphics
- Can show visited link status by changing color
- Are generally better for accessibility: screen readers have an easier time with text and users with poor eyesight can increase the font size
- Can be easier to manage with content management systems

---

6   B.J. Fogg, Cathy Soohoo, David Danielson, Leslie Marable, Julianne Stanford, and Ellen R. Tauber, "How Do People Evaluate a Web Site's Credibility?" *Consumer Reports WebWatch* (2002). *www.consumerwebwatch.org/dynamic/web-credibility-report-evaluate.cfm*.

But graphics have a different quality and aesthetic than plain text. They can also create desired visual priorities and effects. The rounded corners of tabs, for instance, generally need to be created with images. Depending on the goals of the web site, graphics may be appropriate *and* necessary. Graphic images can:

- Give a three-dimensional appearance to buttons and navigation bars
- Make use of fonts that may not be installed on users' computers
- Create rollover effects and other highlighting options not possible with plain text
- Have an overall finer quality and appearance than text links

As the capabilities of CSS improve, more and more of these types of effects are possible without images. In general, you should reduce the use of gratuitous graphics where you can and rely on plain HTML and CSS for improved performance, usability, and accessibility. But at the same time, graphic images can help you reach certain aesthetic goals of your site design. Like so many other aspects of site design, making decisions regarding the use of graphics or plain text is about balance and trade-offs.

Accessibility

Use of graphics is a core concern with web accessibility. To be accessible, all images—*without exception*—must have an `alt` attribute. This gives screen readers an alternative text to display or read aloud. Generally, the `alt` text should be the same as the label on the navigation option. For images that are purely decorative or add nothing to the content, such as spacer images or dividing lines, set the `alt` attribute to an empty double quotes (alt=""). Without these and without an `alt` attribute, screen readers say "image", which is meaningless.

Beyond the question of graphics or no graphics, two other important considerations for navigation design are color and icons.

COLOR

Color is more than just decoration. It can facilitate interaction and help create a sense of priority within navigation options. Layering can be achieved with color, for instance. By using different shades and colors, you can bring some options to the foreground and visually push others to the background. But the use of too many colors can have diminishing returns. When determining the colors for navigation, be careful to enhance the navigation without detracting from it.

One simple use of color in navigation is showing a different color for visited links. By default, most browsers change links that have been followed to a purple color. Other colors are possible, but in general, visited links aren't displayed in the bright and vibrant colors often used for unvisited links; using more muted colors causes the followed links to look dim and "worn out." Because we know that people often exhibit a hub and spoke pattern in navigating, a distinct color for visited links can help orient users and assist in re-finding.

Beyond this, two types of color coding are particularly relevant to navigation design:

Color coding navigation areas by type

Once navigation types are defined, they can be distinguished by color. For instance, main navigation options may have a different color than utility navigation. Or, the background of a navigation area can set it apart from content and other menus. The navigation areas on the Vanguard web site (Figure 10-16, *www.vanguard.com*), a large investment group in the U.S., are consistently distinguished with different colors throughout the site. This increases the sense of coherence of the navigation system:

* The main navigation tabs are dark green
* The utility navigation at the top has a tan background
* An area to log in to the site on the right has a light blue background
* The shortcuts in the bottom right have a gray background.

Figure 10-16 / Consistently colored navigation areas on the Vanguard web site

Further, the colors on the Vanguard site correspond to specific functions. Red is used to show location in the navigation, as well as for page titles and headers. Blue is used for links and also to highlight actions, such as logging on to an account or for the buttons on the page. Overall, red has an orientation function on the Vanguard site, answering questions such as Where am I?, while blue indicates interactive elements, addressing the question Where can I go? or What can I do from here?

Color coding content areas by topic

Another way to apply color coding to navigation is by topic or content area. This type of color coding can also reinforce branding. For instance, T-Online, a German web portal, uses color coding for the main tabs of the site (*www.t-online.de*, Figure 10-17). The content areas for each tab then make use of that color as the main background color of the page. The content area for Service is in magenta, reinforcing the main brand color for Deutsche Telekom, the parent company of T-Online.

Figure 10-17 / Color coding by topic on T-Online.de

In a controlled experiment, these types of color coordination may not reveal any direct, measurable effect on navigation performance, but they certainly add to the consistency and the overall perceived quality of the site. Color-coding can be a subtle but effective way to unify the overall navigation system.

Accessibility

To show location in a site, web designers often change the color of the selected option in a navigation menu. However, accessibility guidelines exclude using color alone to convey information, and screen readers won't pick up on such a distinction. One solution is to explicitly indicate "You are here" in an `alt` or `title` attribute for the currently selected navigation option. A screen reader would then read "You are here: Products" for the selected Products option, for instance. But sighted visitors would just see the color highlighting to show location.

ICONS

The use of icons can increase the scent of information, a topic covered in Chapter 2. This is particularly true when users are quickly scanning lots of information. If given a clear meaning and purpose, icons are more than decoration. They work in conjunction with text to provide a better overall sense of orientation. Icons have many potential advantages:

- Icons can contribute to clarity by reinforcing a label.
- They can aid in both scanning and orientation.
- Icons facilitate the user's ability to learn, understand, and remember functional elements of the site.
- They potentially increase the clickable area of a navigation option.
- By themselves, icons can take up less space than text labels.

But don't expect icons to solve poor labeling problems or take the place of text altogether. There are also disadvantages to using icons:

- They can be ambiguous.

- The interpretation of icons may vary across cultures.

- Icons often don't represent abstract concepts very well.

The Music Australia web site, a service to access information about Australian music and musicians, makes extensive use of icons, primarily to indicate material types: sound files, scores, pictures, and so forth (*www.musicaustralia.org*, Figure 10-18). The large icons are easy to read and fairly clear. People can easily scan a search results list, as shown here, and distinguish material types from the icons alone. Text labels accompany the icons to disambiguate them, and the labels also help visitors learn them quickly.

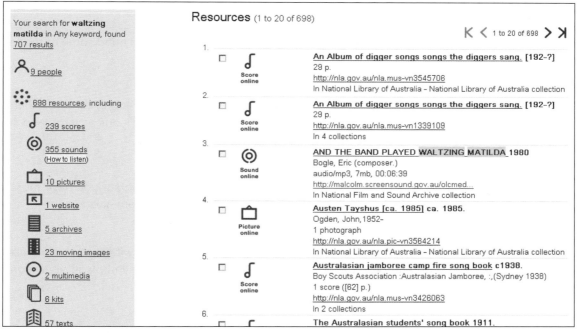

Figure 10-18 / Icons in a results list on the Music Australia web site

CREATING ICONS

Standards for web icons don't exist, but conventions are appearing. Amazon.com has popularized the shopping cart icon in all of their target market countries, for instance, including in Japan and China. Or, links to external web sites are sometimes followed by a box with an arrow, such as those on Wikipedia (Figure 10-19).

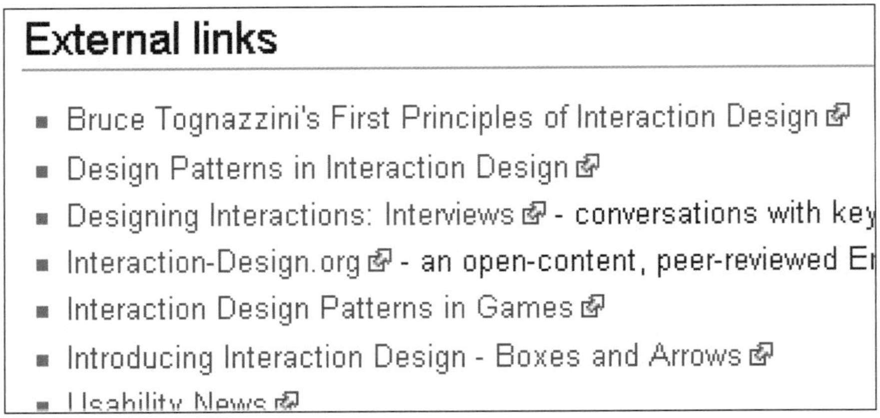

External links

- Bruce Tognazzini's First Principles of Interaction Design ⊡
- Design Patterns in Interaction Design ⊡
- Designing Interactions: Interviews ⊡ - conversations with key
- Interaction-Design.org ⊡ - an open-content, peer-reviewed En
- Interaction Design Patterns in Games ⊡
- Introducing Interaction Design - Boxes and Arrows ⊡
- Usability News ⊡

Figure 10-19 / A commonly seen icon for external links—a small square with an arrow

But in most situations, you'll need to develop icons for your project. If so, keep in mind some of the following qualities of good icons:

Clarity

Do icons say the right things in the right way? Icons should be easy to recognize and understand quickly. They should also be easy to read. It's best to keep the elements of icons as large and simple as possible. With too much detail, they can detract more than they help.

Limited quantity

Don't use too many icons. Generally, six to ten main icons for a site is enough. If you have more than that, they start losing their effect and it becomes hard to distinguish one from another.

Memorable

Can people remember the icons on a site? Don't repeat a similar element within a set of symbols. If you do, exaggerate the differences. If you use a house and a building as symbols in your icons, for instance, make sure there is a noticeable difference at a glance.

Common language

People should be able to look at a group of icons and recognize that they belong together. The balance is keeping icons together as a family of symbols, with sufficient differences to clearly distinguish them. This can achieved through shapes, color, size, and how they are used.

Another distinction to consider when creating icons is whether they are direct or indirect in what they reference.

Direct icons use the object, content, or function in question directly in the symbol. For instance, an icon of a printer is commonly used for a print function. There is little or no abstraction involved.

Indirect icons may use metaphors. For example, an image of a letter may be used to show sending an email, or scissors might represent cutting text. Substitute symbols may be indirect as well. A donkey stands for the Democratic Party in the U.S., or a heart shape can show love.

TESTING ICONS

When in doubt, test icons with potential users of the site. This can be done simply and effectively with a questionnaire or a drawing session. For example, list all of the proposed icons on one side of the page, ask test takers to fill in the blanks on the other side as to what they perceive the icon to represent, then analyze the results for effectiveness of the icons.

Alternatively, you could give participants an oral or written explanation of the concept you want to represent as an icon and ask them to draw that concept; providing a small piece of paper and large pen works best. Afterward, place each drawing for a single concept together and try to identify common patterns (Figure 10-20).

Figure 10-20 / A composite of twelve user-drawn icons for the term "download" from an icon test

SPECIFYING NAVIGATION

Presentation, the title of this chapter, has two meanings. First, it refers to how the navigation will appear on the page to site visitors. But it also refers to communicating your designs to others on the development team. After you've performed analysis, architected the site, determined a layout, and designed the final pages, you must be able to clearly explain your to work to others.

Unlike creating a site map or wireframes, which allow you to consider multiple design directions, this stage in the process is about capturing and documenting the final solution. This is not to say that no revision is involved, but you shouldn't be freely exploring alternatives at this time: it's time to deliver. Note that you probably won't be just specifying navigation, so you'll have to consider other parts of the site's design as well.

To communicate your navigation system effectively, use screen designs and prototypes to show how it will look and user interface specifications to describe how it will work.

Screen designs show the final navigation in context of finished page designs, reflecting and blending layout, alignment, text design, color, icons, imagery, branding, and business goals, among other things. As with wireframes, you needn't show every page in the site; instead, you should generally reflect page types and templates.

Typically, you'll create screen designs in a graphics program such as Adobe Photoshop, which means you're creating static images with fixed proportions. But keep in mind that web pages are flexible and can fit different browser sizes. The "wonderful world of Photoshop" may not correspond to the realities of HTML programming and variable page widths. Make sure that your designs are flexible enough to survive various display configurations on the Web.

Creating HTML *prototypes* is another, perhaps better, way to reflect the design of final pages. In addition to showing color, font, images, icons, and other page elements that might be captured in screen designs, HTML prototypes allow you to work out details of the page construction.

By designing in the same medium as the final product, you get a chance to uncover issues in how pages should best be built. This may cause you to have to make compromises in the navigation in order to ease implementation, but finding this out earlier rather than later is always better. Prototypes help you better gauge whether the desired design is feasible within the project constraints.

USER INTERFACE SPECIFICATIONS

A *user interface specification*, also called a *functional specification* or simply a *UI spec*, is a written document detailing the behavior and interaction of the web interface. It captures all the rules, workflows, and conditions of the navigation and the site as a whole in words. A UI spec often includes screen design images and links to a prototype, if available, as well as site maps, flow diagrams, and even rules for browser titles and URL design. In this sense, it is truly the culmination of many of your design activities up to this point.

In terms of document organization, a UI spec typically details the site page by page. It generally reflects some or all of the following types of information:

- Site map, sections of site maps, and page flows
- The page's ID and title
- A short page description
- The template used for a given page or group of pages
- The main navigation category for the page's content and all local navigation (if not reflected in the site map)
- Detailed tables of all functional elements on the page with descriptions of their behavior
- Business rules that may apply, such as subscription-level access
- Other comments and assumptions

For recurring or global elements, you may want to specify them once in a central location. In the end, the behavior and description of every element on each page needs to be accounted for in some way.

Keep in mind that the overall goal is to communicate to others—usually programmers or engineers—how the site should work. The audience for any kind of specification largely determines how much detail you should include, for example:

- Stakeholders look at final documentation from a business and branding perspective. They want to see if the requirements are met and if there are any risks in meeting the overall business goals.

- Content developers need to see the size and position of text on pages so they can write appropriate texts with fitting lengths.

- Programmers and engineers need detailed information about navigation and expected behaviors for implementation and for testing.

- System testers need to understand how the navigation works to create test scenarios and plans.

While addressing these different needs, you also want to keep documentation to a minimum. One approach is to include as much information as possible in the site maps and page diagrams and to not replicate this information in words in the specification. Overall, be very conscious of how any document you create will be used before setting out to write it. Consider how it fits in with other documents, as well as how you'll update it. If there is a rigorous change control process put in place on the project, updating several lengthy documents throughout the lifecycle of a project may be extremely time-consuming.

A recent trend in web development is to outsource programming to offshore resources, particularly for larger projects with a great deal of technical engineering involved. For the web designer, this often requires painstakingly detailed UI specification documents. You may never have contact with the person doing the actual programming in such situations. Instead, the UI spec must be completely self-contained.

At the same time, agile software development methods are becoming more and more popular. This type of development generally focuses on short iterations of development with little or no documentation. Teams meet daily and have constant communication with one another, essentially circumventing the need for any documentation.

Whatever approach you take, remember to focus on the final product, not the deliverables needed to get there. Fit the documentation and work products you create to the project type and audience for them accordingly.

Accessibility

Don't forget to specify accessibility. If you build a prototype, make it as accessible as you can. Test it with a screen reader or a screen reader simulator, such as Fangs, an extension for the Firefox browser available for free download (*www.standards-schmandards.com/2006/fangs-for-firefox-15*). Include information about accessibility that you can't show in the prototype in a written UI specification.

SUMMARY

People navigate the Web based on a range of cues. Labels provide a great deal of direct information, of course, but there are more subtle aspects that people key in on, such as the page layout and the function of navigation menus. The visual presentation of navigation proves to be critical as well. It's not just about decorating the navigation or coloring it in. Instead, a good visual design can guide visitors through a site.

Existing principles from the field of information design can help you understand how to better present navigation. Be conscious of your use of negative space and don't let chartjunk creep into your design. Layering information allows you to provide clear focus on key information.

The design of text is vital for navigation. Choices of typeface, case, size, text weight, and alignment are all within your control. Use the tools of typography to create a visual hierarchy in the navigation. On well-designed sites, people don't have to hunt for the next logical option: the navigation leads them through it.

But the Web is not static like print media; using the Web requires action. You must consider how people will find and click the links you provide in the navigation. This includes considerations of underlining links, target size, and including rollover effects to enhance that interaction.

Color also plays a role in navigation. In particular, color-coding is a common tactic for distinguishing function or content areas. Color can provide orientation, as well as a sense of movement through a site. Though perhaps not immediately perceivable by visitors, a consistent color scheme improves the overall information experience. Icons can also enhance navigation. If designed effectively, they can serve as visual signposts that facilitate scanning and differentiating navigation options.

Finally, you need to communicate your navigation design to others for implementation. Screen designs, prototypes, and user interface specification documents are three deliverables that capture the final solution. Generally, you want to reduce the amount of documentation you need to produce. Before beginning, discuss which deliverables are needed on the project and create these to fulfill your audience's needs. Outsourced projects may require very detailed specifications, whereas agile projects may have no documentation. In any event, remember to focus your collective team energy on the end product and not the documents needed to get there.

QUESTIONS

1. To simulate the importance of target size, try this: if you're right-handed, use your left hand to operate the mouse; if you're left-handed, use your right hand. Then attempt to navigate through your favorite site. What problems do you have? What would have made user experience in using the site easier?

2. Sketch icons for the following terms commonly found on web sites:

    a) Jobs

    b) Site map

    c) Privacy Policy

    d) Help

e) Home

f) Products

g) Services

h) Support

Which were more difficult than others? Why?

3. Color and text are intertwined. The left and right hemispheres of the brain see different information: the left processes the color, while the right wants to parse the text. To demonstrate this, read the table of colors in Figure 10-21 out loud, but say the color of the text and not the word.

**YELLOW BLUE ORANGE
BLACK RED GREEN
PURPLE YELLOW RED
ORANGE GREEN BLACK
BLUE RED PURPLE
GREEN BLUE ORANGE**

Figure 10-21 / Color and text are closely related

FURTHER READING

Envisioning Information, by Edward Tufte (Cheshire, CT: Graphics Press, 1990).

Visual Explanations: Images and Quantities, Evidence and Narrative, by Edward Tufte (Graphics Press, 1997).

The Visual Display of Quantitative Information (2nd Ed.), by Edward Tufte (Graphics Press, 2001).

These three books are the classic trilogy on information design from Edward Tufte. This is not easy reading, but at times simply mesmerizing. The quality of a graphics in the books is also beyond most other printed works, and the examples are well-researched.

Site-Seeing: A Visual Approach to Web Usability, by Luke Wroblewski (Hungry Minds, 2003).

A site's visual design has a direct and profound impact on how we perceive, use, and navigate web sites. This book contains hundreds of well thought-out examples from the Web to illustrate this point. Wroblewski covers the design of many navigation mechanisms in detail, as well as use of space, color, fonts, and many other visual design elements.

PART III

Navigation in Special Contexts

Navigation is an all-encompassing concept in web site design. Its borders are hard to define, and issues of web navigation span disciplines and job roles. Virtually every aspect of web design has some navigation aspect to it.

For example, keyword searching and navigating aren't necessarily mutually exclusive activities—at least not from a user's perspective. People change their seeking strategies midstream and switch from keyword search to browsing freely. Site search itself has aspects of navigation associated with it.

Or consider tagging, which offers an alternative to traditional means of classification by allowing users to freely apply keywords to web content. When the tags become public and others can see them, a social classification emerges. But in order for a social classification system to be useful, it must be navigable.

Though rich web applications bring more functionality to the Web by simulating the type of interaction found in desktop software applications, navigation again plays an important role. Navigation to and from web applications must be considered in your site design, for instance. And real-time filtering, slider bars, drag-and-drop interaction, and panning and zooming interfaces each bring new challenges to navigation design.

The chapters in this section will help you face the challenges of integrating navigation with rich web applications, tagging, and search tools. Take a closer look:

- Navigation and Search (Chapter 11): Explores ways in which searching and browsing can be integrated, including a review of the faceted browse interface.

- Navigation and Social Classification (Chapter 12): Highlights some of the more important aspects of navigating social tagging systems.

- Navigation and Web Applications (Chapter 13): Reviews key considerations to make when designing navigation for web applications.

Navigation and Search

IN THIS CHAPTER

- Integrating navigation and search
- Navigation before conducting a search
- Navigation after conducting a search
- The faceted browse interface

Searching is commonly considered an alternative to navigating. Basically, a search coordinates a person's keyword query with pages that contain that term or terms. Navigation, on the other hand, allows people to browse to desired content, providing an important overview of a site and helping people determine relevance. But are these alternate or complementary approaches?

From a user's perspective, navigating and searching aren't necessarily contrasting activities. People just want to find the information they need. Integrating navigation and search, then, better supports how people really look for information.

People aren't naturally "search-dominant" or "link-dominant;" instead, whether a person searches or browses is situational. For instance, if you're looking for the manual for your mobile phone on the manufacturer's web site, you might search for the model number directly from the home page (a known-item search). But when you're looking for a new phone to purchase on that same site, you might browse their products (exploratory searching). Information needs dictate the method of seeking.

This chapter considers navigation in the context of keyword searching, suggesting supportive navigation elements and techniques for before and after searches. In addition, the chapter investigates the University of California Berkeley's faceted browse interface, which stands as an example of closely integrating navigation and search.

NAVIGATION PRIOR TO SEARCH

There are potentially many ways to integrate browser mechanisms into the search process, starting with the search form itself. You can include options, such as *search scoping* menus and *words wheels* to let people zero in on target content and pre-filter results, or you can prompt terms for aid in formulating a search query. *Canned searches* combine navigating and searching so that clicking a link actually runs a search in the background. The key is to provide both browsing and searching options, enabling visitors to switch strategies as needed.

SCOPING SEARCH

Some search forms include a scoping option that enables people to set a narrower focus on the search prior to clicking the Go button. Frequently, a drop-down menu contains the site's key content areas, reflecting the main navigation. Visitors select a category from the menu to limit the range of content searched. Sites with distinct content areas or with a lot of content benefit most from the ability to scope a search.

The web site for Eddie Bauer (*www.eddiebauer.com*, Figure 11-1), a large U.S. sportswear manufacturer, provides a simple drop-down menu to scope a search on the home page. The categories in this menu match the main navigation options for the most part. The distinctions are clear, which can help pre-filter results. For instance, a man searching on the term "shoes" could select Men from the menu, and he then wouldn't get women's footwear in his results.

Figure 11-1 / Categories in a search scope menu on the Eddie Bauer web site mirror the site's main categories

WORD WHEEL

A word wheel shows a small piece of a list of terms already in the search system. It dynamically matches user-entered characters and quickly displays the appropriate portion of this list. For example, type N, and a word wheel would show the first five or ten words that begin with N. Then type the letter "A," and the list jumps to the first word beginning with NA, and so forth. At any time, you can select a search term from the word wheel menu. Deleting a character usually jumps back in the list to the matching point.

Answers.com makes use of a type of word wheel. There is a slight delay in producing a list of terms, but the experience is near real-time. Typing a few letters brings up an alphabetical list of matching terms that are displayed as suggestions to the searcher (Figure 11-2). Clicking a term in the list searches it immediately.

Figure 11-2 / Suggested terms on Answers.com in a word wheel display

On Answers.com, this is not a list of previously entered terms that browsers sometime store and display on a historical basis. It is a list of terms indexed by Answers.com that then have associated entries or pages.

A more sophisticated approach involves using what might be called *pattern matching*. With this method, you match not only the first characters of the word, but also match other occurrences of the user-entered string. PubMed.gov (*www.ncbi.nlm.nih.gov*) is a large online database for medical research. The lookup feature for journals in this collection makes use of a pattern matching word wheel. Essentially, after typing at least two characters, the word wheel finds all occurrences of those characters, not just at the beginning of words. In Figure 11-3, typing "cardio" finds *The American Journal of Cardiology* as well as *Cardiology Research,* among others.

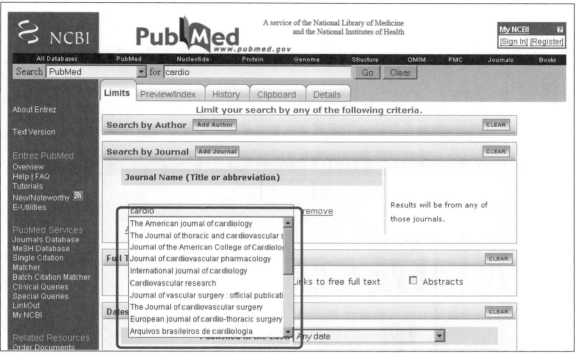

Figure 11-3 / Pattern-matching word wheel on PubMed.gov

Search engines are often very unforgiving of misspellings, alternate spellings, and synonyms. Though automatically searching for variations of words might help, even the best search algorithms can't accommodate all the variations of natural language. Word wheels show the form of existing keywords in a database up front. As people formulate a search query, they can then browse a list of indexed terms, potentially producing better search results.

CANNED SEARCHES

Canned searches are links, such as "Find more resources," that are programmed to contain a search query. Clicking the link automatically conducts that search and presents the results. You usually can recognize that the link is a canned search by the URL, which will contain the search terms as parameters in a string. For instance, a canned search link for the term "web navigation" on the Lycos search engine might look like this:

http://search.lycos.com/?query=web+navigation&x=0&y=0

Often linking between sites, canned searches are particularly helpful when pointing to content you don't own.

Within a site, canned searches can also be useful. Navigation options can lead to search results pages instead of a landing page or gallery, even from the main navigation. This avoids having to manually update these pages. So, as your available products constantly update, your gallery pages will always be current. The downside is that your gallery pages lack the handcrafted quality many users expect.

For example, clicking on Wine Collections in the main navigation of Wine.com (*www.wine.com*) brings up a search results page (Figure 11-4). This is not disguised as a gallery page or landing page, and it even lists the number of results right at the top. Although no search in the traditional sense was conducted, visitors can then use the Narrow Search By feature on the left.

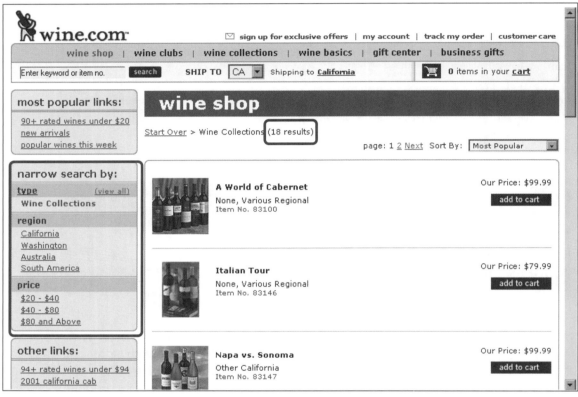

Figure 11-4 / Results page reached from the main navigation of Wine.com

NAVIGATION AFTER SEARCH

Frequently people have a word or phrase in mind and just want to search as quickly as possible without carefully formulating a query. When faced with the results, however, they suddenly discover they need ways to refine the search. Navigation techniques, such as *topics links*, *clustering*, *grouping*, and making *search suggestions*, can help. You've probably already seen many of these without realizing. Navigating search results can aid greatly in narrowing and focusing a search.

TOPIC LINKS

Search results often contain details about each page that was found, as well as the topic of each page. If the topics for each page are linked, clicking one leads to other pages for that category, enabling people to navigate to more stories on a given subject that matches their interests.

For example, each news story found on Digg (*www.digg.com*), a community-driven news story portal, belongs to one of 35 topic categories. Search results include the topic link for each story on the right of the last line for each hit (Figure 11-5). Clicking on topic link shows a new list of items for that category.

Figure 11-5 / Digg.com search results allow people to browse to the topic of any story in the list

CLUSTERING AND GROUPING

More sophisticated search engines automatically group similar results by topic into subsets, sometimes displaying a list of the subsets along one side or the top of the page as a type of navigation. Clicking on a subset then filters the results, displaying a more manageable list of items. You may have already seen such techniques on Amazon.com, for instance, where searching on popular topic like Star Wars provides a staggering main list of results. A look at the left edge of the page, however, provides links for viewing only DVD, Books, or Toys & Game results, among other categories.

Two common methods of producing these subsets are clustering and grouping. Technically, there is a difference between these approaches, although the terms are often used interchangeably.

With *clustering*, categories are automatically derived from a set of results. An algorithm not only finds clusters of like items, it also determines category labels. Because these labels are dynamic, they can change from search to search, even for the same query submitted at a later time. In other words, clustering generates a list of navigable terms on the fly.

With *grouping*, the terms already exist in some kind of index or taxonomy of terms. The results list that is displayed will vary from search to search, but the terms themselves will always appear in the same standardized form. The system either determines the topic of the page and applies an existing label, or the pages already contain category information associated with them. The system then extracts this metadata as navigable categories.

The search engine for the FirstGov web site (*www.firstgov.gov*), the official portal to U.S. government information, uses clusters, displaying its categories in a two-tier hierarchy on the left side of the results set (Figure 11-6). The number of hits in each cluster appears in parentheses after each link. Three tabs at the top change the type of grouping listed in the left pane: by topic, by agency, or by source.

In this example, the automatically generated category names are sometimes accurate. A search for NEA indicates that this abbreviation stands for National Endowment of the Arts, one of the top categories. Other category links are less helpful, however, such as Projects and Council. The cluster for the equally vague Commercial category is expanded in Figure 11-6 to show two sub-clusters. The overall accuracy and utility of clustering can be mixed.

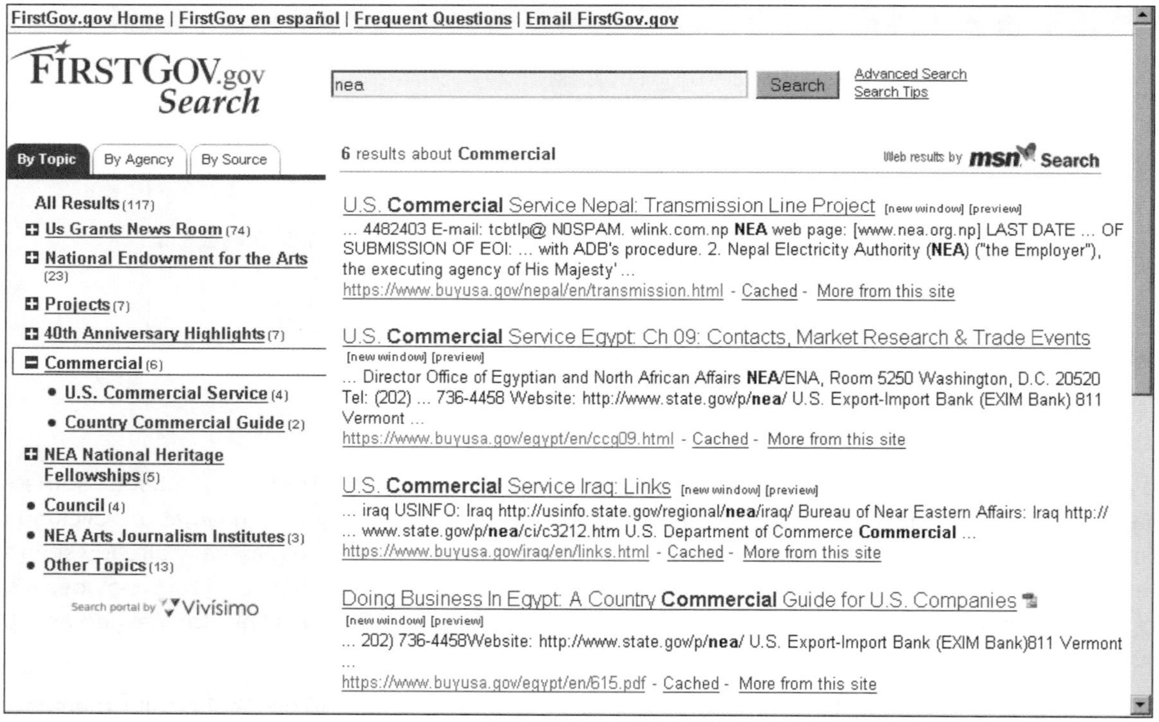

Figure 11-6 / Clustered search results on FirstGov.gov

In contrast, the search results on the Sun web site (*www.sun.com*) are a good example of effective grouping (Figure 11-7). First, tabs along the top filter the results list by predetermined categories. Some of these tabs even have a second level of grouping categories. This closely resembles a main navigation and local navigation, but it's created on the fly. Overall, this example represents a well-integrated approach: it's clearly search results, but the grouping appears and behaves like normal site navigation.

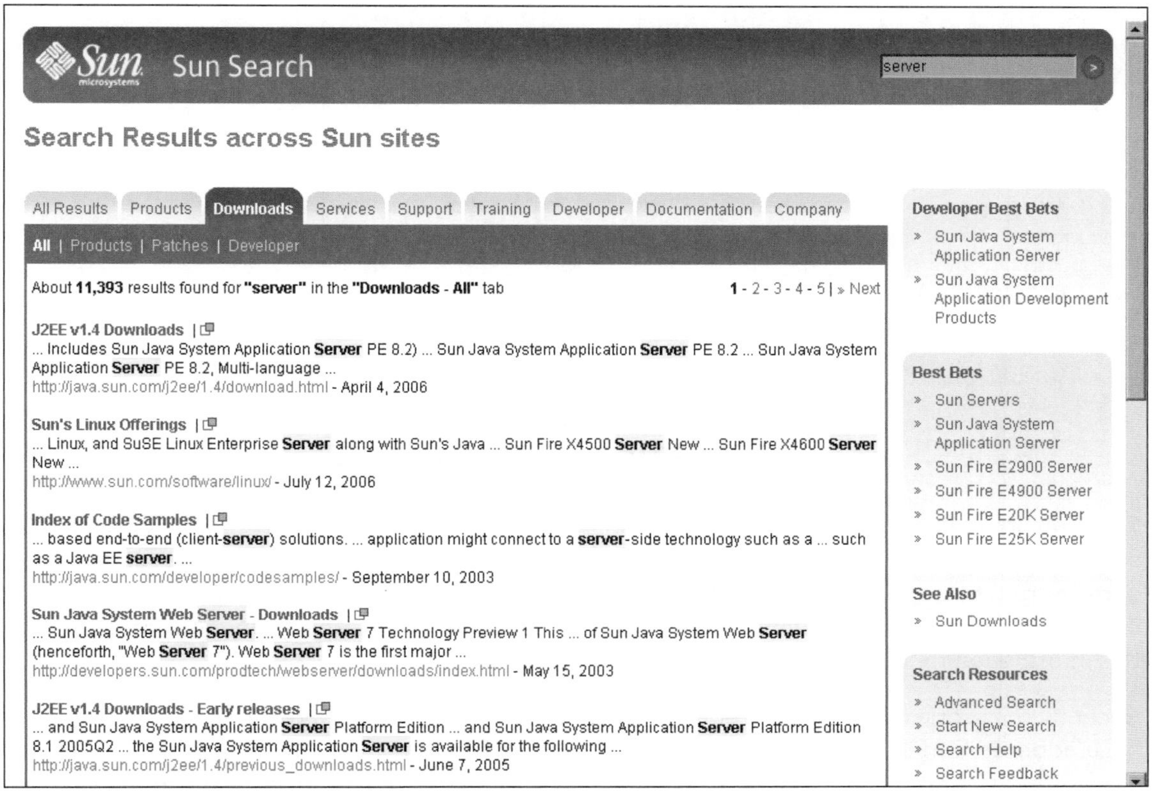

Figure 11-7 / Results grouping on Sun.com

SUGGESTIONS

Search engines can also suggest alternative search terms to use, helping visitors refine or improve a query after it has been conducted. Often a list of words is generated based on the content of the results set. There are different types of suggested terms and different ways of generating a list of suggestions.

Figure 11-8 shows an example of suggested terms for a search for the word "speakers" on eBay.com. The alternative search terms at the top of the box resemble associative navigation. They lead to related content. The lower part of this example is like local navigation in that it provides access to information at a finer level than the term "speakers."

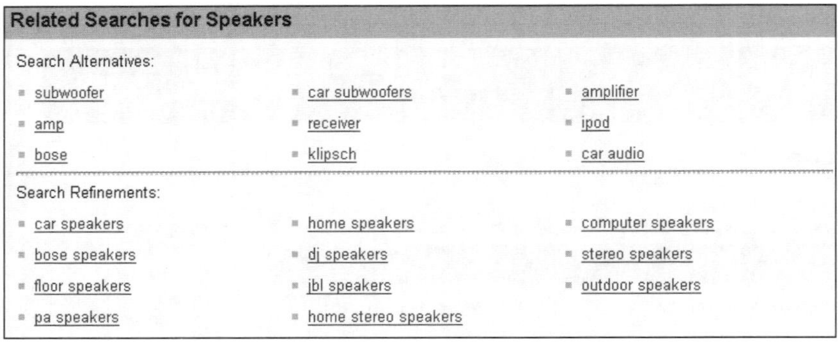

Related Searches for Speakers

Search Alternatives:

- subwoofer
- car subwoofers
- amplifier
- amp
- receiver
- ipod
- bose
- klipsch
- car audio

Search Refinements:

- car speakers
- home speakers
- computer speakers
- bose speakers
- dj speakers
- stereo speakers
- floor speakers
- jbl speakers
- outdoor speakers
- pa speakers
- home stereo speakers

Figure 11-8 / Related searches on the results page for the term "speakers" on eBay.com

Relevance Feedback

Traditionally, *relevance feedback* refers to "an interaction cycle in which the user selects a small set of documents that appear to be relevant to the query, and the system then uses features derived from these selected relevant documents to revise the original query."[1] If someone explicitly indicates that some documents are more relevant than others, the system can incorporate this information to improve the search result.

Recently the scope of relevance feedback has widened. For instance, web-based search engines have adopted a much simpler, one-click More Like This feature. Broadly, then, *relevance feedback* refers to any technique by which the user provides feedback on relevant documents to improve or extend search results.

The underlying principle is that search is an iterative process. Information found in an initial search may reshape a person's overall search strategy. It's kind of like voting for search results that best match your initial query. The problem is that people generally don't want to do this manually unless it's extremely simple, such as with a single click.

Pseudo-relevance feedback, also known as local feedback or blind feedback, is an automatic variation of relevance feedback. The basic idea is to extract terms from the top-ranked documents in a results set. These terms can then be used to run a second search, either automatically or manually.

Ask.com is a public search engine that makes use of pseudo-relevance feedback techniques (Figure 11-9). The system extracts terms from each set of results and presents them as links on the right side under the categories: Narrow Search, Expand Search, and Related Names (not shown in the image). This provides an overview of the semantic makeup of a set. Clicking a link then runs a search for the selected term or phrase. Pseudo-relevance feedback terms are again extracted on the ensuing results set. The cycle is endless.

---

1   Marti Hearst, "User Interfaces and Visualization," in *Modern Information Retrieval* (Chapter 10), by R. Baeza-Yates and B. Ribeiro-Neto (ACM Press, 1999).

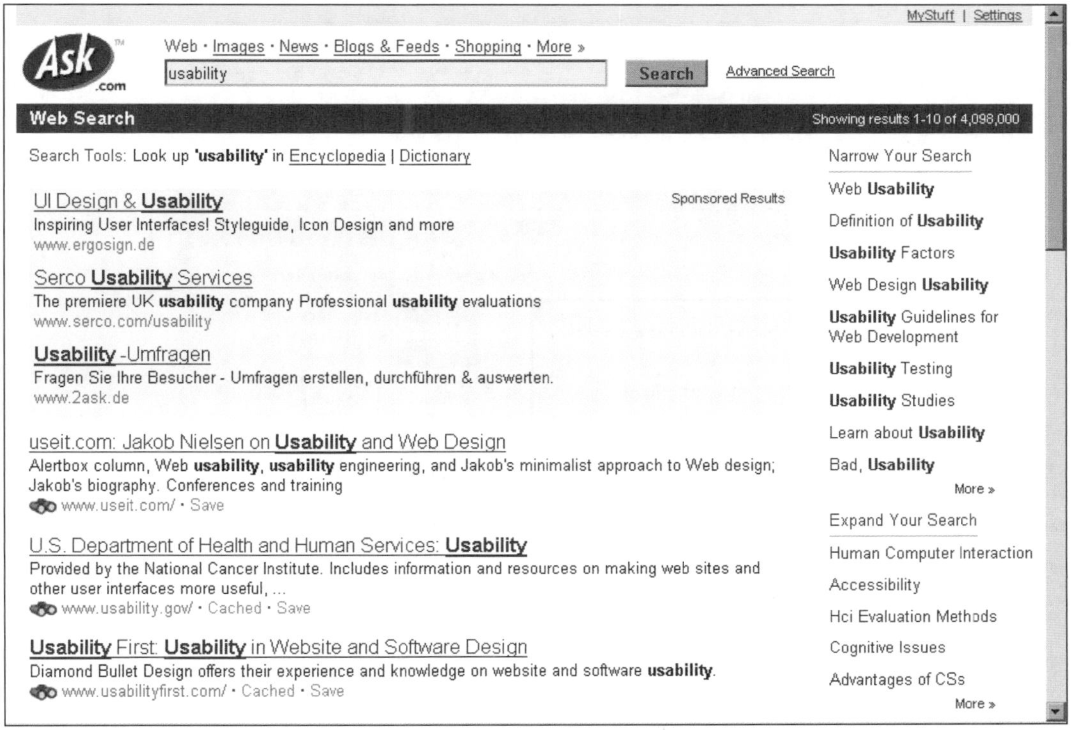

Figure 11-9 / Pseudo-relevance feedback on Ask.com

BEST BETS

Another approach to making suggestions is to predetermine pages that are included in results when certain keywords are entered. These are often referred to as best bets or manual recommendations. Manual recommendations on the right side of the Sun web site (Figure 11-7), for example, are even divided into two categories of best bets.

The BBC web site also includes manual recommendations. These appear at the top of a results list with a slightly different visual treatment than other hits. In Figure 11-10 a search for *Eastenders*, a popular British television show, produces three such links marked with the label "BBC Best Link."

Figure 11-10 / Manual recommendations on the BBC web site

NO RESULTS

What do people see when a search finds no results? A typical approach is to simply present a prominent message indicating that nothing was found. However, there are ways to enhance even these pages with navigation. For one, by matching the entered terms to existing terms in an index, the system could suggest alternate spellings if any are found. Many free search engines on the open web have this feature.

Another strategy is to display categories for browsing or a part of the site map. Apart from misspellings, the assumption is that if the system can't match a person's query, maybe browsing—perhaps by terms unknown to the user initially—is the best way to find information. Additionally, presenting categories when there are no results retrieved gives insight into the scope of site content. Even if people don't click directly on a category link presented on a zero results page, the presence of these navigational elements may help them rework a search.

The search results page for the Hewlett-Packard web site (*www.hp.com*) presents "popular searches" at the bottom of all search results pages, including the zero results page (Figure 11-11). This way people still get an overview of top categories even if nothing is found. There is also a link to an A–Z index at the very end of this list. The no results page then becomes a starting place for browsing and navigating.

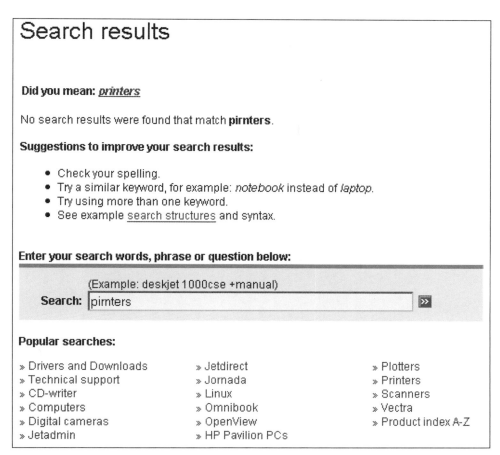

Figure 11-11 / Categories at the bottom of results pages on HP.com, including a link to an A-Z index

FACETED BROWSE

So far, the techniques mentioned in this chapter represent individual approaches to integrating navigation and search that you can merge into an existing web site. The faceted browse interface, on the other hand, which is a system for navigating large bodies of information developed by researchers at the University of California, Berkeley, offers a more holistic integration of search and browse.

This interface relies on facets and faceted classification as a means of structuring information (see Chapter 9). Facets offer an alternative to hierarchical structures. Instead of creating a tree structure and fitting items into that structure, facets seek to describe the properties of a thing.

FACETS

A facet is nothing more than a *category*. But it's the arrangement of categories that is important in faceted classification. Facets are mutually exclusive dimensions or properties of the object they describe. Facet categories then have *values* within each. Unlike hierarchies, these values from different facet categories aren't structurally related to one another. Facet categories can be thought of as independent buckets of values. This allows for any number of ways to approach the objects in a collection.

The classic example for explaining facets is with bottles of wine. There might be several key properties by which to describe wine, such as Region, Type, and Price. Each of these is a mutually exclusive facet. For instance, the values under Region aren't dependent in any way on those in Type or Price. Choosing values from a facet category then filters out all other values from that facet. In other words, a wine can't be both red and white at the same time.

By selecting Napa Valley, CA from the Region facet for a collection of wine, all other values (e.g., France, Italy, etc.) for that facet are omitted. Then selecting Red from the facet Type would filter out all non-red wines. Finally, choosing a price category for Under $20 would limit the number of wines to an even smaller number. You're then left with the intersection of the selected values from those three facets: Napa Valley, red, and under $20.

Facets are generally good at describing and providing access to homogeneous items, such as documents or products. But they may not necessarily be a solution for the main navigation of your site. Further, implementing a faceted browse interface necessarily requires that the data be organized by a faceted classification. This may mean restructuring databases or restructuring information, which can be costly and time consuming.

THE FLAMENCO PROJECT

Facets are potentially very powerful. Large bodies of information collapse into manageable sets in just a few clicks. But it's difficult to expose the power of facets and to navigate them in an interface in a way that doesn't overwhelm and confuse the average web user. The Flamenco project set out to create such an interface that anyone can approach.[2] The researchers write:

" We have developed an innovative search interface that allows non-expert users to move through large information spaces in a flexible manner without feeling lost. The design goal was to offer users a 'browsing the shelves' experience seamlessly integrated with focused search.[3] "

Some advantages of the faceted browse interface include:

Order of selection

People can select values in any order, which supports many ways to achieve the same goal.

Navigating the categories always produces results

This is achieved by updating the available subcategories for any selected category. Non-relevant choices are hidden, as people browse through the categories. A zero results set exists only if the free-text search feature is used.

Deselecting, or disengaging values

Because facets are mutually exclusive, browsing them allows for the recombination of categories. If unsatisfied with the current results, visitors can deselect any value or any combination of values from a facet, thereby expanding the list of results.

---

2   Flamenco stands for FLexible information Access using MEtadata in Novel COmbinations. See the project web site at *http://flamenco.berkeley.edu*.

3   Jennifer English, Marti Hearst, Rashmi Sinha, Kirsten Swearingen and Ka-PingYee, "Flexible Search and Navigation using Faceted Navigation," unpublished manuscript (2002). *http://flamenco.berkeley.edu/papers/flamenco02.pdf*

The basic interaction style of the faceted browser interface mirrors web navigation closely: clicking a link transitions to a new page. Visitors can drill down in the categories naturally. This familiar navigation experience makes it easy to use.

Indication of magnitude

Each of the category values is followed by the number of items in the collection for that value in parentheses. Providing such insight into the size and scope of an ensuing set helps people make navigational decisions. These numbers update automatically to reflect the magnitude of items for the current results set.

Aspects of this approach resemble results grouping, mentioned previously. But with the faceted browse interface, the facet categories and their values are exposed as navigation from the very beginning. You can do a keyword search, but you don't have to in order to get their benefits. It's a more holistic technique to browsing and searching facets. Some implementations of faceted browse are described below to help you better understand.

First, consider this example from the Flamenco project web site: *http://orange.sims.berkeley.edu/cgi-bin/ flamenco.cgi/spiro/Flamenco*. In this case, the interface provides access to the image collection from the University of California, Berkeley Architecture Image Library. This is an example of one the original faceted browse interfaces, representing a comprehensive illustration of all that can be done with facets and demonstrating a close integration of search and browse.

There are three main stages in the browse process: the start page, the results page, and the item page, each discussed in the following sections.

START PAGE

The start page offers a color-coded overview of all facets (Figure 11-12). The top-level values within each are represented as links. The number of items classified by that value follows the link label in parentheses. This display encourages exploration from any starting point. It also familiarizes people with the scope of the image collection.

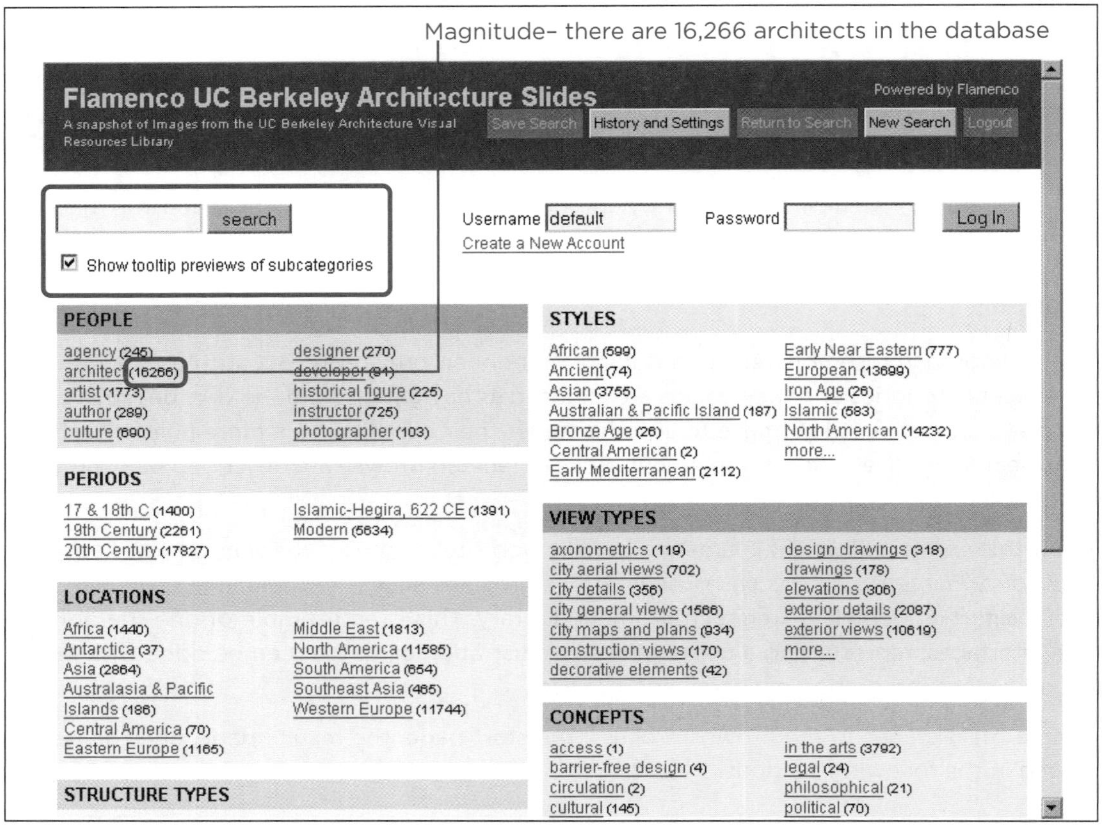

Figure 11-12 / An overview of categories on the Flamenco start page

A keyword search field is also available in the upper left, which provides freedom to choose between searching and navigating. Either way, the results page that follows presents a gallery-like arrangement of links to images in the collection.

RESULTS

The results page contains three main components (Figure 11-13):

Results

> The results occupy most of the page on the right. For this particular collection, thumbnails of images are displayed.

Values

> The facet values that apply only to the current set of results are listed on the left. Clicking a link narrows the focus of the results set and updates the values available. Users can also sort the results set by any of the facets available with the Group Results link. Notice that the corresponding indications of magnitude are updated accordingly as well. For instance, the remaining value under People references 22 architects, whereas the start page lists 16,266.

The path taken to produce a given results set appears at the top. The facet is indicated, followed by the value selected from that facet. For example, in Figure 11-13, Western Europe > France > Paris was selected in the Location facet, and then Buildings in the Structure Types facet. Notice that the color-coding from the start page is applied to each element of the path as well. This path grows as more values are selected. Any portion of the query can be removed at any time by clicking the x icon next to a term.

Overall, the transition from the start page to the results page in terms of layout is great, but seemingly natural. Though visitors have navigated to get here, it has the feel of a results page. More importantly, the Results page allows people to navigate and explore further. They can create their own paths to information. Along the way the navigation available is re-contextualized for the local results set.

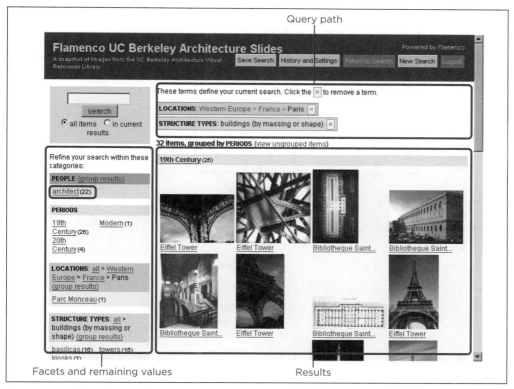

Figure 11-13 / A results page from the Flamenco interface

ITEM PAGE

People can select to view a single item in the collection from the results page. The item page provides a larger image and potentially more detailed information, while still displaying the path taken to reach the item (Figure 11-14).

On the item page, all of the values used to classify the item are displayed on the right in a tree view that expands multiple levels, if present. Users can select one or more of these terms and use them as the basis for a new search with the Find Similar Items button.

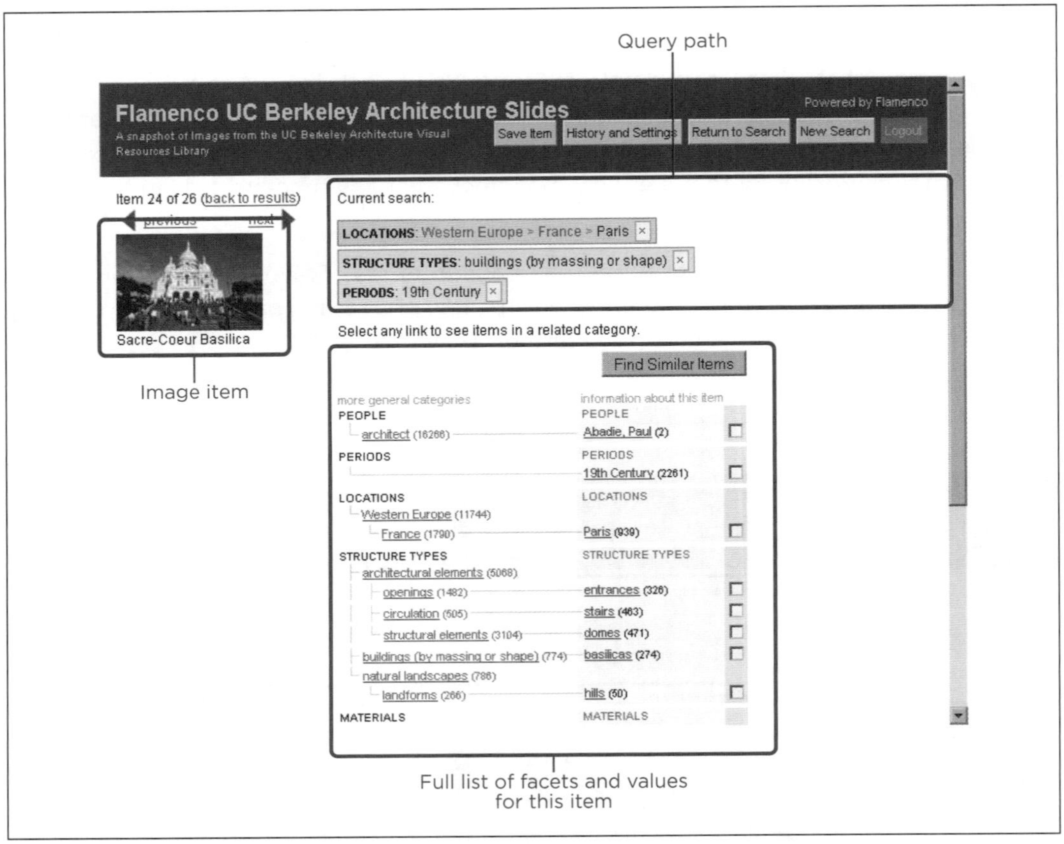

Figure 11-14 / The item view in the Flamenco image collection

EXAMPLES OF FACETED BROWSE

The Flamenco interface represents a comprehensive example of the principles and techniques of faceted browse, but many other sites use variations of the approach. Two of these are discussed below: the NCSU library and Epinions.com.

NCSU LIBRARY CATALOG

A good example of implementing faceted browse in a large collection is the North Carolina State University (NCSU, *www.lib.ncsu.edu*) library catalog, which is powered by "guided navigation" software developed by Endeca (*http://endeca.com*). Consider Figure 11-15's sample search results page; here the entire library catalog is reduced to six items with just four clicks.

To get to this screen, select Astronomy as the first value selected in the Subject category Science. Choose eBook from the Format facet, and then the topic Solar System. You can see these topics in the path at the top of the results list. Any one of these values can be deleted with the small x icon. Other available facets are then displayed on the left. The remaining categories include the number or results for each based on the current results set only.

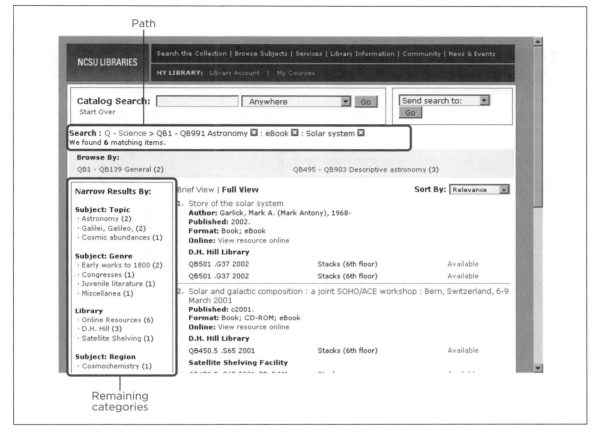

Path

Figure 11-15 / The results view of the NCSU's online library

Click an item in the results list—in this case, *Story of the Solar System*—and basic bibliographic information appears at the top left, with holdings information below that. On the right are some further navigation options (Figure 11-16).

Unlike like the Flamenco example, however, the path followed to get to this book is not shown on the item page, nor are the all of the categories by which this book is classified. Plus, the graphic design makes this page appear more complex than needed, without a clear focus of attention. Although the NCSU library browse represents a good overall example of integrating faceted browse, improvements could be made.

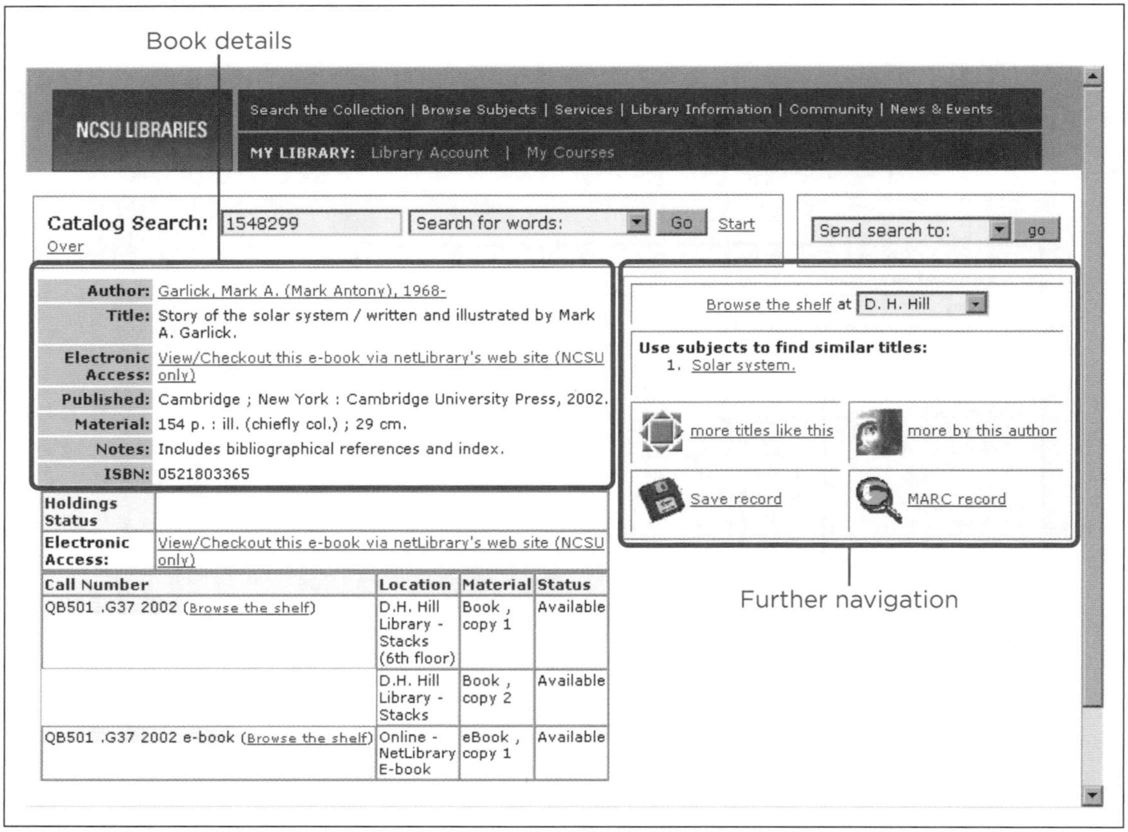

Figure 11-16 / The page for an individual book in the NCSU library

EPINIONS.COM

The category browse feature on Epinions (*www.epinions.com*), an open platform for consumer reviews, also takes a faceted approach. Visitors first pick a product to review or compare. The site then presents an overview of facet categories and their values within that product type.

In Figure 11-17, DVD Players was selected and the relevant facets are displayed. Selecting any link from one of these facets then leads to a results page.

Home > Electronics > DVD Players

DVD Players

Find and Compare

Browse categories in DVD Players. Number of items in parentheses.

View all DVD Players (3248)

by Price Range
Below $50 (71)
$50 - $70 (67)
$70 - $80 (43)
$80 - $90 (39)
$90 - $100 (58)
$100 - $120 (63)
$120 - $130 (47)
$130 - $150 (76)
view more

by Brand
Panasonic (218)
Toshiba (184)
Sony (157)
Samsung (140)
Philips (173)
Coby (86)
Audiovox (71)
JVC (173)
Pioneer (128)
RCA (97)
Denon (54)
Initial (34)
Yamaha (55)
Polaroid (41)
jWIN (40)
view more

by DVD Type
What is DVD Type?
DVD Player (1167)
Portable DVD Player with Screen (415)
DVD Recorder (233)
DVD Player / VCR Combo (224)
DVD Recorder / VCR Combo (73)
Multi-disc DVD Player (166)
Portable DVD Player without Screen (53)
DVD Recorder / HDD Recorder (14)
view more

by Screen Size
Less than 7 in. (98)
7 - 7.9 in. (179)
8 - 8.9 in. (63)
9 in. or More (67)

by Playable Disk Types
3.5" audio CDs (1)
CD (Audio) (2085)
CD+G Karaoke (21)
CD-R (1846)
CD-RW (1807)
DVCD (13)
DVD Audio (288)
DVD Video (1841)
view more

by Progressive Scan
What is Progressive Scan?
With Progressive Scan (1143)
Without Progressive Scan (617)

Or Find and Compare by
Playable File Formats
Video Upconversion

Surround Sound
Number of Discs

Figure 11-17 / The category browse page for DVD Players on Epinions.com

The results page then repeats the most salient facets from the previous screen above the list of search results (Figure 11-18). The top three facets contain links to values, along with the number of results for each in parentheses. Clicking any of these further narrows the results sets. The other facets are present on the far right but without sub-category links broken out on the page. Using them requires an additional click.

Instead of displaying these facets and values on the left, as in the Flamenco and NCSU examples, these facets are displayed horizontally across the top. Nonetheless, visitors can easily and quickly refine search research with this design.

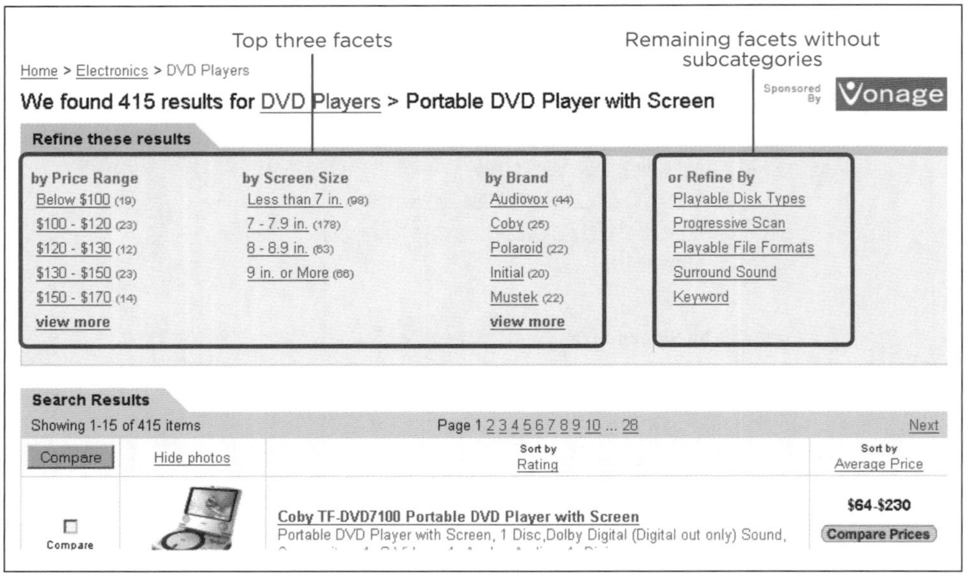

Figure 11-18 / The results page for portable DVD players on Epinions.com

Overall, the Epinions example reflects some of the elements in the Flamenco faceted browse interface. With it, people explore freely from any starting point. Epinions.com successfully exposes the power of facets in a simple interface that provides a navigation experience familiar to the Web.

SUMMARY

Navigation and search need not be mutually exclusive activities. There are potentially many ways to integrate the two. For instance, before conducting a search, navigational elements such as search scope menus and word wheels allow people to browse pre-existing categories. This can help avoid getting no results while communicating the breadth and type of information included in the search. Additionally, navigation links themselves can invoke a search via a canned search. Even main navigation links can be canned searches and lead to a dynamic results page instead of a hand-crafted gallery.

After a search is conducted, techniques such as clustering and grouping allow people to refine the results by browsing categories. Clustering automatically groups results into similar sets and creates a label for each set on the fly. With grouping, search results are sorted into predetermined categories. Suggestions for search terms can also be made on the results side of search, as well as recommending top hits manually (also called best bets).

The overall goal of such approaches is to integrate navigation and search for a richer information experience that mirrors how people naturally seek information; namely, they move around, changing strategies rapidly and switching from navigation to search as needed.

Finally, facets offer a powerful alternative to structuring information than hierarchies. It's difficult, however, to create an interface that exposes facets in a way that novices can understand. Researchers at the University of California, Berkeley, have done just that. The Flamenco interface allows average web users to intuitively search and browse facets in an integrated way. Other examples of the faceted browse approach include the library catalogue for the North Carolina State University library, based on the guided navigation system developed by Endeca, and the search and browse features on Epinions.com.

QUESTIONS

1. Conduct a search for the term "laptop computer" on eBay.com or eBay in the country where you live using the appropriate translation. Which of the following are present before and after doing the search?

    a) Scoping options

    b) Word wheel

    c) Canned searches (browse categories to determine this)

    d) Clustering

    e) Grouping

    f) Suggestions and best bets

    Then do the same search for Amazon.com or Amazon in your country.

    Now purposely misspell the terms, like this: "laptpo computer." How does each site handle misspellings? Which is better? How could both improve?

2. Think back to the last large purchase you made, such as a car, home, or even which school or university to attend. You probably had criteria by which you made that decision. For example, for a car you might have wanted a particular model, within a given price range, and a particular color. What were the primary criteria used in your decision making process? How could these be represented as facets? What were the possible values for each facet?

3. Examine your personal collection of CDs or books. What are all the properties of them that are important to you? For books, the traditional facets are author, title, and subject. What other facets are salient?

    Now suppose you could create a database to catalogue your books or CDs. How would you describe the collection using facets?

FURTHER READING

"Design Recommendations for Hierarchical Faceted Search Interfaces," by Marti Hearst, ACM SIGIR Workshop on Faceted Search (August, 2006). Available online at: *http://flamenco.berkeley.edu/papers/faceted-workshop06.pdf*.

After 13 years of research on faceted browsing, Marti Hearst, head of the Flamenco project at the University of California, Berkeley, summarizes the group's key findings as a set of design recommendations. This article is short and practical. See the many other key publications of the Flamenco Search Interface Project: *http://flamenco.berkeley.edu/pubs.html*.

"How to Make a Faceted Classification and Put it On the Web," by William Denton. (November 2003). Available online at: *http://www.miskatonic.org/library/facet-web-howto.html*.

William Denton offers an excellent summary of facets, as well as practical tips on how to create and use facets on the Web. He references key academic sources, but keeps the text light and readable. This is an excellent starting point to understanding facets with how-to information.

Navigation and Social Tagging Systems

*An understanding of how we categorize is central to any under-
standing of how we think and how we function, and therefore
central to an understanding of what makes us human.*

—George Lakoff
Women, Fire, and Dangerous Things

12

IN THIS CHAPTER

- Tagging
- Social classification
- Navigating social classifications

People naturally tend to categorize things. It's how we make sense of the world—one drawer for socks, another for shirts; food in this kitchen cupboard, dishes in that one. Grouping and labeling helps us find things later.

In the digital world, we create personal systems of organization with computer files and folders. Some intrinsic characteristics of information, such as file type or date, help by enabling you to sort your emails by time received or search for only PDFs, for example. But you also create folders and give files names.

All of this searching and organization relies on *metadata*, which is commonly defined as "data about data." Metadata are the labels used to describe objects: documents, books, photographs, MP3s, web pages, and so forth. They give us handles to grab onto when organizing information. A computer doesn't know that a photo on your hard drive is of the Eiffel Tower taken on your trip to Paris in 2005 unless you tell it so. By attaching metadata to the image, finding it becomes easier.

In the broadest sense of the word, *tagging*, the subject of this chapter, is not a new activity. Librarians and indexers having been "tagging" books with subject headings and keywords for years. Tags are simply metadata we apply to resources and objects on the Web so we can find them later. However, the *way* in which tagging gets done in open, collaborative systems on the Web using such services as del.icio.us and Flickr is unique and innovative.

This chapter looks at social tagging systems and some of the exciting possibilities they bring with them. But to be useful, a tagging system must also be navigable. The discussion here therefore focuses on navigating social tagging systems.

TAGGING

The traditional classification of, say, books relies on standardized classification schemes called *controlled vocabularies*. A controlled vocabulary seeks to clarify language by mapping variant and related terms to a preferred term. In other words, if you had to decide what to call a small, portable computer, a controlled vocabulary might direct you to use notebook and not a variant term such as laptop, lap-top, or even notebook. Overall, this represents a *top-down* approach: The classification scheme is already in place, and when a new item needs to be added, it's assigned a topic, often by a trained professional.

Tagging offers an alternative to controlled vocabularies schemes with a *bottom-up* approach to classification. In tagging systems, any user can assign freely chosen terms to a resource or object on the Web—such as a page, photo, or video—in order to be able to find it again. The terms used to tag a resource can be very informal and personal, and tagging systems lack a predefined structure inherent in controlled vocabularies. If you want to tag a web page with notebook, iBook, and lap-top, you're free to do so, even if your neighbor uses the terms laptop and portable computers.

The use of natural language to describe resources is a strength of tagging systems. Further, with tagging, you apply a keyword to the resource rather than placing the resource in a category. This means a given resource can have any number of tags, allowing for multiple browseable paths through the tagged resources. This potentially overcomes the vocabulary problem discussed in Chapter 5.

But tagging systems often generate what is called "meta-noise" in the classification scheme. This is includes such things as misspelled tags (e.g., bithday, brithday) and unique compound tags (e.g., newyorkcity, programming/php). People also use tags that have no meaning to a wider community (e.g., mydog or mystuff), which may result in single-use tags that appear only once (e.g., bobandsueswedding). Such tags don't contribute to the broader use of the tagging system, but effectively track resources for a given user or group.

With open tagging systems on the Web, the ideals of controlled vocabularies and traditional classification are reversed. Table 12-1 highlights some of these differences.

Table 12-1 / Controlled vocabularies versus open tagging

Classification with controlled vocabularies	Open tagging systems
Consistent word forms and usage	Inconsistent word forms and usage
Relies on an exclusive list of predefined preferred terms	Inclusive; any terms are acceptable
Complete and structured	Incomplete and emergent
Rigid and impersonal	Flexible and highly personal
Trained catalogers apply metadata to resources	Anyone can tag a resource
Generally attempts to represent the intent of the author or creator of an object	The user or community applies metadata that is relevant to them
Requires maintenance from an external party; time intensive and costly to create and maintain	Community driven; workload for producing metadata distributed across the social group

Debates about the value of tagging systems versus controlled vocabularies have raged recently. Ultimately, one approach doesn't replace the other, and each has its place. Controlled vocabularies work well in domains that are small and well defined, where users are experts in the field, and where comprehensiveness in finding information is critical, such as in medical and legal research domains. Company intranets and B2B web sites will also continue to make effective use of controlled vocabularies and traditional means of classification.

On the other hand, large, "open" domains with a wide range of users, such as bookmarking communities on the Web, can clearly benefit from tagging systems. There is no authority to create standardized categories, and no one to maintain a central classification scheme. What's more, finding a few resources by navigating tags may be "good enough" in most cases. When serendipitous discovery is acceptable, tagging systems are appropriate. Tagging represents a way to describe resources and allow people to navigate to them, but it doesn't take the place of traditional types of classification and organization wholesale. Each has their own purpose and use, and each is valuable for different reasons.

Internationalization

Tagging services generally allow tags to be created in any language. However, tagging systems generally don't distinguish between languages. Some taggers have used special tags to mark the language of the resource, such as "lang: fr" for French and "lang: es" for Spanish, and so forth.

Others have suggested that tagging systems employ language-based namespaces to help distinguish between tags from different languages. This could potentially be used to filter tags to only one language. The weighting of terms in a tag cloud, for instance, generally shows the most popular terms from the predominant language of the site. With the ability to distinguish by language, users could see and navigate tags from just one language.

TAGGING SYSTEMS

There are many types of tagging systems, but they all have three key elements:

- *Resources*. The object being tagged, such as a web page or photo
- *Users*. The members of a social tagging system who apply tags to resources
- *Tags*. The terms used to describe a resource

Virtually every resource on the Web can be tagged. An important distinction in how tags are created, maintained, and used deals with the source of the object to be tagged. The origin of the resource to be tagged will affect who will tag it and how it's tagged. Resources to be tagged can be:

- Supplied by participants, such as uploaded photos on Flickr or videos on YouTube
- Supplied by the web site or tagging system, such as artist and album descriptions on Last.fm
- Open resources existing on the Web, such as bookmarking web pages on del.icio.us

Note also that the process for tagging necessarily differs based on the resource in question. Applying tags to a public web page, for instance, is different from applying tags to a photo or video that you upload. With the web page, the system can recognize the resource by its URL and point to other tags people have already used. The text and title of the page can also be used to suggest tags. With a photo or video there is no preexisting descriptive metadata and the system cannot identify that resource until you explain it in words.

Tags can also be either private, so that only the user can see and use them, or public, so that the entire group can use them. Gmail, for example, allows you to tag your emails, but these are never seen by anyone else. Some services allow users to decide whether tags should be private or public, such as del.icio.us and Flickr.

Table 12-2 lists common types of tagging systems, as well as example services for each.

Table 12-2 / Common tagging systems and services

Resource tagged	Service	Description	Source of material	Private or public tags?
Web pages	Del.icio.us http://del.icio.us	A popular social bookmarking service; one of the most widely cited and discussed tagging services; now part of Yahoo!	Open web resources	Private and public
Web pages	Ma.gnolia http://ma.gnolia.com	A social bookmarking service	Open web resources	Private and public
Web pages	CiteULike www.citeulike.org	A social bookmarking service specialized for academic citations	Open web resources	Private and public
Web pages	BlinkList www.blinklist.com	A social bookmarking service that highlights groups and communities; launched by MindValley	Open web resources	Private and public
Web pages	Yahoo Bookmarks http://beta.bookmarks.yahoo.com	A personal bookmarking service with private tags only (i.e., there is no social classification)	Open web resources	Private and public
Web pages	Furl www.furl.net	A free booking services that archives saved pages	Open web resources	Private and public
Photos	Flickr www.flickr.com	The largest photo sharing service with tagging	User-uploaded photos	Private and public
Book records and reviews	LibraryThing www.librarything.com	Allows members to tag records of books in their own personal library as well as review them	Book records and reviews	Public
Music and artists	Last.fm www.lastfm.com	A large music information database that allows subscribers to tag artists, albums, and songs	System-supplied music information	Public
Videos	YouTube www.youtube.com	A popular video sharing system where members can upload videos and tag them	User-uploaded videos	Public
Events	Upcoming http://upcoming.org	Allows members to post and tag events	User-contributed events	Public
Podcasts	Odeo www.odeo.com	This service indexes podcasts and allows users to tag them	System-supplied index of podcasts	Public
Emails	Gmail http://gmail.google.com	A web-based email program that allows users to label emails	System-supplied emails	Private

Services that allow people to navigate the tags from other members are called *social tagging systems* or *collaborative tagging systems*. The resulting set of tags is referred to as a *social classification* or *folksonomy*. Public tags on del.icio.us, for instance, represent a social classification: everyone can see the pages you've bookmarked with a tag and navigate by those tags.

Note that the structure of social classifications is an emergent structure: it grows freely as more and more tags are added to the system. There is generally no hierarchy inherent to the social classification. It's basically a conglomeration of many personal organizing systems that have been made public. And just as your own organization systems grow and change as you use them, so too do social classifications change with use. This brings up new challenges in providing effective navigation systems.

NAVIGATING SOCIAL CLASSIFICATIONS

There are two primary reasons why people tag:

- They want to find something of value at a later point in time.
- They want to share a resource or object with others.

In both cases, navigation plays an important role. To help understand this, consider three distinct activities in the tagging process:

- Creating tags
- Using and managing your own tags
- Using other people's tags

Aspects of navigation involved in each of these steps are discussed in more detail in the following sections.

CREATING TAGS

How tags are created affects whether people can navigate them later. In creating tags, you need to consider such things as access to the tagging service, how suggestions for tags can be made, and the form in which tags can be entered. In general, you want to encourage tagging and lower barriers to creating tags where possible.

ENCOURAGING TAGGING

People like to have their things organized, but at the same time they can be lazy when it comes to doing it. For social classification to be effective, the act of tagging has to be simple. The process of adding tags should be easy enough to overcome any lack of motivation to tag. Flickr, for instance, allows members to tag multiple photos at once while uploading them (Figure 12-1). Requiring users to tag each photo individually is a good way to ensure that few people will bother. Although bulk tagging means that individual objects in the batch end up with more generic tags, the trade-off of convenience for accuracy usually pays off with more tags being added.

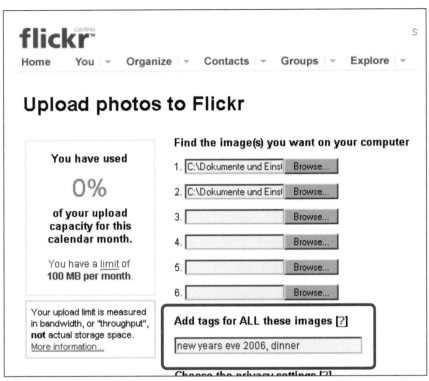

Figure 12-1 / Tagging multiple photos at once on Flickr

The tagging interface should also limit unnecessary navigation steps. Ma.gnolia, for example, dissuades people from tagging by requiring an extra click to display the input field for manually adding a link (Figure 12-2, right side). After visitors add a link, the site states no tag was added, but does not make it clear how to add a tag (Figure 12-2, left side). A more effective approach would be to display a simple Add Tag link for entering tags in place of the "none assigned" message. Exposing the input field for entering tags to begin with, rather than hiding it, would help as well. Avoid complicating the task of adding a tag with even as little as an extra click.

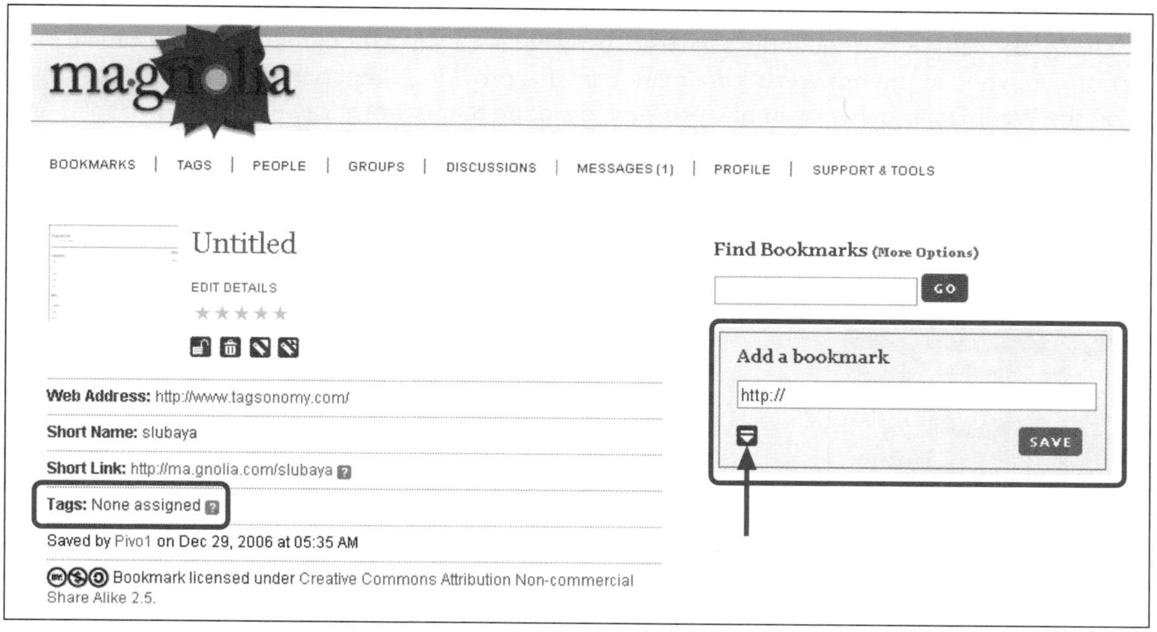

Figure 12-2 / An extra step to tag a page when manually adding a bookmark on Ma.gnolia

A system can also encourage rich tagging by providing large input fields to enter tags. In social tagging systems, more tags for a given resource are generally better than fewer. The smaller the input field, the more likely a tagger will use a word or two only. Technorati, for instance, has a tag input field that allows for only about three short tags (Figure 12-3). A larger input field would encourage taggers to apply more terms. Given the amount of room on this page, there is no reason not to have a large box in which to enter tags. This simple change would promote richer tagging.

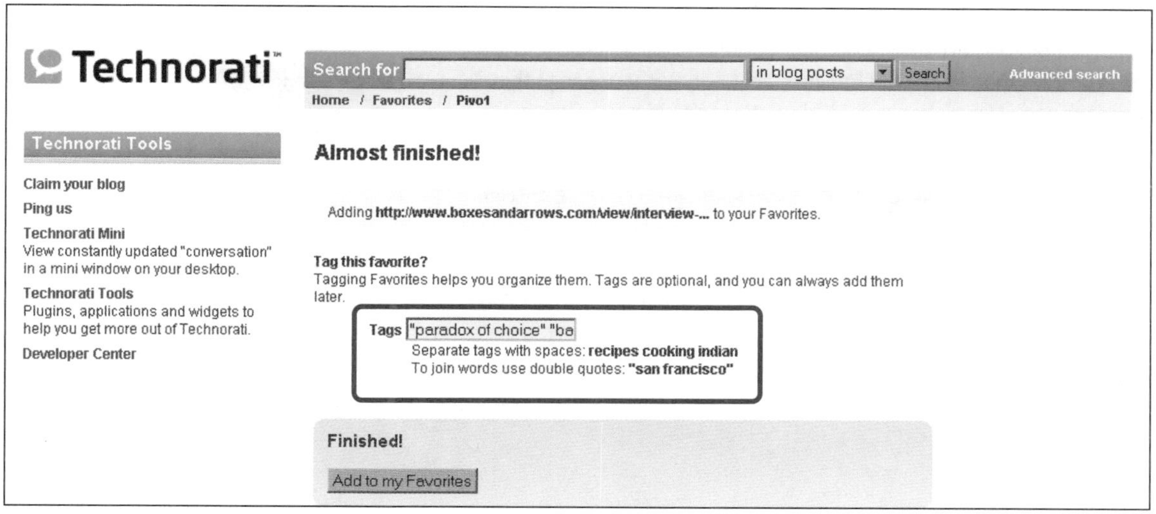

Figure 12-3 / Small entry field for tags on Technorati discourages rich tagging

ACCESSING TAGGING SERVICES

Bookmarking services are frequently accessed by what's called a bookmarklet, or a small piece of JavaScript contained in the browser's bookmark bar. This provides direct access to the service from anywhere on the Web. The process is simple: you surf to a page that is worth saving, click the bookmarklet in your browser, enter tags for that page, and save them.

Figure 12-4 shows the bookmarklet for CiteULike in the toolbar of a Firefox browser. This allows a user to browse the Web and at any point capture a page to the CiteULike service without greatly disturbing normal web navigation.

Figure 12-4 / Quick access from a browser for CiteULike

Some news sites have started adding links to bookmarking services from each article. Though designers of tagging systems can't control this directly, such links also represent another way to access bookmarking services without interrupting web navigation much. Articles on Salon.com, for instance, include direct access to both Digg and Del.icio.us, among other services (Figure 12-5).

The government is reading your mail

But that's nothing new -- a Bush signing statement reminds us how little we know about hush-hush postal-monitoring programs, and how vulnerable they are to abuse.

By Mark Benjamin

Print 🖨 | Email ✉ | Digg it 🎁 | Del.icio.us 🔖 | My Yahoo ➕ | RSS 📶 | Font: S / S+ / S++

Jan. 5, 2007 | WASHINGTON -- There was understandably little fanfare when, just before Christmas, President George W. Bush signed into law the Postal Accountability and Enhancement Act. But attached to this mundane postal legislation was a little-noticed presidential signing statement asserting the government's power to open first-class mail

Figure 12-5 / Direct links to Digg and Del.icio.us from articles on Salon.com

There are two models for navigating to a bookmarking service: *parallel* bookmarking and *sequential* bookmarking (Figure 12-6). With the parallel approach, external access links—such as bookmarklets within a browser—open a pop-up window of some kind so users don't leave the currently viewed page. They view the page being bookmarked in parallel to the bookmarking service, which can be important in conceiving labels for it. The pop-up also allows users to toggle between the resource and tagging service for reference.

In the sequential model, the page for adding bookmarks, such as CiteULike, instead fills the current browser window. After the page is added, users then return to the page they were previously viewing. This sequential navigation for creating tags loses the context of the page being bookmarked while creating a tag label.

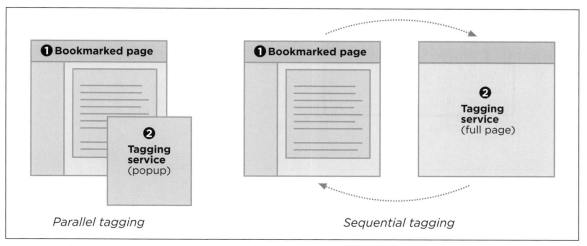

Figure 12-6 / Two models for accessing a bookmarking service

Accessibility

Spawning new browser windows can cause accessibility problems. In general, they can be disorienting to screen reader users as well as people with poor vision and mobility and motor skills limitations. Some accessibility guidelines and legislation discourage their use all together. If you do use pop-ups to navigate between sites or to display content within your site, at least warn users that a link will open a new window. This can be done with an explicit text in the `title` attribute of originating link.

TAG PROMPTING

The act of choosing a tag places a certain cognitive burden on the tagger. People have to stop what they were doing and come up with descriptive words for a resource. In doing so, they may satisfice and just pick anything. To help avoid this, prompt tags where possible.

For instance, BlinkList displays possible tags in a word wheel, enabling visitors to begin typing an idea then select a tag from an existing list quickly (*www.blinklist.com*, Figure 12-7). This also helps keep tags consistent, which can improve navigation when someone tries to find resources again later on.

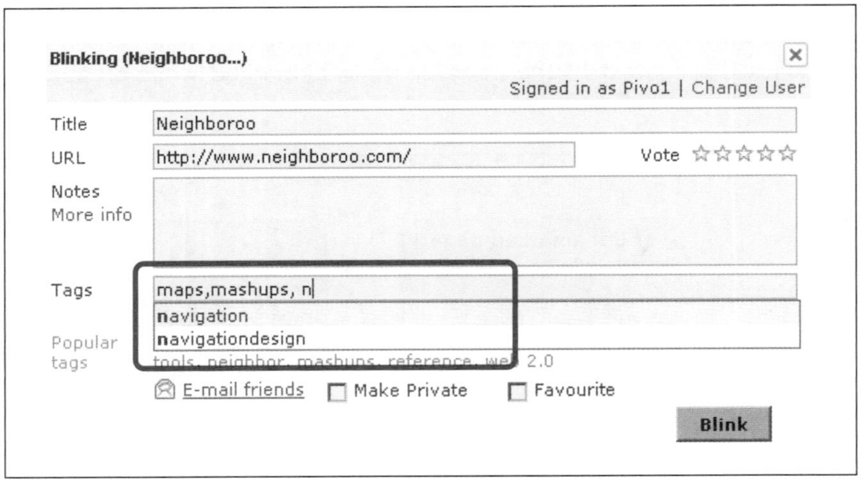

Figure 12-7 / Word wheel to navigate tags on BlinkList

Del.icio.us offers several ways to select from existing tags (Figure 12-8):

- The system shows tags that match the characters being typed under the tag input field.

- The system recommends tags from the visitor's list of tags.

- All of the visitor's tags are displayed and can be sorted alphabetically or by frequency.

- Del.icio.us suggests terms by revealing "popular tags" that others have used for a page or object being tagged.

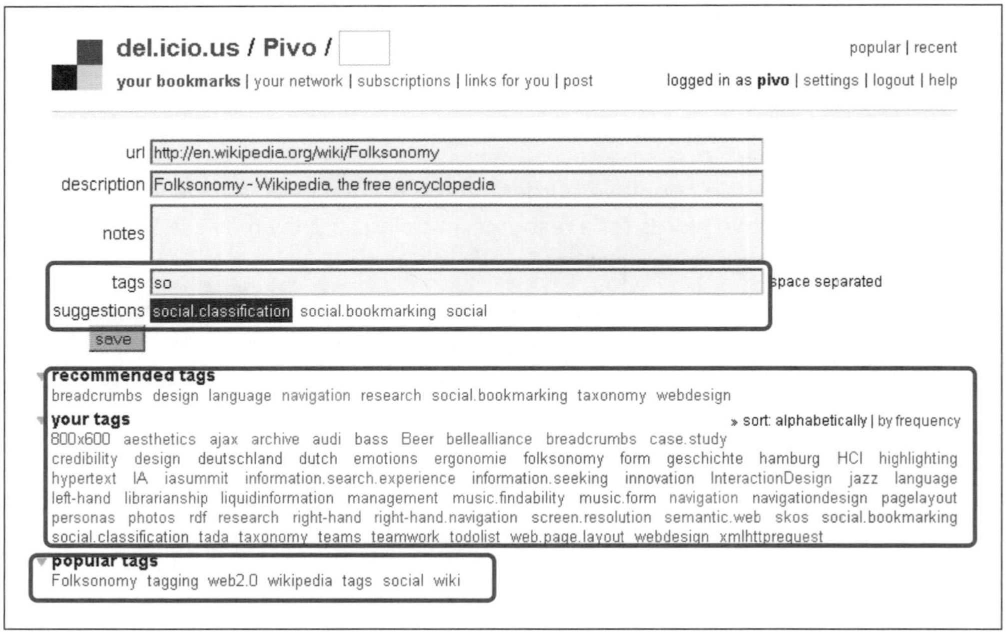

Figure 12-8 / Adding tags on del.icio.us

In each case, clicking the prompted tag adds it to the tag input field, where it can be extended and modified further, if needed. Overall, this approach encourages rich tagging and makes it easier to conceive of tags.

TAG FORM

The form in which tags appear is critical for finding resources. One common problem with some tagging systems is the handling of tag entries that are *spaced separated*. If you enter a tag with two or more words, some systems might encounter the space and separate the words into different entries in your list of tags. To get around this, users resort to using underlines, dots, or dashes to join multiple words into one tag or eliminating spaces entirely: to-read, social.software.programs, or newyearseveparty2007. Some systems allow the use of quotes to form phrases, but this is an extra task that may hinder creating good tags.

A better alternative is for a service to support *comma-separated* tag entry, in which the system separates words into new tags when it encounters a comma. This is more natural way of conceiving of descriptive labels and allows the user to type in multiple terms and phrases as they would normally. The system then keeps track of the multiword phrase as a compound tag.

An extension of the comma-separated tag entry is to offer individual fields for each tag. The Yahoo! Bookmarks service provides this type of entry, making it clear when forming compound tags which words go together (Figure 12-9).

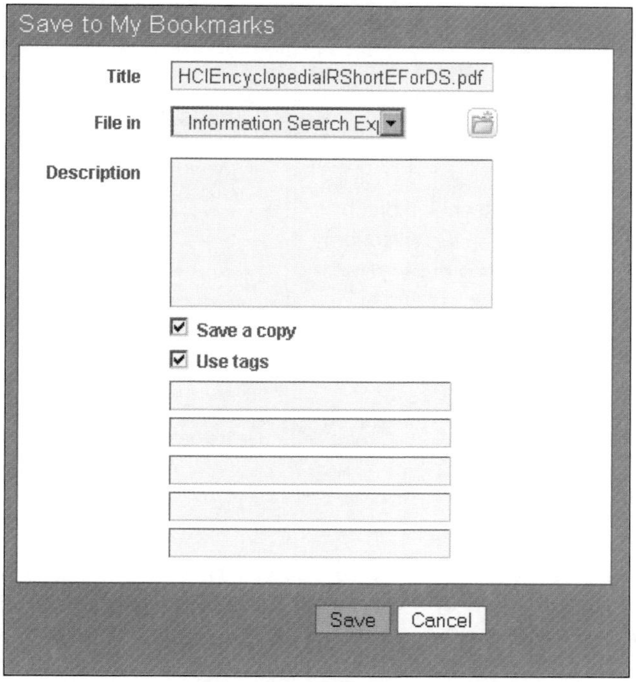

Figure 12-9 / Multiple fields for multiple tags with Yahoo! bookmarks

The form of the tag will effect navigation. For instance, a tag cloud won't accurately reflect the actual frequency of a compound term represented in several different ways. Or, a list of personal tags might include noise words such as "of" or "for," when they are meaningless without context. To improve navigation, the system should support normal creation of multiple word tags that mirrors people's natural language use.

Because a key motivation for tagging is to be able to get back to a resource, navigating your own tags is critical. An avid tagger may have hundreds of tags to wade through to find resources. The system should provide the ability to view tags in various ways, find related tags, and combine tags, as well as edit and manage tags in general.

VIEWING TAGS

Tagging systems often provide simple controls for filtering and sorting the list in various ways, including alphabetical, reverse chronological, popular tags, and so forth. These are generally effective and give users control over the use of their own tags.

BlinkList offers a tabbed navigation to four arrangements of personal tags (Figure 12-10): a favorites list, a popularity-based list, a chronological list, and a tag cloud. The tabs are easy to learn and understand, and this approach makes good use of screen real estate. The Favorites feature is particularly good for creating a subset of higher-priority tags.

Figure 12-10 / Four different views of personal tags on BlinkList

COMBINING TAGS

The ability to combine tags can be a powerful tool for locating a resource. It can reduce a large set of tagged items quickly, resembling the combination of facet values discussed in Chapter 11.

Del.icio.us enables users to combine tags and hone in specific tagged web pages. To do this, the system also presents related tags on the right side of the page when displaying a list of resources (Figure 12-11). These can then be combined to further reduce the set of bookmarked links. If you want to only see items tagged with "innovation" and "diffusion," you can click on the plus sign (+) next to one of the related tags. After viewing the combined set of resources, you can also remove either of the combined tags.

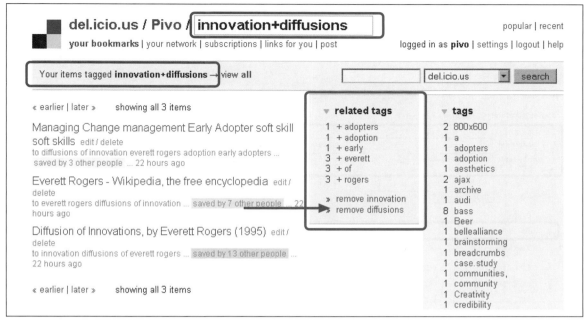

Figure 12-11 / Combining tags: a powerful way to filter resources

NAVIGATING RESOURCES

A tagging system should make it easy to browse through the tagged resources, as well as the tags. Frequently, the resources are presented in a table resembling a search results list. The standard practice is to list the user's recent tagged items in reverse chronological order. But further controls to manipulate this list help people find specific resources, including such things as:

- Filtering or reducing the number of items to look at by focusing on one aspect of the collection

- Sorting or ordering the list of tagged items in different ways

- Searching or directly finding tags or resources with a keyword search

Furl.net allows members to do all three. It provides a simple search that includes some filtering options (Figure 12-12, middle), as well as a table of bookmarks that can be sorted by Title, Date, Topic, Rating, and Views by clicking on the column headers (Figure 12-12, bottom). Overall, these controls allow people to navigate quickly to saved pages using any number of access points or strategies.

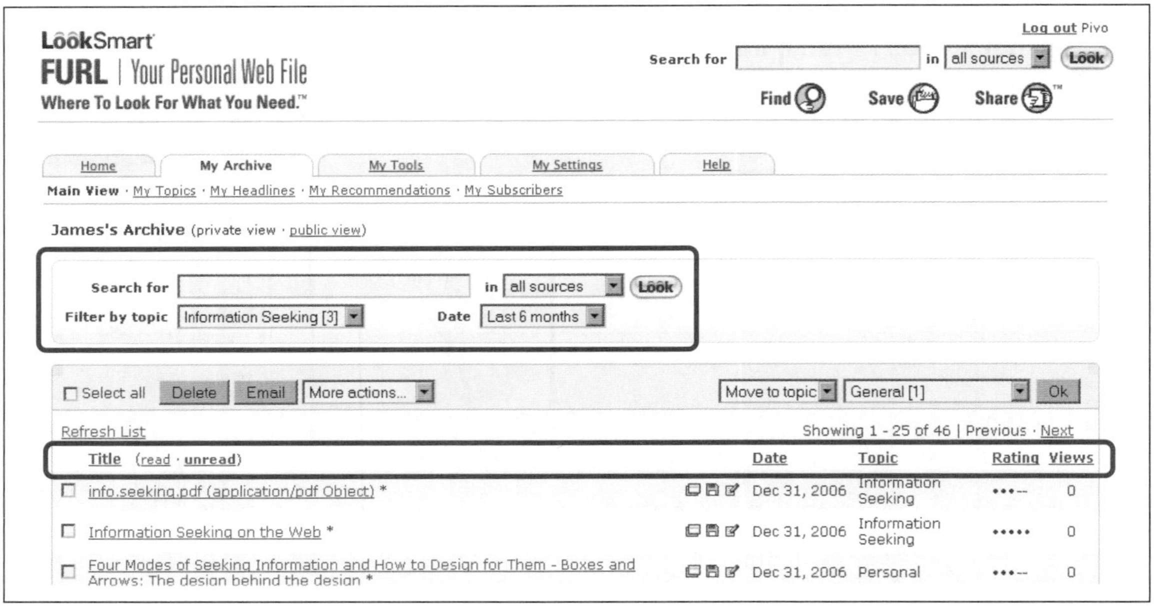

Figure 12-12 / Searching, filtering, and sorting your tags on Furl

NAVIGATING OTHER PEOPLE'S TAGS

The second reason people tag is to share resources with others. But have you ever tried to find a specific file on someone else's computer? It's often not that easy. Personal organization schemes are just that: personal. As a collection of personal organization schemes, social classifications present some interesting challenges in navigation.

Generally, browsing tagged resources via a social classification is exploratory in nature, leading to seren-dipitous discovery. Collaborative filtering and adaptive navigation therefore prove to be important tech-niques in exposing social classifications within a tagging system. What's more, you also need to consider social aspects of tagging. Linking to other people and viewing their tagged resources also becomes impor-tant in navigating social classifications.

ADAPTIVE NAVIGATION

Tag clouds are the most frequent way of presenting tags from social classification. Because there is not an intrinsic or stable hierarchy involved in a social classification system, it's generally not possible to display a limited set of top-level categories. And because tagging systems track millions of tags, displaying them all at once is also not possible. Often, a limited set of tags are shown in tag clouds, truncated chronologi-cally (Today's Tags or Tag in the last 7 days) or by popularity (Top 100 Tags).

Technorati offers several different views of tags in the system in one overview (Figure 12-13). Both the Tags this Hour and Top 100 Tags from A to Z views are types of adaptive navigation and will change as the social classification changes. In Figure 12-13, you can see that the iPhone was clearly a hot topic among bloggers at the time this screen shot was taken. In this case, the navigation options potentially change on an hourly basis.

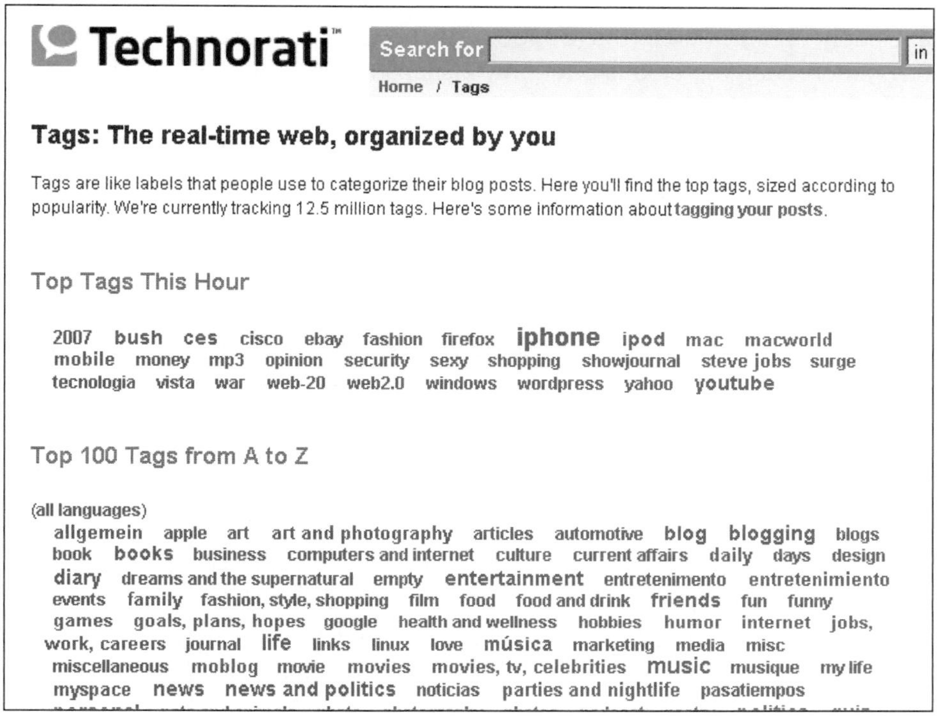

Figure 12-13 / Basic views of a social classification as tag clouds on Technorati

In another example, del.icio.us displays popular tags in a view that can be ordered alphabetically or by text size (i.e., popularity). Red tags are those that a user shares in common with everyone else (Figure 12-14).

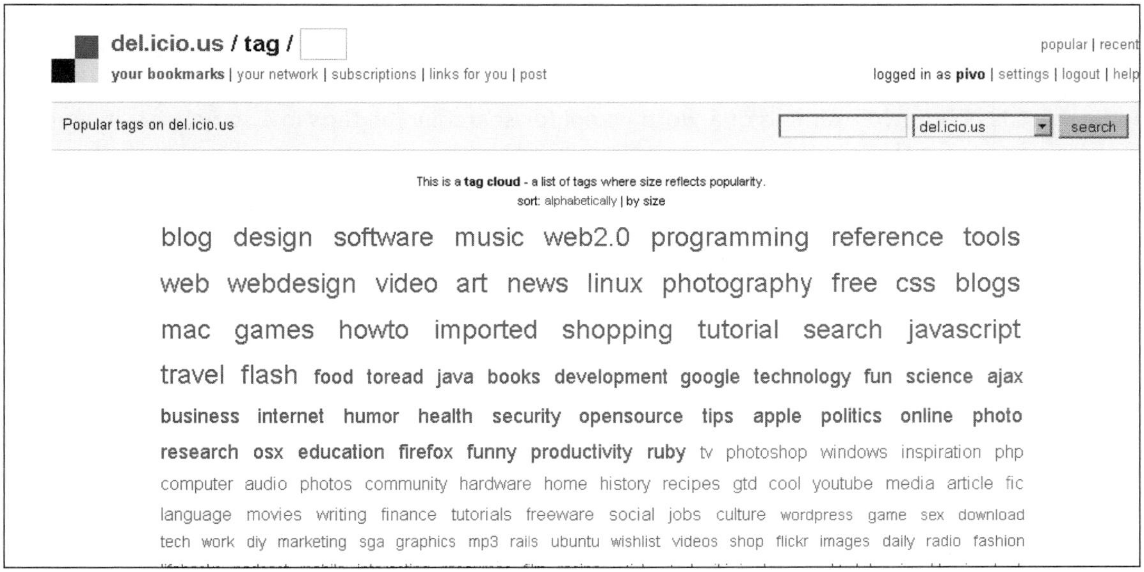

Figure 12-14 / Sorting by the size of tags in a tag cloud on del.icio.us

But some social classifications have millions of tags. Technorati claims to be tracking 12.5 million tags at this writing, for instance. Limiting a tag cloud to the top 100 tags shows a small fraction of the social classification. As adaptive navigation, such tag clouds offer only a snapshot of the tagging of the group at a given point in time. For this reason, LibraryThing even calls their adaptive navigation "Zeitgeist" in the main navigation (Figure 12-15). Notice in this example that the numerous adaptive navigation mechanisms show various types of information, such as reviewed books and authors, in addition to tags, which are much lower on the page and not shown in the figure.

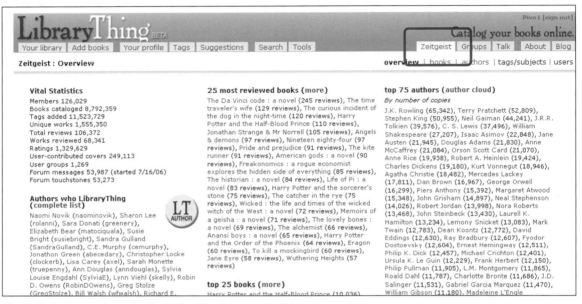

Figure 12-15 / Adaptive navigation under Zeitgeist on LibraryThing

Because social classifications can be so large, searching is another primary way of accessing tags. A word wheel (see Chapter 11) could help so that people could essentially access the list of tags for browsing. Currently, there is no known example of a word wheel for searching all tags in a social classification.

Collaborative filtering techniques can be used to make recommendations as well. This really exposes the power of a social tagging system. For any given resource bookmarked on Furl, for instance, users can see related tagged resources. Figure 12-16 shows the "People who furled this, also furled" feature. Color-coding helps distinguish the most popular links on a scale of a cool-warm-hot.

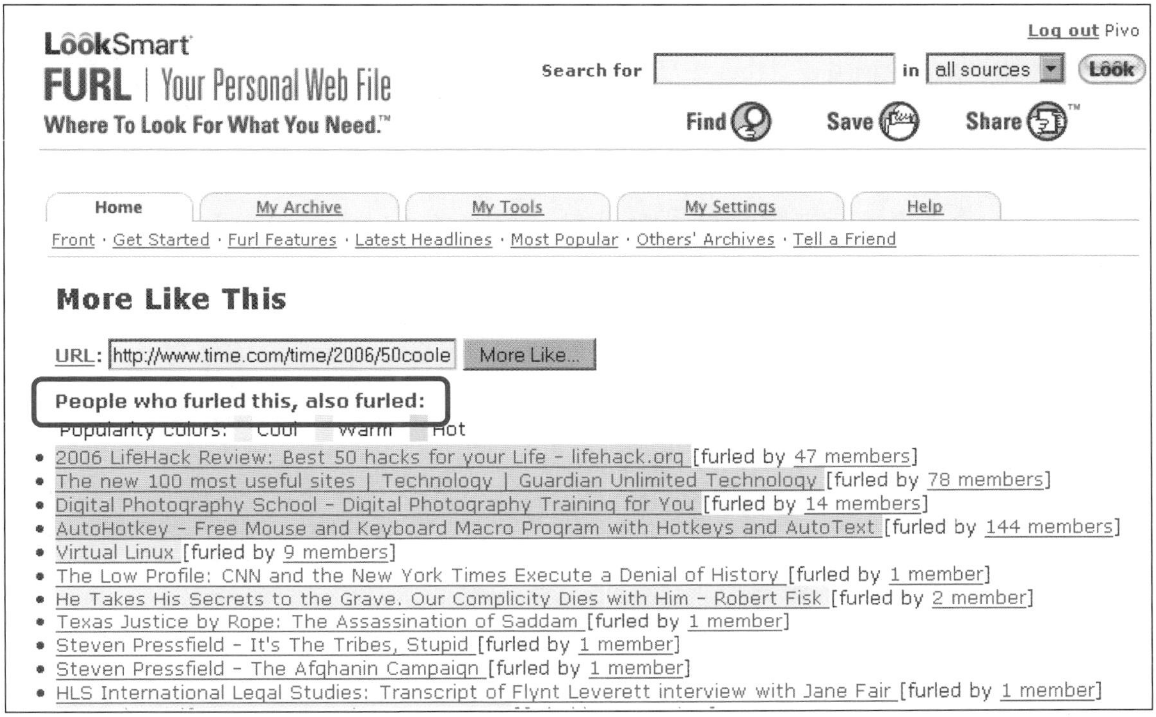

LookSmart
FURL | Your Personal Web File
Where To Look For What You Need.™

Log out Pivo

Search for [   ] in [all sources ▼] (Look)

Find 🔍   Save 💾   Share 🗐™

| Home | My Archive | My Tools | My Settings | Help |

Front · Get Started · Furl Features · Latest Headlines · Most Popular · Others' Archives · Tell a Friend

More Like This

URL: [http://www.time.com/time/2006/50coole] More Like...

People who furled this, also furled:

Popularity colors: Cool   Warm   Hot

- 2006 LifeHack Review: Best 50 hacks for your Life – lifehack.org [furled by 47 members]
- The new 100 most useful sites | Technology | Guardian Unlimited Technology [furled by 78 members]
- Digital Photography School – Digital Photography Training for You [furled by 14 members]
- AutoHotkey – Free Mouse and Keyboard Macro Program with Hotkeys and AutoText [furled by 144 members]
- Virtual Linux [furled by 9 members]
- The Low Profile: CNN and the New York Times Execute a Denial of History [furled by 1 member]
- He Takes His Secrets to the Grave. Our Complicity Dies with Him – Robert Fisk [furled by 2 member]
- Texas Justice by Rope: The Assassination of Saddam [furled by 1 member]
- Steven Pressfield – It's The Tribes, Stupid [furled by 1 member]
- Steven Pressfield – The Afghanin Campaign [furled by 1 member]
- HLS International Legal Studies: Transcript of Flynt Leverett interview with Jane Fair [furled by 1 member]

Figure 12-16 / Collaborative filtering on Furl

Furl is also able to recommend resources other people have tagged based on what any given user has tagged (Figure 12-17). Removing a recommendation with a red X provides relevance feedback, which is then used to provide better recommendations. This allows users to navigate and explore additional resources they may not have been aware of. Additionally, related "Furlmates," or other members with similar bookmarks, are also suggested on the right.

Accessibility

Just as you should avoid using color to communicate information on the Web, so too should you refrain from relying on the visual size of text to have a particular meaning, as with the terms in tag clouds. To make weighted text in tag clouds accessible, you have to add additional semantic information in the code to reflect the importance of a tag. First, you need to ensure that the tag cloud can be read by as a screen reader sequentially as a list of items. Then, you need to indicate the number of items indexed with each tag, such as in Figure 12-19, or in some other way show the relative magnitude of tags in the cloud. This information need not be shown in the interface and can be hidden so only screen readers can access it, if needed.

NAVIGATING TAGS FOR A GIVEN RESOURCE

Because tagging systems can contain so many tags, some tags may appear only when a user views a resource within the tagging system, such as for a bookmarked page or a video. Showing the tags others have used for that item is an important type of associative navigation that leads to discovery. When viewing artist information on Last.fm, for instance, tags from the social classification for that resource are shown on the right (Figure 12-18). At first only the most popular tags are shown, but visitors can click the See More link to view all tags. This exposes tags that may otherwise never be accessed through other means of navigation on the site.

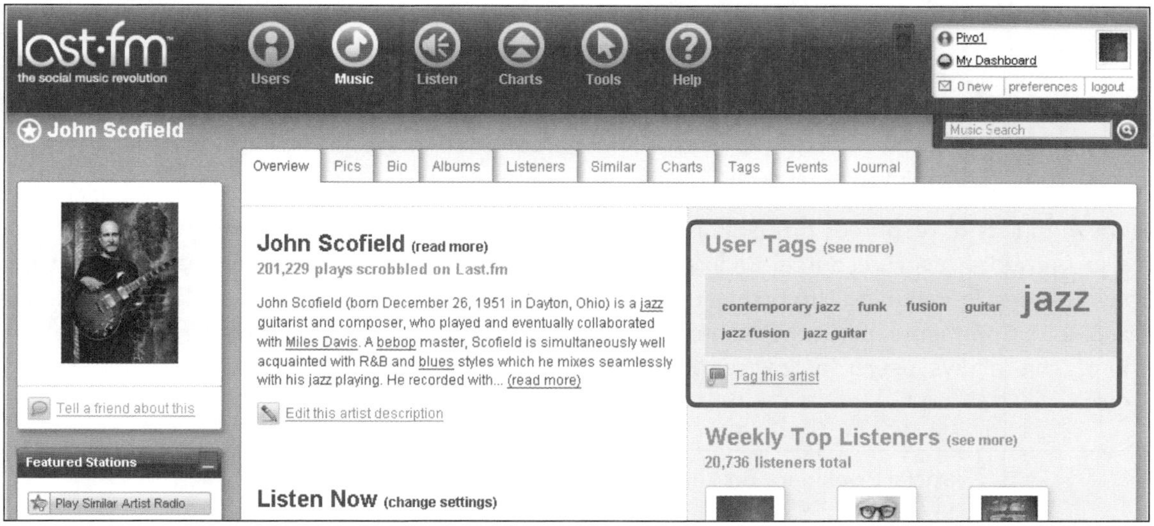

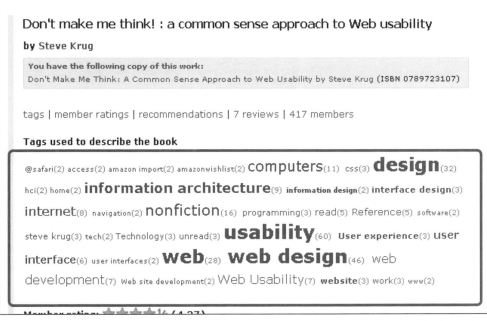

Figure 12-18 / Showing other peoples' tags for a given artist on Last.fm

LibraryThing even allows members to view the number of items associated with each tag in a tag cloud for a given item. This provides potentially valuable information about whether following that tag for more information will be fruitful or not. A tag with many items associated with it may be more appealing that a tag with only one thing. In Figure 12-19 the tags with their corresponding numbers for the book *Don't Make Me Think!* by Steve Krug.

Figure 12-19 / Tag cloud for an individual item on LibraryThing with indications of number of other books for each tag

LINKING TO OTHER PEOPLE

Inherent in a social tagging are the direct relationships between users of the system. When creating navigation mechanism for a social classification, try to expose these social connections where possible. This may be important for discovering new resources. The basic idea is that if a two people use similar tags, there is a good chance that those two people share a common interest. Viewing the other's tags might reveal new resources of interest to both.

While viewing lists of resources on BlinkList, for instance, there is a clear indication of other people who have also tagged a given resource. Clicking the corresponding link provides information about people who have tagged it, including the first person to have tagged and the last five people to have tagged it (Figure 12-20). Comments about the resource are also included, each with a link to the person making the comment. This allows users to link to others with possible similar interests and view their tagged resources.

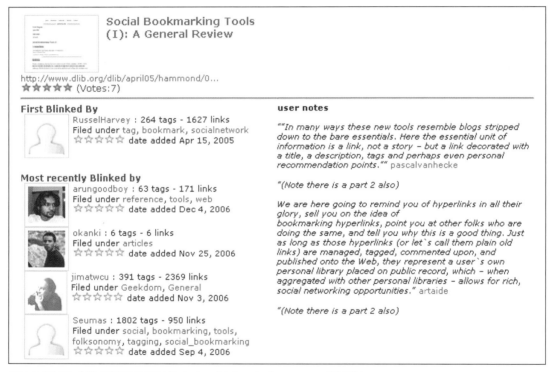

Figure 12-20 / Social information for a given bookmarked resource on BlinkList

Or, on CiteULike you can browse the resource libraries of other members, as well as their tags (Figure 12-21). If you find that another member (here: Icequeen) is saving similar material as you, for instance, you can even get notified of new resources added to her library with the Watch feature.

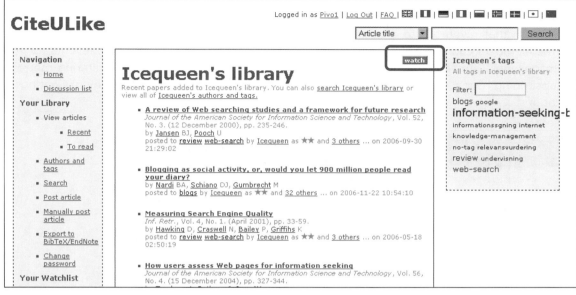

Figure 12-21 / Viewing someone else's library on CiteULike

Groups are another part of social tagging systems. Flickr is well-known for its discussions groups, for instance. Ma.gnolia does a particularly good job of exposing tags for groups. This provides yet another snapshot of a yet a smaller segment of the overall tagging population. The tag cloud for the Web Design group on Ma.gnolia in Figure 12-22 reveals that accessibility is currently a prominent topic amongst members.

Figure 12-22 / A tag cloud for the Web Design group on Ma.gnolia

SUBSCRIBING TO A TAG VIA RSS

Many tagging services enable members to subscribe to a tag via RSS. This will "push" newly added resources with that given tag to a user's RSS feed reader. Figure 12-23 shows an example of this on Upcoming. Members can subscribe to a tag to receive updated events. In this case, events for the tag "museumsgalleries" are shown. Unfortunately, the service doesn't seem to enable filtering metro areas when subscribing. Subscribing to a tag via RSS, however, is an important part of navigating social classifications.

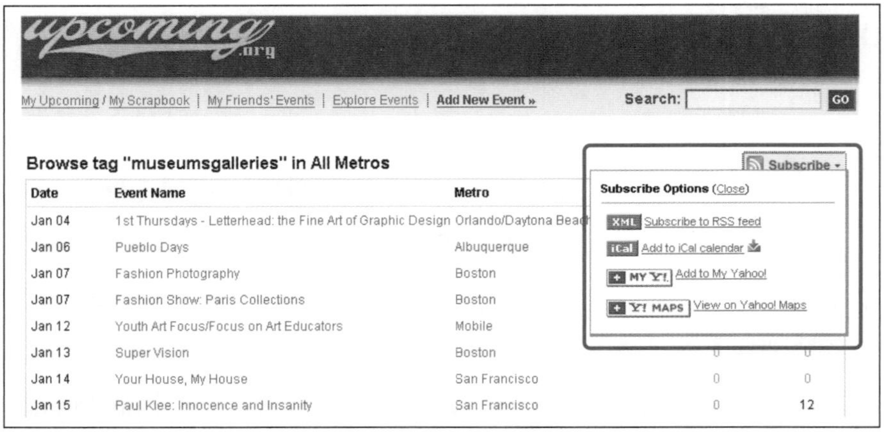

Figure 12-23 / Subscribing to tagged events via RSS on Upcoming

INTEGRATING APPROACHES: TOP-DOWN AND BOTTOM-UP

Not only do traditional ways of classification and tagging serve different purposes, as mentioned previously, but the two can also be integrated. We are already seeing large, open tagging systems benefiting from categorization. As they continue to grow, the need to navigate smaller chunks of tags emerges. Flickr has introduced something called clusters, for example (Figure 12-24). These are groups of related photos with a common theme. Even though such clusters may be automatically generated, the categories nonetheless provide an important aspect of navigation.

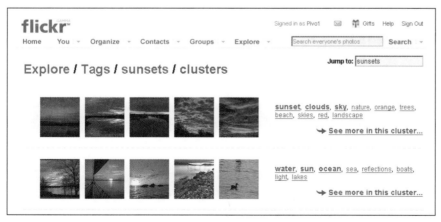

Figure 12-24 / Clusters for sunsets on Flickr

Flickr also allows navigation of photos by many other categories. Take a look at the options in the Explore menu in the main navigation shown in Figure 12-25. You can browse by:

- Time or chronologically (e.g., Most Recent Photos, A Year Ago Today)
- Geography (World Map)
- Copyright permissions (Creative Commons)
- Popularity (Popular Tags)
- "Interestingness" (Last 7 Days Interesting)

Such categorizations will likely continue to grow as the collection of photos and tags on Flickr grows.

Figure 12-25 / Flickr's Explore menu

Other systems have introduced the notion of folders or groups of tags, thus introducing hierarchy into tagging structures. See the bundle feature or the category "minimum use" for organizing your own tags on del.icio.us for an example. Further, as tagging systems grow, we may even start seeing domain specific services crop up. CiteULike already points in that direction, where bookmarks are academic in nature. This increases the value of the overall service to users and provides a certain focus that might otherwise be lost with open social classifications that have millions of tags on any every subject possible. Language-centric tagging systems may also emerge.

In a final example, Italian information architects Andrea Resmini, Emanuele Quintarelli, and Luca Rosati have developed an interesting application that blends top-down classification of bookmarked resources with bottom-up tagging, as discussed in the sidebar "FaceTag."

FaceTag

By Andrea Resmini, Emanuele Quintarelli, and Luca Rosati

FaceTag (*www.facetag.org*) is a working prototype of a semantic collaborative tagging tool conceived for bookmarking specialized domains. Using a lightweight structure, FaceTag aims to solve some of the linguistic issues currently plaguing social tagging tools such as polisemy (when a single word has many meanings), synonymy (when different words have the same meaning), and homonymy (when two words sound or are spelled alike but have different meanings).

The linear approach provided by traditional flat tag clouds is replaced by a multidimensional decomposition of the information domain in which each concept (bookmark) is described through aspects or facets (such as taste, color, size) that can be later combined as criteria to build a navigation system or to search the system. Each tag is associated with one of the facets (i.e. red to the facet color) and may have an arbitrary number of more specific sub-tags (dark red can be a specialization of red). The blend of facets and tags augments the information scent, adds context, helps avoiding ambiguity, and allows for improved navigation.

The placement of tags in hierarchies and facets is basically a byproduct of user activity—saving and collecting bookmarks—but the resulting social navigation is an engaging and powerful way to share and discover documents other users are working on. Facets guide the user along different conceptual dimensions at the same time, with the ability to easily add and remove criteria (i.e., tags) to restrict or broaden the result set.

Browsing and searching are seamlessly integrated, enhancing the overall usability, browsability, and findability of large collections of tagged resources.

In terms of navigation, the most relevant parts of the user interface are the search box and the sidebar. The sidebar lists facets and pertaining first-level tags. If a user clicks on a tag, FaceTag returns the results set of all corresponding resources. Similar to the faceted browse interface discussed in Chapter 11, the facets in the sidebar adjust to offer only those tags available, and a breadcrumb path is displayed with the active facet and the engaged (selected) tag or search term.

At each additional step these are updated to reflect the state of the query, and they can be individually leveraged to retrace an information path (disengaging) or to start a new exploration from scratch. Obviously, users may start searching for a keyword and then adjust results set using facets, combining the two approaches in any way they prefer until they reach a satisfactory answer.

Figure 12-26 show the resources for the tag "intranet design" in this given collection of tagged pages. This list can be narrowed by adding tags from other facets list in the sidebar on the left. In Figure 12-27, the user added article and shiv singh to the engaged tags and found a final result set. The facets and tags adjust accordingly. The items in the breadcrumb at the top of the screen list all engaged tags, which can be disengaged in any order by clicking the X icon.

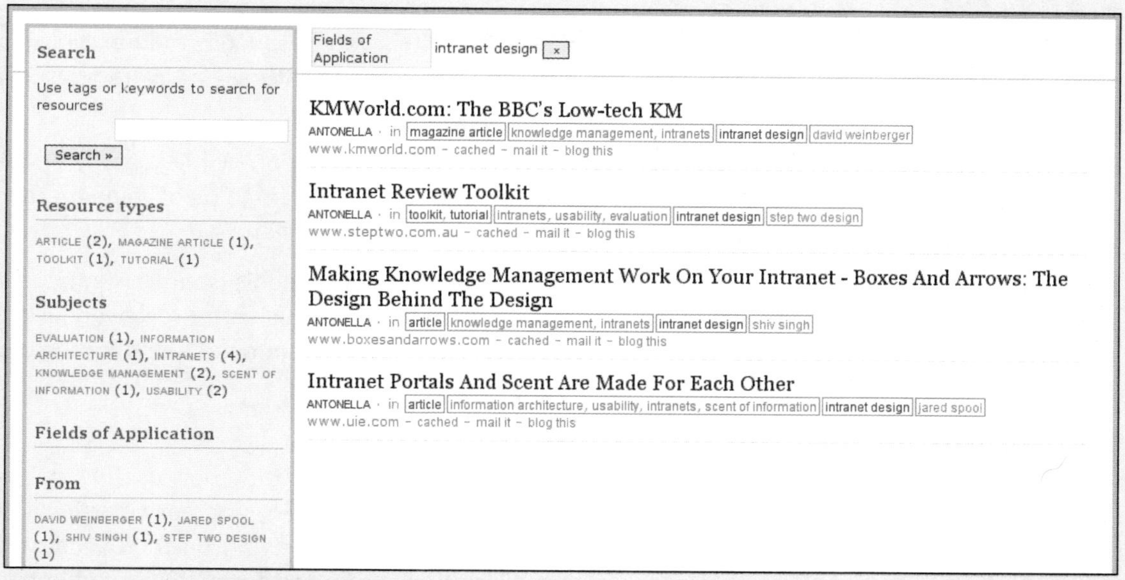

Figure 12-26 / FaceTag: bookmarks for intranet design

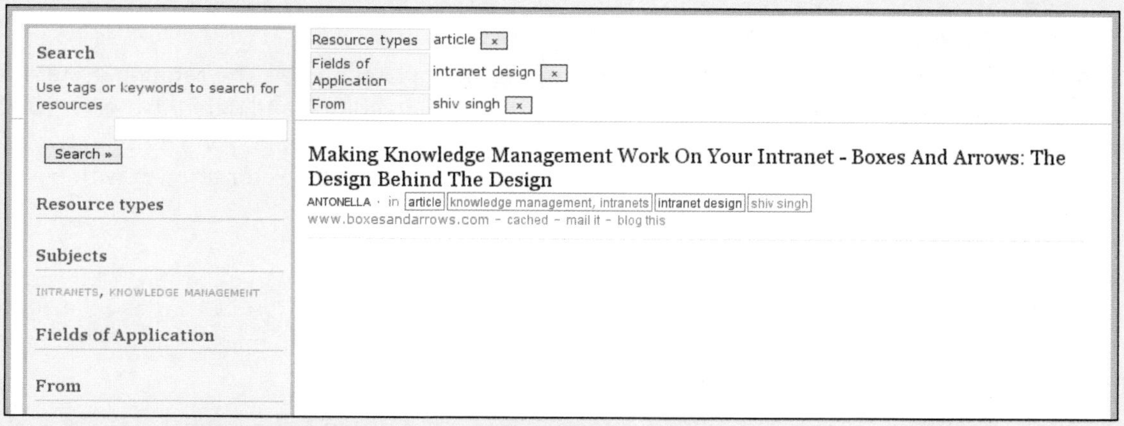

Figure 12-27 / FaceTag: bookmarks for article, intranet design, and shiv singh

FaceTag is ongoing work and planned future steps include extensive user testing to verify outcomes and emergent patterns of use and the introduction of social network analysis to study and leverage the user behavior. See the FaceTag web site for more details: www.facetag.org.

Andrea Resmini is an architect and information architect. An IT professional since 1989, he's now a PhD candidate at CIRSFID, the Department of Computer Sciences and Law at the University of Bologna, Italy.

Emanuele Quintarelli is an IT consultant, customer experience expert and information architect with Reed Business Systems.

Luca Rosati is freelance Information Architect and assistant professor in Informatics for Humanistic Science at University for Foreigners of Perugia (Università per Stranieri di Perugia), in Italy.

SUMMARY

Social tagging systems offer a new alternative way to classify digital, web-based information. Unlike controlled vocabularies, which are rigid and impersonal, tagging systems grow naturally as average users add personal tags to resources.

When tags become public for an entire community to use, a social classification or folksonomy emerges. Social classifications have many inherent relationships and links, but for a system to be of value these must be exposed and apparent to users of the system. Navigation plays a key role here.

Three key activities in the tagging process are important for effective navigation systems for social classifications: creating tags, using your own tags, and navigating others' tags. This chapter reviewed just some of the techniques and best practices currently in place, resulting in some recommendations for the design of social tagging systems:

Creating tags

Generally, the system should encourage tagging and lower barriers to creating rich, useful tags where possible. One way to do this is by making access to a tagging service quick and easy, particularly for bookmarking services. You can also prompt for tags, where possible, relying on the user's existing tags as well as tags from others. Finally, the system should allow for tag forms to resemble natural language as close as possible

Navigating your own tags

A primary reason for tagging is so that you can return to a resource later. The tagging system must therefore allow people to effectively manage their tags, including editing and deleting them. Providing options for filtering, sorting, and searching are common ways to let people navigate effectively. The ability to combine tags is also an important way to hone in target resources for taggers with hundreds of tags.

Navigating tags from other users

In navigating other users' tags, adaptive navigation proves to be helpful. You can expose the zeitgeist of the group, highlighting current trends and topics in the navigation. With collaborative filtering, tagging systems can also make recommendations.

Beyond this, exposing tags at the page level for a given topic is an important means of navigating a social classification. And because of the social aspect of tagging, you should consider how to provide rich linking to other members of the tagging community.

These are just some of the ways in navigation design can improve the experience of tagging systems. They are many other aspects to consider beyond the scope of this book, and we will likely see new and innovative uses of tagging in the future. There are many opportunities for you to consider ways of exposing metadata, links between tags, and links between people. For instance, at the time of printing this book, no bookmarking system allows users to browse saved pages by the domain name in the URL. It might be very useful to be able to see the top tagged sites in the Web Design group on Ma.gnolia (Figure 12-22).

Finally, consider ways in which top-down classification and bottom-up tagging can inform each other. The FaceTag example suggests concrete ways to integrate the two, but there are likely others.

QUESTIONS

1. Apart from those listed in Table 12-1, name three other web-based resources that could be tagged. What are potential unique aspects of tagging those resources? How would navigation to those resources be improved with tagging?

2. Consider the four modes of information seeking proposed by Donna Maurer as outlined in Chapter 2. How does a social tagging system handle each?

    a) Known-item searching

    b) Exploration

    c) Don't know what you need to know

    d) Re-finding

3. Search tags on a popular service such as del.icio.us or Flickr for a compound phrase, such as "cell phone" or "web design" or any other two-word phrase. Be sure to search tags only. Then vary the form of that term by joining and combining the words, such as cell-phone, cellphone, and cell-phone. Use the plural forms as well and search tags only again. Compare the resulting resources that are returned for each.

    a) What are the differences?

    b) What is gained or lost by changing the form of the word?

    c) Is something missed by changing the word form? Is that a problem?

4. Create an account for two popular bookmarking services, such as del.icio.us, BlinkList, Ma.gnolia, or CiteULike, if you aren't already registered. Bookmark at least ten new pages in each. Compare the process of:

    a) Creating tags

    b) Navigating your own tags

    c) Navigating other peoples tags

    What aspects are better or worse in each service? Why? If you were to make your top three recommendations to the owners of each service to improve each of the above, what would they be?

FURTHER READING

"Position Paper, Tagging, Taxonomy, Flickr, Article, ToRead," by Cameron Marlow, Mor Naaman, Danah Boyd, and Marc Davis (position paper, 2006). *www.rawsugar.com/www2006/29.pdf.*

> This is an excellent overview of how tagging systems work in general. Though unpublished, it provides a solid academic discussion of tagging.

"What is a Controlled Vocabulary?," by Fred Leise, Karl Fast, Mike Steckel (*Boxes and Arrows*, Dec. 2002). *www.boxesandarrows.com/view/what_is_a_controlled_vocabulary.*

> This is a well-written primer on otherwise difficult concepts. The discussion is easy-to-follow and uses real world examples. For anyone looking to learn more about controlled vocabularies, this is a great starting point. Also see from the same authors:

"All About Facets & Controlled Vocabularies" (*Boxes and Arrows*, Dec. 2002). *www.boxesandarrows.com/view/all_about_facets_controlled_vocabularies.*

"Controlled Vocabularies: A Glosso-Thesaurus" (*Boxes and Arrows*, Oct. 2003). *www.boxesandarrows.com/view/controlled_vocabularies_a_glosso_thesaurus.*

Women, Fire, and Dangerous Things, by George Lakoff (University of Chicago Press, 1987).

> Lakoff comes out swinging hard in this book, challenging the classical theory of classification. Using many examples he shows, for instance, that categories aren't always mutually exclusive with clear boundaries. This is a dense text that isn't that easy to get through. Though fairly old, its arguments are still salient and timely.

"Usage Patterns of Collaborative Tagging Systems," by Scott Golder and Bernardo A. Huberman (*Journal of Information Science*, 32(2), 2006): 198-208). *www.hpl.hp.com/research/idl/papers/tags/tags.pdf.*

> This is a brief, but more scientific article that statistically analyzes patterns of tagging on del.icio.us. Along the way, the authors make some interesting observations about tagging systems in general.

Navigation and Rich Web Applications

"No matter what the subject be, there is only one course for the beginner; he must at first accept a discipline imposed from without, but only as the means of obtaining freedom for, and strengthening himself in, his own method of expression."

—Igor Stravinsky

13

Consider for a moment the difference between surfing the web and using a program native to your computer, such as a word processor. At the heart of web navigation is the hyperlink, which connects pages by URL addresses. The interaction involved is fairly straightforward: clicking a link sends a request to a server at the corresponding address. After the requested files are returned, a browser renders a static page, which may contain more links leading to more web pages.

With desktop programs, you typically access files you've created that are stored locally on your computer. Clicking menu options such as Paste or Save doesn't take you to another document via a link, but instead performs an action. Sure, there is help text and you can link documents together, but for the most part, software navigation is about editing, saving, and manipulating text, graphics, or a file in some way. Compared to web navigation, this type of interaction is more dynamic, and it introduces the concepts of behavior and functionality.

But as new web technologies evolve, designers can increasingly simulate the type of interaction found in desktop software online. Consequently, the Web is becoming more and more interactive. This increase in highly functional web sites marks a shift in how navigation works and extends the possibilities for accessing information.

For the web designer, this means new issues to consider when creating a navigation system. Single-page interactions like those found in desktop software replace the basic idea of linking two static pages together, as is typical on the Web. The navigation design must necessarily take into account dynamically updated content and interactive features.

Existing techniques from fields such as interaction design, which has a long tradition in software application development, provide potential solutions. But creating interactive applications online isn't just desktop software design for the Web. Designers must embrace the constraints of the Web and support users in a way that makes sense in online environments. This chapter offers a look into just some of the new challenges and general considerations of creating navigation for rich applications on the Web.

RICH WEB APPLICATIONS

Technically, a *web application* is any feature on a web site that performs a function. A site search is a web application. So too, is a shopping cart or the checkout process on an e-commerce site. But these are fairly simple and commonplace examples. *Rich web applications*, also referred to as rich Internet applications (RIAs), however, are a class of more sophisticated web applications that behave similarly to software programs. Compared to normal web pages, they are rich in interaction, rich in content, and rich in functionality. Ultimately, rich web applications are a breed of their own.

The primary advantage of rich web applications is an enhanced user experience. Instead of the clicking from one page to the next with reloads in between each, rich web applications often make use of a single-page model in which updated information is quickly brought into the page (Figure 13-1). With this method, reorientation to navigation options is minimal or not present at all. Overall, rich web applications are more responsive and allow for quicker ways to find information, while potentially lessening the "lost in hyperspace" effect.

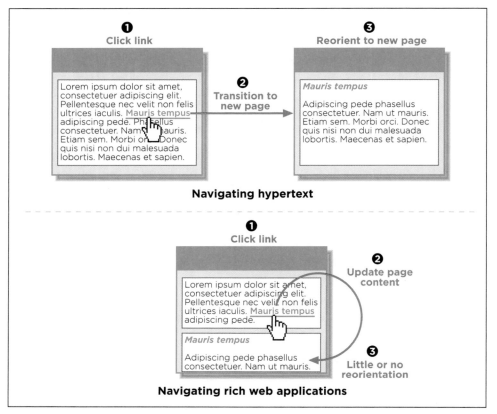

Figure 13-1 / Page-to-page hypertext linking compared to single-page interaction of rich web applications

For an example of these differences, compare the process for selecting cars on the General Motors (GM) site (*www.gm.com*) and on the Ford web site (*www.ford.com*), which features a rich web application.

GM offers a showroom of its vehicles that allows visitors to browse by different criteria in the tabs across the top: by brand, by body style, by model, or by price (Figure 13-2). Selecting an option under one of the tabs, such as the brand Saturn, transitions to a new page where all Saturn models are presented (Figure 13-3). After this new page loads, you experience a brief moment of reorientation to the new navigation options there. To view another brand, you would have to go back to the showroom's start page and make another selection.

Figure 13-2 / Page 1 in the GM vehicle showroom: select criteria

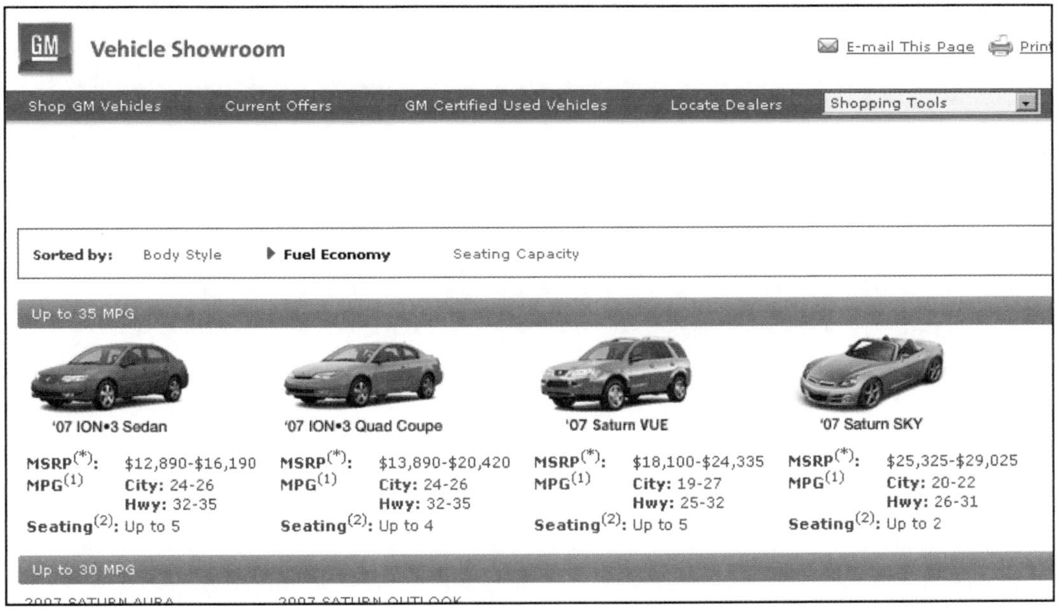

GM Vehicle Showroom

Shop GM Vehicles   Current Offers   GM Certified Used Vehicles   Locate Dealers   Shopping Tools

Sorted by: Body Style   ▶ Fuel Economy   Seating Capacity

Up to 35 MPG

'07 ION•3 Sedan	'07 ION•3 Quad Coupe	'07 Saturn VUE	'07 Saturn SKY
MSRP$^{(*)}$: $12,890-$16,190	MSRP$^{(*)}$: $13,890-$20,420	MSRP$^{(*)}$: $18,100-$24,335	MSRP$^{(*)}$: $25,325-$29,025
MPG$^{(1)}$ City: 24-26	MPG$^{(1)}$ City: 24-26	MPG$^{(1)}$ City: 19-27	MPG$^{(1)}$ City: 20-22
Hwy: 32-35	Hwy: 32-35	Hwy: 25-32	Hwy: 26-31
Seating$^{(2)}$: Up to 5	Seating$^{(2)}$: Up to 4	Seating$^{(2)}$: Up to 5	Seating$^{(2)}$: Up to 2

Up to 30 MPG

2007 SATURN AURA   2007 SATURN OUTLOOK

Figure 13-3 / Page 2 in the GM vehicle showroom: select a model

Ford.com also has a showroom, but this one makes use of a Flash-based rich web application (Figure 13-4). After selecting a brand, you can filter models with the slider bars on the left. A matching list is displayed on the right without a page reload. Selecting another brand doesn't result in a page reload, and, if you do change brands, the filter settings are kept. The process of narrowing or broadening a search is seamless and immediate within a single page.

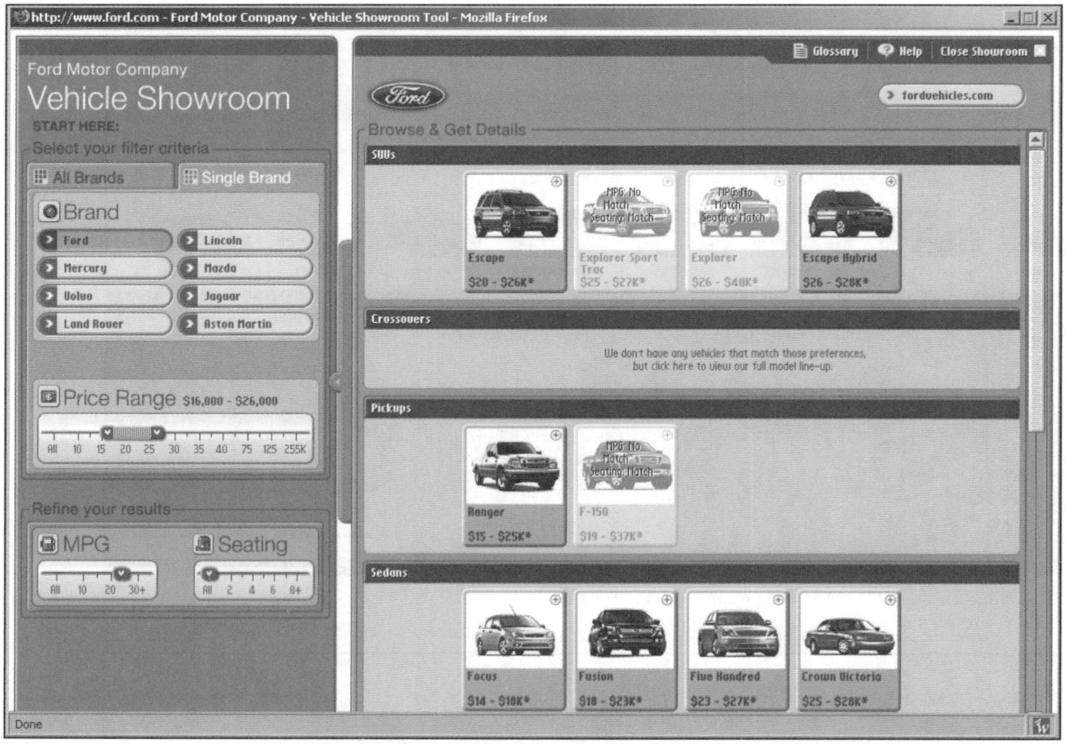

Figure 13-4 / Ford vehicle showroom: a Flash-based rich web application

The difference in interaction in these two examples illustrates the potential power of rich web applications. By avoiding page reloads, the Ford showroom feels more like a desktop software application, offering a richer, smoother, and more engaging experience. But this example also brings new patterns of user thinking that the design must address. When creating a navigation system for such applications, it's important to understand some of the key differences in navigating rich web applications and navigating normal hypertext links on the Web.

NAVIGATING RICH WEB APPLICATIONS

Most web users have developed a mental model of how navigation works:

- Navigating information is primarily done by clicking links.
- Clicking on a link brings up a new page.
- The back button returns to the previous screen.
- Each page has its own URL that can be linked to or bookmarked.

In emulating desktop applications, however, rich web applications introduce some twists into these basic assumptions and challenge the very model of the web as a hypertext system. With rich web applications, there may not be a transition to a new page with each action, screens may not have their own URL, the back button may erase a previous transaction, and interacting with information is more dynamic than a simple click of link. The next sections take a detailed look at these differences.

A key aspect of rich web applications is that they shift some of the processing of information from the server to the client, or local computer. This important technical difference changes the resulting web experience dramatically. Technically, there are two basic ways in which rich web applications circumvent the process of having to reload pages with each click. They either:

Load the data all at once

Some web applications simply load all the necessary information needed to interact with application to the user's browser at once. Filtering, sorting, and manipulating data then doesn't require a page reload. This is how the filters in the Ford showroom works in Figure 13-4: all of the model descriptions, images, and parameters are loaded at once, and filtering via the slider bars is done within the browser without a call to a server. You may have seen this elsewhere on the Web with a "please wait while loading" message before an application starts. Apart from an initial delay, this approach offers very quick interaction with information.

Load parts of the page incrementally

Another technique is to update only parts of a rich web application with new data without reloading the whole page. Often the navigation areas of the page remain static, so there is little or no reorientation to the navigation. The Ajax programming technique, which has gained popularity in recent times, relies on this approach. Ajax is discussed briefly in Chapter 7.

Google Maps (*http://maps.google.com*) is an example of a rich web application that makes use of Ajax. Quickly moving a map around on the page, the application must load sections incrementally to give the sense of a single map. There is a very brief pause in the display of the full map as the new sections are retrieved from the server. Figure 13-5 shows this with gray squares as temporary place holders on the left side. Notice the browser is loading the necessary pieces as the map is panned to the right. But while this is going on, the rest of the page with the navigation at the top does not refresh.

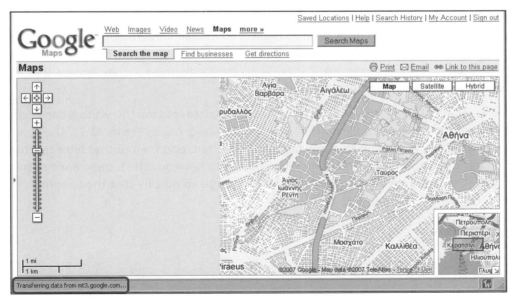

Figure 13-5 / Partial page loading with Ajax technologies on Google Maps

The results page on the A9 search engine also eliminates the need for screen refreshes with incremental page-loading techniques (*www.a9.com*). As visitors scroll down a long list of results, the next chunk of hits is requested and integrated into the page after a very brief pause (Figure 13-6). The experience is as if all the results appear in one long list, and it does away with paging navigation altogether.

Figure 13-6 / Incremental page load with results lists from the A9 search engine

But also keep in mind that the transition from page to page is so fundamental to our normal web experience that we've come to expect it. When designing rich web applications, you need to account for this by indicating to users that changes have occurred. If there is no feedback given, it may appear that a click has no effect or users may overlook updated information.

For instance, on the Serenata Flowers site, a large online flower distributor in the UK, visitors can find flowers quickly and easily with a rich web application (*www.serenataflowers.com*, Figure 13-7). They can first filter flower bouquets by selecting from one of the facets on the right, and then further filter by color on the ensuing page. In this case, however, unchecking blue appears to have no effect: there are currently no blue bouquets on the screen and the application refreshes the page so quickly that the user receives no feedback indicating that something has happened.

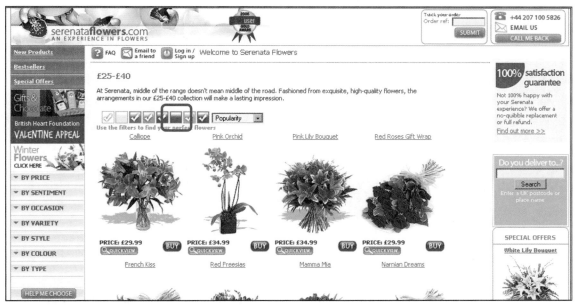

One way to call attention to parts of a page that have changed dynamically is to use the yellow fade technique, developed by 37signals (*www.37signals.com*). This highlights an updated region, which then slowly fades out over a few seconds. It provides necessary feedback to users about new content on the page without being intrusive.

TadaLists, a free to-do list service from 37signals, demonstrates the yellow fade technique (*www.tadalist. com*). Figure 13-8 shows a simple example of this when adding an item to a list of chores. After adding an item, it appears with a yellow highlighted background that then fades away until the background is white again.

Figure 13-8 / Yellow fade technique: after an item is added, highlighting slowly fades away

As mentioned in Chapter 3, browsers have their own navigation controls. These sometime interfere with rich web applications, particularly the back button. On static pages, the back button, as expected, moves to the previously visited web page. But for web applications with dynamically generated content and user-entered data, the back button becomes problematic.

If, for instance, a visitor has entered information in a long form and clicks the back button without having submitted that data, it may get lost unless the application is programmed to retain it. Or, if someone has just configured a computer online and clicks the back button, all of the selections may be lost. It's safe to assume that people will click the back button while surfing the web, so plan around this common user behavior. You have several options for dealing with the so-called *back button problem* in rich web applications:

Preserve user-entered data and selections

> If effectively used, programming scripts and session history management can preserve user-entered data and selections. Using the back button should retain the user's work to the degree possible.

Include explicit navigation controls in the web application

> Even if you effectively support the browser's back button, you may also want to include explicit navigation options to move forward and backward in the application, potentially dissuading people from having to use the browser controls at all. In general, don't require people to use the back button with your web application and provide alternative navigation mechanisms.

Warn visitors if they will lose settings or input

> If user-entered data can't be protected, warn users that it may be lost and give them a chance to go back and save changes without penalty. Google Docs & Spreadsheets (*http://docs.google.com*) is a very robust and highly interactive web interface that handles the back button and other browser controls well. If people use the back button, close the browser, access a bookmark, type in a new URL, or try to navigate away from the page in any other way, a warning message appears (Figure 13-9).

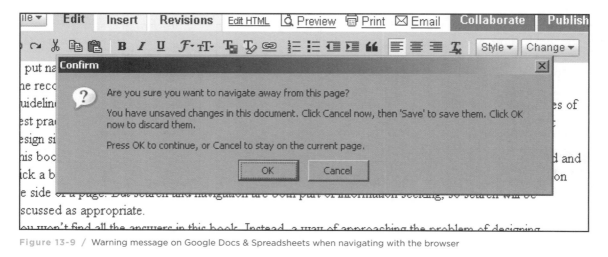

Figure 13-9 / Warning message on Google Docs & Spreadsheets when navigating with the browser

Also keep in mind that clicking the right mouse button in most browsers provides access to navigation options, as well as keyboard commands. Even if the application is in a secondary window with no browser controls, users may still have access to a back function, as well as the print, save, and reload commands.

POP-UP WINDOWS AND EXTERNAL LINKS

To get around problems with the back button and other browser controls, designers sometimes open rich web applications in new browser windows that have no controls. For example, consider the custom candle application for Yankee Candle (*www.yankeecandle.com*, Figure 13-10). This Flash-based application provides smooth interaction for assembling custom candles for weddings, parties, and events. But because it opens in separate browser window, it is separated from the rest of the web site. The experience is detached from the main site.

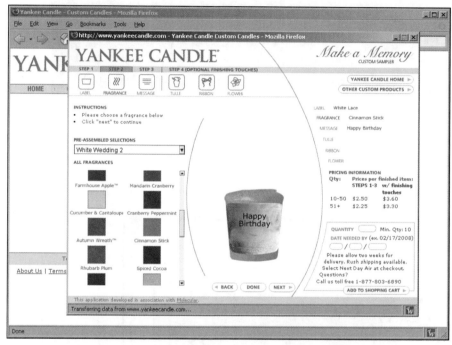

Figure 13-10 / Yankee candle's custom candle application in a new browser instance

External links tend to be problematic for rich web applications that open in a separate browser window because they very often open yet another browser instance. This can further confuse navigation to and from an application, and may leave a user's desktop littered with browser windows.

In a particularly convoluted example, the House of Blues Hotel in Chicago has an online reservations system that opens in a secondary browser window from the home page (*www.houseofblueshotel.com*). Within this rich web application is a link back to the home page. But clicking it displays the home page in the same window as the application, so that the simple navigation pattern of *Home > Reservations > Home* results in two browsers, each with the same page (Figure 13-11). Simple programming can avoid such navigation issues by targeting the parent browser window from the application.

Figure 13-11 / Circular navigation pattern moving to and from the reservation application for the House of Blues Hotel in Chicago

Of course, there may be other situations where detaching the web application from the main site to which it belongs is desired. Pandora, on online radio service, allows users to launch its music player in a separate window (*www.pandora.com*, Figure 13-12). They can then surf the Web normally while listening to their favorite music. In this case, a secondary window is a necessity and provides a convenience to users.

Figure 13-12 / The Pandora music player in a pop-up window

The point is that although rich web applications themselves offer a smoother interaction, navigating to and from them shouldn't be complicated or disorienting. You need to consider how you will access the web application and plan a logical flow with a normal web navigation experience.

TYPES OF INTERACTION

Rich web applications extend the types of interactions possible on the web. Examples include such things as real-time filtering with sliders, configuring objects with drag-and-drop, and panning across large surfaces or zooming in on images. Such actions also require new kinds of mechanisms and controls compared to normal web navigation.

REAL-TIME FILTERING

Rich web applications can filter information in real-time, with immediate updates to content. This is often done with sliders, or small controls resembling levers that you can move back and forth. Blue Nile, a large online retailer of diamonds and jewelry, provides a rich web application to find diamond rings (*www.bluenile.com*, Figure 13-13). A series of sliders filters matching rings by a number of criteria, and the list updates automatically without a page reload. With this interface, visitors are able to zero in on the highest-quality diamonds with the desired cut and price range in a matter of seconds.

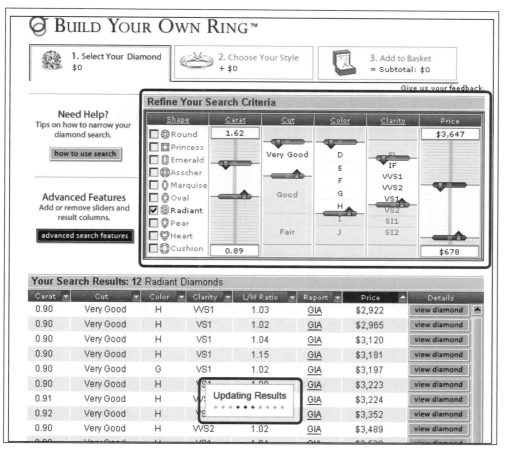

Figure 13-13 / Sliders for real-time filtering on the Blue Nile web site

DRAG-AND-DROP CUSTOMIZATION

Desktop software programs have long made use of drag-and-drop interaction. It's is a good way to allow people to visually arrange screen elements to their liking and to perform actions quickly. Though drag-and-drop is an uncommon action on the web, rich web applications now make this possible. The feature for organizing photos on Flickr.com, for instance, effectively employs drag-and-drop interaction within a web interface (Figure 13-14). Users can easily add or delete photos to a workspace in the center of the screen, where they can be edited as a group.

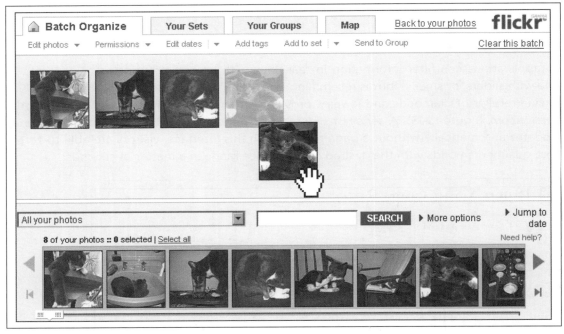

Figure 13-14 / Drag-and-drop on Flickr

One problem with drag-and-drop in general is that there is no conventional way to visually indicate that an element can be dragged, even for desktop applications. The beveled edges of button may make them look clickable and underlining links is a well-known convention, but nothing really looks ready for dragging. It's either a learned behavior or people must simply try it to figure it out. Because drag-and-drop is not an assumed type of interaction on the web to begin with, it's a good idea to explicitly call this capability out in a note or instruction on screen. Flickr does this with a prominent message (Figure 13-15). If you include drag-and-drop capability in your rich web application, be sure that you clearly communicate it in some way.

Figure 13-15 / A clear message to indicate drag-and-drop interaction on Flickr

PANNING AND ZOOMING

Some rich web applications allow users to pan across an object, such as a photo or map, by grabbing it and moving it around the page. Releasing the mouse stops the panning action. Zooming in on a photo or map is also possible, allowing visitors to view an object up close or from a distance.

Maps available on the Microsoft Live site include both types of interaction (*www.live.com*, Figure 13-16). Visitors can grab a map and push it in any direction to view other areas. A zooming tool allows for views that range from 5000 miles away to 80 yards (around 73 meters).

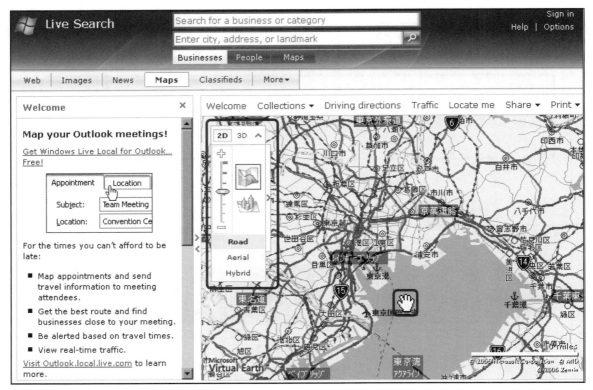

Figure 13-16 / Panning and zooming maps on Live.com

Overall, these types of interactions—filtering, drag-and-drop, panning, and zooming—are examples of the distinctions between using rich web applications and navigating static HTML web pages. But they also bring potentially conflicting interactions as well. For instance, zooming can often be done with the mouse's scroll wheel on some rich web applications. But the scroll wheel is normally used to scroll pages. In the case of Microsoft Live maps, the scroll wheel zooms *and* scrolls the page simultaneously, resulting in an unexpected and undesired effect. When creating new types of interaction on the web, consider normal behaviors and functions of web navigation, and design accordingly to avoid conflicting interactions.

PAGE SCROLLING

Scrolling long, text-based web pages is generally trouble-free. Book pages on Amazon.com, for instance, can be a dozen pages long without presenting an issue for customers. With web applications, however, longer pages become more problematic. Because people are entering data and manipulating elements on the screen, they may need the content and the controls in sight at the same time. It's harder to get an overview of all the functions on a page if you have to constantly scroll within rich web applications.

One way to avoid scrolling is to have collapsible components for controls, such as those on Kayak, an online travel service (*www.kayak.com*). The results page for flights has many helpful filters that are expanded by default on the left side (Figure 13-17, left). Each of these components can be collapsed to save space and bring into view more filters that were initially off screen. The Flight Duration component, for instance, is far down on the page when all the components are open. But in the collapsed state, its slider bar works quickly and accurately, filtering results instantaneously (Figure 13-17, right).

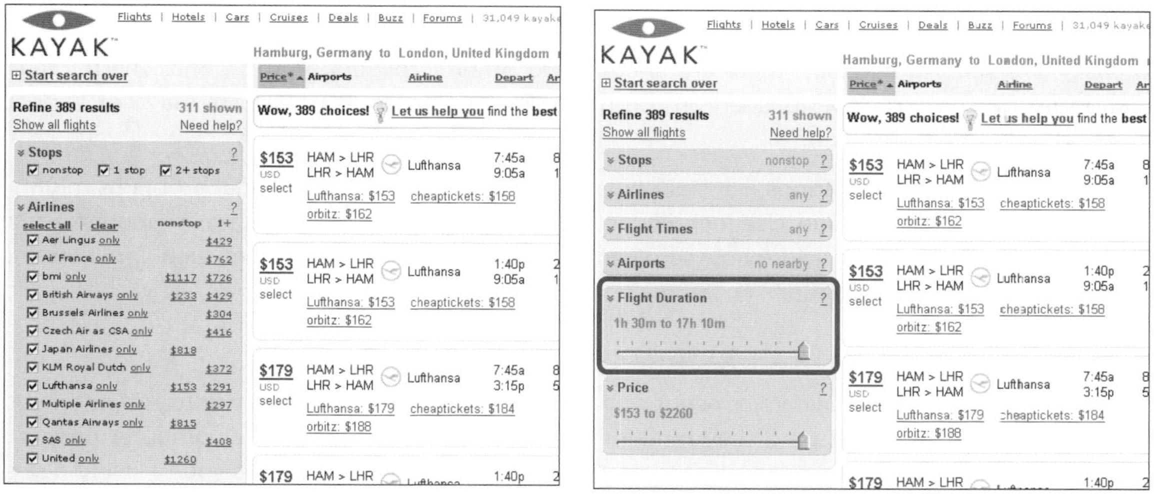

Figure 13-17 / Collapsible and expandable components on Kayak.com

Another technique to address scrolling is to create smaller regions of a page that scroll instead of scrolling the whole page. This approach is good for keeping one set of options or content in view while scrolling others, allowing for quick comparison. But you should implement embedded scrolling with the application only if you have to. The Nike online shoe store allows visitors to customize running shoes online with an embedded scrolling region on the right (*www.nike.com*, Figure 13-18).

Figure 13-18 / Embedded scrolling in a web application on the Nike web site

However, note that a small tip with the word "More" indicates there are more options below the scroll line. This may be necessary because of the non-standard appearance of the orange scrollbar, which customers could easily oversee. Additionally, there are already two other scrollbars on this page: one for the Nike store and one for the HTML page, seen on the right side of Figure 13-18. Visitors may not expect yet another and therefore overlook it.

When creating rich web applications, consider how pages scroll and what potential problems might arise when controls are set off the page. Use techniques such as expanding and collapsing components to optimize screen real estate. Also consider how scrolling regions embedded within a rich web application work with other scrollbars on the screen.

CAPTURING AND RE-FINDING INFORMATION

Normal web pages are static. Dynamic menus and similar mechanisms may add a sense of interaction in the interface, but, for the most part, they remain in the same state on the user's computer once downloaded. Further, each page has a permanent location with a single URL. This allows you to link to a specific page as well as to bookmark it.

Rich web applications are dynamic. They respond to user input to change the display of information on the fly. Though a web application may also have a URL, this usually points to the application itself and not a specific arrangement of information or objects within the application. Users' selections, sort order, and filter combinations, for instance, are generally not reflected in the URL of rich web applications. This makes it harder to point to a given set of content and, in many cases, once you close out of the application, your configuration of options is lost.

Technical workarounds can preserve the state of data in a web application. These usually involve creating a static URL for the given state of an application in some way. Yahoo! Maps, for instance, dynamically writes the coordinates of a given view of a map into the URL, including view type (map or satellite view) and zoom level (*maps.yahoo.com*, Figure 13-19). Any view of a map can then be sent via email or bookmarked and tagged on del.icio.us, if desired. The downside of this approach, however, is that the back button now recounts each action in panning and zooming the map instead of returning to the previous page.

Figure 13-19 / Permanent URL for each view on Yahoo! Maps

In another example, the interactive Index Returns Charts on the iShares web site, a division of the global financial giant Barclays, provides other ways to save configurations of data (*www.ishares.com*, Figure 13-20):

- Subscribers can save any chart they configure under the My Benchmarks feature on the left.

- Toward the bottom, there are options for downloading and printing a given index returns chart.

- Users can set a given chart as the default view, so upon returning, their preference is shown automatically.

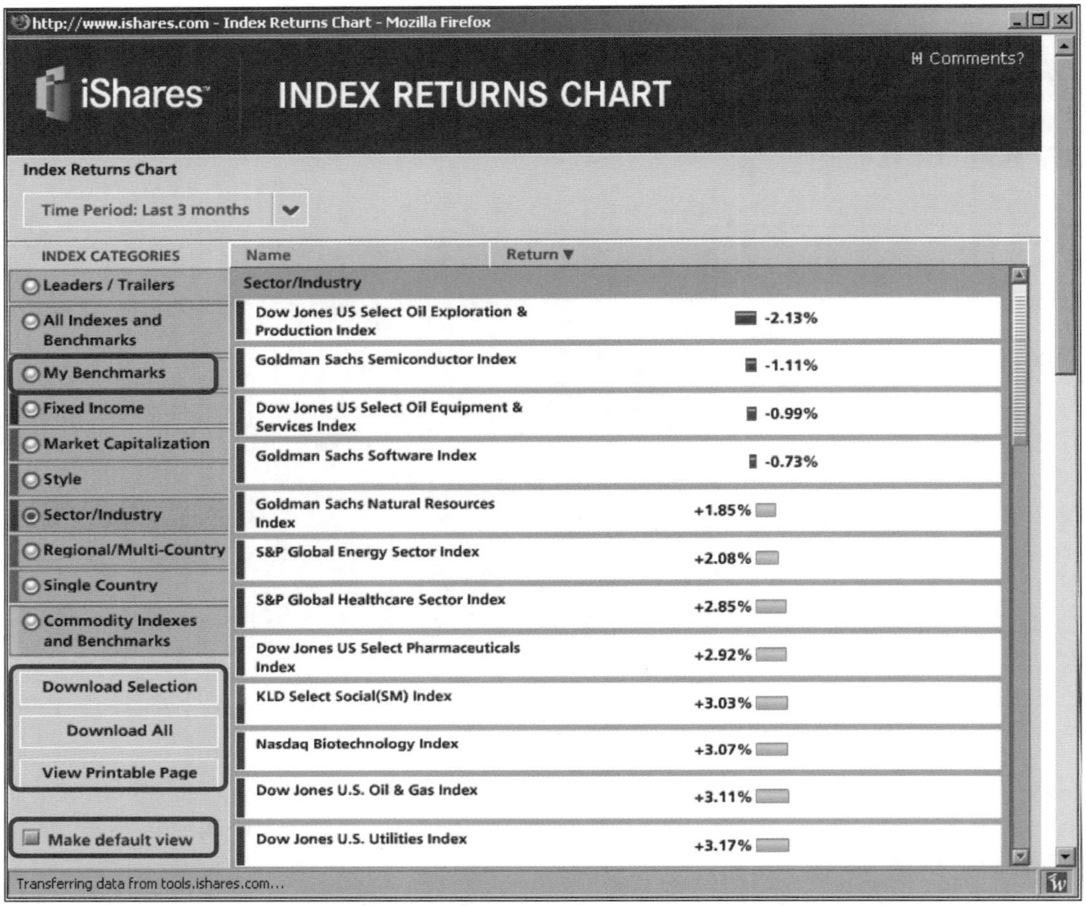

Figure 13-20 / Various ways to capture and re-find information with the iShares Index Returns Chart application

Overall, although rich web applications enhance the interaction with information, current examples often fail at allowing users to print, download, or otherwise save information for later use. Finding information with rich web applications may be easy, but re-finding is often difficult. By removing browser controls—which many web application do—even printing from a browser may not be possible. Consider how people will re-find, save, and share information, and then design to support these behaviors.

Accessibility

Rich web applications complicate web accessibility greatly. Assistive technologies such as screen readers generally don't handle dynamic applications well. They are built to read a static HTML page from top to bottom, and then allow users to jump back and forth in the page as needed. But if a region of the screen in a rich web application updates content after it's been read, there is no way for the screen reader to know this unless the application explicitly communicates a change.

Many web applications also rely on heavy use of JavaScript and other client-side scripting. These are not handled consistently by screen readers and may render an application inaccessible. Cross-browser compatibility is problematic with many rich web applications. Be careful about accessibility issues when embarking on a rich web application project.

The W3C began an initiative to help web developers make dynamic content accessible (Web Accessibility Initiative–Accessible Rich Internet Application Roadmap, or WAI-ARIA Roadmap). See the first "public working drafts" for more on this effort: *http://w3.org/TR/2006/WD-aria-roadmap-20060926*.

The article "Accessibility of AJAX Applications" also provides a good overview of some of the issues; see *http://webaim.org/techniques/ajax*.

DESIGNING RICH WEB APPLICATIONS

The overall process for designing rich web applications looks similar to the framework outlined in Part 2 of this book:

- Investigate user goals and business goals, and derive product requirements.
- Structure the product logically to meet those goals and requirements.
- Explore alternative design directions and capture these in screen layouts.
- Design the final screen presentation, considering such things as font, color, and icons.
- Evaluate and test designs as you go along.

Of course, specific implementation teams will have their own methods and phases, but they are usually variations of the above, even when working in fast iterations on agile projects. Design processes in general move from abstract to concrete; this progression is no different for rich web applications.

Many of the deliverables for creating rich web applications are similar to those mentioned in previous chapters. Personas and scenarios are important artifacts to define and communicate user needs. Site maps allow you to plan the structure of the application. Wireframes are good tools for identifying and working through different design directions. And screen designs, prototypes, and UI specifications document the final solution.

But compared to information-rich sites, where the content and its organization are main design concerns, rich web applications allow for transactions and dynamic displays of information. In creating rich web applications, you must therefore consider the behavior of the application and how people with interact with it.

Interaction design is a broad field that deals with designing the behavior of products. It encompasses everything from interacting with a computer program to interacting with a physical product such as a mobile phone. The field has gained particular importance and prominence in web design because of the increase of rich web applications and new technologies that allow for more transactions on the web.

Existing techniques help bridge the gap between conventional web site design and rich web application design. Some important differences to consider include:

Structure

The core of a web site is typically a hierarchical structure. Rich web applications, however, often rely on hub and spoke structures and linear workflows, both discussed in Chapter 8. Wizards represent a typical linear structure, for instance, where screens appear sequentially. With a hub, there is a main page for viewing information and controlling the application and single pages extending from it.

Consider any online email program, such as Google Mail, Hotmail, or Yahoo! Mail. You typically have a main inbox, and from there you can get to screens to compose an email, set preferences, view contacts, or manage folders, among other things. This is a basic hub and spoke structure (Figure 13-21).

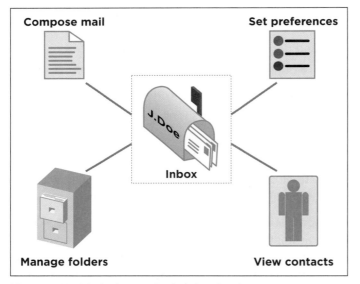

Figure 13-21 / A simple example of a hub and spoke structure

Hybrids of these types of structures are also common, such as those that Bob Baxley calls *guides* in his book *Making the Web Work*. He explains: "Similar to wizards, [guides] lead users through a sequence of forms. However, once the sequence is finished, they behave like hubs, providing non-sequential access to form."[1] In Figure 13-22, the Review screen becomes a hub only after each step in the linear structure is completed.

---

1   Bob Baxley, *Making the Web Work* (New Riders, 2003): 137.

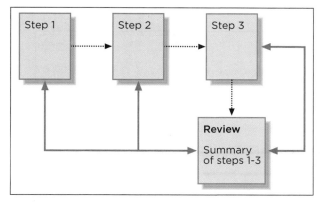

Figure 13-22 / The guide structure: a mix of linear and hub and spoke structures

State and persistence

Because rich web applications are dynamic, the *state* of the screen now becomes important. This includes such things as filter settings, sort order, user-selected criteria, and the position of elements on the page. Unlike normal static web pages, rich web applications have conditional situations that you must take into account.

Having the current state persist is important for saving work or configurations. When using a customizable home page, as with Netvibes (*www.netvibes.com*), you'd expect the last arrangement of components on the screen to persist the next time you visit the site. Or, if you sort a list of emails, you might expect that sort order to be retained while using an online email service. But unless programmed to remember your last settings, the service won't be able to retain a given state of the application.

There are three different levels of persistence to for you to consider:

- Persistence within a workflow, or retaining settings only as people move through a particular process or procedure with the application
- Persistence within a session, or maintaining settings as long as a user is logged in or has accessed the service
- Persistence across sessions, or persistence of options even after the person logs out, closes the browser, and restarts the computer

Note that none of these is better than the other, and creating persistence rules for an application involves a mix of different types.

Each time you log into the Yahoo! Mail service, for instance, you start on the Home tab regardless of where you left off in your last session. In other words, there is no persistence of the last screen you viewed. However, the last state of your inbox does persist across sessions, including the sort order of emails and the width of panels on the screen. When composing a new email, you can show or hide the Bcc: line. But this stays open only while writing the current email. If you compose another email, the Bcc: line returns to its default closed state (Figure 13-23). These are all expected behaviors of persistence that take into account user needs and context of use. Keep in mind that over-persisting options can be as annoying as not retaining them at all, so balance is the key.

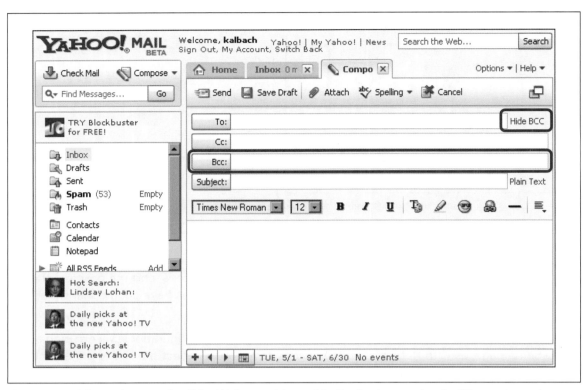

Figure 13-23 / Composing an email on Yahoo! Mail: no persistence of the Bcc: line (open or closed) within or across sessions, as expected

Note that on the Web it can be problematic to retain settings and session data because of the volatile nature of the connection to users. Cookies are the most common way to do this without having a user account. If users are required to log in, state and persistence can be tracked through their profiles. Find out about the constraints of your system regarding persistence during an analysis of the technologies involved, and design accordingly.

Errors

Navigating the Web via normal hyperlinks generally won't produce any errors that prohibit people from moving forward. Either a link works or it doesn't. Of course, the user could make an error and select the wrong link, but even then, navigation will not stop. With rich web applications, however, user input and selections could produce situations that are impossible to process, thus stopping users and asking them to correct values. Dates, email addresses, and mandatory menu selections are examples of input that can cause errors.

Generally, strive to avoid user-caused errors where possible. One approach is to gray out options until mandatory input is entered. Or, as in Google Docs & Spreadsheet, hide options that will cause errors until the user takes a required action. Figure 13-24 shows the Actions menu opened with no checked items in a list of documents. Instead of showing the options in this menu, which would cause an error without anything selected, a simple message is displayed. Compare this to the same menu after an item has been checked (Figure 13-25).

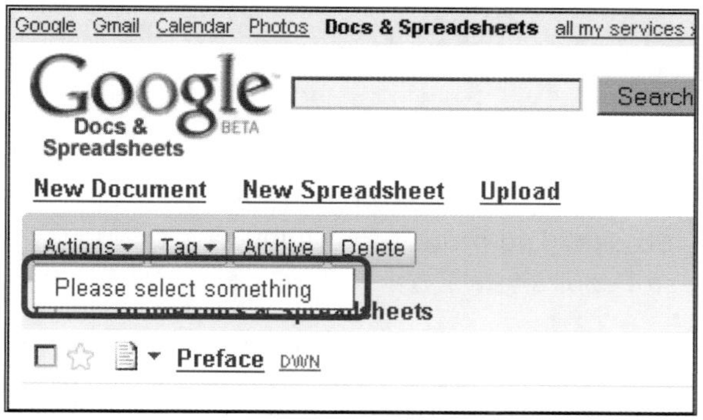

Figure 13-24 / Actions menu with no items selected

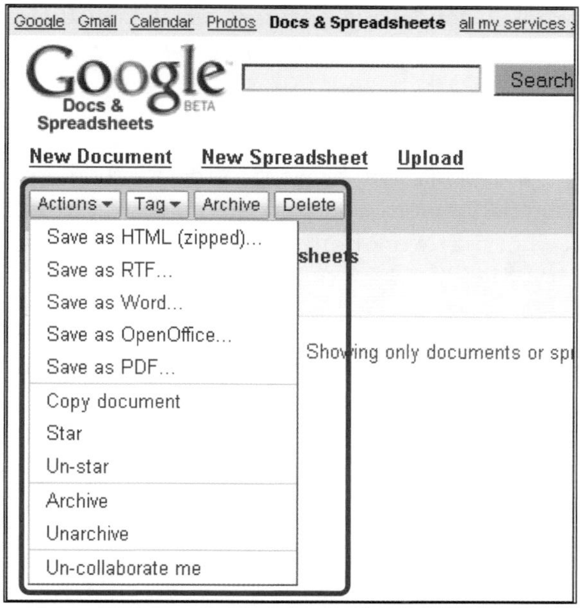

Figure 13-25 / Actions menus with items selected

In many situations, there is no choice but to stop the user's workflow and require them to fill in missing data or correct entries and selections before proceeding. When designing rich web application, you must take error conditions into account.

Traditional desktop software interfaces have relied on these and other principles of interaction design for a long time. Much of the knowledge for designing software interfaces can be applied to rich web applications. But the web has its own constraints and contexts that make it unique: page loads, client-server technology, and its overall hypertext environment. Designing web applications is not just about recreating a desktop application on the web—it's about creating an application for the web, taking into account the expectations of web surfers and constraints of the medium.

For more on interaction design in general, see Dan Saffer's *Designing for Interaction* and Alan Cooper and Rob Reimann's *About Face 2.0*, cited at the end of this chapter.

Specifying Navigational Behavior

By Mark Edwards

As for conventional web sites, *task flows* for rich web applications are the steps users follow to achieve their goals while interacting with your web site. The more thoroughly you understand your users' needs and task flows, the more successful your site will be.

To analyze how users might approach your rich web application, observe and interview people trying to reach similar goals on your competitor's sites. You can capture the sequence of tasks in a written narrative, often called a *scenario*, or model it in a sequence of steps. Tasks flows can be a straightforward sequence of steps, loop back on themselves, or have branches in them, showing where users choose different ways to meet their goal. A good way to capture a task flow, therefore, is to use a set of cards, because you can easily rearrange them as you discover complexity.

How users go about achieving their goals in these situations is constrained by the way the sites have been put together. Although it is useful to know how people use existing sites that have a similar purpose, what you should strive to uncover is the ideal way they want to achieve their goal. After conducting observational interviews with a number of users, you can determine what works well for given types of user, and you can discuss what may work better, enabling you to model ideal task flows.

For example, a user visits your site with the goal of finding and printing properties with at least two bedrooms and a garden that are within a specific price range and area of London. The user's ideal task flow while using your rich web application for property sales might be:

1. Choose postcodes that encompass the area of interest.

2. Submit search and view a list of results.

3. Filter results to houses with two or more bedrooms.

4. View matching houses on a map.

5. Filter to houses within the price range with gardens.

6. Browse around the map, viewing details of potential houses within the page.

7. Add desired houses to a basket, and exclude others from being seen again.

8. View and print a list of all desired houses.

Remember, however, that other visitors may have different goals, and that all the main goals need to be identified and understood to design the rich web application.

Once you have the ideal task flows, for the set of goals to be supported, you can convert these into *screen flows* (or page flows) for the web developers to use while building the site (Figure 13-26). These flows map out the routes through your rich web application, and you should aim to have at least one for each goal. You can break down goals into numerous screen flows for complex task flows.

Much detail is required to fully specify the behavior of rich web applications. You should specify:

- Entry and exit points in the flow
- Each page in the flow, including pop-ups
- Labeled links between pages
- Actions within the page resulting in dynamic data updates
- Branching points that require server-side decisions, including error conditions
- Annotations to explain functionality

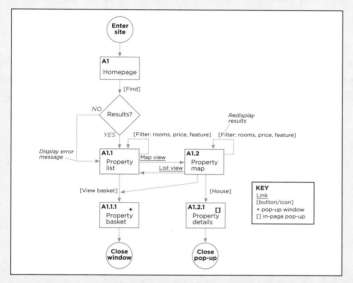

Figure 13-26 / An example screen flow for a property sales rich web application

Give each page a unique name and ID, so they can easily be identified, and use symbols to differentiate window pop-ups, in-page pop-ups, and pages external to the site, from the main pages. Label links as they are labeled in the accompanying page designs, and indicate buttons and icons with square brackets and standard links with underlined text. Show dynamic data updates, such as filtering, by offering links back to the same page. To avoid overloading the diagram, exclude links common to most pages, such as global navigation, specifying these once in their own diagram. Finally, use annotations to explain key application functionality.

Although Figure 13-26 is a simple example, specifying a rich web application fully in this manner, when combined with detailed page designs, provides web developers most of what they need to build a web site. This approach to specification accounts for both conventional web site navigation and dynamic behavior in an effective, diagrammatic format, thereby keeping the amount of text that needs to be written in a user interface specification to a minimum.

Dr. Mark Edwards is a user experience consultant working for LexisNexis in the UK, and an advocate of lightweight, effective specifications. You can contact him at dredwards@acm.org.

Learning curves on the web must necessarily be quick. People won't spend a lot of time to learn how to use your site. This contrasts the expected learning curves for desktop software applications, for instance. Programs that you own and have installed on your computer may be used more frequently and for different purposes than a rich web application on an e-commerce site. Desktop software may even come with a manual and, in some cases, require training. But you'd hardly expect to have to read a manual to purchase an article on an e-commerce site.

An approach to creating applications that addresses a need for very quick learning curves and infrequent usage is called *inductive user interface*, pioneered by designers at Microsoft, most notably in their MS Money 2000 software program.[2] A few key guidelines and principles of this technique are particularly relevant to web application design:

Limit each screen to one primary task

Inductive design techniques take a wizard-like approach to structuring the task flow of an application by breaking complex actions into smaller, comprehensible steps. In this sense, inductive design works well with the page by page style of navigation inherent to the web.

State each task clearly and explicitly

Label the primary task of the page prominently and obviously. Don't keep people guessing the purpose of a link, button, or navigation option. Embed instructions into the interface and make labels explicit.

Make the next step obvious

There should be clear ways to complete a task and move on to a new one. This creates a sense of closure to the task and can reduce uncertainty as well.

Amazon is a particularly good example of inductive design. No manual or help files are needed to purchase a book there: instructions are explicitly given directly onscreen. Figure 13-27 reflects many of the principles of inductive design during the checkout process on Amazon.com:

- The overall process is broken down into individual steps to guide the shopper through the checkout.
- There is a clear instruction at the top of the page for the primary task on the page.
- The options themselves are explicitly labeled and require no further explanation.
- There is one clear option to move to the next step.

---

2 Microsoft Corporation, "Microsoft Inductive User Interface Guidelines" (February 9, 2001). *http://msdn.microsoft.com/library/default.asp?url=/library/en-us/dnwui/html/iuiguidelines.asp*.

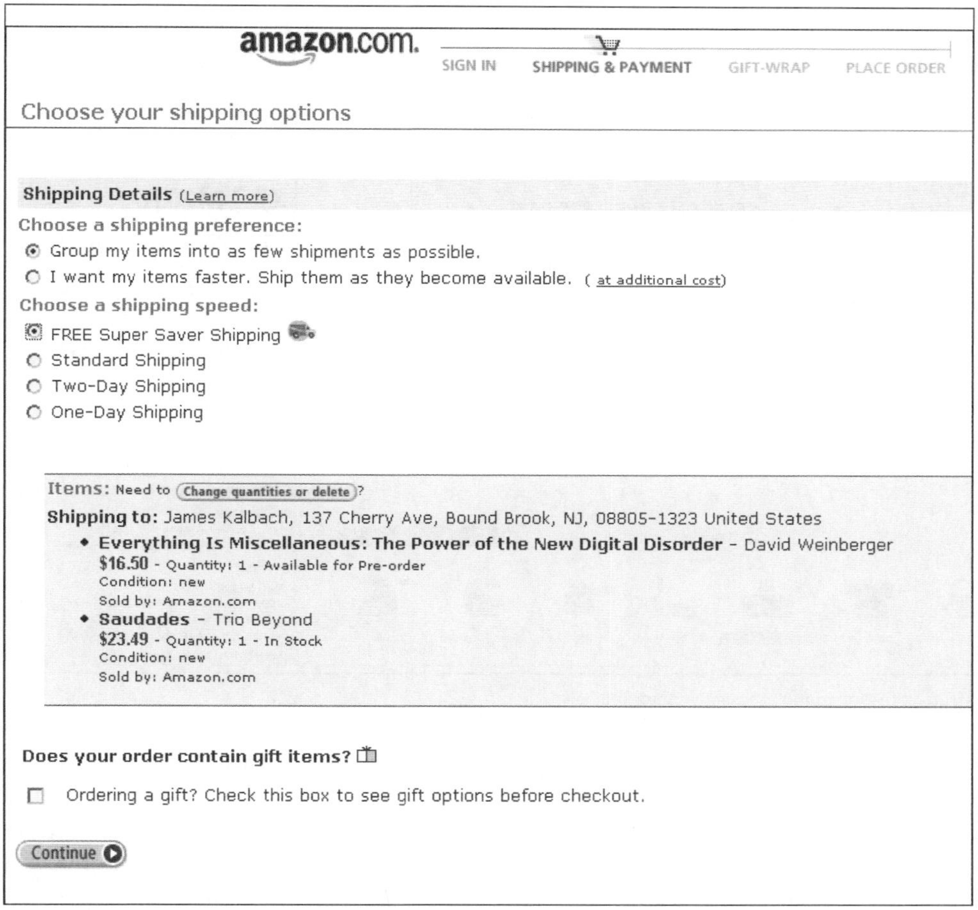

Figure 13-27 / Inductive user interfaces during the checkout process on Amazon

Other rich web applications, such as the customized computer feature on Dell, also break up the process of building your own computer into several steps (*www.dell.com*, Figure 13-28). The navigation across the top moves users through the process in five steps. The components within each of those categories are listed in a row of icons along the bottom. A prominent green button moves from one component to the next sequentially. The primary purpose of each screen is labeled in the page title (here it's Select My Wireless Cards). This is a good way to lower the learning curve of a potentially complex process so that average users can successfully complete the tasks.

Figure 13-28 / Discrete steps for configuring a computer online

The inductive user interface design technique is particularly good for applications that are used infrequently by novice users. Of course, for specialized rich web applications, such as in business-to-business applications or scientific research services, a longer learning phase may be the norm, and training may be required. Expert users might even find an inductive user interface inefficient and would prefer less on-screen prompting. Instead, providing more control on each page and displaying more data or options may be desirable. But on the Web, the time to learn an application is often immediate, and the inductive user interface design approach proves quite useful.

SUMMARY

Within a decade and a half, the Web has moved from a small hypertext system used for sharing scientific documents to a worldwide phenomenon, fundamentally changing the way we do business and lead our lives. More robust means of accessing information, such as the type of interaction offered by rich web applications, represent another step in this evolution.

The single most important advantage of rich web applications over static web pages is a smoother, more fluid user experience. Web applications allow people to filter, sort, and manipulate information dynamically, as well as perform functions. This maximizes users' time and provides a more satisfying information experience overall.

The new possibilities that technologies such as Flash and Ajax offer also bring new challenges in navigation. The notion of linking from page to page—a fundamental part of web navigation—is replaced by single-page applications and dynamic interaction more akin to desktop software. But unlike these programs, web applications have several distinctive considerations that make them uniquely web-based products:

- Rich web applications reside within another application: the web browser. The designer of a web application must consider how the controls of the browser work together with the application itself, particularly the back button.

- Web applications that are launched in a secondary browser complicate window management and detach the application from the experience on the rest of the site.

- Examples of new types of interaction previously uncommon to the web are filtering with slider bars, drag-and-drop interactions, panning, and zooming.

- While scrolling is acceptable in static web pages, it is problematic for web applications, which use techniques such as collapsible and expandable components to maximum screen real estate.

- Although rich web applications may increase the ease and efficiency with which people find information, their dynamic nature makes it harder to save, bookmark, print, share, and re-find information.

The process for designing rich web application looks similar to the framework outlined in Part 2 of this book, but has some differences. The architecture of web applications generally makes use of linear and hub and spoke structures, rather than hierarchies. Designers also have to take into account conditional states of screens and error messages. Overall, interaction design is a mature field that can inform the development of rich web applications.

Inductive user interface design techniques help break tasks in a complex web application into comprehensible steps. Processes that can be broken down into wizard structures, such as checkout processes and online configurations, benefit from this design approach in particular. Create one screen per task and give it a clear, instructive title. If the title doesn't indicate the screen's purpose right away, you need to either find a better title or redesign the page. Then provide a clear way to complete the task at hand and move to the next step.

Because they potentially offer a much better experience, you can expect to see more and more rich web applications on the web. But note that they don't necessarily replace traditional hypertext navigation systems for content-rich web sites wholesale. People must still be able to navigate to and from a rich web application within a site, for instance. And content will be a driver for much of the need for rich web applications to begin with. The two—normal hypertext web sites and rich web applications—go hand-in-hand.

Advances in technology may continue to blur the line between the web and the computer desktop, opening up new possibilities in navigating information. Relying solely on browsers to access web content, for instance, may become a thing of the past. Instead, web sites or parts of sites may appear as standalone applications on our desktops. But as long as there is information to organize and access, and as long as it doesn't fit on one screen, we will need navigation. New technologies don't remove the need to understand fundamentals of navigation or the basics of human information needs. Ultimately, the success or failure of your navigation relies not on a deep understanding of specific technologies, but on how the navigation gets used. A methodical approach to solving your design problems helps you create effective web navigation systems.

QUESTIONS

1. Using the Web, find out about the following technologies. Indicate their possible implications for rich web applications. What do they enable beyond conventional HTML page design and construction? How do these possibilities affect the design of navigation? How do they extend or eliminate the page metaphor inherent to the Web?

    a) XForms

    b) ActiveX

    c) Java Applets

    d) Adobe Flex

    e) Adobe Apollo

2. Open a common software program on your computer, such as a word processor or email program. Then find the home page for the web site of the manufacturer of that software. Compare the navigation between the two and answer the following questions:

    a) What are the main navigational mechanisms that appear in each?

    b) What are differences in approaches to labeling in each?

    c) What role does branding (e.g. logo, colors, etc.) play in each of the navigations?

    d) What role does location or knowing your location within the product's structure play in each?

    e) What are the assumed learning curves of each? How much time would you invest in learning the navigation of the web site? Of the software program?

3. Create a document in an online word processor or spreadsheet application such as Google Docs & Spreadsheets (*http://docs.google.com*) or NumSum (*www.numsum.com*).

    a) How does the application handle the following:

        *   Back button

        *   Scrolling

        *   Capturing and saving information

        *   Navigating away from the page

        *   Pop-up windows

        *   URLs and bookmarking

        *   Retaining different states of the application

    b) What types of actions can you take to cause errors? How are the error messages presented?

    c) Other than the controls and options to create documents, what other types of navigation menus are present? How do they relate to the options in the application itself?

FURTHER READING

About Face 2.0: The Essentials of Interaction Design, by Alan Cooper and Robert Reimann (Wiley, 2006).

This book offers a very deep look at the various aspects of interaction design, including user research, persona and scenario development, and a painstakingly detailed review of interface mechanisms, widgets, and screens. Chapter 11 discusses navigation for desktop software applications in particular.

Designing for Interaction, by Dan Saffer (New Riders, 2006).

This is a concise but broad overview of the field of interaction design. Discussions include the design of digital interfaces, mobile devices, physical products, and even service design.

Making the Web Work, by Bob Baxley (New Riders, 2003).

Baxley offers a thorough look at designing web applications by structuring this book around a process for designing them. It includes discussions of problem analysis and audience research, as well as structuring the web application. The text is easily approachable for novices, but substantial enough for experts to get something out of it.

Web Application Design Handbook, by Susan Fowler and Victor Stanwick (Morgan Kaufmann, 2004).

Weighing in at over 650 pages, this book presents a thorough look at application design. It serves as a good reference source for anyone developing web applications. It describes how web applications are different than web sites, but in doing so relies on references to desktop applications perhaps too often.

References

Bates, Marcia. "The Design of Browsing and Berrypicking Techniques for the Online Search Interface." *Online Review* 13 (1989): 407-424. *http://www.gseis.ucla.edu/faculty/bates/berrypicking.html.*

Bates, Marcia. "Toward an Integrated Model of Information Seeking." *The Fourth International Conference on Information Needs, Seeking and Use.* Lisbon, Portugal (September, 2002). *http://www.gseis.ucla.edu/faculty/bates/articles/info_SeekSearch-i-030329.html.*

Baxley, Bob. *Making the Web Work* (New Riders, 2003).

Belkin, Nicholas. "Anomalous States of Knowledge as the Basis for Information Retrieval." *Canadian Journal of Information Science* 5 (1980): 133-143.

Benway, Jan Panero and David M. Lane. "Banner Blindness: Web Searchers Often Miss Obvious Links." *Internetworking* 1.3 (1998). *http://www.internettg.org/newsletter/dec98/banner_blindness.html.*

Bernard, Michael. "Developing Schemas for the Location of Common Web Objects." *Usability News* 3.1 (2001). *http://psychology.wichita.edu/surl/usabilitynews/3W/web_object.htm.*

Bernard, Michael, Melissa Mills, Michelle Peterson, and Kelsey Storrer. "A Comparison of Popular Online Fonts: Which is Best and When?" *Usability News* 3.2 (2001). *http://psychology.wichita.edu/surl/usabilitynews/3S/font.htm.*

Bernard, Michael, Shannon Riley, Telia Hackler, and Karen Janzen. "A Comparison of Popular Online Fonts: Which Size and Type is Best?" *Usability News* 4.1 (2002). *http://psychology.wichita.edu/surl/usabilitynews/41/onlinetext.htm.*

Birkhoff, George D. *Aesthetic Measure* (Harvard University Press, 1933).

Blythe, Mark, Overbeeke, K., Andrew Monk, and P.C Wright. *Funology: From Usability to Enjoyment* (Kluwer Academic Publishers, 2003).

Boiko, Bob. *The Content Management Bible*, Second Edition (John Wiley & Sons, 2004).

Bowker, Geoffrey C. and Susan Leigh Start. *Sorting Things Out: Classification and Its Consequences* (The MIT Press, 2000).

Brown, Dan. *Communicating Design* (New Riders, 2006).

Bush, Vannevar. "As We May Think." *Atlantic Monthly* (1945). *http://www.theatlantic.com/doc/194507/bush.*

Bruce, V. and P.R. Green. *Visual Perception: Physiology, Psychology and Ecology,* Second Edition (Lawrence Erlbaum Associates, 1990).

Card, Stuart K., Jock Mackinlay and Ben Shneiderman (Editors). *Readings in Information Visualization: Using Vision to Think* (Morgan Kaufmann, 1999).

Catledge, Lara and James Pitkow. "Characterizing Browsing Strategies in the World Wide Web." *Computer Systems and ISDN Systems: Proceedings of the Third International World Wide Web Conference* 10, Darmstadt, Germany (1995): 1065-1073. *http://www.igd.fhg.de/archive/1995_www95/papers/80/userpatterns/UserPatterns.Paper4.formatted.html*.

Choo, Chun Wei and Don Turnbull. "Information Seeking on the Web: An Integrated Model of Browsing and Searching." *FirstMonday* 5, 2 (2000). *http://firstmonday.org/issues/issue5_2/choo/index.html*.

Clark, Joe. *Building Accessible Websites* (New Riders, 2003).

Cockburn, Andrew and Bruce McKenzie. "What Do Web Users Do? An Empirical Analysis of Web Use." *International Journal of Human-Computer Studies* 54, 6 (2000): 903-922. *http://www.cosc.canterbury.ac.nz/andrew.cockburn/papers/ijhcsAnalysis.pdf*.

Conklin, Jeff. "Hypertext: an Introduction and Survey." *IEEE Computer* 20, 9 (1987): 17-41.

Cooper, Alan. *The Inmates Are Running the Asylum* (Sams, 1999).

Cooper, Alan. "Navigating isn't Fun," *Cooper Interaction Design Newsletter* (October 2001). *http://www.cooper.com/newsletters/2001_10/navigating_isnt_fun.htm*.

Cooper, Alan, and Robert Reiman. *About Face 2.0: The Essentials of Interaction Design* (Wiley, 2006).

Cremers, Iris. "Merge Your Site Map with Your Home Page." *Forrester Report* (November 18, 2005).

Danielson, David R. "Transitional Volatility in Web Navigation." *IT&Society* 1, 3 (2003): 131-158. *http://www.stanford.edu/group/siqss/itandsociety/v01i03/v01i03a08.pdf*.

Dervin, Brenda. "From the Mind's Eye of the User: The Sense-Making Qualitative-Quantitative Methodology. " *Qualitative Research in Information Management*. J. D. Glazier and R. R. Powell (Editors) (Libraries Unlimited, 1992).

Dervin, Brenda, and Michael S. Nilan. "Information Needs and Uses." *Annual Review of Information Science and Technology* 21 (1986): 3-33.

Dillon, Andrew and Misha Vaughan. "It's the Journey and the Destination: Shape and the Emergent Property of Genre in Evaluating Digital Documents." *New Review of Multimedia and Hypermedia* 3 (1997): 91-106. *http://www.ischool.utexas.edu/~adillon/publications/journey&destination.pdf*.

Dumas, Joseph and Janice Redish. *A Practical Guide to Usability Testing* (Intellect, Ltd, 1999).

Eisenberg, Brian. "Do You Want to Inform or Persuade?" *ClickZ Network* (October, 2002). *http://www.clickz.com/showPage.html?page=1474771*.

Eisenberg, Bryan and Jeffrey Eisenberg. *Waiting for Your Cat to Bark? Persuading Customers When They Ignore Marketing* (Nelson Business, 2006).

Ellis, David. "A Behavioral Model for Information Retrieval System Design." *Journal of Information Science* 15 (1989), 237-247.

English, Jennifer, Marti Hearst, Rashmi Sinha, Kirsten Swearingen and Ka-Ping Yee. "Flexible Search and Navigation Using Faceted Navigation." Unpublished manuscript (2002). *http://flamenco.berkeley.edu/papers/flamenco02.pdf*.

Fitts, Paul M. "The Information Capacity of the Human Motor System in Controlling Amplitude and Movement." *Journal of Experimental Psychology*, 47 (1954): 381-391.

Fitts, Paul M. and J. Peterson. "Information Capacity of Discrete Motor Responses." *Journal of Experimental Psychology* 67 (1964): 103-112.

Flanders, Vincent. "Mystery Meat Navigation." *Web Pages That Suck*. *http://www.webpagesthatsuck.com/mysterymeatnavigation.html*.

Fleming, Jennifer. *Web Navigation: Designing the User Experience* (O'Reilly, 1998).

Fiorito, David and Richard Dalton. "Creating a Consistent Enterprise Web Navigation Solution." Presentation at the Information Architecture Summit, Austin, TX, 2004. *http://www.iasummit.org/2004/finalpapers/73/73_Handout_or__final__paper.ppt*.

Fiorito, David. "Thinking Navigation." Presentation at Information Architecture Summit, 2005, Montreal, QC. *http://www.iasummit.org/2005/finalpapers/101_Presentation.ppt*.

Fogg, B.J. *Persuasive Technology* (Morgan Kaufmann, 2003).

Fogg, B.J., Cathy Soohoo, David Danielson, Leslie Marable, Julianne Stanford and Ellen R. Tauber. "How Do People Evaluate a Web Site's Credibility?" *Consumer Reports Webwatch* (2002). *http://www.consumerwebwatch.org/dynamic/web-credibility-report-evaluate.cfm*

Foss, Carolyn. "Tools for Reading and Browsing Hypertext." *Information Processing and Management* 25 (1989): 407-418.

Foster, Alan. "A Non-linear Model of Information-Seeking Behavior." *Information Research* 10, 2 (2005). *http://InformationR.net/ir/10-2/paper222.html*.

Fowler, Susan and Victor Stanwick, *Web Application Design Handbook* (Morgan Kaufmann, 2004).

Furnas, George, T.K. Landauer, L.M. Gomez, and Susan Dumais. "The Vocabulary Problem in Human-System Communication." *Communications of the ACM* 30, 11 (1987): 964-971.

Garrett, Jesse James. "The Psychology of Navigation." *Digital Web Magazine* (December 2002). *http://www.digital-web.com/articles/the_psychology_of_navigation/*.

Garrett, Jesse James. *Elements of the User Experience* (New Riders, 2003).

Garrett, Jesse James. "Ajax: A New Approach to Web Applications." *Adaptive Path Essays* (February, 2005). *http://www.adaptivepath.com/publications/essays/archives/index.php*.

Golder, Scott and Bernardo A. Huberman. "Usage Patterns of Collaborative Tagging Systems." *Journal of Information Science*, 32, 2 (2006): 198-208. *http://www.hpl.hp.com/research/idl/papers/tags/tags.pdf*.

Goleman, Daniel. *Emotional Intelligence* (Bloomsbury, 1995).

Hackos, JoAnn, and Janice Redish. *User and Task Analysis for Interface Design* (John Wiley & Sons, 1998).

Hackos, JoAnn. *Content Management for Dynamic Web Delivery* (John Wiley & Sons, 2002).

Hammond, Tony, Timo Hannay, Ben Lund, and Joanna Scott. "Social Bookmarking Tools—A General Overview." *D-Lib Magazine* 11, 4 (April 2005). *http://www.dlib.org/dlib/april05/hammond/04hammond.html*.

Hearst, Marti. "User Interfaces and Visualization." In *Modern Information Retrieval* (Ch. 10), by R. Baeza-Yates and B. Ribeiro-Neto. (ACM Press, 1999).

Hedden, Heather. "A-Z Indexes to Enhance Site Searching." *Digital Web Magazine* (April 2005). *http://digital-web.com/articles/a_z_indexes_site_searching*.

Hurst, Mark. "Interview with Marissa Mayer, Product Manager, Google." October, 2002. *http://www.goodexperience.com/blog/archives/000066.php*.

Instone, Keith. "Location, Path, and Attribute Breadcrumbs." Last updated November, 2004. *http://user-experience.org/uefiles/breadcrumbs*.

Instone, Keith. "Navigation Stess Test." *http://user-experience.org/uefiles/navstress/*.

Kalbach, James and Tim Bosenick. "Web Page Layout: A Comparison Between Left- and Right-justified Site Navigation Menus." *Journal of Digital Information* 4, 1. (April 2003). *http://jodi.ecs.soton.ac.uk/Articles/v04/i01/Kalbach/*.

Krug, Steve. *Don't Make Me Think* (New Riders, 2000).

Kuhlthau, Carol C. "Inside the Search Process: Information Seeking from the User's Perspective." *Journal of the American Society for Information Science* 42, 5 (1991): 361-371.

Lakoff, George. *Women, Fire, and Dangerous Things* (University of Chicago Press, 1987).

Lamantia, Joe. "Analyzing Card Sort Results with a Spreadsheet Template." *Boxes and Arrows* (August 26, 2003) *http://www.boxesandarrows.com/view/analyzing_card_sort_results_with_a_spreadsheet_template*.

Lash, Jeff. "Persuasive Navigation" *Digital Web Magazine* (December 2002). *http://digital-web.com/articles/persuasive_navigation*.

Lash, Jeff. "More That Just a Footer." *Digital Web Magazine* (February 2004). *http://www.digital-web.com/articles/more_than_just_a_footer*.

Leise, Fred, Karl Fast, and Mike Steckel. "What is a Controlled Vocabulary?" *Boxes and Arrows* (December 2002). *http://www.boxesandarrows.com/view/what_is_a_controlled_vocabulary*.

Lida, Bonnie, Spring Hull, and Katie Pilcher. "Breadcrumb Navigation: An Exploratory Study of Usage." *Usability News* 5.1 (2003). *http://psychology.wichita.edu/surl/usabilitynews/51/breadcrumb.htm*.

Lindgaard, Gitte, Gary Fernandes, Cathy Dudek, and J. Brown. "Attention web designers: you have 50 milliseconds to make a good first impression!" *Behaviour and Information Technology* 25, 2 (March-April 2006): 115-126.

Lippell, Helen. "The ABCs of the BBC: A Case Study and Checklist." *Boxes and Arrows* (December 2005). *http://www.boxesandarrows.com/view/the_abcs_of_the_bbc_a_case_study_and_checklist*.

Lynch, Patrick and Sarah Horton. *Web Style Guide*, Second Edition (Yale University Press, March 2002). *http://www.webstyleguide.com*.

Marchionini, Gary N. *Information Seeking in Electronic Environments*. (Cambridge University Press, 1995). *http://www.ils.unc.edu/~march/isee_book/web_page.html*.

Marlow, Cameron, Mor Naaman, Danah Boyd, and Marc Davis "Position Paper, Tagging, Taxonomy, Flickr, Article, ToRead," (Position paper, 2006). *http://www.rawsugar.com/www2006/29.pdf*.

Maurer, Donna. "Four Modes of Seeking Information and How to Design for Them." *Boxes and Arrows* (14 March 2006). *http://www.boxesandarrows.com/view/four_modes_of_seeking_information_and_how_to_design_for_them*.

Maurer, Donna and Todd Warfel. "Card Sorting: A Definitive Guide." *Boxes and Arrows* (April 2004). *http://www.boxesandarrows.com/view/card_sorting_a_definitive_guide*.

Microsoft Corporation, "Microsoft Inductive User Interface Guidelines" (February 9, 2001). *http://msdn.microsoft.com/library/default.asp?url=/library/en-us/dnwui/html/iuiguidelines.asp*.

Miller, Craig S.. and Roger W. Remington.. "Modeling Information Navigation: Implications for Information Architecture." *Human-Computer Interaction* 19, 3 (2004): 225-271.

Mintzberg, Henry, Bruce Ahlstrand, and Joseph Lampel. *Strategy Safari: A Guided Tour through the Wilds of Strategic Management* (Free Press, 1998).

Morville, Peter and Louis Rosenfeld. *Information Architecture for the World Wide Web*, Third Edition (O'Reilly, 2006).

Mulder, Steve with Ziv Yaar. *The User Is Always Right: A Practical Guide to Creating and Using Personas for the Web* (New Riders, 2006).

Nielsen, Jakob. *Usability Engineering*. (Morgan Kaufmann, 1993).

Nielsen, Jakob. "Heuristic Evaluation," In *Usability Inspection Methods*, edited by Jakob Nielsen and Robert L. Mack. (John Wiley & Sons, 1994). *http://www.useit.com/papers/heuristic/heuristic_evaluation.html*.

Nielsen, Jakob and Marie Tahir. *Homepage Usability: 50 Websites Deconstructed* (New Riders, 2000).

Norman, Donald A. *The Design of Everyday Things* (Doubleday, 1990).

Norman, Donald A. *Emotional Design: Attractive Things Work Better* (Basic Books, 2003).

Ojakaar, Erik. "Users Decide First; Move Second." *UIE Tips* (October, 2001) *http://www.uie.com/articles/users_decide_first/*.

Olsen, George. "Making Personas More Powerful: Details to Drive Strategic and Tactical Design." *Boxes and Arrows* (September 2004). *http://www.boxesandarrows.com/view/making_personas_more_powerful_details_to_drive_strategic_and_tactical_design*.

Pagendarm, Magnus and Heike Schaumberg. "Why Are Users Banner-Blind? The Impact of Navigation Style on the Perception of Web Banners." *Journal of Digital Information* 2, 1 (2001). *http://jodi.tamu.edu/Articles/v02/i01/Pagendarm*.

Peterson, Eric T. *Web Site Measurement Hacks* (O'Reilly, 2005).

Pirolli, Peter and Stuart Card. "Information Forgaging in Information Access Environments." *Human Factors in Computer Systems: Proceedings of CHI95* (1995). *http://www.acm.org/turing/sigs/sigchi/chi95/Electronic/documnts/papers/ppp_bdy.htm*.

Pruitt, John and Tamara Adlin. *The Persona Lifecycle: Keeping People in Mind throughout Product Design* (Morgan Kaufmann, 2006).

Reiss, Eric L. *Practical Information Architecture: A Hands-on Approach to Structuring Successful Websites* (Addison-Wesley, 2000).

Robbins, Jennifer Niederst. *Learning Web Design*, Third Edition (O'Reilly, 2007).

Rogers, Bonnie Lida and Barbara Chaparro. "Breadcrumb Navigation: Further Investigation of Usage." *Usability News* 5.2 (2003). *http://psychology.wichita.edu/surl/usabilitynews/52/breadcrumb.htm*.

Rubin, Jeffery. *Handbook of Usability Testing: How to Plan, Design, and Conduct Effective Tests* (Wiley, 1994).

Saffer, Dan. *Designing for Interaction* (New Riders, 2006).

Schroeder, Manfred. *Fractals, Chaos, Power Laws* (W.H. Freeman & Co., 1991).

Shaikh, A. Dawn and Kelsi Lenz. "Where's the Search? Re-examining User Expectations of Web Objects." *Usability News* 8.1 (2006). *http://psychology.wichita.edu/surl/usabilitynews/81/webobjects.htm*.

Snyder, Carolyn. *Paper Prototyping: The Fast and Easy Way to Design and Refine User Interfaces* (Morgan Kaufmann, 2003).

Spiteri, Louise. "A Simplified Model for Facet Analysis: Ranganathan 101." *Canadian Journal of Information and Library Science* 23 (1998): 1-30. *http://iainstitute.org/pg/a_simplified_model_for_facet_analysis.php*.

Spool, Jared. "Users Continue After Category Links." *UIEtips* (4 Dec 2001). *http://www.uie.com/articles/continue_after_categories*.

Spool, Jared. "Evolution trumps usability." *UIEtips* (September 2002). *http://www.uie.com/Articles/evolution_trumps_usability.htm*.

Spool, Jared, Christine Perfetti, and David Brittan. "Design for the Scent of Information. " *UIE Fundamentals*. User Interface Engineering, 2004.

Taylor, Robert S. "Value-added Processes in Document Based Systems: Abstracting and Indexing Services." *Information Services and Use* 4, 8 (1984): 127-146.

Taylor, Robert S. "Information Values in Decision Contexts." *Information Management Review* 1, 1 (1985): 47-55.

Tidwell, Jenifer. *Designing Interfaces* (O'Reilly, 2006).

Thatcher, Jim, Cynthia Waddell, Shawn Henry, Sarah Swierenga, Mark Urban, Michael Burks, Bob Regan, Paul Bohman. *Constructing Accessible Web Sites* (Peer Information Inc., 2002).

Toms, Elaine. "Recognizing Digital Genre." *Bulletin of the American Society of Information Science and Technology* 27, 2 (2001). *http://www.asis.org/Bulletin/Dec-01/toms.html*.

Toms, Elaine G. and D. Grant Campbell. "Genre as Interface Metaphor: Exploiting Form and Function in Digital Environments." *Proceedings of the 32nd Hawaii International Conference on System Sciences*. (1999).

Tufte, Edward. *Envisioning Information* (Graphics Press, 1990).

Tufte, Edward. *Visual Explanations: Images and Quantities, Evidence and Narrative* (Graphics Press, 1997).

Tufte, Edward. *The Visual Display of Quantitative Information*, Second Edition (Graphics Press, 2001).

Quack, Till. "How to Succeed with URLs." *A List Apart* (October, 2001). *http://www.alistapart.com/articles/succeed*.

Van Dijck, Peter. *Information Architecture for Designers: Structuring Websites for Business Success* (Roto Vision, 2003).

Vaughan, Misha and Andrew Dillon. "Why Structure and Genre Matter for Users of Digital Information: A Longitudinal Experiment with Readers of a Web-Based Newspaper." *International Journal of Human-Computer Studies*, 64 (2006): 502-526.

Wade, N. J. and M. Swanston. *Visual Perception: An Introduction* (Routledge, Chapman, and Hall, Inc., 1991).

WebAIM. "Accessibility of AJAX Applications." *http://webaim.org/techniques/ajax*.

Weinreich, Harald, Hartmut Obendorf, Eelco Herder, and Matthias Mayer, "Off the Beaten Tracks: Exploring Three Aspects of Web Navigation," *International World Wide Web Conference 2006*, Edinburgh (2006). *http://www2006.org/programme/files/xhtml/18/p018-weinreich/p018-weinreich.html*.

Wilson, Tom D. "Models in information behaviour research." *Journal of Documentation* 55, 3 (1999): 249-270. *http://informationr.net/tdw/publ/papers/1999JDoc.html*.

Wodtke, Christina. *Information Architecture: Blueprints for the Web* (New Riders, 2003).

Wroblewski, Luke. *Site-Seeing: A Visual Approach to Web Usability* (Hungry Minds, 2003).

Yunker, John. *Beyond Borders: Web Globalization Strategies* (New Riders, 2002).

Index

SYMBOLS

Colophon

The animal on the cover of *Designing Web Navigation* is a margay cat (*Leopardus wiedii*). Native to Mexico, Panama, Colombia , Peru, and Paraguay, these smallish (9-20 pound) cats live in humid ever-green forests. They love to climb, and can rotate their hind legs 180 degress, which lets them run head-first down trees in a manner similar to squirrels. The margay is also able to hang from branches using only a hind foot.

The large eyes of a margay help them hunt at night; their diet consists of small mammals, birds, and fruit. Their pelts are prized by humans, and hunting, combined with destruction of their natural habitats, has led to their endangerment. Margays can live for up to 20 years, but do not have large litters of kittens and reproduce only once every two years. Once listed as vulnerable to extinction, preservation efforts have have helped to increase the margay population throughout the world. Though they remain on the list of endangered species, the outlook for their survival is positive.

The cover image of *Designing Web Navigation* is from *Wood's Animate Creation*. The cover font is Adobe ITC Garamond. The text font is Hoefler Gotham.